R. Gupta's®

POPULAR MASTER GUIDE

KVS Limited Department Examination (LDE)

PRINCIPAL
VICE-PRINCIPAL

Tier-I Exam

Also Useful for

KVS Principal/Vice-Principal Tier-II
Direct Recruitment Exam

by
RPH Editorial Board

2027
EDITION

RAMESH PUBLISHING HOUSE, NEW DELHI

Published by
O.P. Gupta *for* Ramesh Publishing House

Admin. Office
12-H, New Daryaganj Road, Opp. Officers' Mess,
New Delhi-110002 ✆ 23275224, 23245124

E-mail: info@rameshpublishinghouse.com
For Online Shopping: www.rameshpublishinghouse.com

Showroom
- Balaji Market, Nai Sarak, Delhi-110006 ✆ 23282525 📱 9354373464
- 4457, Nai Sarak, Delhi-110006

Book Code: R-1973

ISBN: 978-93-87918-20-7

Price: ₹ 295

Printed at: Guruji Printers, New Delhi-110096

CONTENTS

❑❑❑

THE TYPE OF EXAMINATION

Pattern of Subject Knowledge Examination (Combination of Pen-paper and OMR Based)

Component of the Test	No. of Questions		Total Marks		Duration of the Test
	Objective	Descriptive	Objective	Descriptive	
Perspectives on Education and Leadership; Administration and Finance; Management, Supervision and Leadership	60	10	60	40	2½ hours

- There will be no negative marking.
- There will be interview of 100 marks for the post of Principal & Vice-Principal.
- The Selection for Interview (wherever applicable) will be on the basis of seniority cum qualifying the written examination. Such candidates will be called for interview in the ratio of 1 : 3 as per the vacancies notified for the post.

Sample Paper

Kendriya Vidyalaya Sangathan (KVS)–LDE

PRINCIPAL / VICE-PRINCIPAL

Tier-I Recruitment Exam

(Objective Test)

1. National Education Policy 2020, has included age group 3 - 6 years under school curriculum because:

A. parents wanted it.

B. anganwadi system had become superfluous.

C. it is recognized as crucial stage for development of mental faculties of a child.

D. it is helpful in enhancing motivation levels of children.

2. A never enrolled child of 13 years of age has to be mainstreamed, in which class she/he would be admitted as per provisions of Right of Children to Free and Compulsory Education Act, 2009?

A. Class 4 B. Class 5
C. Class 6 D. Class 7

3. A document titled "Challenge of Education - A Policy Perspective" was published by Ministry of Education in ______.

A. 1985 B. 1986
C. 1992 D. 2005

4. The Right of Children to Free and Compulsory Education Act, 2009 provides for a full time head teacher for a school of VI to VIII class with students strength exceeding one hundred besides a teacher-pupil ratio of:

A. 1 : 30 B. 1 : 35
C. 1 : 40 D. 1 : 45

5. The school curriculum should be planned to agree with:

A. the available text books in various subjects.

B. the goals, purposes and interests of the students.

C. the general culture of the school in the past.

D. the training and interest of teachers.

6. A teacher first tells the rule and then cites examples to explain a concept she/he is adopting:

A. explanatory approach

B. inductive approach

C. deductive approach

D. investigatory approach

7. In the context of social development, most of the basic social attitudes of an individual are determined in the:

A. nursery school years.

B. years of adolescence.

C. first two years.

D. primary school years.

8. In the context of human growth, which one of the following is an incorrect statement?

A. Growth is limited to the description of quantitative changes.

B. The results of growth are very specific.

C. Growth continues throughout one's life.

D. Growth is a self-system of development.

9. A student is studying in class VII. In the context of Kohlberg's theory of moral development, he cannot be expected at which stage of moral reasoning?

A. Exchange of favours
B. Social contract
C. Law and order
D. Punishment avoidance and obedience

10. According to Vygotsky, _________ is the difference between what a child can do alone and what that child can do with help.

Fill in the blank with the correct option:

A. habituation
B. metamemory
C. zone of proximal development
D. scaffolding

11. In which of the following approaches there is no scope for debate and discussion among students?

A. Teacher centred approach.
B. Learner centred approach.
C. Constructivist approach.
D. Competency based approach.

12. Which one of the following is not a process of observational learning?

A. Observer must pay attention.
B. Observer must use trial and error approach for rehearsals.
C. Observer must reproduce and refine the observed behaviour.
D. Observer must perform learned behaviour under appropriate motivational conditions.

13. In which of the following situations 'assessment as learning' is possible?

A. Group learning
B. Collaborative learning
C. Group test
D. Unit test

14. Role of teacher in trans-disciplinary integration is that of a:

A. Generalist
B. Co-planner
C. Facilitator
D. Specialist

15. Inclusive education signifies having the same __________ for all children in the class.

Which one of the following option CAN NOT fill the blanks?

A. teacher
B. teaching methodology
C. learning outcomes
D. assessment standards

16. You have a class which is very hetetrogeneous in height. You should allow seating arrangement which:

A. is purely based on height.
B. has taller students on one side of the class.
C. allows smaller students to sit such as they can see and participate easily in class activities.
D. is random.

17. Institutional planning should not be based on:

A. Survey of resources
B. Stakeholder's views
C. Principle of flexibility
D. Time constraints

18. A good Head of an educational institution, is one who:

A. allows full freedom to students and teachers.
B. is concerned with good administration and deals with strong hand.
C. is a disciplinarian and does not compromise misconduct.
D. is flexible in her/his approach and uses human touch.

19. In order to correct the undesirable behaviour of a student, the most effective method is to:

A. punish her/him.
B. inform her/his parents.
C. find out reasons and provide appropriate remedies.
D. ignore her/him.

20. Which of the following characterizes best teaching episode?

A. Pin drop silence in the class
B. Full attendance of students
C. Number of students passing the examination
D. Meaningful questions asked by the students

21. Which of the following is/are correct?

(*i*) When there are no emergencies of work, leave can be claimed as a malter of right.
(*ii*) Once granted, leave cannot be revoked.

A. Only (*i*)
B. Only (*ii*)
C. Both are correct
D. Both are incorrect

22. Which of the following is/are correct?

When an employee is transferred from one organization to another, which has made separate rules, his joining for the journey to that organization shall be governed by which rules:

(*i*) Those of the borrowing organization
(*ii*) Different provisions if expressly made by mutual agreement between the lending and the borrowing authorities.

A. Only (*i*)
B. Only (*ii*)
C. Both are correct
D. Both are incorrect

23. Which of the following is/are correct?

An employee is appointed to another post in Government on acceptance of technical navigation. Later on he rejoins his earlier post. The period spent in another department will:

(*i*) Not count for promotion but will count for seniority in the earlier post
(*ii*) Neither count for promotion nor for seniority in the earlier post

A. Only (*i*)
B. Only (*ii*)
C. Both are correct
D. Both are incorrect

24. Which one of the following Articles of the Constitution of India provides that backlog will be treated as a class in itself and will not be considered for the limit of 50% reservation limit

A. Article 16 (4)
B. Article 16 (4A)
C. Article 16 (4B)
D. Article 16 (6)

25. Which of the following is/are correct?

(*i*) If reservation applies, the extended zone for filling reserved vacancies will be 5 times the number of vacancies
(*ii*) The extended zone will be the same in promotion by selection within Group A

A. Only (*i*)
B. Only (*ii*)
C. Both are correct
D. Both are wrong

26. Which of the following is/are correct?

(*i*) Own merit concept means selection on the same standard as applied to general candidates
(*ii*) Candidates appointed on their own merit will lose their status of SC/ST in future promotion, if any

A. Only (*i*)
B. Only (*ii*)
C. Both are correct
D. Both are wrong

27. Which of the following is/are correct?

(*i*) Urgent dak means dak marked "Immediate", "Priority" etc

(*ii*) Classified dak means dak bearing a security grading

A. Only (*i*)

B. Only (*ii*)

C. Both are correct

D. Both are wrong

28. Which of the following are not constitutional bodies?

(*i*) Central Vigilance Commission

(*ii*) Central Information Commission

(*iii*) Minorities Commission

A. Only (*i*) and (*ii*)

B. Only (*i*) and (*iii*)

C. Only (*ii*) and (*iii*)

D. (*i*), (*ii*) and (*iii*)

29. The term members of family include which of the following interms of CCS (Conduct) Rules, 1964?

(*i*) A wholly dependent step-daughter not residing with the Government servant

(*ii*) A judicially separated wife not dependent on the Government servant

A. Only (*i*)

B. Only (*ii*)

C. Both are correct

D. Both are incorrect

30. Which of the following is/are correct:

(*i*) Subject to the provisions of the RTI Act, no Govt. servant shall communicate any official document to anyone to whom he is not authorized to communicate such document

(*ii*) No prior sanction is necessary for raising of funds in persuance of philanthropic purposes

A. Only (*i*)

B. Only (*ii*)

C. Both are correct

D. Both are incorrect

31. Which of the following is/are correct?

If the transaction is with a person having official dealing with the Govt. servant

(*i*) Prior permission is necessary irrespective of the value of the immovable property

(*ii*) Prior permission is necessary irrespective of the value of the movable property

(*iii*) Only intimation is necessary in the case of movable property if the value does not exceed two months basic pay

A. Only (*i*)

B. Only (*ii*)

C. (*i*) and (*ii*)

D. (*ii*) and (*iii*)

32. Which of the following are true?

During suspension an employee can:

(*i*) be given House Building Advance

(*ii*) function as Defense Assistant

(*iii*) not retain lien

A. Only (*i*) and (*ii*)

B. Only (*i*) and (*iii*)

C. Only (*ii*) and (*iii*)

D. (*i*), (*ii*) and (*iii*)

33. No Government Servant shall ordinarily be granted leave of any kind for a continuous period exceeding:

A. One year

B. Three years

C. Five years

D. Ten years

34. A Government servant in receipt of existing grade pay of ₹ 10,000 (level 14 in the pay matrix) is entitled to which of the following type of residences?

A. V - B (D-I)

B. VI - A (C-II)

C. VI - B (C-I)

D. V - A (D-II)

35. In respect of which of the following types of accommodation, unified waiting list shall be prepared?

A. Type I to type IV (s)
B. Type I to type VI
C. Type I to type VII
D. Type I to type VIII

36. In which of the following cases, a Govt. servant is required to furnish security in the form of a Fidelity Bond?

(*a*) A Govt. servant actually handling cash
(*b*) A Govt. servant entrusted with the custody of stores
(*c*) A Govt. servant entrusted with the custody of stores, which in the opinion of the competent authority are not considerable
(*d*) Librarian and Library staff

Select the correct answer using the code given below:

A. (*a*) & (*b*) only
B. (*a*), (*b*) & (*d*) only
C. (*b*), (*c*) & (*d*) only
D. (*a*), (*b*) & (*c*) only

37. Consider the following statements in the context of Demands for Grants:

(*a*) The Demands for Grants represent the estimates for expenditure for which vote of Lok Sabha is required.
(*b*) One Demand for Grant is presented in respect of each Ministry or Department irrespective of the size of Ministries or Departments
(*c*) The Demand for Grants shall be presented to parliament at two levels.

Which of the above statement(s) is/are correct?

A. (*a*) & (*c*) only
B. (*b*) only
C. (*b*) & (*c*) only
D. (*a*) & (*b*) only

38. As a general rule and without the prior approval of the Department of Expenditure, Ministry of Finance, no Global Tender Enquiry (GTE) shall be invited for tenders upto:

A. ₹ 100 crore
B. ₹ 200 crore
C. ₹ 300 crore
D. ₹ 500 crore

39. In respect of which of the following types of Dental treatment obtained at Government hospitals recognized under CS (MA) Rules, the expenses incurred by the Central Government employees are reimbursable?

(*a*) Extraction
(*b*) Scaling and gum treatment
(*c*) Root canal treatment
(*d*) Treatment of pyorrhoea

Select the correct answer using the code given below:

A. (*a*) & (*b*) only
B. (*b*), (*c*) & (*d*) only
C. (*a*), (*c*) & (*d*) only
D. (*a*), (*b*), (*c*) & (*d*)

40. "Consideration" in relation to the supply of goods does not include which of the following?

A. Any payment mode for supply of goods by recipient
B. Any payment made for supply of goods by any other person (on behalf of recipient)
C. Amount of subsidy given by the Central Government
D. Deposit given in respect of supply of goods where supplier applies such deposit as consideration for the said supply

41. Father of Modern Management theory is _____.

A. Henry Fayol
B. F.W. Taylor
C. Henry Gantt
D. None

42. School of Management recognizes the existence of a centralized body of knowledge for the Management:

A. System approach
B. Empirical
C. Contingency
D. Operational

43. Koontz and O'Donnel are the advocates of _______ approach to management.

A. System approach
B. Empirical
C. Contingency
D. Operational

44. An organisation structure is effective if it enables individuals to contribute to the objectives of the enterprise. This is known as:

A. Scalar Principle
B. Principle of functional definition
C. Principle of unity of objectives
D. None of these

45. Which one of the following orders indicates the correct logical order of managerial functions?

A. Organising, planning, directing, staffing, coordination and control
B. Planning, organising, staffing, directing, coordination and control
C. Planning, directing, organising, staffing, control and coordination
D. Organising, planning, staffing, directing, control and coordination

46. Management by exception introduces:

A. selective, responsibility oriented reporting
B. reporting of significant variances
C. requirement of full reports on performance
D. computation of actuals in different spheres of performance

47. Control refers to:

I. Establishment of standards
II. Measurement of actual performance against the set standards
III. Correction for deviation from standards

Of these statements:

A. I alone is correct
B. III alone is correct
C. I and II are correct
D. I, II, and III are correct

48. If a general manager asks the sales manager to recruit some sales men on his behalf, it is an instance of:

A. division of authority
B. decentralisation of authority
C. delegation of authority
D. delegation of responsibility

49. "Human Relating Approach" to management was origined by:

A. Henery Fayol
B. Winslow Taylor
C. Elton Mayo
D. Peter F. Drucker

50. The famous book "The Philosophy of Management" was written by:

A. Henery Fayol
B. Oliver Sheldon
C. F. W. Taylor
D. Urwick

51. Control function of management implies:

A. to bring harmony in various activities
B. to keep the work force content
C. taking corrective course of action
D. to provide sufficient finance

52. General manager has delegated authority to production manager for achieving budgeted production. Who is responsible for low production to Board of Directors?

A. Production Supervisors
B. Production Manager
C. General Manager
D. None of these

53. Which of the following functions of management are more closely related?

I. Planning
II. Co-ordination
III. Motivation
IV. Control

A. I and II
B. II and III
C. II, III, and IV
D. I, II, and IV

54. Which of the following constitute manpower planning?

I. Determining human resource requirements both quantitatively and qualitatively.
II. Finding the sources of talented individuals.
III. Planning for the human resource needs of an organisation.
IV. Reaching out to the right source for procuring the right people.

Select the correct answer using the codes given below:

Codes:

A. I, II and IV
B. II and III
C. I and III
D. I, II, III and IV

55. Which is the most fundamental function of Management?

A. Planning
B. Organising
C. Staffing
D. Controlling

56. Consider the following statements:

I. MBO is a control technique in which managers devote time only on the areas of deviation.
II. MBO integrates the individual with the organisation and the organisation with the environment.
III. In MBO the control over people is Shifted to control over operations.
IV. The MBO Principle must be accompanied in practice by the principle of critical – point control.

Of these statements:

A. I and II are correct
B. II and III are correct
C. III and IV are correct
D. I and IV are correct

57. Techniques of managerial control are useful in:

A. Selection of plant location
B. Identifying appropriate technology.
C. Profit planning
D. Conducting share holder's meetings.

58. When management pays attention to more important areas and when the day-to-day routine problems are looked after by lower level management, it is known as:

A. Management by Objectives
B. Management by Exception
C. Participative Management
D. Critical Path Method

59. The following steps are involved in managing by objectives:

I. Preliminary setting of objectives at the top
II. Setting subordinates objectives
III. Tying resources with the goals
IV. Clarifying the organisational steps is

A. I, II, III, IV
B. I, II, IV, III
C. I, III, II, IV
D. I, IV, II, III

60. Which one of the following is the most appropriate management control technique for timely completion of a project?

A. Organisation chart
B. Management by objectives
C. PERT
D. Span of control

ANSWERS

1	2	3	4	5	6	7	8	9	10
C	D	A	B	B	C	C	C	B	C
11	**12**	**13**	**14**	**15**	**16**	**17**	**18**	**19**	**20**
A	B	B	B	B	C	D	D	C	D
21	**22**	**23**	**24**	**25**	**26**	**27**	**28**	**29**	**30**
D	D	A	C	A	A	C	D	A	A
31	**32**	**33**	**34**	**35**	**36**	**37**	**38**	**39**	**40**
C	A	C	B	B	A	A	B	D	C
41	**42**	**43**	**44**	**45**	**46**	**47**	**48**	**49**	**50**
A	D	D	C	B	B	D	C	C	B
51	**52**	**53**	**54**	**55**	**56**	**57**	**58**	**59**	**60**
A	C	D	C	A	B	C	B	A	C

◆ ◆ ◆ ◆ ◆

PERSPECTIVES ON EDUCATION AND LEADERSHIP

UNDERSTANDING THE LEARNER

CONCEPT OF DEVELOPMENT AND ITS RELATIONSHIP WITH LEARNING

The discipline of Child Development is concerned with the changes in the behaviour of children over time and explains why and how they occur. It aims to describe and explain development in the areas of physical, social, emotional, language and cognitive functioning.

Development and Growth

The term 'development' is used for changes in a person's physical and behavioural traits that emerge in orderly ways and last for a reasonable period of time. The three main characteristics of these changes are progressive, orderly and long lasting. Development refers to both quantitative as well as qualitative changes. It includes changes not only in structure but also in function.

'Growth' refers to physical increase in the size of the body. Increase in weight, height and internal organs is growth. Growth refers to a quantitative change, that is, a change that can be measured.

Growth is only one aspect of the larger process of development. Development continues even when physical changes are not visible. Physical growth slows down considerably after adolescence but development does not.

Stages of Development

The human life span has been divided into the stages of infancy, childhood, adolescence and adulthood.

The period from birth to two years of age is referred to as the period of infancy. In this period the child is totally dependent on the caregiver for the fulfilment of his needs. After birth, this is the period of most rapid growth and development. The child's skills and abilities increase. By the end of infancy he is able to walk, run, communicate his needs verbally, feed himself, identify family members, recognise himself and venture confidently in familiar surroundings.

The period of childhood is from two to twelve years of age. Development at this stage is not as rapid as during infancy. During this period the child refines the skills he has acquired during infancy and learns new skill as well. During childhood he also learns the ways of behaviour that are considered appropriate by the society. The child meets many people outside the family and forms attachments with more people. As the child grows and his thinking capacities mature, he realises that he can do many things. This gives him a feeling of confidence. During this period he becomes more independent though adult guidance is constantly needed. The period of childhood is divided into two stages: the period of early childhood (2–6 years) and middle childhood (6–12 years). The period of early childhood is also referred to as the preschool age because at this age the child is learning skills that will help him to do tasks associated with schooling. The preschooler has mastered the words to ask questions about things and people. He learns about numbers, colours, shapes and the reasons for everyday events. All these concepts develop from actually seeing things and doing various activities. The child in the age group 6–12 years has matured a great deal and is expected to behave more responsibly than the preschooler.

The next stage is referred to as the period of adolescence (12–18 years). The beginning of this period is marked by puberty. Puberty refers to the stage around 11–14 years of the age, when there is a spurt in physical growth. This results in a rapid increase in height and weight and the emergence of secondary sexual characteristics. These rapid physical changes lead to a need for emotional readjustment.

At this age the peer group becomes very important and the adolescent follows the rules and the codes of her group. Feelings of loyalty and pride for the group are very strong. At times the values of the peer group may become more important than those of the family. During adolescence thinking develops further and becomes more complex. The individual can understand and deal with varied situations. He can think of abstract problems and work out their solutions. All this helps him to prepare for the roles and responsibilities, which he will be expected to carry out as an adult.

After the age of 18 years the person is referred to as an adult. Physical changes are completed in this stage and person becomes mature.

Theories of Child Development and Learning

Maturationist Theory

The maturationist theory was advanced by the work of Arnold Gessell. Maturationists believe that development is a biological process that occurs automatically in predictable, sequential stages over time. This perspective leads many educators and families to assume that young children will acquire knowledge naturally and automatically as they grow physically and become older, provided that they are healthy.

School readiness, according to maturationists, is a state at which all healthy young children arrive when they can perform tasks such as reciting the alphabet and counting; these tasks are required for learning more complex tasks such as reading and arithmetic. Because development and school readiness occur naturally and automatically, maturationists believe the best practices are for parents to teach young children to recite the alphabet and count while being patient and waiting for children to become ready for kindergarten. If a child is developmentally unready for school, maturationists might suggest referrals to transitional kindergartens, retention, or holding children out of school for an additional year. These practices are sometimes used by schools, educators, and parents when a young child developmentally lags behind his or her peers. The young child's underperformance is interpreted as the child needing more time to acquire the knowledge and skills needed to perform at the level of his or her peers.

Environmentalist Theory

Theorists such as John Watson, B.F. Skinner, and Albert Bandura contributed greatly to the environmentalist perspective of development. Environmentalists believe the child's environment shapes learning and behaviour in fact, human behaviour, development, and learning are thought of as reactions to the environment. This perspective leads many families, schools, and educators to assume that young children develop and acquire new knowledge by reacting to their surroundings.

Kindergarten readiness, according to the environmentalists, is the age or stage when young children can respond appropriately to the environment of the school and the classroom (*e.g.*, rules and regulations, curriculum activities, positive behaviour in group settings, and directions and instructions from teachers and other adults in the school). The ability to respond appropriately to this environment is necessary for young children to participate in teacher-initiated learning activities. Success is dependent on the child following instructions from the teacher or the adult in the classroom. Many environmentalist-influenced educators and parents believe that young children learn best by rote activities, such as reciting the alphabet over and over, copying letters, and tracing numbers. This viewpoint is evident in kindergarten classrooms where young children are expected to sit at desks arranged in rows and listen attentively to their teachers. At home, parents may provide their young children with workbooks containing such activities as colouring or tracing letters and numbers—activities that require little interaction between parent and child. When young children are unable to respond appropriately to the classroom and school environment, they often are labelled as having some form of learning disabilities and are tracked in classrooms with curriculum designed to control their behaviours and responses.

Constructivist Theory

The constructivist perspective of readiness and development was advanced by theorists such as Jean Piaget, Maria Montessori, and Lev Vygotsky. Although their work varies greatly, each articulates a similar context of learning and development. They are consistent in their belief that learning and development occur when young children interact with the environment and people around them. Constructivists view young children as active participants in the learning process. In addition, constructivists believe young children initiate most of the activities required for learning and development. Because active interaction with the environment and people are necessary for learning and development, constructivists believe that children are ready for school when they can initiate many of the interactions they have with the environment and people around them.

Constructivist-influenced schools and educators pay a lot of attention to the physical environment and the curriculum of the early childhood classroom. Kindergarten classrooms often are divided into different **learning centers** and are equipped with developmentally appropriate materials for young children to play with and manipulate. Teachers and adults have direct conversations with children, children move actively from one center to another, and daily activities are made meaningful through the incorporation of children's experiences into the curriculum. At home, parents engage their young children in reading and storytelling activities and encourage children's participation in daily household activities in a way that introduces such concepts as counting and language use. In addition, parents may provide young children with picture books containing very large print, and toys that stimulate interaction (such as building blocks and large puzzles). When a young child encounters difficulties in the learning process, the constructivist approach is neither to lable the child nor to retain him or her; instead, constructivists give the child some individualized attention and customize the classroom curriculum to help the child address his or her difficulties.

Today, most researchers have come to understand child development and the learning process as articulated by the constructivists. However, this view has not been widely translated into practice. Many kindergarten teachers and parents still believe that young children are not ready for school unless they can recite the alphabet, count, and have the ability to follow instructions from adults.

PRINCIPLES AND THEORIES OF CHILD DEVELOPMENT

Studying and understanding child growth and development are important parts of teaching young children. No two children are alike. Children differ in physical, cognitive, social and emotional growth patterns. Even identical twins, who have the same genetic makeup, are not exactly alike. They may differ in the way they respond to play, affection, objects and people in their environment.

Knowledge of the areas of child development is basic to guiding young children. Linked to this is the understanding of healthy brain development. These stimuli begin at birth. Therefore, it is vital for children to have loving caregivers. Young children need dependable, trusting relationships. They thrive in environments that are predictable and nurturing. Understanding theories about how people develop helps form your knowledge base in caring for young children.

Child Development

Development refers to change or growth that occurs in children. It starts with infancy and continues to adulthood. By studying child development, you will form a profile of what children can do at various ages.

Different names are used to describe young children at different ages. From birth through the first year, children are called **infants.** **Toddlers** are children from age one up to the third birthday (Because of an awkward style of walking, the name toddler describes this age group). The term **preschooler** is often used to describe children ages three to six years of age.

Areas of Development

The study of child development is often divided into three main areas. These include physical, cognitive and social-emotional development. Dividing development into these areas makes it easier to study.

Physical development refers to physical body changes. It occurs in a relatively stable, predictable sequence. It is orderly, not random. Changes in size and weight are also part of physical development.

Physical skills, such as crawling, walking and writing, are the result of physical development. These skills fall into two main categories:

1. **Grossmotor development :** It involves improvement of skills using the large muscles in the legs and arms. Such activities as running, skipping and bike riding fall into this category.
2. **Fine-motor development :** It involves the small muscles of the hands and fingers. Grasping, holding, cutting and drawing are some activities that require fine-motor development.

Environmental factors also affect what children can do physically. These factors include proper nutrition and appropriate toys and activities.

Cognitive development, sometimes called **intellectual development,** refers to processes people use to gain knowledge. Language, thought, reasoning and imagination are all included. Identifying colours and knowing the difference between one and many are examples of cognitive tasks.

Language and thought are a result of cognitive development. These two skills are closely related. Both are needed for planning, remembering and problem solving. As children mature and gain experience with their world, these skills develop.

The third area of development is called social-emotional development. These two areas are grouped together because they are so interrelated. Learning to relate to others is social development. Emotional development, on the other hand, involves feelings and expression of feelings. Trust, fear, confidence, pride, friendship and humor are all part of social-emotional development. Other emotional traits include timidity, interest and pleasure.

Learning to express emotions in appropriate ways begins early. Caregivers promote this learning when they positively model these skills. A person's self-concept and self-esteem are also part of this area. As children have success with all skills confidence flourishes. This leads to a healthy self-concept and sense of worth.

The physical, cognitive and social-emotional areas of development are linked to one another. Development in one area can strongly influence another area. For instance, writing words requires fine-motor skills. It also requires cognitive development. Language, a part of cognitive development, is needed to communicate with others. It is also necessary for growing socially and emotionally.

Principles of Development

Although each child is unique, the basic patterns or principles of growth and development are universal, predictable and orderly. Through careful observation and interaction with children, researchers and those who work with children understand the characteristics of the principles that follow:

1. Development tends to proceed from the head downward. This is called the **cephalocaudal principle.** According to this principle, the child first gains control of the head, then the arms, then the legs. Infants gain control of head and face movements within the first two months after birth. In the next few months, they are able to lift themselves up using their arms. By 6 to 12 months of age, infant start to gain leg control and may be able to crawl, stand or walk.

2. Development also proceeds from the center of the body outward according to the **proximodistal principle**. Accordingly, the spinal cord develops before other parts of the body. The child's arms develop before the hands and the hands and feet develop before the fingers and toes. Fingers and toes are the last to develop.

3. Development also depends on maturation. **Maturation** refers to the sequence of biological changes in children. These orderly changes give children new abilities. Much of the maturation depends on changes in the brain and the nervous system. These changes assist children to improve their thinking abilities and motor skills. A rich learning environment helps children develop to their potential.

Children must mature to a certain point before they can gain some skills. For instance, the brain of a four-month-old has not matured enough to allow the child to use words. A four-month-old will babble and coo. However, by two years of age, with the help of others, the child will be able to say and understand many words. This is an example of how cognitive development occurs from simple tasks to more complex tasks. Likewise, physical skills develop from general to specific movements. For example, think about the way an infant waves its arms and legs. In a young infant, these movements are random. In several months, the infant will likely be able to grab a block with his or her whole hand. In a little more time, the same infant will grasp a block with the thumb and fore finger.

SOCIALISATION PROCESS

As a child grows up, there is a deliberate and conscious effort made through active training to make the child learn the values and expectations of the society he or she lives in. The child has to learn to adjust and accommodate her behaviour according to the rules for appropriate behaviour in the society. Parents, teachers, elders as well as the peers (same age group children) all influence and control the behaviour of a child.

According to the Indian view, a child comes to this world with certain behavioural tendencies which carry over from previous birth. The role of the family is to bring up the child in such a way that her positive capacities are developed fully and negative tendencies are controlled. Apart from the family, there are also other influences on the child from the outside environment. The important agents of socialisation include media, day-care centers, peer group, school and religion.

Parents have the most direct effect on the socialisation of the child. They are role models for children. Their responses to child behaviour, giving approval or disapproval etc. mould the personality of child and plays a very important role in acquiring rules. In addition, parents arrange the environment of a children in different ways. They take the child outside in specific settings like museum, church, temple, mosque, hill station, sea beach. The grand parents and aunts and uncles of the child also contribute in the socialisation process. Children learn manners and skills by observing parents. During the life span of a person, at different ages, specific rituals are performed. These rituals represent the changes in the child from one stage to another. They contribute in forming the identity of the child.

The influence of the **peer group** of the child, particularly during middle childhood is very important. In the interactions with the children of the same age group, a child learns the importance of team work, sharing and trust. One of the significant effects of this is that the child learns to adjust and accommodate to the view point of the others.

The school which the child attends is another very important socializing agent. The child learns different types of social, intellectual and physical skills in school. The school provides the child with a miniature society where he or she has to learnt the right values and rules and follow them. Values such as honesty, democracy and fairness etc. are learnt in the school setting.

Now-a-days, children search and know the world through TV, magazines, books, comics, radio and films. This media influences the socialisation of the child in significant ways. A positive influence can be learning the importance of family values by watching good and informative programmes. Watching aggressive programmes and programmes based on violence can influence the child negatively.

In the present way of life, when both parents are doing jobs, very young children have to be left at day-care centers. These centers, therefore, play an important role in the socialisation of the child because the child will learn many things about appropriate behaviour in the society. For children from poor background the Aganwadis under the programme of Integrated Child Developments (ICDs) help children to learn about appropriate social behaviour and the importance of community life.

Theories of Development

Psychologists continue to study human development. They are learning more about what people are like and how they develop. Over the past century, many psychologists have provided theories that are considered practical guides. A theory is a principle or idea that is proposed, researched and generally accepted as an explanation. Developmental theories provide insights into how children grow and learn. Theories are helpful for understanding and guiding developmental processes.

Theories can be useful decision-making tools. Since a variety of theories exists, teachers need to understand these different approaches for working with children. Theories will help you understand strategies for promoting children's development. Four major theories about how children learn are important. These include theories of mid-twentieth century psychologists Erik Erikson, Jean Piaget and Lev Vygotsky. The final theorist, Howard Gardner, is a twenty first century developmental psychologist. These theories are based on observation and experiences with children.

Erikson's Psychosocial Theory

Erik Erikson proposed a theory of psychosocial development. He believed development occurs throughout the life span. His theory provided new insights into the formation of a healthy personality. It emphasizes the social and emotional aspects of growth. Children's personalities develop in response to their social environment. The same is true of their skills for social interaction.

Erikson's theory includes eight stages. At each stage, a social conflict or crisis occurs. These are not generally tragic situations; however, they require solutions that are satisfying both personally and socially. Erikson believed that each stage must be resolved before children can ascend to the next stage.

Maturity and social forces help in the resolution of the crisis or conflict. Therefore, teachers and parents play a powerful role in recognizing each stage. By providing social opportunity and support, teachers and parents can help children overcome each crisis. Following table contains the first four stages of Erikson's theory. These stages occur during the early childhood years. The paragraphs that follow give a brief overview of these early stages.

Erikson's Stages of Development During Early Childhood		
Stage	**Approximate Age**	**Psychosocial Crisis**
I	Birth–18 months	Trust versus mistrust
II	18 months–3 years	Autonomy versus shame and doubt
III	3–5 years	Initiative versus guilt
IV	6–12 years	Industry versus inferiority

Note : *The first four stages of Erikson's theory concern children from birth to twelve years.*

PIAGET'S COGNITIVE DEVELOPMENT THEORY

Jean Piaget's thinking has challenged teachers to focus on the *ways* children come to know as opposed to *what* they know. His theory of cognitive development focuses on predictable cognitive (thinking) stages. Piaget believed that thinking was different during each stage of development. His theory explained mental operations. This includes how children perceive, think, understand and learn about their world.

Piaget believed that children naturally attempt to understand what they do not know. Knowledge is gathered gradually during active involvement in real-life experience. By physically handling objects, young children discover that relationships exist between them. Terms Piaget used to describe these processes were *schemata, adaptation, assimilation* and *accommodation.* These processes occur during each stage of development.

Schemata are mental representations or concepts. As children receive new information, they are constantly creating, modifying, organizing and reorganizing schemata.

Piaget's theory includes four stages: sensorimotor, preoperational concrete, and formal operations. The first three stages occur during early childhood and the early school-age years. The following paragraphs describe these stages.

Piaget's Stages of Development

The **sensorimotor stage** takes place between birth and two years of age. Infants use all their senses to explore and learn. In this way, sensory experiences and motor development promote cognitive development. Babies' physical actions, such as sucking, grasping and hitting, help them learn about their surroundings. Movements are random at first. Gradually they become intentional as behaviours are repeated. Children begin to learn that objects still exist even when they are out of sight. This is known as *object permanence.* Through exploration and exposure to new experiences, new concepts are learned.

The **preoperational stage** takes place between ages two and seven. Children during this stage are very *egocentric*. This means that they assume others see the world the same way they do. Children do not yet have the ability to see others' points of view. During this time, representation skills are learned. These skills include language, symbolic play, and drawing. Children learn to use symbols and internal images, but their thinking is illogical. It is very different from that of adults. Children begin to understand that changing the physical appearance of something does not change the amount of it. They are able to recognize the difference between size and volume. For example, a ball of clay can be stretched into a long rope. Even if the physical appearance changes, the amount of the object does not change. This skill is called *conservation.* At this stage, children can also classify groups of objects and put objects in a series in order.

During the ages of seven to eleven years, **concrete operations** begin. Children develop the capacity to think systematically, but only when they can refer to actual objects and use hands-on activities. Then they begin to internalize some tasks. This means they no longer need to depend on what is seen. They become capable of reversing operations. For example, they understand that 3 + 1 is the same as 1 + 3. When real situations are presented, they are beginning to understand others' points of view.

The fourth stage, *formal operations,* takes place from eleven years of age to adulthood (the age range you are in right now). According to Piaget, young people develop the capacity to think in purely abstract ways. They no longer need concrete examples. Problem solving and reasoning are key skills developed during this stage.

VYGOTSKY'S SOCIOCULTURAL THEORY

Both Jean Piaget and Lev Vygotsky believed that children build knowledge through experiences. Piaget believed this happened through exploration with hands-on activities. Vygotsky, on the other hand, believed that children learn through social and cultural experiences. Interactions with peers and adults help children in this process. While interacting with others, children learn the customs, values, beliefs, and language of their culture. For this reason, families and teachers should provide plently of social interaction for young children.

Vygotsky believed language is an important tool for thought and plays a key role in cognitive development. He introduced the term ***private speech***, or self-talk. This refers to when children "think out loud". After learning language, children engage in this self-talk to help guide their activity and develop their thinking. Generally, self-talk continues until children reach school age.

One of Vygotsky's most important contributions was the *zone of* ***proximal development*** (ZPD). This concept presents learning as a scale. One end of the scale or "zone" includes the tasks that are within the child's current development level. The other end of the scale includes tasks too difficult for children to accomplish, even with help. In the middle are the tasks children cannot accomplish alone. These are achieved with help from another knowledgeable peer or adult. The term used for this assistance is ***scaffolding***. Just as a painter needs a structure on which to stand and point a building, scaffolding provides the structure for learning to occur. For example, a teacher could scaffold a child's learning while constructing a puzzle. The teacher might demonstrate how a piece fits or provide clues regarding colour, shape or size. The "zone" is constantly changing. In contrast to Piaget, Vygotsky believed that learning was not limited by stage or maturation. Children move forward in their cognitive development with the right social interaction and guided learning.

KOHLBERG'S THEORY OF DEVELOPMENT

According to him moral development of the child proceeds in sequential but distinctive stages. These stages are given below:

(a) **Stage-I :** In the early years of a child's life (from zero-four years) the physical consequences of an action determines its goodness or badness. If fire burns the child, he does not touch it. The child is ego-centric and standards of morality are external here.

(b) **Stage-II :** The child gives importance to his own point of view, (his self) and is able to take account of other's roles insofar as he can use them in his own way. This is a period of make belief. Right action is what which satisfies the needs of the child. The role of others is also important in the sense that a child does only what can bring approval of others. Thus, only that behaviour is moral which can satisfy not only self needs of the child but it must please others also.

(c) **Stage-III :** At this stage the child adopts the view pints of others on the basis of their consequences. He does not question the views of others. The child considers only that thing as right which are considered as right by others. Thus, the child is totally conformist to the standard of the society.

(d) **Stage-IV:** At this stage, the child is able to make any moral decision on his own without caring for the thinking of others. Though he considers laws and regulations set by the society as the essence of morality, yet he

develops his own principles of morality on various occasions. Thus, he is a non-conformist to the norms of the society to a great extent.

(e) **Stage-V :** Standards and norms are more internalized here. The adolescents examine various view points prepared by different societies and recognize them. They think that the laws prepared by their own society are correct. Other societies may have good moral principles that must be adopted after careful appraisal.

(f) **Stage-VI :** This is the last stage of moral development according to Kohlberg. Here the universality of the view points of the individual is seen. He formulates his own universal moral principles which he thinks that all societies should adhere to it. True understanding of right and wrong is developed at this stage.

Gardner's Multiple Intelligences Theory

Howard Gardner has helped teachers rethink how they work with young children. Traditional intelligence tests mainly focus on language and math/logic skills. In contrast, Gardner's theory of **multiple intelligences** emphasizes that there are different kinds of intelligences used by the human brain. Gardner believes intelligence is the result of complex interactions between children's heredity and experiences. This theory focuses on how cultures shape human potential.

Gardner claims that children learn and express themselves in many different ways. In the process, they are using several types of intelligence. Each intelligence functions separately, but all are closely linked. According to Gardner, a potential intelligence will not develop unless it is nurtured. Learning can best be achieved by using a child's strongest intelligence. Gardner claims, however, that all children need opportunities to develop all areas of intelligence.

The multiple intelligence theory allows teachers to see the positive attributes of all children. Teachers also view Gardner's theory as a meaningful guide for making curriculum decisions. It gives them a chance to assess children's learning strengths. From this data, teachers can plan a wide variety of learning experiences.

Theories of Intelligence

1. Faculty theory of intelligence:

This is the oldest theory of intelligence given during the period of pre-experimental psychology. According to this theory mind is made up of different faculties like reasoning, logic, memory, imagination and discrimination. These faculties are independent of each other and can be developed by rigorous mental exercises of the difficult subject-matter.

This theory does not take the hereditary factors of intelligence into account and thus this theory was discarded by the later psychologists who believed that we can never improve the intellectual capacity of a person if he is mentally slow by birth.

2. Unifactor theory:

According to Alfred Binet (1916) intelligence is a general intellectual ability which is made up of several discrete abilities. These abilities include

(i) to reason well with abstract material

(ii) to comprehend well

(iii) to have a clear direction of thoughts

(iv) to relate thinking with the attainment of a desirable end and

(v) to be self-critical.

All these abilities combined together is called general mental ability. Thus, intelligence is a single but complex mental process which can be measured by different kinds of materials designed for the purpose.

3. Two factors theory:

This theory was developed by an English psychologist, **Charles Spearman** in 1904. According to him, intellectual abilities consist of two factors, general ability known as 'G' factors and specific abilities known as 'S' factors.

Characteristics of G factors

(i) It is universal inborn ability.

(ii) It is general mental energy.

(iii) It is constant, *i.e.*, it remains the same in all the individuals and does not change with time.

(iv) The amount of G differs from person to person depending on his genes.

(v) It is used in every life activity.

(vi) Greater the amount of G in an individual, larger is the chance of his success in life.

Characteristics of 'S' factors

(i) It is learnt and hence acquired in the environment.

(ii) It varies from activity to activity in the same individual.

(iii) The amount of S also differs from person to person due to his accessibility to learning situations.

(iv) 'S' factors are related to the specific activity. A low correlation between two or more functions or activities indicates the presence of 'S' factor involved in the activity. A person can be expert only in one or few activities because of the specific factors involved in the activity.

According to Spearman, out of these two factors 'G' factor is more important and thus it is an important measure of intelligence. So, any intelligence test should measure only 'G' factor because it provides most important basis of predicting a person's behaviour in different situations. Raven's Progressive Matrices and Catell's Culture Fair Test both measure 'G' factor.

Spearman has explained his theory with the help of a tetrad equation which is given below :

$rap \times rbq - raq \times rbp = 0$

Here,

a = opposites
b = discrimination
p = completion
q = cancellation

Thus, rap means correlation between opposites and completions, rbq means correlation between cancellation and discrimination, raq means correlation between opposite and cancellation and rbp means correlation between discrimination and completion. This theory can also be explained with the help of a diagram given below :

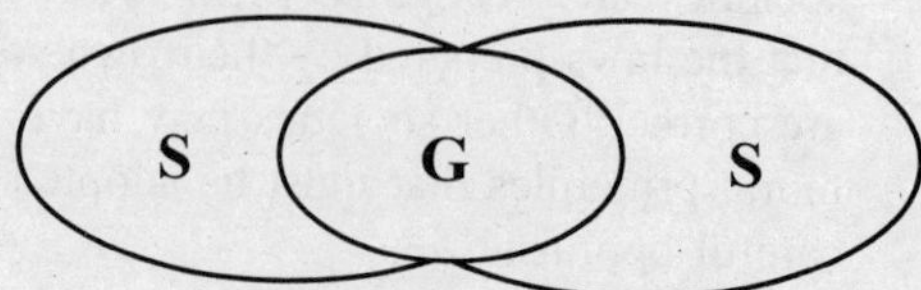

4. Multi-factors theory :

This theory was developed by an American psychologist, **E.L. Thorndike.** He opposed the theory of general intelligence by saying that there are specific stimuli and specific mental responses. Intelligence is nothing more than a potential specific connections between these stimuli and responses. Differences of intelligence among people are due to the different number of such connections in the neurological system. This theory is also called **atomistic theory** of intelligence. There are **four attributes of intelligence** according to him:

(a) *Level :* It refers to the difficulty of a task that can be removed by using intelligence. If different tasks are arranged in increasing difficulty order, then the height that a person can attain determines his level of intelligence. It is a kind of power test.

(b) *Range :* It refers to the number of tasks of the same difficulty value that a person can do in a certain period of time. Theoretically, an individual possessing a certain level of intelligence should be able to solve the whole range of tasks at a given level. It is a kind of speed test.

Range and level can not be completely isolated from each other. We can not measure range without altitude (level) and vice versa.

(c) *Area :* It refers to the total numbers of situations at each level to which the individual is able to respond. Area is the

summation of all ranges at each level of intelligence. Area = Level × Range.

(*d*) *Speed :* It refers to the rapidity with which an individual can respond to a test items. Speed and level are positively correlated. It is different from range in the sense that no specific time is given here to complete a task.

Every intelligence test should consist of these four attributes.

5. Group factor structure of intelligence (PMA Test) :

This theory was developed by **L.L. Thurstone.** According to him, intelligence is not an expression of general factor but a combination of group of traits. They are intermediate factors, *i.e.*, they are not so universal as 'G' factor and they are not so specific as 'S' factor. This primary group of factors give the common mental abilities, a functional cohesiveness and then constitute a group. Another group of common mental abilities is said to have another primary factor and so on. In this way, there are a number of groups of mental abilities each of which has its own primary factors. On the basis of factor analysis of these groups, Thurstone identified the following seven group factors which are termed as primary mental abilities (PMA).

1. Number factor (N) : It is the ability to do numerical calculations rapidly and accurately.
2. Verbal factor (V) : They are related to the operations involving verbal comprehension.
3. Space factor (S) : It is related to the tasks in which subject manipulates an object imaginary in space.
4. Word fluency factor (W) : It is involved to the situation when the subject is asked to think of isolated words at a fast rate.
5. Reasoning factors (R) : It is used in those tasks that require the subject to discover a rule or principles involved in series or groups of letters.
6. Rote memory (M) : It is the ability to memorize a fact quickly.
7. Perceptual speed (P) : It is the ability to note perceptual (visual) details rapidly.

The point to be noted here is that these seven abilities are significantly correlated with each other.

6. Structure of intelligence (SI) model :

This model was given by **J.P. Guilford** in 1966 in the University of California on the basis of factor analysis of many tests. According to him human mind is composed of at least three dimensions—operations, contents and products, and each dimension of intellect is sufficiently distinct which can be detected by factor analysis. These three dimensions of mind are given below:

(A) **Operations :** Operations can be divided into five major groups of intellectual abilities.

- **Cognition :** It includes discovery, recognition of informations and new understanding of the facts.
- **Memory :** It is the ability to recognize or recall previously learnt material.
- **Divergent thinking :** This operation is closely associated with creative potential. It refers to the ability to search out and think in a novel out of track way.
- **Convergent thinking :** It refers to the generation of information from given information and drawing conclusion from the given facts.
- **Evaluation :** It is the ability to make judgement on the basis of merits and demerits of a phenomenon. Here, value judgement on knowledge and thoughts is placed after critically examining them.

(B) **Contents :** Five kinds of contents are involved here. Operations are performed on these contents.

- **Figural content :** It is the concrete material perceived through the senses. Visual materials have three properties, size, form and colour.

- **Auditory content :** It includes nature and characteristics of sound perceived.
- **Symbolic content :** It includes letters, digits and other conventional signs usually organised in general pattern.
- **Semantic content :** It refers to those verbal meanings, ideas and concepts for which no examples are necessary.
- **Behavioural content :** It includes knowledge regarding other persons.

(C) Products : When five operations are applied to five types of contents, six kinds of products are made.

- **Units :** It refers to the production of a single word, definition or isolated bits of informations.
- **Classes :** It refers to the production of a concept.
- **Relations :** It refers to the production of any form of relationship, such as, analogy, opposite or similar ones.
- **System :** It refers to the production of internally consistent set of classification of various forms.
- **Transformation :** It refers to the production of changes in meaning, organisation or some other arrangement.
- **Implication :** It refers to the production of such information which is beyond the data given.

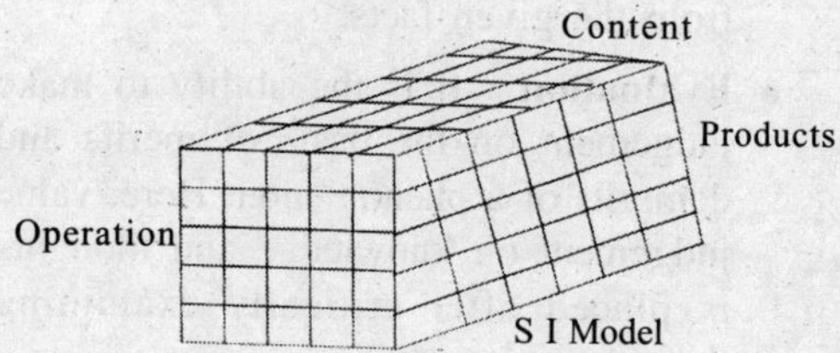

On the basis of the model given above it can be stated that there are 5 × 5 × 6 = 150 factors involved in intelligent acts.

7. Two Level Process Theory of Intelligence :

This theory was developed by **Jensen** in 1968. According to him intelligence is a combination of two levels of processes. One is associative intelligence and the other is abstract intelligence. Associative intelligence includes those kinds of tests that depend upon memory and simple verbal association. Abstract intelligence includes those factors as concept learning, thinking, problem solving skills, multiple discrimination, principle learning etc.

8. Burt and Vernon's hierarchy theory :

Burt (1940) separated four factors of intelligence by using statistical techniques :

- General factors (common to all traits)
- Group factors (common to some of the traits)
- Specific factors (limited to few traits)
- Error factors (limited to a particular trait when it is measured)

When human mind is put at the top, there will be 5 level hierarchical model of intelligence where general factors will come next to intelligence and error factors will come in the last.

Vernon, on the other hand, suggested that intelligence tests measure an overall factor G as well as two other mental abilities. First are related to verbal, numerical and educational. Second are related to practical, mechanical, spatial and physical. These two major factors can be divided into minor group factors. These minor factors can further be divided into various specific factors and so on.

UNDERSTANDING ADOLESCENCE

The word adolescence is derived from Latin word "adolescere" meaning "to grow up" or "to mature."

It is a period of transition between childhood and adulthood that involves a number of changes in body and mind.

World Health Organization (WHO) defines adolescence as a phase of life between 10-19 years of age characterized by physical growth, emotional, psychosocial and behavioural changes, thus, bringing about transformation from childhood to adulthood. These changes usually occur a year or two earlier in girls than boys. Some of the changes are externally visible and some are internal. These changes are normal and natural and are due to release of various hormones in both boys and girls.

Adolescence : A Period of Change

I. Physical Changes in Adolescent Boys

Physical changes in adolescent boys are:

- Growth spurt occurs
- Shoulders broaden
- Muscles develop
- Skin becomes oily
- Voice deepens
- Growth of moustaches and beard
- Growth of underarm, chest and genital hair
- Penis and testes enlarge
- Sperm production begins in the testes and ejaculation occurs

II. Physical Changes in Adolescent Girls

There are different changes in girls:

- Growth spurt occurs
- Breasts develop
- Skin becomes oily
- Hips widen
- Waistline narrows
- Growth of underarm and genital hair
- External genitals enlarge
- Uterus and ovaries enlarge
- Ovulation occurs and menstruation begins.

III. Sexual Changes in the Boys

During adolescence the adolescents become sexually active. So it is very important to know the sexual changes. The sexual changes in boys are:

- Penis, testes and scrotum enlarge
- Pubic, axillary and bodily hair appears
- The voice of the young boys breaks and attains a deeper tone
- The body itself becomes more distinctly muscular
- Sexual urge begins
- Sperm production begins in the testes and ejaculation occurs.

IV. Sexual changes in the girls

The sexual changes in girls are:

- Menarche, the appearance of the first menstruation is a dramatic event in the life of a female. The menstrual cycle, initially, may be irregular but becomes regular over a period of time.
- Budding of the breasts takes place, which becomes progressively bigger and fuller
- Auxiliary and pubic hairs start appearing
- The hips become wider and the body shape changes
- Sexual urge begins.

V. Emotional and Social Changes during Adolescence

These are the changes which are not observable as physical but definitely the behaviour of adolescents changes due to emotional and social changes happening in their body and mind. These changes are:

- Emotional instability
- Preoccupied with body image
- Frequent mood changes
- Curiosity and experimentation
- Self-exploration and evaluation
- Concerns and worries about the body changes
- Conflicts with family/elders over control
- Development of abstract thinking but confusion at times
- Attraction towards opposite sex
- Day dreaming and fantasizing
- Relationships tend to be oriented from parents to peers.

Developmental Stages in Adolescence

Adolescence may be divided into early, middle and late periods, which are respectively the 10-14, 15-17 and 18-19-year age groups. These periods roughly correspond with the phases in physical, social and psychological development in the transition from childhood to adulthood.

Stages of Adolescent Development

Stage of Adolescence	Physical Development	Cognitive Development	Social-Emotional Development
Early Adolescence **Approximately 11-13 years of age**	• Puberty: grow body hair, increase perspiration and oil production in hair and skin, Girls – breast and hip development, onset of menstruation Boys – growth in testicles and penis, wet dreams, deepening of voice • Tremendous physical growth: gain height and weight • Greater sexual interest	• Growing capacity for abstract thought • Mostly interested in present with limited thought to the future • Intellectual interests expand and become more important • Deeper moral thinking	• Struggle with sense of identity • Feel awkward about one's self and one's body; worry about being normal • Realize that parents are not perfect; increased conflict with parents • Increased influence of peer group • Desire for independence • Tendency to return to "childish" behaviour, particularly when stressed • Moodiness • Rule- and limit-testing • Greater interest in privacy
Middle Adolescence **Approximately 14-18 years of age**	• Puberty is completed • Physical growth slows for girls, continues for boys	• Continued growth of capacity for abstract thought • Greater capacity for setting goals • Interest in moral reasoning • Thinking about the meaning of life	• Intense self-involvement, changing between high expectations and poor self-concept • Continued adjustment to changing body, worries about being normal • Tendency to distance selves from parents, continued drive for independence • Driven to make friends and greater reliance on them, popularity can be an important issue • Feelings of love and passion
Late Adolescence **Approximately 19-21 years of age**	• Young women, typically, are fully developed • Young men continue to gain height, weight, muscle mass, and body hair	• Ability to think ideas through • Ability to delay gratification • Examination of inner experiences • Increased concern for future • Continued interest in moral reasoning	• Firmer sense of identity • Increased emotional stability • Increased concern for others • Increased independence and self-reliance • Peer relationships remain important • Development of more serious relationships • Social and cultural tradition regain some of their importance

Characteristics of Adolescence

Growth spurt

Adolescents mature at varying rates of speed and are highly disturbed by body changes. They are physically vulnerable because of poor health habits or risky experimentation with drugs and sex.

Self discovery

The adolescent is in the process of discovering self and it fluctuates across situations and times. The adolescent finds herself moody and understanding, ugly and attractive, introverted and fun loving.

Desire for independence and prove their identity

Adolescents have a great desire for independence and want to be treated like adults. Anxiously searching for identity, adolescents attach great importance to status symbols, as reflected by their possessions and clothing. Rebellion seems to be inevitable, so they can be different from their parents and defy them.

Egocentrism

This is the heightened self-consciousness of adolescents, which is reflected in their belief that others are as interested in them as they are themselves. They have attention seeking behaviour- the attempt to be noticed, visible and "onstage" and consider them unique. This, according to some writers, is responsible for drug use, suicides and failure to use contraceptives during sex.

Emotionally unstable

Their emotions outpace their rational thinking, they are so intertwined that adolescents have difficulty distinguishing between feeling and thinking.

Curiosity and experimentation

Adolescents are curious, innovative, exploring and experimenting. Fascinated by "adult" behaviours; they are motivated to try out forbidden activities like rash driving, sex and experiments with drugs.

Peer influence outweighs parental affection

Adolescents need frequent validation by others and they desperately seek peer affiliation and acceptance. They are fiercely loyal to peer group values and peers' opinions become most influential and guide the flow of their life.

Changing focus of relationships

Parents no longer are the major focus of the teenagers' world. Adolescents shift from same-sex best-friend relationships to having close interactions and increasing interest in both sexes. They are often aggressive and argumentative.

Idealism and confrontation with religion, traditions and moral value

Adolescents are idealistic and have strong sense of fairness. They criticize, challenge and confront moral values and ask frequent, ambiguous questions about the meaning of life.

Absence of long-term thinking about life and the world

The absence of abstract thinking makes the present most precious and self – the most important. The future seems far away and immediate gratification becomes more important.

Desire to be considered as an asset rather than a problem

The moral and spiritual development leads the adolescent to find a bigger role for himself while questioning the behaviour of elders.

Adolescence is characterized by turbulent changes in self and complex interaction with the environment. On the other hand it makes them vulnerable and often leads to conflicts and undesirable and socially unacceptable behaviour. The society needs to be empathetic and understand adolescents to harness their potential and energy.

Challenges of Adolescence

The period of adolescence usually is an eventful one. However, it poses various challenges for the adolescents and society. These challenges are:

- **Challenges related to Physical Development:** Physical changes are an essential part of adolescence. While these changes are part of a normal process of maturation, it is a challenging process for the individual especially when these changes are early or late compared to their peers. The process of physical maturation often creates problems for adolescents.
- **Challenges related to Cognitive Development:** The adolescents develop a capacity for abstract thinking, discover how to think about relationship issues, discerns new ways of processing information and learns to think creatively and critically.
- **Challenges related to Psychosexual Development:** The adolescent is no longer a child. He is a new person emerging into an adult. This process of understanding self and seeking meaning and direction leads to identity formation. The adolescent constructs concepts of self within the context of relations with others, yet he is also seeking to establish an independent entity. This journey of self-discovery is both stressful and anxiety-provoking for them.

- **Challenges related to Social Development:** Adolescents need to find their place in society and gain a sense of fitting in it. This is a process of socialization involving an adolescent's integration with society. This process socialization enhances the sense of personal identity, and the development of personal identity helps the adolescent to deal with society's expectations and standards and norms.
- **Moral and spiritual challenges:** The processes of social development and the formation of a personal identity go hand in hand with moral and spiritual development. The adolescent finds it difficult to choose between self-sacrifice and social conformity. The process of identity formation, peer pressure, desire to form relationships and exploration of their sexuality pose difficult challenges.

Thus, adolescence by virtue of its nature of change, pose innumerable challenges both for adolescents as well as society. Awareness generation, providing correct and scientific information may help to face these challenges up to a great extent.

*****

UNDERSTANDING TEACHING LEARNING

THEORETICAL PERSPECTIVES ON LEARNING BEHAVIOURISM

Behaviourism is among the most dominant of modern theories of learning. According to behavioural theories, learning is viewed as the ability to perform new behaviours which are established as goals. There is an effort to create conditions which will enable the learners to demonstrate these behaviours.

The early behaviourist, Edward L. Thorndike has put forward three main laws of learning: The law of effect, the law of readiness and the law of exercise. The law of effect stresses the importance of the effect of a stimulus-response (S-R). Satisfying results reinforce the response while inadequate results weaken it. Reward and punishment are, therefore, important ingredients of learning. The law of readiness indicates the learner's willingness to make (S-R) connection while the law of exercise is related to the strengthening of the connection through practice.

Educational Implications

The behaviourist approach to learning has greatly influenced modern educational practices. Behaviourists have conceived of teaching as a manipulation of the environment in order to produce desired behavioural changes in learners and thus make education more effective. They suggest the adoption of the following three principles towards making a teaching-learning transaction yield desirable results.

- knowledge of results and use of positive reinforcement,
- minium delay in reinforcement, and
- elaboration of complex behaviour by dividing learning into a series of small steps.

Skinner's Theory of Operant Conditioning

Skinner (1958) propagated a theory related to stimulus-response relationship and reinforcement. In his view, learning is a change in behaviour. As the learner learns, his/her responses in terms of changed behaviour increase. Learning is, therefore, formally defined by him as a change in the likelihood or probability of a response.

Operant conditioning is a learning force which effects the desired response more frequently by providing a reinforcing stimulus immediately following the response. The most important principle of this type of learning is that behaviour changes according to its immediate 'consequences'. Pleasurable consequences strengthen behaviour while unpleasant consequences weaken it.

In *operant conditioning*, learning activities are divided into many small steps/tasks and reinforced one by one. The operant-the response/behaviour or act – is strengthened so as to increase the probability of its recurrence in the future. Three external conditions – reinforcement, contiguity and practice.

Reinforcement

The most important aspect of Skinner's theory of learning relates to the role of reinforcement. An organism/learner is presented with a particular stimulus – a reinforcer – after it makes a response. In a given situation, the organism/learner will tend to repeat responses for which it is reinforced.

Skinner made a distinction between positive and negative reinforcements. Positive reinforcement is a stimulus which increases the probability of desired responses. Usually, it is a positive reward. Praise, smiles, or a prize, are examples of positive reinforcement. In negative reinforcement, the desired behaviour is more likely to occur if such stimulus/ reinforcement is removed.

Educational implications

The basic implication of *operant conditioning* for instructional activities is their dependence on observable behaviour. For Skinner, reinforcement facilitates learning. Further, he thinks that the most effective control on human learning requires instrumental aids. Broadly, Skinner's theory has made the following contributions to the practice of education:

(*a*) **Teaching Machines:** Teaching machines, in the sense of systematic approaches to teaching with the help of machines, deserve attention as they have strongly influenced distance education both in theory and in practice. In this method, machines present the individual learners with a series of questions to be answered, problems to be solved, or exercises to be done. In addition, they provide automatic feedback to the learners.

(*b*) **Programmed Instruction:** Programmed instruction is a self-learning system in which the subject matter is broken up into small bits and presented in logical sequences. Each step builds deliberately upon the preceding one. A learner progresses through the sequence of steps at his/her own pace. Each step presents some new information about the theme that is being taught through the programme. At the end of each step there is a question to be answered by the learner. After the question is answered, the learner is expected to check his/her answer with the correct answer supplied in the programme. This correct answer functions as a reinforcing stimulus.

THEORETICAL PERSPECTIVES ON LEARNING COGNITIVE APPROACH

The cognitive approach is concerned with the individual's inner psychological functioning, and it strongly contends the behaviourist's emphasis on overt behaviour.

Cognitive theorists have made investigations to show that people learn by perceiving, comprehending and conceptualising problems. The comprehension of concepts and rules is transferable to the solution of new problems or from one situation to another. The cognitivists in arguing that people grasp things as a whole, are, therefore opposing the behaviourist approach to teaching which employs drills to memorise the information.

Cognitivists believe that learning is a question both of insight formation and of successful problem solving, and not a mechanical sequence of stimuli and responses. And so, teaching, according to them, should encourage understanding based on problem solving and insight formation.

Information Processing

The contemporary cognitivists equate human mental activities with the process that goes on in a 'computer' in operation. They conceptualise human beings as information processing systems. The following discussion explains the process of information system and the three different types of memories, each of which serves a different function in the total process. The three different types of memories are: (*i*) the sensory memory, (*ii*) short-term memory and (*iii*) the long-term memory. The sensory memory receives information into the system either visually or in an auditory form. This type of memory refers to the active mental process by which knowledge is coded or represented. The short-term memory refers to the process by which knowledge is organised, stored and accessed. The long-term memory refers to the mental process by which the information is integrated with previously stored information in short-term memory.

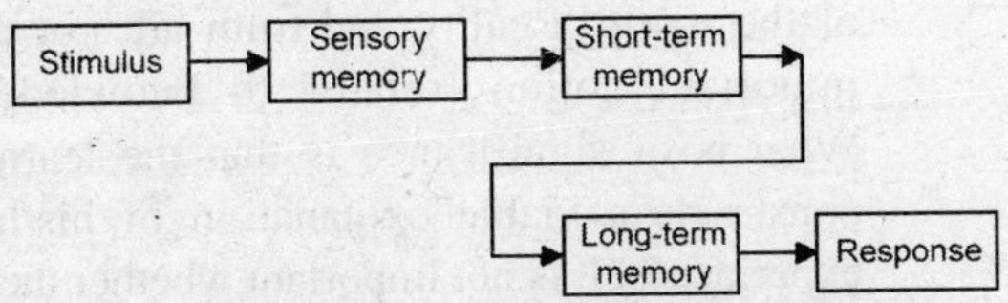

An Information Processing Model

Educational Implications

Major educational implications of this approach are:

(i) The most important aspect of the cognitive approach to education relates to promoting retention of knowledge acquired through learning.

(ii) Teaching materials should be planned on the basis of the theory of discovery. Instructional methods should, therefore, emphasize the learners' competence for spontaneous discovery, which implies that active learning methods should be adopted to motivate the learner to rediscover the facts or to find solutions to the problems.

(iii) This approach emphasises appropriate decisions regarding the instructional objectives, the analysis of prerequisite behaviour, and the teaching methods.

(iv) Such an approach also stresses problem-oriented learning. By raising problems and then solving them, it tells us how to teach in a reflective way.

(v) Lastly, it emphasises the study of learner characteristics which can be used by the teacher to expand the quality and quantity of the student's insights.

Bruner's Discovery Learning

Jerome S. Bruner (1966) is a proponent of cognitive learning and a developmental psychologist who is primarily interested in the development of mental abilities. His approach to psychology is eclectic (*i.e.* he selects the best or the most useful features from the various conflicting theories available). He looks at human being as information processors, thinkers and creators, and treats the learner as a reactive organism who actively selects, structures, retains and transforms learning/information to achieve certain goals.

Learning as a cognitive process

In Bruner's view, the *cognitive process* encloses three almost simultaneous processes:

- Acquisition of new knowledge/information
- Transformation of acquired knowledge
- Checking the adequacy of the new knowledge.

The modes of cognitive development are described by Bruner in terms of three hierarchical levels/ modes.

Autonomous learning

Bruner advocates autonomy in learning. He suggests that when the learner is allowed to approach learning as an act of discovery, s/he will increasingly engage him/herself in learning, with the autonomy of self-reward. In other words, the learner provides for his/ her own stimulation and in this way arouses his or her own curiosity.

According to Bruner, learning should be flexible and exploratory. Institutions should arouse learners' curiosity, minimise the risk of failure and make the activities relevant to them.

Bruner's theory of instruction

Bruner defines learning as a process in which a learner achieves instructional objectives with little or no help from the teacher. He emphasises 'the training of students in the use of mind' with confidence, energy and honesty. Thus, a theory of instruction should take into account:

(a) the ways of structuring knowledge,

(b) the presentation sequence,

(c) the motivating experience, and

(d) the nature of pacing of rewards and punishment.

In his theory of instruction, Bruner puts forth his original ideas concerning the most effective way of achieving knowledge and skills.

THEORETICAL PERSPECTIVES ON LEARNING CONSTRUCTIVISM THEORY

Constructivism has emerged as an influential doctrine in education in the last two decades. As an area of study it has roots in multiple disciplines, like philosophy, psychology, sociology, education, cognitive science and cybernetics. Its earliest votary was an Italian Philosopher Giambattista Vico, who proposed a constructivist theory of knowledge in which he regarded knowledge purely as a by product of human construction. This is evident in his words that "The known is the made."

In the words of Martin Dougiamas (1998), a student of science education at Curtin University of Technology on Internet Technologies, Australia, observed:

"Constructivism is building on knowledge known by the student. Education is student-centered; students have to construct knowledge themselves. Explanations can use metacognition to explain via metaphor. Semiotics, or meanings of words, are important to keep in mind. Constructivism is a theory, a tool, a lens for examining educational practices."

Bruner defines constructivism as a learning theory in which learning is seen as an active process in which learners construct new ideas or concepts based upon their current and past knowledge.

Principles of Constructivism

Two main ideas that can be termed as the principles of constructivism are as follows:

- The learner is not a passive entity but an active cognizing subject. He/she plays an important role in learning and development of knowledge. Knowledge is not passively received or absorbed by the learner but actively built by him/her. What more this implies is that knowledge cannot be transmitted from one learner to another. Learners have to construct this knowledge themselves.
- The function of cognition is not the discovery/representation of the world but adaptation. That is to say that cognition performs the function of organizing the learner's experiences of the world. Reality and truth are not the important notions related to knowledge. What is of significance is that the learner constructs a viable explanation of his/her experiences. It is not important whether these explanations are factually correct or mirror the reality, but rather that they are self-constructed by the individuals. The goal of cognition is thus not the representation of an objective independent reality but our own attempt to understand and organize it. In order to do so we create a version of it by our own selves. This is the process of construction of knowledge.

Constructivism in Education Theory

Some of the reasons that have fuelled the popularity of constructivism are the following:

- Educators are increasingly rejecting the philosophical basis of behaviourism. The assumption of the passive learner is especially unacceptable. Almost all the contemporary writers on education regard children as active and inherently educable. The dominant modern view of child nature is completely opposite of behaviourism. With increasing disenchantment with behaviorism, constructivism offers a refreshingly contrasting alternative.
- Children's knowledge often involves systematic errors and misconceptions. Constructivism alone accounts for their formation. The formation of personal constructs, misconceptions and errors will become obvious to you.
- It explains variability in meaning, perception and understanding that learners attach to objects and events.
- In philosophy of science, doubts have developed about the accessibility of objective

reality in the area of modern physics. If objective reality is not knowable even in an area as objective as physics, then the constructivist skepticism of objective knowledge is well founded.

- Constructivist theory is compatible with the interactional and cultural emphasis of theorists like Vygotsky and Bruner.

Types of Constructivism

There are three types of constructivism:

- **Trivial Constructivism:** Vorr Glasersfeld first coined this term in 1990 calling it the simplest type of constructivism. One can say that trivial constructivism is contained in all other types of constructivism, which will become obvious. It also parallels the argument of personal constructivism.

  Trivial constructivism agrees only with the first of the two main principles of constructivism, that is, the learner is an active player in the process of construction of knowledge.

- **Radial Constructivism:** This complex and difficult to describe notion is well summarized in the words of its most ardent advocate Glasersfeld (1990), who wrote, "Coming to know is a process of dynamic adaptation towards viable interpretations of experience. The learner does not necessarily construct knowledge of a 'real' world."

  Radical constructivism does not deny the objective reality, but considers it unimportant. According to Glasersfeld we do not even have a way of knowing this objective reality. It is colored by the lenses of the learner's eyes by way of his/her experiences.

- **Personal and Social Constructivism**

  Personal Constructivism: Theorists and researchers located in this position can often be identified by the fact that they call themselves as constructivist and not social constructivist. So what are the identifying features of this version of constructivism? As evident from the title it regards the individual learner as the constructor of knowledge and prioritizes the individual aspects of learning. Learning and cognitive development involve individual sense making in an experiential world.

  Social Constructivism: Social constructivism is founded on the thesis that social processes are central to learning and cognitive development. It regards knowledge as a social construct and prioritizes the social aspects of learning and cognitive development. Some of these social aspects are language, culture, everyday practices, material objects, interpersonal interaction, peer interaction, tools and symbols.

TEACHING

Teaching is one of the instruments of education and is a special function to impart understanding and skill. The main function of teaching is to make learning effective. The learning process would get completed as a result of teaching. Thus, teaching and learning are very closely related.

Meaning of Teaching

Teaching is a process in which one individual teaches or instruct another individual. Teaching is considered as the act of imparting instructions to the learners in the classroom situation. It is watching systematically.

Dewey: considers it as a manipulation of the situation, where the learner will acquire skills and insight with his initiation.

Important Definition of Teaching

According to this analysis, we can define teaching as:

1. **H.C. Morrison:** Teaching is intimate contact between the more mature personality and a less mature one.
2. **Jackson:** Teaching is a face-to-face encounters between two or more persons, one of whom (teacher) intends to effect certain changes in the other participants (students).

3. **J.B. Hough and James K. Duncan:** Teaching is an activity with four phases, a curriculum planning phase, an instructing phase, and an evaluating phase. This definition presents the organizational aspect by which can describe and analyze the teaching process.
4. **N.L. Gage (Democratic point of view):** Teaching is interpersonal influence aimed at changing the behaviour potential of another person.
5. **Clerk:** Teaching refers to activities that are designed and performed to produce in students behaviour.

Nature and Characteristics of Teaching

Teaching is a social and cultural process, which is planned to enable an individual to learn something in his life. We can describe the nature and characteristics of teaching in the following way:

- **Teaching is giving information:** Teaching tells students about the things they have to know and students cannot find out themselves. Communication of knowledge is an essential part of teaching.
- **Teaching is a complete social process:** Teaching is undertaken for society and by society. With ever-changing social ideas, it is not possible to describe the exact and permanent nature of teaching.
- Teaching is a process of development and learning.
- **Teaching is an interactive process:** Teaching is an interactive process between the student and the teaching sources, which is essential for the guidance, progress, and development of students.
- Teaching is from memory level to reflective level.
- Teaching is a continuum of training, conditioning, instruction, and indoctrination.
- Teaching causes a change in behaviour.
- Teaching is an art as well as science.
- Teaching is face to face encounter.
- Teaching facilitates learning.
- Teaching is observable, measurable and modifiable.
- **Teaching is a skilled occupation:** Every successful teacher is expected to know the general methods of teaching-learning situations.
- Teaching is both a conscious and an unconscious process.

Characteristics and Basic Requirements

Characteristics of Teaching

- **A system of action:** Teaching is a system of actions varied in form and related with content and pupil behaviour under the prevailing physical and social conditions.
- **A professional activity:** It is a professional activity involving teacher and student with a view to the development of students personality. Professionalism helps students in being regular and making harmony with their objects towards those they are concentrated.
- **Subjected to analysis and assessment:** Teaching can be analysed and assessed and analysis and assessment provide a feedback for further improvement.
- **An interactive process:** Teaching is highly dominated by the communication skills. Teaching is an interactive process carried with purpose and objectives.
- **A specialized task:** It is a specialized task and may be taken as a set of skills for realization of certain objectives.
- **A collection of various modes:** Teaching is a collection of various modes of itself. It is a broader term. Terms like conditioning, training, instruction, indoctrination denote a kind of teaching. They are a part of

teaching but not a synonym with teaching. These are various modes of teaching contributing towards teaching.

Basic requirement

The teaching process involves following variables.

1. **Dependent Variable:** The student is a dependent variable. He is subjected to changes and developments through the efforts of the teacher and teaching process. In the teaching process the dependent variable plays the functional or active role.
2. **Independent Variable:** The teacher is an independent variable. He is responsible for the functioning of students, the dependent variables. The teacher is free to act in the process while students are quite dependent on him. He plans, leads, organizes and controls the teaching process. Like dependent variables, independent variables also play the functional or active role.
3. **Intervening Variables:** The desirable interaction between the dependent and the independent variables to achieve the goals of teaching is needed. This role is played by the intervening variables. The content of teaching, methods and techniques, strategies and tactics management of instructional material and teaching environments, etc., are the Intervening Variables.

Some basic requirements of teaching are:

1. Teacher's devotion to teaching, and also on the other hand, student's devotion to learning
2. All the three variables of teaching
3. Professionalism
4. Suitable environment
5. Teacher-student relationship
6. Student's discipline.

LEARNER'S CHARACTERISTICS

A Learner is someone who is consistently learning. We all are the learner at some or the other time in our daily life. To be precise, a learner at a particular time is that person who is learning about a particular subject.

For a decision maker, it is important to know the learner's characteristics. It is essential to know what factors affect their learning. Learning can be described as the process of acquiring new or modifying existing knowledge, skill values, behaviour and preferences.

Learning is strongly based on the intellectual level, cognitive ability, perception, personality and attitude of a learner. As individual many factors affect the learning of a person. They are bound to get influenced by the social arena, cultural habits, and willingness of a person to adopt change. No successful outcome strategy can be expected without analyzing learner characteristics. Learner characteristics can be identified by collecting the information based on their cognitive, physiological, affective and social characteristics. Different methods are used to collect information about learners such as surveys, interviews, observation, current knowledge/skill levels and performance result.

Definitions of Learning

- **Gardener Murphy:** *"The term learning covers every modification in behaviour to meet environmental requirements."*
- **Henry P. Smith:** *"Learning is the acquisition of new behaviour or the strengthening or weakening of old behaviour as the result of experience."*

Learning means a permanent change in the behaviour of the learner through experience, instructions, and study. It is very difficult to measure the learning but the result of learning can be measured.

Learner characteristics can be described as measuring the characteristics of learners such as behavioural nature, attitudes and psychological towards everything related to learning. In learner characteristics aptitude is defined according to Cronbach and Snow as "any characteristic of a person that forecasts his probability of success under a given treatment" or "whatever makes a person ready to learn rapidly in a particular situation (or, more generally, to make effective use of a particular environment)". Various components were described in learner characteristics such as gender, attitude, motivation, learner style and cultural background.

There are the few characteristics of learners given below:

- **Habit of Readiness:** Learners should have habit of readiness. This habit is also known as law of motivation. Woodworth calls it law of mental set. The teacher should arouse the attention and interest of the students by asking suitable questions. Curiosity is indispensable for learning.
- **Habit of Exercise:** "Practice makes a man perfect" is a well known proverb. This habit is also known as law of practice or law of use and disuse.
- **Habit of Effect:** It is also called the law of pleasure and pain or law of satisfaction and annoyance. The activities which are associated with pleasure or satisfaction becomes more effective. Activities which are associated with pain, punishment are not repeated and their strength is decreased.

FACTORS AFFECTING TEACHING

Some factors influencing teaching aptitude, which are discussed as under:

- **Ability to maintain discipline:** This factor is to reveal if a prospective teacher can handle the class effectively. This would also bring out the authoritarian or democratic attitude in him/her.
- **Activeness:** Activeness is to judge how far an aspirant teacher is respective to any situation, action or work that comes up before him/her.
- **Adaptability:** This factor is to see if an aspirant teacher is adaptable to all such ideas and situations which are not contrary to the spirit and nature of his/her profession.
- **Attitude Towards Children:** Attitude towards children includes attitude of teacher towards the needs, nature, problems, behaviour (of his/her students or fellow teachers), in a group or as individual, inside the school or out of it. This goes to show how a teacher reacts to the children in various situations.
- **Attitude Towards Community:** This is to know a teacher's attitude towards society in general and towards his/her colleagues, students, principal, authorities, parents, friends, environment and so on in particular.
- **General Knowledge:** This is needed in a person aspiring to be a teacher for he shall often be required to talk on and even to guide in matters of general knowledge.
- **Health:** Good health is definitely necessary for having sound mind in a sound body. It is required to keep a teacher active and fresh both-in teaching and in guidance.
- **Honesty:** This hardly needs any explanation. A prospective teacher should be honest/ not only in the matters of money, but more so in his/her words and deeds.
- **Impartiality:** This is to know if he/she is impartial enough to treat all his/her students equally as also to know the extent to which he/she would be objective in his/her teaching and in his/her treatment.
- **Initiative:** A real teacher cannot rest with doing the work assigned to him/her. He/she would be zealous, industrious and insightful to take the lead. He/she should not be only respective to new ideas, but should take the initiative in discussions.
- **Interest in Profession:** It is obvious that if one has interest in this profession, one would naturally have interest in reading because one cannot be up to the mark without having interest in reading. A person having interest in profession would take interest in matters related to education.
- **Interest in Reading:** Reading is in fact the food for the teacher. It would keep him/her

in touch with the latest trends in his/her profession as also with general knowledge. If food is a must for the body, reading is a must for the mind.

- **Intelligence:** Intelligence is a term with a very wide connotation, comprising of a number of traits. The term here is used in limited sense of recognising with swiftness word analogy, number series and word relation.
- **Knowledge of Subject Matter:** It is to be noted that a secondary school teacher has to teach particular subject in the standard given by his/her head. This means he should have full command over the contents of the subject. Even otherwise, content is more important for thorough teaching with full command and confidence.
- **Personal Appearance:** This factor indicates the physical outlook of the teacher.
- **Professional Information:** This is related to the teacher's built in equipness beliefs and reaction on the methods of teaching, medium of instruction, evaluation techniques, curriculum, co-curricular activities, behaviour with children, school inspection, classroom interaction and school administration.
- **Sincerity:** This is to judge how far a prospective teacher is sincere in his/her work, views and temperament.
- **Skill in Teaching:** Skill in teaching is the fact that a teacher possesses in teaching his/her subject. This is something more than the method of teaching. A skilful person would always lead his/her students to learn with three Es—Easiness, Effectiveness and Economy. He/she would teach without making his/her student feel that they are being taught.
- **Teacher-Pupil Relationship:** It is to judge the extent to which a teacher is able to establish cordial relations with his/her students, and yet is able to keep a certain distance from his/her students.
- **Technical Skill:** The knowledge of pedagogy does not make a good teacher. It is the implementation of the knowledge in classroom that makes a good teacher. So a teacher having a repertoire of various skills can make a good teacher. Hence technical skill of a teacher is a great asset that would make him/her an effective teacher.
- **Attitude towards Social Work:** Social work cannot be initiated by imitating other people. One must have a positive attitude towards the work. By having positive attitude for social work in ample quota, he would make a successful and efficient teacher. A teacher is always ready to go an extra miles for other people or society.
- **Emotional Stability:** A stable teacher is an asset to any society. Emotionally matured teachers are most wanted when a country passes through a transition period. The change in society creates upheaval of great consequence which affect the immature minds of the pupils. To mould such pupils to the desired goal is the work of an emotionally stable teacher. Hence, maturity and stability are the precursors of a good stable teacher.

Teaching Styles

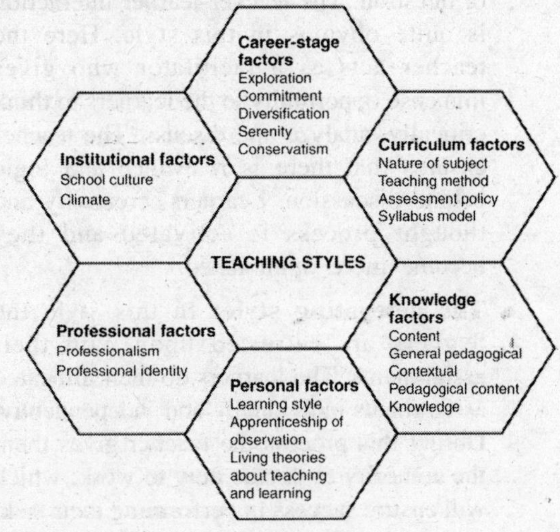

As the above figure clarifies, all teachers try different styles of teaching according to the situations and there are factors which affect the teaching styles. All the mentioned factors are like personal, professional, knowledge, curriculum, institutional and career-stage factors. Actually, dominance of any one or more of these factors in teaching process decides the style. Thus we can say that there is no such fixed teaching style which will lead to effective and successful teaching.

Effective teachers use mixture of styles and they are well aware of how and when to choose the most suitable one for teaching.

Thornton, B. Paul (2013) has suggested three basic teaching style:

- **The directing style:** This style is basically based on instructional based teaching. The teacher guides the learners through whole teaching learning-process going on in the classroom. Usually methodologies used during teaching are lecture, demonstration, lecture-cum-demonstration, AV presentation, reading, writing etc. In this style the teacher ensures that all the learners follow instructions and guidelines properly. This is almost traditional type of teaching.
- **The discussing style:** In this style the learners get a bit more freedom of speech and open environment to discuss their point or question. The teacher-learner interaction is quite obvious in this style. Here the teacher acts as a facilitator who gives immense opportunity to the learners to think critically, analyze and discuss. The teacher ensures that there is relevance and logic behind discussion. Learners' creativity and thought process is activated and they become more opinionated.
- **The delegating style:** In this style the learners are entrusted upon with their assignments. The learners do their allocated assignments individually and independently. During this process the teacher gives them the authority to decide how to work; which will ensure success in performing their task.

Teaching Models

"School faculties and individual teachers create life in schools by models of teaching, they choose and create."

—***Bruce Joyce***

One needs a good teaching style but with that the teacher must be aware of the teaching models that should be used in classroom. The teaching has to be given a direction and for this a proper draft or format is helpful which we can call as teaching model. As an architect makes a detailed plan of the building to be constructed on a paper, similarly, a teacher has to be prepared with a design or idea before teaching the learners.

Paul D. Eggen has rightly stated that models are prescriptive teaching strategies designed to accomplish particular instruction goals. A teaching model helps a teacher to reach out to all the learners effectively and successfully.

Features of a Good Teaching Model

- It should complement the content which is to be taught.
- It should have both philosophical and psychological background.
- It should help for better performance of both teacher and learners.
- It should be interactive in nature.
- It should help in building interesting and motivating environment in the classroom.
- It should help in developing creativity and innovative ideas in teacher as well as learners.
- It should help in bringing out the expected behavioural changes in the learners.
- It must be viable in recognizing the strengths and weaknesses of the learners and assess them by their feedbacks.

Fundamentals of Teaching Models

(i) **Focus:** It is the axis of any teaching model i.e., the main objective for whom it is to be used.

(ii) **Syntax:** All the dimensions of the model are organized sequentially.

(iii) **Principle of Sensation:** The concept of action-reaction is to be maintained to create a bond between teacher and learner.

(iv) **Social System:** The bond and interaction between teacher and learners should prepare them for the society by bringing behavioural change according to the norms of society.

(v) **Support System:** The model should be as a supplement to the regular teaching process which enhances the teaching effectiveness and learning experiences.

(vi) **Application Perspective:** The use and presentation of the model should be according to the content to be taught.

Teacher

If the learner stands on one end of the ongoing teaching-learning process as one of the pole then teacher act as the other pole for the desired flow of the teaching learning activities in classroom. Therefore, teacher related factors play quite signicant role in the process of teaching. Following are the teacher related factors in the teaching learning process.

(i) **Subject Knowledge:** There is a saying that a teacher is only as good as what they know. If a teacher lacks knowledge in a subject, that dearth of understanding is passed along to the students. A teacher who knows his subjects well can only play a decisive role in leading the journey of the teaching learning process. How effectively the task of teaching learning will be carried out that depend merely on the scholarly nature and mastery over the subject matter demonstrated by a teacher in the class or work situations.

(ii) **Knowledge of learners:** This is a broad category that incorporates knowledge of the cognitive, social and emotional development of learners. It includes an understanding of how students learn at a given developmental level; how learning in a specific subject area typically progresses like learning progressions or trajectories; awareness that learners have individual needs and abilities; and an understanding that instruction should be tailored to meet each learner's needs.

(iii) **Teaching Skills:** A teacher may know his subject well but for sharing, communicating and interacting various experience related to the learning of the subject, he needs specific teaching skills. The proficiency and deficfiency possessed by a teacher in this regard are quite responsible for turning the teacher learning process a big success or failure.

(iv) **Friendliness and Approachability:** Because it's the teacher's job to help students learn, they must be easy to approach. Students will have questions that can't be answered if the teacher isn't friendly and easy to talk to. The unapproachable, mean, arrogant, rude, teacher can't last long. If the students think of their teacher as their enemy, they certainly won't learn much. The best teachers are the most open, welcoming, and easy to approach. A good teacher possess good listening skills and take time out of their busy schedule to solve all kinds of problems of their students.

(v) **Personality and behaviour:** A teacher as a leader has to lead his students in the teaching learning process through the magnetic influence and incredible impression left on the minds of the students on the basis of his personality traits and behaviour. He is a role model for his students. His actions, behaviour pattern and personality traits carry a great meaning to his students for being imitated and brought in to practice.

(vi) **Level of Adjustment and Mental health of the teacher:** How adjusted a teacher feel in his personal and professional life and the state and level of mental health maintained

by the teacher carries much weight in influencing his teacher behaviour and teacher effectiveness needed for the effective control and management of the teaching, learning process. While a teacher possessing poor mental health and lack of adjustment in his personal and professional life may prove totally failure in realization of teaching learning objective, a teacher possessing good mental health and adjustment may prove an ideal image to his students and boon to the effectiveness of the teaching learning process.

(vii) **Discipline:** In a classroom, a teacher uses discipline to ensure routine is maintained, school rules are enforced, and the students are in a safe learning environment. A great teacher has effective discipline skills and can promote positive behaviours and change in the classroom. Without discipline, learning cannot be accomplished.

Learner

The learner is the key figure in any teaching – learning task. How will he learn or what will he achieve depends heavily on his own characteristics and way of learning. Such factors related with him can be described as below:

(i) **Learner's physical and mental health:** Teaching-Learning is greatly affected by the learner's physical and mental health maintained by him particularly at the time of teaching task. A simple headache or stomach ache can play a havoc with the process and products of learning. Children who did not keep up with satisfactory physical health of the learner at the time of learning become potent factor in deciding the outcome of the learning. A tense, emotionally and mentally disturbed learner cannot be expected to show satisfactory results in learning.

(ii) **Basic potential of the learner:** The results achieved by learner through teaching-learning task depend heavily upon his basic potential to undergo such learning. Such potential may consist of the following things:

- Learner's innate abilities and capacities for learning a thing.
- Learner's basic potential in terms of general intelligence and specific knowledge, under-standing and skills related to particular learning area.
- Learner's basic interests, aptitudes and attitudes related to the learning of a particular thing or area.

(iii) **The level of aspiration and achievement motivation:** Learning is greatly influenced by the level of aspiration and nature of achievement motivation possessed by the learner. The teacher has to maintain the level of his aspiration and achievement motivation to a reasonable level neither too high causing frustration for non-achievement nor too low as not to try for the things for which he is quite capable. In this way, one's level of aspiration and achievement motivation works significantly towards gains in learning.

(iv) **Goals in life:** The philosophy and immediate as well as ultimate goals of one's life affect the process and products of learning. His mode and ways of looking towards the things, his inclination towards the learning in a particular area and patience and persistence maintained for continuing his learning despite the heavy odds all depend upon his goals and philosophy of life.

(v) **Readiness and will power:** Learner's readiness and power to learn is a great deciding factor about his results in learning. Now power on earth can make a learner learn if he is not ready to learn. Contrarily, if he has a will to learn a thing then automatically, he will himself find the way for its effective learning.

Support Material

The availability and use of the study material, audios and videos, online courses, online tests and other teaching aids also increase the effectiveness of the teaching and learning. These materials aim to support teachers and students in achieving the learning outcomes. The teacher alone cannot provide all the needed condition for an effective teaching and learning process, other supporting materials should be provided.

Instructional Facilities

These include the classrooms, laboratories, seminar rooms, oncampus clinics, cybraries and other spaces used principally for the purpose of delivering formal instruction to students.

Their availability ensures effective teaching and if these are not available in adequate amount as per the number of students, then students will not be able to learn properly.

Learning Environment

Learning environment refers to the diverse physical locations, contexts, and cultures in which students learn. Since students may learn in a wide variety of settings, such as outside-of-school locations and outdoor environments, the term is often used as a more accurate or preferred alternative to classroom, which has more limited and traditional connotations—a room with rows of desks and a chalkboard. The term also encompasses the culture of a school or class—its presiding ethos and characteristics, including how individuals interact with and treat one another—as well as the ways in which teachers may organize an educational setting to facilitate learning. Effectiveness of teaching also depends upon the learning environment. If the teacher and learner are comfortable in the surrounding environment, then the learning will be effective; else, both the teacher and students will be distracted, leading to ineffective learning. In a noisy class, no matter how well-qualified the teacher is, he will not be able to teach effectively.

Institution

Effectiveness of teaching is also affected by the policies framed by institutions. These policies can give autonomy to the teacher or can control the classroom activity. If the teacher feels extremely controlled, then his performance will suffer. On the other hand, autonomy to teachers to choose teaching methods and classroom activities will bring an element of flexibility.

TEACHING SUPPORT SYSTEM

Today, in the 21st century understanding is more important than ever. That is why it is vital for educators to use methods or techniques in teaching that will enable learners to use their knowledge efficiently to solve problem in their daily lives.

The rapid growth of Information and Communication Technologies (ICT) has challenged the traditional method of teaching and changed the educational landscape globally. The teaching method is now divided into two different ways of thinking on education, one is traditional and other one is ICT Method.

Most of the teachers and experts have explored new methods of teaching and believe that modern methods or the ICT method is better than the traditional method of teaching.

When we talk about teaching methods then our society divides into three groups; one group favours the traditional teaching methods, second group favours modern teaching methods and third group is the one who supports the combination of both for effective teaching.

A teaching aid is something a classroom teacher uses in her class to help students improve reading and other skills, reinforce a skill, or to make learning fun. Teaching aids can be used in any of the core classes. There are several types of teaching aids to be utilized in a classroom.

Classification of Teaching Aids

Teaching aids can be classified in many different ways. Some of these classifications.

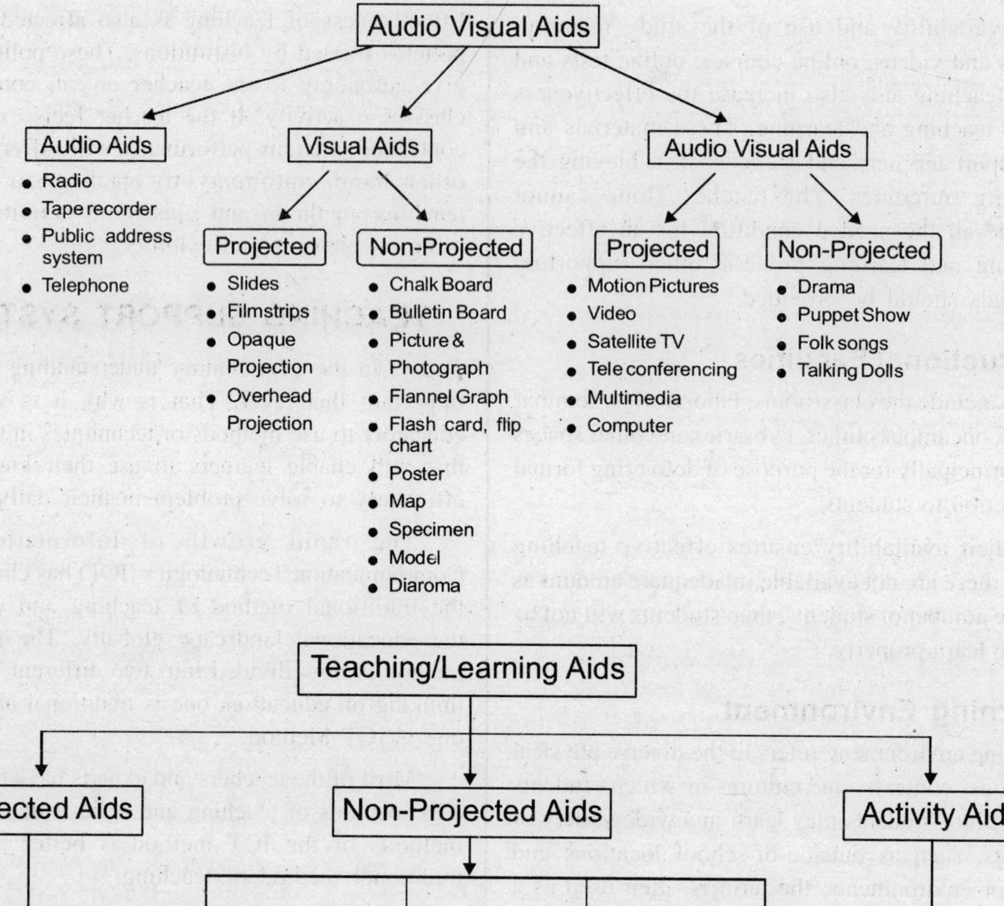

Teaching/Learning Aids

Projected Aids

1. Film & Film Projector
2. Film strips & Film strip Projector
3. Slides & Slide Projector
4. Episcope & Epidiascope
5. OHP
6. Television
7. LCD Projector
8. DPL Projector

Non-Projected Aids

Graphic Aids

1. Graphs
2. Diagrams
3. Posters
4. Maps
5. Cartoons
6. Comics
7. Flash Cards
8. Pictures & Photographs
9. Charts
10. Time line

Display Boards

1. Black Board
2. Roll-up Board
3. Peg Board
4. Hook & Loop Board
5. Flannel Board
6. Magnetic Board
7. Plastigraph Board
8. Bulletin Board
9. Marker Board

3-D Aids

1. Models
2. Objects
3. Specimen
4. Diorama
5. Puppets
6. Globes

Audio Aids

1. Radio
2. Tape Recorder
3. Public Address System

Activity Aids

1. Field Trip & Excursions
2. Exhibition
3. Demonstration
4. Dramatization
5. Museum
6. Planetarium
7. Aquarium
8. Terrarium
9. Vivarium
10. Teaching Machine
11. Programmed Learning
12. CAI

Hardware and Software in Teaching Aids

Educational technology can be classified into two categories, i.e., the hardware approach and software approach.

- **Hardware Approach:** It is based on the application of engineering principles for developing electromechanical equipments for instructional purposes. This approach is the result of the impact of scientific and technological development during the 20th century. Hardware approach mechanizes the process of teaching so that teachers would be able to deal with more students with less expenditure in educating them. Hardware:
    1. Computer
    2. Epidiascope
    3. Magic lantern
    4. Motion pictures
    5. Overhead projector
    6. Radio
    7. Slide and Film projector
    8. Tape recorders
    9. Teaching machines
    10. Television
- **Software Approach:** This uses the principles of psychology for building in the learner a complex repertoire of knowledge modifying his/her behaviour. It has originated from the pioneering work of Skinner and other behaviourists. The programmes that such a technology produces are often called 'Software'. Software approach is characterized by task analysis, writing precise objectives, selection of appropriate learning strategies, immediate reinforcement of responses and constant evaluation. Newspapers, books, magazines, educational games, flash cards may also form part of software.

EVALUATION SYSTEM

Evaluation covers a wider purpose than the testing. The testing only aims at knowing the achievement of the pupils in a particular subject during a specified period. Again, testing confines to the memorisation of knowledge only and does not test the application, skills, abilities, interests and other objectives of teaching of a subject. On the other hand, evaluation not only aims at knowing the achievements but helps in improving curriculum and methods also. It is never static but is dynamic and its methods and materials changes according to the changes in needs of the individual and society. Because education is a process of growth and development and its aims are changing from time-to-time, it is essential that our evaluation techniques should also change. So evaluation aims at improving the whole educational process in the following way:

1. Evaluation tests the genuineness of objectives and helps in their modification. It does not test the content learnt but the objectives. If the objectives are not achieved, it tries to find out the reason for that. It may be that the objectives are ambitious or below the standard. It is, therefore, necessary to modify the objectives in the light of the needs of the individual and of the society.
2. Evaluation helps in judging the effectiveness of the methods of teaching in terms of the objectives of teaching. The methods of teaching are also modified if they do not help in achieving the objectives.
3. Evaluation also helps in finding out the psychological and logical soundness of the material. Because curriculum is the base for success of the education process, it is essential that it should be dynamic and broad based and should be modified according to changing objectives.
4. It test the all-round development of the child and helps in predicting the future success of the student in a particular field. So it serves the diagnostic and prognostic purpose and thus serves as a basis for guidance to the teacher and the taught.
5. Evaluation helps in the improvement and modification of the evaluation tools and

techniques which should not be static but should change from time-to-time.

The scope and interrelation of evaluation with objectives, methods and curriculum can be shown in the following diagram:

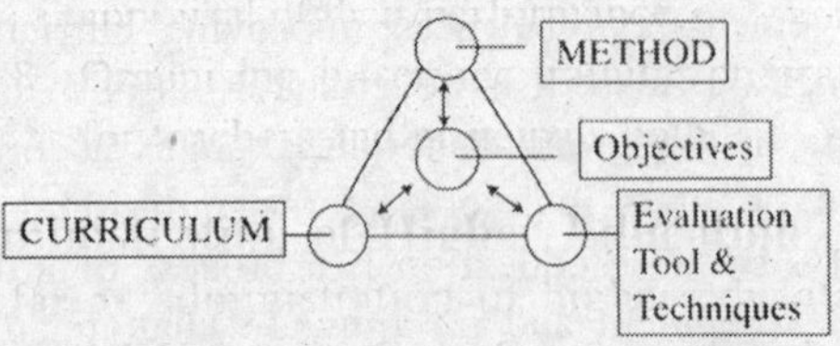

Fig. *Triangular Process of Evaluation*

Evaluation procedure should not delimit its scope to only paper and pencil aspect for this may not reveal most of the inherent qualities of the child's personality and his participation in the day-to-day activities of the school programme. So it is essential to maintain the systematic records of the pupil's progress in theoretical studies, practical work and the various co-curricular activities which form an integral part of educative process. This will give a true picture of the child's progress throughout the year and will thus give reliability and validity to the evaluation programme which is based upon the objectives of the teaching subject.

For this, every school should maintain diaries of pupils, anecdotal records and cumulative records. Children's diaries throw much light to their appreciations, attitudes and interests and attitudes and their personal and social problems. Anecdotal records is the teacher's description of significant pupil behaviour in an incident on critical behaviour.

Cumulative Record assist the teacher to discover the growth of students in different directions. Every type of information regarding each child is entered in this card from time to time. This will reveal the whole history of the child and the assessment done in this way should be counted at the time of final assessment. Cumulative records will also help the vocational guidance services in determining the future vocations of the pupils.

Purpose of Evaluation

In broad sense, the purpose of evaluation can be classified into two categories:

1. **The Educational Purpose of Evaluation:** The educational purpose of evaluation is basically with Quality Control in relation to:

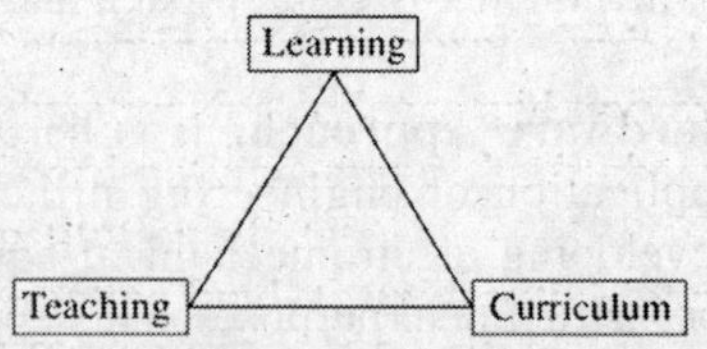

2. **The Administrative Purpose of Evaluation:** The administrative purpose of evaluation is concerned with the accountability to:

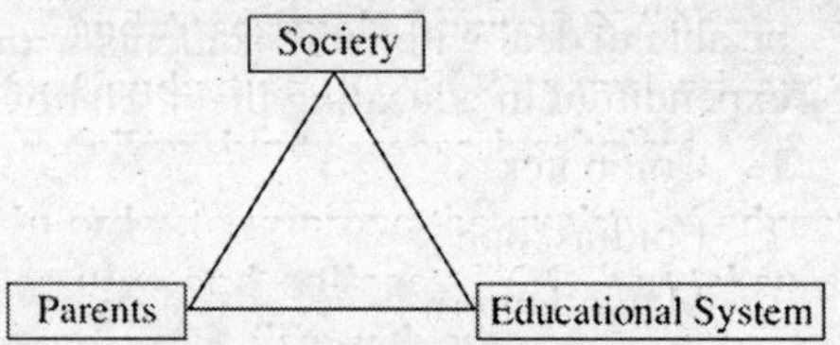

According to Moffatt: "Evaluation is a continuous process and is concerned with more than the formal academic achievement of the students. It is interested in the development of the individual in terms of the desirable behavioural changes in relation to his feelings and actions."

Characteristics of Evaluation Systems in Education

- **Continuous process:** Evaluation is a continuous process. It leads together with Teaching-learning process.
- **Comprehensive:** Evaluation is comprehensive as it includes everthing can be evaluated.
- **Learners-Centered:** Evaluation is a learner-centered process which gives importance to the learning process, not to the teaching process.
- **Remedial:** Evaluation comments on the result which helps in remedial work it is not a remedy. Evaluation is remedial in nature.
- **Cooperative process:** Evaluation is a cooperative process involving students, teachers, parents, and peer-groups.

- **Teaching Methods:** Effectiveness of teaching methods is evaluation.
- **Common practice:** Evaluation is a common practice among the proper growth of the childern mentally and physically.
- **Multiple Aspects:** It is concerned with the total personality of students.

Elements of Evaluation Systems

Five essential elements of evaluation systems:

1. Audience,
2. Purpose,
3. Questions,
4. Scope, and
5. Resources

To determine these elements, the following questions should be considered:

- For what audience is the evaluation being conducted?
- For what purpose is the evaluation being conducted?
- What question will be asked in the evaluation?
- What is the scope of the evaluation?
- What resources are available to conduct the evaluation?

Types of Evaluation

Evaluation can be classified into 3 groups as:

1. **Formative Evaluation:** It is concerned with making decisions relating to forming or development of students as well as of the courses. It provides feedback at appropriate stages of teaching-learning process which helps in making changes in the curriculum, teaching strategies and the learning environment, formative evaluation is done during the process of teaching-learning with the following purposes:
   (*a*) To monitor student learning for the purpose of providing individualized instruction.
   (*b*) To evaluate teaching effectiveness.
   (*c*) To evaluate courses and curricula with the purpose of modification, updating or replacement, if necessary.
   (*d*) To evaluate curriculum materials.
   (*e*) To evaluate the learning environment with a view to improving it.
2. **Diagnostic Evaluation:** This type of evaluation is generally done in the beginning of teaching-learning process in order to findout the specific weaknesses, either or an individual or at class level, and also to findout particular strengths. It helps to design the courses and curricula according to the capabilities of the learner to help him overcome his deficiencies in knowledge, skills, and abilities.
3. **Summative Evaluation:** It is concerned with making judgements about a finished product or process. Terminal examinations—whether internal or external—are a good example of summative evaluation. But summative evaluation must not necessarily be terminal in nature. Cumulative assessments, where they are undertaken solely for the purposes of selection, promotion, prediction, recording and such other administrative purposes, should be considered as a series of summative evaluation.

The Evaluation Process

The process of evaluation has the following stages:

1. Formulating and selecting worthwhile objectives of teaching in a subject.
2. Classifying and defining objectives in terms of expected learning outcomes or behavioural changes in the pupils.
3. Developing appropriate Learning experiences or activities.
4. Devising and adopting suitable assessment procedures to collect adequate and trustworthy evidences about the pupil's achievement.
5. Evaluating the outcomes on the basis of evidences collected and modifying the necessary aspects of the entire system for better results.

* * * * *

CREATING CONDUCIVE LEARNING ENVIRONMENT

INCLUSIVE EDUCATION: DEFINITION AND CONCEPT

Inclusive Education denotes that all children irrespective of their strengths and weaknesses will be part of the mainstream education. Thus, inclusive education means, "the act of ensuring that all children despite their differences, receive the opportunity of being part of the same classroom as other children of their age, and in the process get the opportunity to being exposed to the curriculum to their optimal potential."

Every child is special for his/her parent and, every child has a special need for love, acceptance and a feeling of belongingness. Here, we call **children with special needs** to those who are "different" from their cohorts. They are born equal with some limitations and with the help of inclusion be able to actively participate as equal citizens in all aspects of society and community life. Thus, children with special needs refer to "all those children who require adaptations to the normal process of education due to problems of vision, hearing, movement, learning and intellect." In other words, these children have some kind of **disability**.

Disability: Definitions

Disability refers to any limitations experienced by the disabled in comparisons to able persons of similar age, sex and culture. The UN Declaration on the Rights of Disabled Persons has defined disabled person as "any person unable to ensure by himself or herself, wholly or partly, the necessities of a normal individual and/or social life, as a result of a deficiency, either congenital or not, in his or her physical or mental capabilities".

DISTINCTIONS AMONG IMPAIRMENT, DISABILITY AND HANDICAP

The World Health Organisation (WHO) has made distinctions between the definitions of impairment, disability and handicap as follows:

- Impairment is any loss or abnormality of psychological, physiological or anatomical structure or function generally taken to be at organ level. Impairment is a damage to tissue due to disease or trauma.
- A disability is any restriction or lack of ability (resulting from an impairment) to perform an activity in the manner or within the range considered normal for a human being.
- A handicap is a disadvantage for an individual, resulting from impairment or disability that limits or prevents fulfilment of a role that is normal (depending on age, sex and social cultural factors) for that individual. Handicap is a condition or burden, which is imposed on the person confronted with the disability.

Types of Disability According to PWD Act, 1995

The PWD Act, 1995 has given the following seven types of disability as:

1. Blindness
2. Low Vision
3. Leprosy-cured
4. Hearing impairment
5. Locomotor disabilities
6. Mental retardation
7. Mental illness

EDUCATIONAL PROVISIONS FOR CHILDREN WITH SPECIAL NEEDS

The last two decades of the 19th century has witnessed the knowledge and processes of educating the disabled children through Christian Missionaries. The first school for the deaf was established in Mumbai in 1883 and the first school for the blind in Amritsar in 1887. At that time, it was believed that children with disabilities could not be educated alongwith normal children. Therefore, education to disabled children was offered through special school. This trend continued early sixties of the last century with the help of some international agencies who developed programme of integrated education. Here, children disabilities were placed in regular school so that they could study alongwith their non-disabled 'peers". The integrated education adopts various models for service deliver. Presently the emphasis is on the need to provide education for all in appropriate environment with inclusive philosophy through inclusive education.

Integrated Education for the Disabled Children (IEDC)

With the development of science and technology and improvement in Medical Services and Aggressive neo-natal intervention has ensured that a large number of babies who would earlier have not survived but often with different abilities. The number of differently abled children is on the increasing trend but it is not possible to create the required number of special schools throughout the country to meet this challenge due to the high cost and also due to the fact that the population is so scattered. The best alternative under these situations is to make use of the infrastructural facilities already present in terms of regular schools and integrate children into the mainstream of education.

Consequent on the success of international institutions in introducing differently abled children in regular schools, the planning commission, Govt. of India, in 1971 includes in its plan a programme for integrated education. In 1974, the Union Government introduced a scheme called "Integrated Schools" to do just this. This scheme was later revised and a plan of action formulated. The important aims of IEDC includes:

- Provide educational opportunity to differently abled children in regular schools.
- Facilitate retention of differently abled in the school system.
- Integrate children from special school to common schools.

The scope of the scheme of IEDC includes pre-school training, counselling for the parents, and special training in skills for all kinds of differently abled children. It provides facilities in the form of books, stationary, uniforms and allowances for transport, reader and escort etc.

Project Integrated Education for the Disabled (PIED)

This scheme was launched by MHRD Govt. of India in collaboration with UNICEF in 1987 to strengthen the integration of differently abled into regular schools. Under this scheme, a cluster instead of individual school is given importance. This scheme is an improvement over the special schools in one or many ways and provides a way towards universalisation of elementary education and Education for All including for differently abled children.

ASSUMPTION ABOUT INTEGRATED EDUCATION

Integrated education assumes a process of bringing disabled children into mainstream schools, where the system remains the same. As per the system, the child is the problem. So, it is essential to change the child where the resources are focused on the individual child. The failure is due to the child's problem; he is not able, not ready, not good enough to cope up with the system.

In integrated education; it is the children with disabilities who are seen as the problem, who must be "fixed", "changed" & "adapted" to suit the existing regular, mainstream school. It is the disabled child who is seen as a square peg in a round table. The system remains the same. The onus for successful integration therefore, is on the disabled child.

ASSUMPTION ABOUT INCLUSIVE EDUCATION

Assumptions of inclusive education is opposite to integrated education. Inclusive education assumes that changes the system to fit the child. It is essential to addresses all types of individual needs, not just disability. Teachers and schools are held responsible for children's learning. It focuses on flexibility of curriculum, teacher training and change in environment. Failure is the problem with the system not with the child. It is quite essential to assume that all children can learn and that all children need their learning to be supported in diverse ways.

In this model of inclusive education, it is not the child, but the education system, which is seen as a problem. Therefore, it is the system (with all its components) which should be changed, modified & made flexible enough to accommodate the diverse needs of all learners, including children with disabilities. The onus for success is therefore on the flexibility of the system. It focuses on the environment, as the "disabling" cause because it fails to provide appropriate access to equal opportunities for all persons to participate fully in social life.

Though integrated education of differently abled children has gained momentum all over the country since 1974, there are some other possibilities too for these children to get education. For example, the NIOS (National Institute of Open Schooling) offers education which have the advantage of being specially adopted to the needs of every child as well as aimed at giving the child every opportunity to progress at his/her pace. Another example is alternative schooling and community-based rehabilitation programmes.

EDUCATION FOR A COHESIVE SOCIETY

Despite more than half a century of independence, India is struggling for freedom from various kinds of biases and imbalances such as rural/urban, rich/poor, and differences on the basis of caste, religion, ideology, gender etc. Education can play a very significant role in minimising and finally eliminating these differences by providing equality of access to quality education and opportunity.

Equality of opportunity means ensuring that every individual receives suitable education at a pace and through methods suited to his/her being. Children of the disadvantaged, and socially discriminated groups and also those suffering from specific challenges must be paid special attention.

Provision for equal opportunity to all not only in access, but also in the conditions for success is a precondition for the promotion of equality. The curriculum must create an awareness of the inherent equality of all with a view to removing prejudices and complexes transmitted through the social environment and the factor of birth.

EDUCATION OF GIRLS

Equality among sexes is a fundamental right under the constitution of India. The state, however, also has the right to exercise positive protective discrimination in favour of the disadvantaged population groups including women. Emphasis in education has moved from 'Equality of Educational Opportunity' (NPE, 1968) to 'Education for Women's Equality and Empowerment' (1986). As a result, the curricular and training strategies for the education of girls now demand more attention. Besides, making education accessible to more and more girls, especially rural girls, removing all gender discrimination and gender bias in school curriculum, textbooks and the process of transaction is absolutely necessary. There is a need to develop and implement gender inclusive and gender sensitive curricular strategies to nurture a generation of girls and boys who are equally competent and are sensitive to one another, and grow up in a caring and sharing mode as equals, and not as adversaries.

EDUCATION OF LEARNERS FROM DISADVANTAGED GROUPS

For achieving a cohesive society it would be essential to respond to specific educational needs of learners from different sections of the society with special emphasis on the Scheduled Castes, the Scheduled Tribes and the other socially and economically disadvantaged groups. In order to do so, there is a need for integrating the socio-cultural perspectives partly by showing concern for their linguistic specificities and pedagogic requirements. Implications of the multilingual and multicultural environment shall have to be taken care of through specifically devised methodology. Contextualisation of curriculum shall have to be effected through curricular materials. The fundamental rights of the disadvantaged groups have to be consciously incorporated in the curriculum. Even the problem of educating the migrating population shall have to be handled through specific condensed educational programmes based on the main ingredients of the national curriculum.

EDUCATION OF THE GIFTED AND TALENTED

An educational system has the dual role of promoting equality as well as excellence. Education is increasingly called upon to liberate all the creative potentialities of human consciousness. Man essentially fulfils himself in and through creation. It is in the context of this, that education of gifted and talented children assumes great importance. A curricular programme while on the one hand should identify such children, on the other it should also nurture their diverse creative abilities by paying them special attention. It is also important that the identification and nurturance begins right from the earliest stage of education. Moreover, the task of identifying the gifted and talented must be accomplished on the basis of a broad conceptualisation of the process from multiple perspectives rather than as a search for a unitary human attribute. Not only their IQ (Intelligence Quotient) but also their EQ (Emotional Quotient) and SQ (Spiritual Quotient) ought to be assessed.

NATIONAL LEVEL POLICY AND LEGISLATION

Kothari Commission (1964-66)

The Kothari Commission first suggested that the education of handicapped children has to be organised not merely on humanitarian grounds, but also an aspects of utility. The commission also specifically emphasised that the education of children with disability should be "an inseparable part of the general education system. The commission also specifically emphasised the importance of integrated education in meeting this target as it is cost effective and useful in developing mutual understanding between children with and without disabilities.

National Policy on Education (1986)

The National Policy on Education was adopted by Indian Parliament in 1986. The policy emphasized the removal of disparities, and ensuring equalisation of educational opportunity under its para education of the disabled.

The Rehabilitation Council of India (RCI) Act, 1992

This Act was passed in 1992 for the purpose of constituting the Rehabilitation Professionals and for maintenance of a Central Rehabilitation Register. It was amended by Rehabilitation Council of India (Amendment) Act, 2000 to provide for monitoring the training of rehabilitation professionals and personal, promoting research in rehabilitation and special education as additional objectives of the council.

Persons with Disabilities (Equal Opportunities, Protection of Rights & Full Participation) Act, 1995

Landmark legislation in the history of special education in India is the persons with Disabilities Act, 1995. This comprehensive Act covers seven disabilities, namely blindness, low vision, hearing impaired, loco-motor impaired, mental retardation, leprosy cured and mental illness.

National Policies for Persons with Disabilities (2006)

This recognises that persons with disabilities are valuable human resources for the country and seek to create an environment that provides them equal opportunities, protection of their rights and full participation in society.

The Rights of Persons with Disabilities Act, 2016

The Rights of Persons with Disabilities Act, 2016 was enacted in 2016 replacing the erstwhile Persons with Disabilities (Equal Opportunities, Protection of Rights and Full Participation) Act, 1995. As per Section 2(s) of the Rights of Persons with Disabilities Act, 2016 "person with disability" means a person with long term physical, mental, intellectual or sensory impairment which, in interaction with barriers, hinders his full and effective participation in society equally with others. The new Act is right based whereas the earlier Act was welfare based.

The RPwD Act, 2016 provides for various rights and entitlements for persons with disabilities. These rights and entitlements include equality and non-discrimination, community life, protection against cruelty and inhuman treatment, access to justice, legal capacity, right to live in family and community, reproduction rights, etc. The types of disabilities have increased from the erstwhile 7 to 21.

The Act mandates the appropriate governments to frame schemes and programmes in the area of inclusive education, skill development, social security, health, rehabilitation, recreation and sports for effective empowerment and inclusion of persons with disabilities. Special provisions in the area of education, employment and social security have been made for persons with benchmark disabilities.

The Act also focuses on creating accessible environment for PwDs in built-up environment, transportation system and ICT ecosystem in time bound manner. It also mandates the Central Government and State Governments to set up broad based Central & State Advisory Boards on Disability as policy recommending bodies. The Act provides for penalties for offences committed against persons with disabilities to ensure effective implementation.

* * * * *

SCHOOL ORGANIZATION AND LEADERSHIP

LEADERSHIP

Educational Organizations should be considered socio-technical systems. They are unique organizations whose basic components are the individuals and technology. There is, however, little technology used by educational organizations. Largely, it is the manpower and human resource on whose manipulation they survive and make progress. The individuals constitute, by and large, the most important unit of these organizations.

These organizations are established for the purpose of achieving certain specific goals. In general, all of them bear a responsibility to impart knowledge to the pupils, develop in them skills and certain human qualities.

The importance of leadership in management of any educational organization can never be minimized. Achievement of organizational goals very much depends on how effectively leadership is exercised in the organization. Organizational leaders are the key figures who can so change the work climate that all the employees are motivated to work hard with the result that the goals are achieved.

Definition

Bolman and Deal (1991) suggest that when people are asked "what is leadership", answers seem to fall into one of these categories:

- ability to get others to do what you want (power);
- motivate people to get things done-mostly through persuasion;
- provide a vision;
- leadership is facilitation; and
- empower people to do what they want.

There are problems with all of these but overall they convey the notion that we expect a leader to influence through non-coercive means, to produce some degree of cooperative effort, and to pursue goals that transcend his/her own narrow self-interest.

Theories of Leadership Style

- **The Laissez-faire Style or Delegative Style:** The laissez-faire "leave it be" leadership (Lewin, Lippit & White, 1939) is the leadership style that gives no continuous feedback or supervision because the employees are highly experienced and need little supervision to obtain the expected outcome. On the other hand, this type of style is also associated to leaders that don't lead at all, failing in supervising its team members, resulting in lack of control and higher costs, bad service of failure to meet deadlines.
- **The Bureaucratic Style:** The bureaucratic leader (Weber, 1905) is very structured and follows the procedures as they had been

established. This type of leadership has no space to explore new ways to solve problems and is usually slow paced to ensure approval of the leader stated by the company. Leaders ensure that all the steps had been followed prior sending it to the next level of authority. Universities, schools, colleges and government organisation usually require this type of leader in its organizations to ensure quality, increase security and minimise malpractices. Leaders that try to speed up the process usually leads to frustration and anxiety.

- **The Charismatic Style:** The charismatic leader (Weber, 1905) leads by infusing energy and eagerness into their team members. This type of leader has to be committed to the organization for the long run. Otherwise, charismatic leaders are a risk for the institution when they decide to resign for other opportunities because his/her staff only saw the success of the department is linked to the leader and not the team. It takes time and hard work to gain the team members confidence back with other type of leadership.

- **The Autocratic Style**: In the case of autocratic leadership (Lewin, Lippitt & White, 1939) we could say that the leader has been given the power to take decisions, having total authority. This leadership style is good for employees that needs close supervision to perform certain tasks. Educational institutions do not prefer and resent this type of leadership, due to the creative and personal commitment of the teachers and other staff in carrying out their duties. A rigid, structured and formal supervision is not being able to enhance processes or decision making, resulting in job dissatisfaction.

- **The Democratic or Participative Style:** The democratic leader (Lewin, Lippitt & White, 1939) means that even though you want to listens to your team's ideas, you as the leader will study those ideas and will take the final decision. Team member contributes to the final decision thus increasing satisfaction and ownership by their members, feeling their input was considered when the final decision was taken. When change arises, this type of leadership help the team assimilate the changes better and rapidly than other styles, knowing they were part and parcel to the decision making process, minimizing resis-tance and intolerance.

- **The People-Oriented Style:** People-Oriented leader (Fiedler, 1967) is the one that in order to comply with effectiveness and efficiency, support, train and develop his personnel increasing job satisfaction and genuine interest to do a good job.

- **The Task Oriented Style:** Task oriented leaders (Fiedler, 1967) are those who focus on the job, and concentrate in the specific tasks assigned to each employee to reach goal accomplishment. This leadership style suffers the same motivation issues as autocratic leadership, showing no involvement in the team's needs. It requires close supervision and control to achieve expected results.

- **The Servant Style:** A servant leader (Greenleaf, 1977) is the leader that facilitates goal accomplishment by giving its team members what they need in order to be productive. It is an instrument employees uses to reach the goal rather than a commanding voice that moves to change. This leadership, as well as democratic leadership tends to achieve the results in a slower motion than other styles, although employee engagement is higher.

- **The Transaction Style:** In transaction leadership (Burns, 1978) the power is given to a certain person to perform certain tasks and rewards or punish for the team's performance. It gives the opportunity to manager to lead the group and the group agrees to follow his/her leader to accomplish a predetermined goal in exchange of something else. Power is given to the leader to evaluate, rectify the train his/her subordinates when productivity is not up to the desired results and reward effective-ness when expected outcome is reached.

- **The Transformation Style:** A transformation leader (Burns, 1978) is the one who motivates his/her team to be effective and efficient. Communication is the base for goal achievement focusing the group in the final desired outcome or goal attainment. This leader is highly visible and uses chain of command to get the job done. Transformational leaders focus on the vision, needing to be surrounded of followers or group who carry out the future plan of actions or tasks. The leader is always looking for ways to ideas that moves the organization to reach the company's vision.

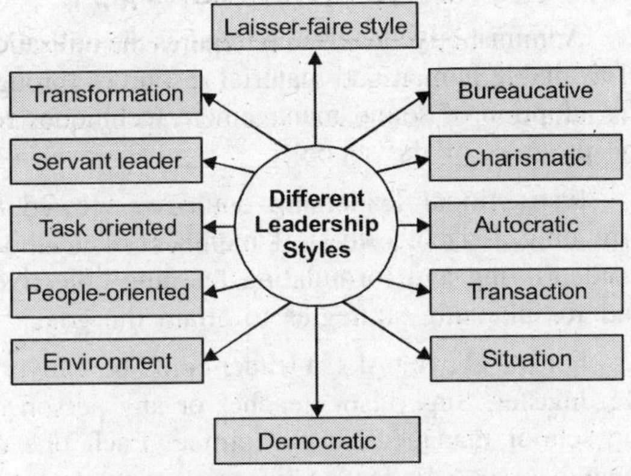

Different Leadership Styles

- **The Environment Style:** The Environment Leader (Carmazzi, 2005) is the one who nurtures group or organizational environment to affect the emotional and psychological perception of an individual's place in that group or organization. This leadership style relies on creating an education matrix where groups interactively learn the fundamental psychology of group dynamics and culture from each other. The leader uses this psychology, and complementary language, to influence direction through the members of the inspired group to do what is required for the benefit of all.
- **The Situation Style:** The situation leader (Joseph Praveen Kumar, Hersey, Blanchard & Johnson, 2008) is the leader that uses different leadership styles depending on the situation and the type of employee that is being supervised.

Leadership Style Vis-A-Vis Educational Institution

Leaders in the education system have the ability to transform the system. Generally leaders in the education system can:

- Set the pattern and guide the outcomes of co-operative action
- Guide educational programs, but rely on shared decisions
- Give common understanding to common purposes and goals
- Produce cohesiveness without which co-operation is impossible
- Communicate with all concerned personnel with a sense of mutual understanding and mutual loyalty to the ideals of education
- Generate enthusiasm for project and inspire working towards their completion
- Resolve the differences which frequently arise in growing organizations
- Lead by example and inspiration
- Contribute to the group by advancing useful suggestions.

Thus, based on the assessment of the needs in the school or any other educational institutions, each leader must decide the leadership style that needs to be opted for the smooth functioning of the educational institution in all circumstances. It is essential to remember that a single style cannot solve or resolve all the *issues* in the educational system. In order to run the school successfully by giving adequate importance and opportunities to the members of the school, the leadership style followed must be flexible and with a mixed approach.

Leadership at Different Levels of School Hierarchy

School is a formal setup of education, wherein teachers and students interact with each other for achieving pre-determined objectives. It is through this interaction that students learn. The quality of interaction enhances the quality of learning outcomes. Classroom processes and interaction depends upon many factors in a classroom, like regularity in classroom activities, discipline, motivation of students, resources available, and so on.

The usual leadership positions that exist in a school are given below:

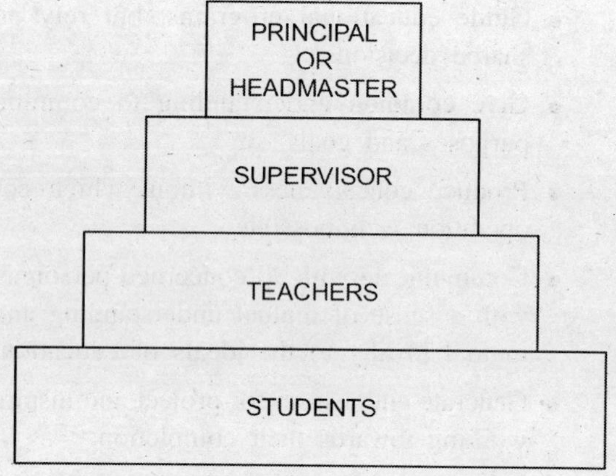

Leadership Position in a School

The Headmaster of the school is considered to be the leader of the school, because he/she looks after all academic, non-academic and administrative functions of the school. You must have seen in schools where the Headmaster stands in front of students during morning prayers. You must also have seen the Headmaster's room, wherein the whole plan of school activities is displayed.

Similarly, teachers prepare unit plans, instructional plans, evaluation techniques and other co-curricular activities in the school. Recall your school days and remember your teacher sitting in the staff room and preparing for the next class, correcting note books, etc.

Students also have a different type of leadership role in the school. They are the assets of a school. The detailed description of the different leadership roles is given in subsequent sections.

People involved in different positions at school hierarchy tend to perform leadership roles.

Nature of School Leadership

Management of school means managing different activities in the school which are directly or indirectly affecting student learning. Leadership is important in planning, organizing, directing, supervising and evaluating school programmes.

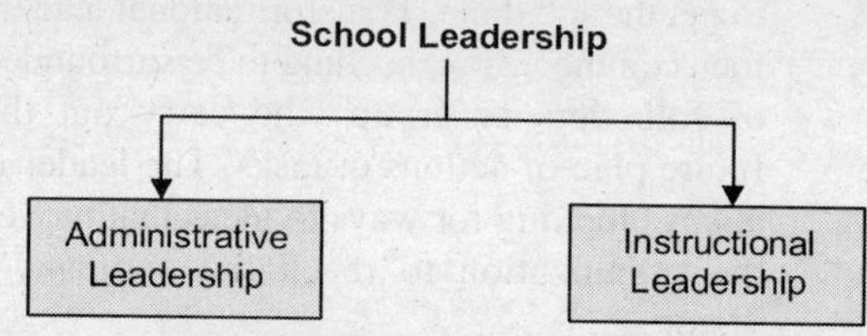

Kinds of School Leadership

Administrative leadership requires the utilisation of available human and material resources through the adoption of sound management techniques for the progress of the school.

Instructional leadership could be viewed as providing assistance to staff members of a school in identifying and formulating learning objectives and for planning strategies to attain the goals.

For the above tasks, a leader could be - anyone Headmaster, Supervisor, teacher or any person of the school management committee. Each one of them has specific leadership roles to perform in school administration. The administrative process of a school always emphasises learning by students. In fact, administrative functions are the support service for academic functions. Coordination between these two functions needs to be maintained.

Teacher as Leader

The National Policy on Education, 1986 stated that "No system of education can rise higher than its teachers". A teacher is the most important element in the educational process. A teacher is the vital component in teaching-learning process. Before identifying the teacher as leader in the instructional process, we have to understand the process of classroom interaction.

The Secondary Education Commission (1952-53) stated, "We are convinced that the most important factor in the contemplated educational reconstruction is the teacher". A teacher usually performs three different types of activities in a classroom. They are pre-active, interactive and post-active functions.

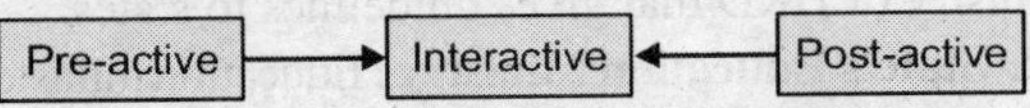

Functions of a Teacher in Classroom

Pre-active functions are those which are to be performed before going to the classroom. They are:

- Planning curricular and co-curricular programmes,
- Organizing programmes,
- Selecting appropriate strategy of teaching,
- Preparing lesson plans, assignments and teaching aids, etc.

In the interactive phase the leadership role of a teacher is directive. Here a teacher is the leader of the overall transaction. Let us list the different functions of the teacher in the interactive phase.

- Creating an appropriate classroom climate for better learning
- Explaining, illustrating and questioning
- Providing motivation and positive reinforcement
- Getting feedback from students, and
- Evaluating students' learning.

A teacher perfoms the above activities in the classroom. During classroom teaching, a teacher acts as a leader and guides the classroom instructional process.

The post-active phase of teaching consists of the following:

- Supervision and guidance,
- Communicating with parents,
- Maintenance of cumulative records,
- Preparation of evaluation reports/progress reports,
- Organization of tutorial classes, and
- Maintaining inter-personal relations.

Role of Headmaster

A Headmaster in a school is vital to school administration. He/she is the leader for both administrative and instructional processes. Now, we shall discuss the position of the Headmaster in a school and his/her responsibilities.

He is a leader to all the sub groups in the school, working for the achievement of the goals.

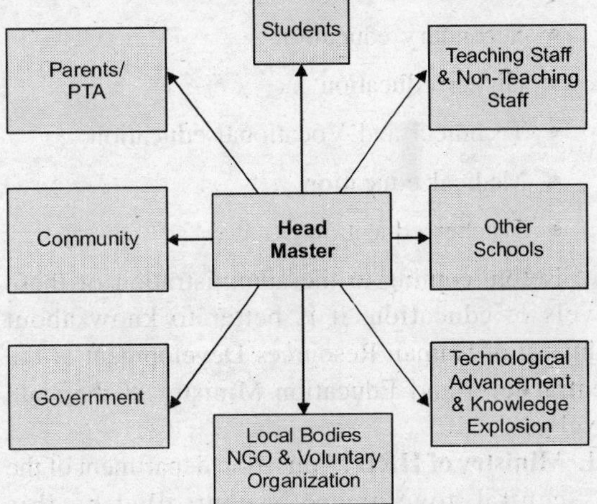

Multiple Responsibilities of a School Headmaster

Headmaster preforms in schools:

- He plans and organizes school activities,
- Allocates duties to staff and non-teaching staff,
- Maintains relationship with parents, community and Government,
- Develops networking with other schools,
- Acquaints himself with recent trends in technology and information,
- Organizes social activities,
- Procures infrastructure and material resources,
- Mobilises available resources for the development of the school,
- Visualises future of the school in the society,

- Coordinates different school activities,
- Appraises performance of the teaching staff, non-teaching staff and students, and
- Organizes staff meetings on various aspects for decision-making.

EDUCATIONAL ADMINISTRATION IN INDIA

We can divide the total education system in India into the following categories :

- Primary education
- Secondary education
- Higher education
- Technical and Vocational education
- Medical education
- Teacher education

Before coming to the administration of these levels of education, it is better to know about ministry of Human Resources Development at the central level and Education Ministry at the state level—

1. **Ministry of HRD :** Education department of the central government is controlled by this ministry. This department takes all decisions related to education. Secretariat of this department is headed by Education Secretary, Additional Secretaries and education advisors are also there to assist him.

Education department has been divided into different bureaus and divisions. Every bureau is headed by joint secretary who is assisted by division officers. Education advisor is the administrative head of the department of education.

A number of advisory boards and commissions have been created to organise education in the country from primary to higher level.

Since education is in the concurrent list of subjects, this makes ministry of HRD more powerful than the state education ministries. Education was put in the concurrent list in 1976 by 42nd amendment of the constitution. At present both centre and states can make laws on matter related to education and if there is any controversy and contradiction between the two, only the law made by the Indian Parliament will prevail. Generally centre does not interfere in the affairs of states as far as education is concerned but in order to create a unified and symmetrical system of education throughout the country, it is the ministry of HRD that gives guidelines to states.

2. **State's Education Ministry :** Education minister and one or two deputy ministers look after this ministry. Education minister is responsible to all levels of education in the state. Education minister is assisted by two officers-education secretary and director of education.

Education secretary is the head of secretariate of education. He is assisted by deputy secretaries. Group officers work under deputy secretaries and section officer assist group officer.

Education secretary is an IAS. He issues directions to implement education policies of states formulated by education minister. He also gives advices to the minister regarding the matters of education. Decisions regarding the recognition of a school or about the salary of teachers can not be taken without the consent of the education secretary.

Orders of the secretariat (state govt.) are enforced by the directorate of education. If secretariate is policy making body, directorate is an executive body. It works as a link between state's school and colleges and secretariate. Director of education is assisted by joint directors and education officers. It consists of three divisions

- Directorate of higher education.
- Directorate of secondary education.
- Directorate of primary education

All three officers are headed by separate directors but director, higher education works as a co-ordinator.

1. Administration of Primary Education

Primary education is mainly controlled and administered by the state department of education through Basic Siksha Parishad and local government (Municipalities and Panchayat). The role of central government is only advisory here.

Important functions of Basic Shiksha Parishad are given below :

1. Controlling over primary teachers and other related staff.
2. Appointment and transfer of primary teachers and other related staff.
3. Arrangement of examination materials and declaration of results.
4. Developing curriculum for primary education and preparing text books for children.
5. Doing arrangement for training of teachers.
6. Recognizing private primary schools.
7. Organization and control of basic schools, normal schools and units of basic certificates.
8. Development of primary education in the state.
9. Receiving grants from the state govt. and distributing them to different schools.
10. Construction and maintenance of primary schools.

As far as role of central government for promotion of primary education is concerned, it is performed by All India Council of Primary Education (AICPE). It was established in 1957. The purpose of establishment of this council was to take necessary steps to provide free and compulsory education to children in the age group of 6-14. Whatever action is taken by the central government in this regard, it is taken by this very council.

The main functions of AICPE are as follows :

1. Giving suggestions to all primary education institutions managed by the central and state governments regarding primary education.
2. Conducting researches on the administrative, financial and educational problems related to primary education and publishing the results and conclusions.
3. Preparing literature and text books for the improvement of primary education.
4. Giving the declaration of free and compulsory education upto the age of 14 a practical shape through its policies and suggestions.
5. Giving suggestions to central government for the development of primary education and for bringing cooperation between the centre and states.
6. Preparing programmes for the development of primary education in the states and forcing the states to implement them.

2. Administration of Secondary Education

We can divide the administration of secondary education into two sections—

State Administration

All educational institutions that impart secondary education in states can be classified into the following categories—

- Schools maintained by universities for practice teaching of B.Ed. trainees. State government does not have any direct control over them.
- Government Inter Colleges and Government Girls Inter Colleges maintained by the state government.
- Government aided colleges managed by private organizations and societies. 100% grants are given to these schools by the state government and appointment of teachers and other staff is also done by Madhyamic Siksha Parishad.
- Hindi and Sanskrit colleges maintained by the state government.
- Minority colleges maintained by the state government by giving them 100% grants but they are managed by minorities. Appointment of teachers and other personnel is done by the management committee here. They are autonomous institutions.
- Unaided but recognised schools.
- Unaided and unrecognized schools like Madarsahs and Pathshalas. Their certificates are recognised by some universities of India.

Administration of all recognised schools is the responsibility of state department of education (Madhyamic Siksha Nideshalay) through Madhyamic Siksha Parishad . Parishad performs the following functions here—

1. It prepare norms for the recognition of schools with the Madhyamic Siksha Boards and gives its recommendation after the inspection of a school to the directorate for recognition.
2. It prepares secondary school curriculum and text books for secondary classes.
3. It also determines the limits of grants in aid or its curtailment for a particular school.
4. It prepares programmes for in-service training of teachers.
5. It publishes magazines and journals for the improvement of education system.
6. As far as examinations of high schools and inter-mediates are concerned, they are conducted by Madhyamic Siksha Board and results are also declared by it.

Administration by the Centre

A number of central schools for central government employees, army schools, railway schools, Navodaya Vidyalays and a large number of private schools affiliated to CBSE or ICSE are administered by the central government through its agencies. All these schools were opened to bring about uniformity in the pattern of secondary education throughout the country to benefit those employees whose jobs are transferable across the country and change in boards for their wards was really a problem for them because of the following reasons—

- Standard and quality of education were not uniform in all state boards.
- Standard and quality of education were very poor in many states and government employees could not afford this loss.

Central Board of Secondary Education (CBSE) was established by the central government to solve this problem and a number of schools were affiliated with this board. At present, there are 24,000 schools affiliated with this board, out of them about 50% are private schools.

In order to provide quality education to rural pupils free of cost from class VIth to XIIth our Late Prime Minister Mr. Rajeev Gandhi started hundreds of Navodaya schools across the country. Provision was made that at least one Navodaya Vidyalaya will be opened in every district and admission in these schools will be given on the basis of an aptitude test.

Important agencies working at the central level for the administration and improvement of secondary education are given below :

***(a)* National Council of Educational Research and Training (NCERT) :**

It was established in 1961 at the recommendation of Secondary Education Commission (1952-53). The purpose of establishment of NCERT was to lead the nation in the field of research in education and teaching and in the preparation of text books for all classes from Ist to 12th. Following departments were established by the government for this purpose.

- National Text Book and Research Bureau (1954)
- National Elementary Education Institute (1956)
- National Fundamental Education Institute (1956)
- National Education Extension Directorate (1959)
- National Audio Visual Education Institute (1959)

However, irony of the fact was that all the above institutes could not realize the objectives identified by Secondary Education Commission. As a result NCERT was established in 1961 and in order to lessen its work loads State Council of Educational Research and Training (SCERT) were also established in states. NCERT is an autonomous body of the central government and it has been set up in order to achieve the following objectives—

1. To study the problems of school education in the country.
2. To organize extension programmes in the field of secondary education. Such programmes consists of pre-service and in-service training programmes.
3. To lead every field of secondary education at the central level such as preparation of text books, teaching strategies, evaluation etc.
4. To provide extension services to teachers in teacher training colleges across the country.
5. To help the states to establish Model Teacher Training Centres.

6. To conduct educational surveys across the country and publish the results.
7. To work as a distribution centre for innovative educational concepts.
8. Discovering best teaching strategies and techniques and introducing them all over the country.
9. To prepare standard text books, to publish and distribute them from its counters. All schools affiliated to CBSE New Delhi prefers these text books to the books published by private agencies.

The functions of NCERT can be divided into four units—

(a) **Organizational committee :** This committee manages all the four regional colleges of NCERT. These training colleges are in Ajmer, Mysore, Bhopal and Bhuvanesvar. These colleges run B.Ed., BPEd., M.Ed., Ph. D. and integrated three year, courses. They provide training to teachers of their respective regions and guide them in the field of secondary education.

(b) **National Educational Institute :** There are 12 departments in this institute. The main function of this institute is to further research, training and extension programmes.

(c) **Secondary Education Extension Directorate:** This directorate is controlled by NCERT but it has been affiliated to Delhi University for degree and other formalities.

(d) **Educational Administration Board :** This board has three permanent committees. First committee considers research projects and gives its report to the main body. Second committee coordinates different programmes, projects and researches. Third committee takes care of the four regional colleges of NCERT.

All India Council of Secondary Education

This Council was established in 1955. The purpose of this council was to bring about qualitative improvement in secondary education. It is an advisory body. It studies the problems of secondary education across the country and gives relevant suggestions to states for the solution of these problems. Education Advisor of the government of India is the head of this council. There are 22 other members in the Council who come from the following departments—

- Representatives of ministry of HRD.
- Representatives of the finance ministry.
- One representative from Indian Council of Pravidhik Shiksha.
- One representative from All India Council of Primary Education.
- One representative from University Grants Commission.
- One representative from All India Teachers' Community.
- One representative from All India Council of Teachers Education.
- Representative of the States

Central Board of Secondary Education (CBSE)

It is an autonomous body of the central government which controls 24,000 schools across the country and overseas and conducts examinations for them. Thus character of CBSE is global in nature. CBSE has its headquarters at Delhi with Sixteen Regional Offices at Delhi (East), Panchkula, Prayagraj, Ajmer, Guwahati, Dehradun, Patna, Bhubaneswar, Chennai, Thiruvananthapuram, Delhi (West), Noida, Chandigarh, Bhopal, Bengaluru and Pune. It has also Seventeen Centre of Excellence for Teachers at Ajmer, Prayagraj, Bhubaneswar, Chennai, Dehradun, Delhi (East), Guwahati, Kakinada, Panchkula, Patna, Delhi (West), Thiruvananthapuram, Noida, Chandigarh, Bhopal, Bengaluru and Pune.

The main functions of CBSE are as follows:

1. Determining affiliation norms for affiliating private schools to CBSE.
2. Inspecting CBSE schools even after affiliation.
3. Giving affiliation to new schools after inspection.
4. Preparing necessary text books for CBSE affiliated schools. This work is done by the academic cell of the board.

5. Conducting examinations for all CBSE affiliated schools and declaring results.
6. Developing curriculum for its affiliated schools.
7. Awarding talented teachers every year after appraisal of their performance.
8. Organising in service training programmes for teachers and principals both.

Administration of Higher Education

As far as administration of higher education is concerned, University Grant Commission is the main and autonomous body. It controls all universities, 55 Central and 456 State Universities by preparing curriculum for them and by sanctioning or restricting grants for them. Universities are also autonomous bodies at their own level. They are responsible not only for the maintenance and advancement of university education but they also control the education imparted by affiliated degree and PG colleges of the states whether they are government aided or private colleges.

University Grants Commission (UGC) was established in 1945 on the recommendation of Sargent Report (1944). Higher Education Commission (1948-49) recommended to develop it as an autonomous body. Consequently a bill regarding this was passed in Indian Parliament in 1954 and University Grants Commission (UGC) was made an autonomous body.

UGC had 9 members apart from chairman and vice chairman at that time. Out of these 9 members, three of them were university Vice Chancellors, two of them were government representatives and remaining two were prominent educationists of the country. The number of these members were raised to 12 in 1966. They are nominated by the government for a period for six years.

There are six sections working in UGC as-

- Humanities and Social Science Department
- Science and Technology Department
- Central Universities, Coordination, Administration and Finance Department'
- Higher Studies Centre and Scholarship Department
- Statistics, Publication and Information Section
- Pay Scale Section.

Main Functions of UGC

1. Determining the norms and standard of education for colleges and universities.
2. Coordinating among the higher education institution of states.
3. Granting funds to universities for performing different types of functions.
4. Preparing norms for pay scale
5. Evaluating the performance of universities and colleges through National Accreditation and Assessment Council (NAAC)
6. Conducting JRF/NET exams and sanctioning fellowship to research scholars.

In order to improve the quality of education in universities and colleges UGC has taken several other measures also such as:

- College Humanities and Social Science Institute Programme
- College Science Institute Programmes
- Universities Leadership Programme
- Setting up committees for assessment of different programmes
- Establishment of Examination Reform Cell in Universities in order to improve quality of examination.
- Implementing the recommendations of pay commissions for improving the pay scale of teachers and other personnel.
- UGC has also stressed on setting up and development of Women's Studies Centres.

Grants by the UGC are given for the following purposes—

1. Grants for development such as appointment of additional staff, establishment of libraries and laboratories, purchase of books, furniture and equipments, construction of hostels and buildings.
2. Grants for improvement in the standard of education such as setting up of advanced studies centres in universities, research works, in service training programmes, establishment of resource centres and academic staff colleges etc.

3. Grants for regional studies such as study of historical, social and economic conditions of the country and abroad.
4. Grants for exchange programmes of teachers.
5. Special grants given to retired teachers in order to take the benefit of their long experiences.
6. Grants given to universities and colleges for the construction of staff quarters.
7. Grants given for the purpose of student's welfare Programmes, i.e., constructing health care centres and hostels for them, arrangement of fellowship, sanction of research project etc.

Apart from giving grants to universities, UGC is also giving special grants to 62 colleges of science and technology, 19 higher studies science centres and 35 higher studies centres of humanities and social sciences.

As far as appointment of teachers are concerned UGC, Central or State government do not interfere in the affairs of universities and autonomous colleges. However, teachers in government aided colleges are appointment by Higher Education Commission of States and pay scale is determined by the State department of education. For the convenience of administration, these colleges are affiliated to any nearby university of the state.

*****

PERSPECTIVES IN EDUCATION

ROLE OF SCHOOL IN ACHIEVING AIMS OF EDUCATION

School education is a deliberate and more-o-less external intervention in the life of a child. Although much learning and teaching takes place at home, in the neighbourhood community, and in actual living communities in rural and tribal India, the school introduces the child to an environment of teaching and learning that, quite by design, marks itself off from the rest of the child's environment. Tagore's experience of his first day at school is repeated with greater or less intensity in most children's first encounter with school: "...all of a sudden I found my world vanishing from around me, giving place to wooden benches and straight walls staring at me with the blank stare of the blind."* While the school must perhaps have boundaries of its own—as the life of the school cannot just be merged with the life of the community around it—these boundaries must not become barriers. They must, on the other hand, facilitate the creation of vital links between children's experiences at home and in the community and what the school offers them.

Self-knowledge is diametrically opposed to self-ignorance and self-deception. To be deceived by others is bad but to be deceived by oneself is even worse. However, unfortunately, we deceive ourselves much of the time. The big fat ego, which most of us have, can remain fat only on a daily diet of self-deception. Self-knowledge can be achieved only through the knowledge of the other, and one cannot know the other without being just to the other. Education must be a continuous process of self-discovery, of learning the truth about oneself.

There is need to convince the child or the adolescent of the superiority of a life of virtues to a life of vice and wickedness. The only way to do this is to effectively demonstrate that genuine human happiness can spring only from a life lived in accordance with virtues. But, how is this to be done? How is one to counter the opposite belief that it is not the virtues but power and wealth that are constitutive of true happiness? In a world where the latter belief is pre-dominant, it may be impossible to teach the value of virtues to our children. We need, therefore, to create the possibility of profound questioning of our social structure, and show in various ways the deep connection between human discontent and a life devoid of virtues.

Value education must be a part of the education system, values or virtues must be integral to the whole process of education. Value education cannot be imparted as a separate bit of education; the whole of education has to be value education. Here, we need powerful reminders, in a variety of ways, of the Gandhian ideas of ahimsa, peace, and harmony.

Cultural diversity is one of our greatest gifts. To respect and do justice to others is also to respect and do justice to their respective cultures or communities. We, therefore, need to radically change the centre versus periphery perspective on intercultural relationships in our country. Cultures on the so-called periphery must receive as much attention as cultures in the centre. As for education, its implication is that ways of life other than one's own must be imaginatively and effectively presented as deserving of as much respect as one's own.

Individual differences are as important as cultural differences. Individual children frequently have capacities and skills which do not find adequate recognition in the school environment. Development and flourishing of these skills and capacities would not only enhance the individual's life but also enrich the life of the community. Education must therefore promote and nourish as wide a range of capacities and skills in our children as possible. The gamut of such skills include the performing arts (music, dance, drama, and so on), painting and crafts, and literary abilities (weaving stories, wielding language to portray different aspects of life, a flair for metaphorical and poetic expression, etc.). Also, skills as diverse as some children's special capacity to bond with nature— with trees, birds, and animals— need to be nurtured.

Knowledge is not a unitary concept. There are different kinds of knowledge as well as different ways of knowing. The idea that objectivity, which is a necessary constituent of knowledge, can be achieved only if knowledge is free from emotions (care, concern, and love) must be abandoned. One implication of this for education is that literary and artistic creativity is as much part man's epistemic enterprise as is seeking knowledge through laboratory experiments or deductive reasoning. The former frequently enables us to see the truth in a way that the paradigmatic scientific quest cannot.

Education must be seen as a liberating process; otherwise, all that has been said so far will be rendered pointless. The process of education must therefore free itself from the shackles of all kinds of exploitation and injustice (e.g., poverty, gender discrimination, caste and communal bias), which prevent our children from being part of the process.

It is very important that school teaching and learning takes place in an environment that is aesthetically pleasing. It is also essential that children take an active part in creating such an environment for themselves.

It ought to be possible for every child to be proud of his or her nation. But, one can be proud of something only if it is an achievement of one's own or if one is very intimately connected with those whose achievement it is. We can be proud of our own achievements, or the achievements of our children or friends. If we feel an intimacy with God or nature, we can be proud of even the skies and the whole universe. It is therefore very important that education fosters within the child an intimacy with people who are directly connected with achievements which are part of our national heritage.

NATIONAL EDUCATION POLICY (NEP), 2020

NEP 2020 is the first education policy of the 21st century and replaces the thirty-four year old National Policy on Education (NPE), 1986. Built on the foundational pillars of Access, Equity, Quality, Affordability and Accountability, this policy is aligned to the 2030 Agenda for Sustainable Development and aims to transform India into a vibrant knowledge society and global knowledge superpower by making both school and college education more holistic, flexible, multidisciplinary, suited to 21st century needs and aimed at bringing out the unique capabilities of each student.

The policy has been formulated after a very detailed consultative process, unprecedented in depth and scale. Consultation involved over 2 lakh suggestions from 2.5 lakhs Gram Panchayats, 6600 Blocks, 6000 ULBs, 676 Districts. The MHRD had initiated a collaborative, inclusive, and highly participatory consultation process from January

2015. In May 2016, 'Committee for Evolution of the New Education Policy' under the Chairmanship of Late Shri T.S.R. Subramanian, Former Cabinet Secretary, submitted its report. Based on this, the Ministry prepared 'Some Inputs for the Draft National Education Policy, 2016'. In June 2017, a 'Committee for the Draft National Education Policy' was constituted under the Chairmanship of eminent scientist **Padma Vibhushan, Dr. K. Kasturirangan,** which submitted the Draft National Education Policy, 2019 to the Hon'ble Human Resource Development Minister on 31st May, 2019.

School Education

Ensure Universal Access at All Levels of schooling from pre-primary school to Grade 12

NEP 2020 aims to achieve 100% Gross Enrollment Ratio in school education by 2030. The initiatives that will be undertaken for this include provision of effective and sufficient infrastructure, alternative and innovative education centres to ensure that children who are dropping out of school are brought back into mainstream education, universal participation in school by carefully tracking students, as well as their learning levels. Counsellors or well-trained social workers connected to schools/school complexes and teachers will continuously work with students and their parents to ensure that all school-age children are attending and learning in school.

Early Childhood Care Education

NEP 2020 emphasises on the criticality of the early years to ensure quality early childhood care and education for all children between 3-6 years by 2025. The children in the ages of 3-5 will be catered to by the current system of anganwadis and pre-schools, and age 5-6 will be included with the schooling system in a seamless integrated manner, with a play-way based curriculum to be prepared by the NCERT. A National Curricular and Pedagogical Framework for Early Childhood Care and Education (NCPFECCE) for children up to the age of 8 will be developed by NCERT. The planning and implementation of early childhood education will be carried out jointly by the Ministries of HRD, Women and Child Development (WCD), Health and Family Welfare (HFW), and Tribal Affairs.

New Curricular and Pedagogical Structure

With emphasis on Early Childhood Care and Education, the 10+2 structure of school curricula is to be replaced by a 5+3+3+4 curricular structure corresponding to ages 3-8, 8-11, 11-14, and 14-18 years respectively. This will bring the hitherto uncovered age group of 3-6 years under school curriculum, which has been recognized globally as the crucial stage for development of mental faculties of a child. The new system will have 12 years of schooling with three years of Anganwadi/pre schooling. The new system will cover four stages:

Foundational Stage (in two parts, that is, 3 years of Anganwadi/pre-school + 2 years in primary school in Grades 1-2; both together covering ages 3-8),

Preparatory Stage (Grades 3-5, covering ages 8-11), **Middle Stage** (Grades 6-8, covering ages 11-14), and **Secondary Stage** (Grades 9-12 in two phases, *i.e.,* 9 and 10 in the first and 11 and 12 in the second, covering ages 14-18).

The curricula will aim for **holistic development of learners,** equipping them with the key 21st century skills, reduction in curricular content to enhance essential learning and critical thinking and greater focus on **experiential learning**. Students will have increased flexibility and choice of subjects so that they choose their own paths according to their talents and interests. There will be **no rigid separations between arts and sciences, between curricular and extra-curricular activities, between vocational and academic streams**. The objective is to give equal emphasis on all subjects-science, social sciences, art, languages, sports, mathematics - with integration of vocational and academic streams in school. A new and comprehensive **National Curricular Framework for School Education**, NCFSE 2020-21, will be developed by the NCERT.

High-quality textbook materials will be developed by NCERT and SCERTs. States will prepare their own curricula and prepare textbooks incorporating state flavour and material. The availability of textbooks in all regional languages will be a top priority. Reducing the weight of school bags and textbooks will also be ensured by suitable changes in curriculum load.

Attaining Foundational Literacy and Numeracy

A National Mission on Foundational Literacy and Numeracy will be set-up on priority to focus on early language and mathematical skills from Grades 1 to 3 by 2025. Strategies include: developing school readiness through interim 3-month play-based school preparation module for all Grade 1 students; increased focus on reading, writing, speaking, counting, arithmetic, and mathematical thinking; continuous assessment and adaptive testing; national repository of high-quality resources on foundational literacy and numeracy; filling teacher vacancies; peer-tutoring and volunteer activities; setting up school libraries in every village; A National Book Promotion Policy will be formulated, and initiatives to ensure the availability, accessibility, quality, and readership of books across geographies, languages, levels, and genres will be undertaken.

Multilingualism and the power of language

NEP 2020 lays great emphasis on promoting multilingualism so that children know and learn about the rich and vast array of languages of their country. The medium of instruction until at least Grade 5, but preferably till Grade 8 and beyond, will be the home language/ mother tongue/local language/regional language. Every student in the country will participate in a fun project/activity on 'The Languages of India', sometime in Grades 6-8, such as, under the *'Ek Bharat Shrestha Bharat'* initiative. Sanskrit will be offered at all levels of school and higher education as an important, enriching option for students, including as an option in the three-language formula. Other classical languages and literatures of India, including Tamil, Telugu, Kannada, Malayalam, Odia, Pali, Persian, and Prakrit, will also be widely available in schools as options for students. Foreign languages, such as Korean, Japanese, Thai, French, German, Spanish, Portuguese, and Russian, will also be offered at the secondary level. Indian Sign Language (ISL) will be standardized across the country, and National and State curriculum materials developed, for use by students with hearing impairment.

Assessment Reforms

There will be a shift from summative assessment to regular and formative assessment, which is more competency-based, promotes learning and development, and tests higher-order skills, such as analysis, critical thinking, and conceptual clarity. Board exams for Grades 10 and 12 will be continued, but be reformed to eliminate the need for taking coaching classes. Board exams will be redesigned to encourage holistic development; and will also be made 'easier', by testing core capacities/ competencies. All students will be allowed to take Board Exams on up to two occasions during any given school year, one main examination and one for improvement, if desired. All students will take school examinations in Grades 3, 5, and 8 which will be conducted by the appropriate authority.

A new **National Assessment Centre, PARAKH (Performance Assessment, Review, and Analysis of Knowledge for Holistic Development)**, will be set up as a standard-setting body for setting norms, standards, and guidelines for student assessment and evaluation for all recognized school boards of India, guiding the State Achievement Survey (SAS) and undertaking the National Achievement Survey (NAS), monitoring achievement of learning outcomes and encouraging and helping school boards to shift their assessment patterns towards meeting the skill requirements of the 21st century.

Equitable and inclusive Education

NEP 2020 aims to ensure that no child loses any opportunity to learn and excel because of the circumstances of birth or background. Special emphasis will be given on Socially and Economically Disadvantaged Groups(SEDGs) which include: gender identities (particularly female and transgender individuals), socio-cultural identities (such as Scheduled Castes, Scheduled Tribes, OBCs, and minorities), geographical identities (such as students from villages, small towns, and aspirational districts), disabilities (including learning disabilities), and socio-economic conditions (such as migrant communities, low income households, children in vulnerable situations, victims of or children of victims of trafficking, orphans including child beggars in urban areas, and the urban poor).

A **separate Gender Inclusion fund** will be created as also **Special Education Zones** for disadvantaged regions and groups.

Every State/District will be encouraged to establish **"Bal Bhavans"** as a special daytime boarding school, to participate in art-related, career-related, and playrelated activities. The unutilized capacity of school infrastructure will be used to promote social, intellectual, and volunteer activities for the community and to promote social cohesion during non-teaching / schooling hours and may be used as a "**Samajik Chetna Kendra**".

Teacher recruitment and career path

Teachers will be recruited through robust, transparent processes. Promotions will be merit-based, and a mechanism for multi-source periodic performance appraisals will be put in place. Progression paths to become educational administrators or teacher educators will be available for the teachers. A common **National Professional Standards for Teachers (NPST)** will be developed by 2022, by the National Council for Teacher Education, in consultation with NCERT, SCERTs, teachers from across levels and regions, expert bodies in vocational education, and higher education institutions etc.

Higher Education

Quality Universities and Colleges

- Higher education plays an extremely important role in promoting human as well as societal wellbeing and in developing India as envisioned in its Constitution - a democratic, just, socially conscious, cultured, and humane nation upholding liberty, equality, fraternity, and justice for all.
- Higher education must form the basis for knowledge creation and innovation thereby contributing to a growing national economy. The purpose of quality higher education is, therefore, more than the creation of greater opportunities for individual employment. It represents the key to more vibrant, socially engaged, cooperative communities and a happier, cohesive, cultured, productive, innovative, progressive, and prosperous nation.

Institutional Restructuring and Consolidation

- The main thrust of this policy regarding higher education is to end the fragmentation of higher education by transforming higher education institutions into large multidisciplinary universities, colleges, and HEI clusters/Knowledge Hubs, each of which will aim to have 3,000 or more students.
- Moving to large multidisciplinary universities and HEI clusters is thus the highest recommendation of this policy regarding the structure of higher education.
- Autonomous degree-granting College (AC) will refer to a large multidisciplinary institution of higher learning that grants undergraduate degrees and is primarily focused on undergraduate teaching though it would not be restricted to that and it need not be restricted to that and it would generally be smaller than a typical university.

- A stage-wise mechanism for granting graded autonomy to colleges, through a transparent system of graded accreditation, will be established.
- With appropriate accreditations, Autonomous degree-granting Colleges could evolve into Research-intensive or Teaching-intensive Universities, if they so aspire.

Over a period of time, it is envisaged that every college would develop into either an Autonomous degree-granting College, or a constituent college of a university - in the latter case, it would be fully a part of the university.

In addition to **teaching and research**, HEIs will have **other crucial responsibilities**, which they will discharge through appropriate resourcing, incentives, and structures. These include **supporting other HEIs** in their development, **community engagement** and **service**, contribution to various fields of **practice**, **faculty development** for the higher education system, and **support to school education**.

Curricular Structure

Imaginative and flexible curricular structures will enable creative combinations of disciplines for study, and would offer multiple entry and exit points, thus, removing currently prevalent rigid boundaries and creating new possibilities for life-long learning.

Flexibility in curriculum and novel and engaging course options will be on offer to students, in addition to rigorous specialization in a subject or subjects. This will be encouraged by increased faculty and institutional autonomy in setting curricula. Pedagogy will have an increased emphasis on communication, discussion, debate, research, and opportunities for cross-disciplinary and interdisciplinary thinking.

Environment education will include areas such as climate change, pollution, waste management, sanitation, conservation of biological diversity, management of biological resources and biodiversity, forest and wildlife conservation, and sustainable development and living.

(a) Structure of Degree Programme

The undergraduate degree will be of either **3 or 4-year duration**, with multiple exit options within this period, with appropriate certifications, e.g., a certificate after completing 1 year in a discipline or field including vocational and professional areas, or a diploma after 2 years of study, or a Bachelor 's degree after a 3-year programme.

The **4-year multidisciplinary Bachelor's programme**, however, shall be the preferred option since it allows the opportunity to experience the full range of holistic and multidisciplinary education in addition to a focus on the chosen major and minors as per the choices of the student.

An **Academic Bank of Credit (ABC)** shall be established which would digitally store the academic credits earned from various recognized HEIs so that the degrees from an HEI can be awarded taking into account credits earned. The **4-year programme** may also lead to a degree **'with Research'** if the student completes a rigorous research project in their major area(s) of study as specified by the HEI.

(b) Model Public Universities

Model public universities for holistic and multidisciplinary education, at par with IITs, IIMs, etc., called MERUs (Multidisciplinary Education and Research Universities) will be set up and will aim to attain the highest global standards in quality education. They will also help set the highest standards for multidisciplinary education across India.

(c) Research and Innovation

HEIs will focus on research and innovation by setting up start-up incubation centres; technology development centres; centres in frontier areas of research; greater industry-academic linkages; and interdisciplinary research including humanities and social sciences research. HEIs will develop specific hand holding mechanisms and competitions for promoting innovation among student communities.

Internationalization

Courses and programmes in subjects, such as Indology, Indian languages, AYUSH systems of medicine, yoga, arts, music, history, culture, and modern India, internationally relevant curricula in the sciences, social sciences, and beyond, meaningful opportunities for social engagement, quality residential facilities and on-campus support, etc. will be fostered to attain the goal of global quality standards, attract greater numbers of international students, and achieve the goal of 'internationalization at home'.

Credits acquired in foreign universities will be permitted, where appropriate as per the requirements of each HEI, to be counted for the award of a degree.

Student Activity and Participation

Students are the prime stakeholders in the **education system** and hence they will be given plenty of opportunities for participation in sports, culture/arts clubs, eco-clubs, activity clubs, community service projects, etc.

In every education institution, there shall be counselling systems for handling stress and emotional adjustments. Furthermore, a systematized arrangement shall be created to provide the requisite support to students from rural backgrounds, including increasing hostel facilities as needed. All HEIs will ensure quality medical facilities for all students in their institutions.

Teacher Education

Teacher education is vital in creating a pool of school teachers that will shape the next generation. Teacher preparation is an activity that requires multidisciplinary perspectives and knowledge, formation of dispositions and values, and development of practice under the best mentors.

By 2030, only educationally sound, multidisciplinary, and **integrated teacher education programmes** shall be in force. All teacher education programmes must be conducted within composite multidisciplinary institutions. Hence, universities and colleges will also run B.Ed. programmes, in collaboration with other departments such as psychology, philosophy, sociology, neuroscience, Indian languages, arts, music, history, literature, physical education, science and mathematics.

All stand-alone TEIs will be required to convert to multidisciplinary institutions by 2030, since they will have to offer the **4-year integrated** teacher preparation programme.

"The 4-year integrated B.Ed. offered by such multidisciplinary HEIs will, by 2030, become the minimal degree qualification for school teachers."

Reimagining Vocational Education

This policy aims to overcome the social status hierarchy associated with vocational education and requires integration of vocational education programmes into mainstream education in all education institutions in a phased manner.

- Beginning with vocational exposure at early ages in middle and secondary school, quality vocational education will be integrated smoothly into higher education.
- It will ensure that every child learns at least one vocation and is exposed to several more.
- This would lead to emphasizing the dignity of labour and importance of various vocations involving/Indian arts and artisanship.
- By 2025, at least 50% of learners through the school and higher education system shall have exposure to vocational education, for which a clear action plan with targets and timelines will be developed.
- The number of students in vocational education will be considered while arriving at the GER targets. The development of vocational capacities will go hand-in-hand with the development of 'academic' or other capacities.
- Higher education institutions will offer vocational education either on their own

or in partnership with industry and NGOs.

- The B.Voc. degrees introduced in 2013 will continue to exist, but vocational courses will also be available to students enrolled in all other Bachelor's degree programmes, including the 4-year multidisciplinary Bachelor's programmes.
- HEIs will also be allowed to conduct short-term certificate courses in various skills including soft skills.
- The possibility of offering vocational courses through ODL mode will also be explored.
- Vocational education will be integrated into all school and higher education institutions in a phased manner over the next decade.

Transforming The Regulatory System of Higher Education

The regulatory system of higher education will ensure that the distinct functions of regulation, accreditation, funding, and academic standard setting will be performed by distinct, independent, and empowered bodies.

This is considered essential to create checks-and-balances in the system, minimize conflicts of interest, and eliminate concentrations of power.

- The first vertical of Higher Education Commission of India (HECI) will be the National Higher Education Regulatory Council (NHERC).
- It will function as the common, single point regulator for the higher education sector including teacher education and excluding medical and legal education, thus eliminating the duplication and disjunction of regulatory efforts by the multiple regulatory agencies that exist at the current time.

Accreditation

The primary mechanism to enable above mentioned regulation will be accreditation. The second vertical of HECI will, therefore, be a 'meta-accrediting body', called the **National Accreditation Council (NAC)**.

- Accreditation of institutions will be based primarily on basic norms, public self-disclosure, good governance, and outcomes, and it will be carried out by an independent ecosystem of accrediting institutions supervised and overseen by National Accreditation Council (NAC).
- The task to function as a recognized accreditor shall be awarded to an appropriate number of institutions by NAC.
- In the short term, a robust system of graded accreditation shall be established, which will specify phased benchmarks for all HEIs to achieve set levels of quality, self-governance, and autonomy.
- In turn, all HEIs will aim, through their Institutional Development Plans (IDPs), to attain the highest level of accreditation over the next 15 years, and thereby eventually aim to function as **self-governing degree-granting institutions/ clusters**.

General Education Council

The fourth vertical of HECI will be the General Education Council (GEC), which will frame expected learning outcomes for higher education programmes, also referred to as 'graduate attributes'.

- A National Higher Education Qualification Framework (NHEQF) will be formulated by the GEC and it shall be in sync with the National Skills Qualifications Framework (NSQF) to ease the integration of vocational education into higher education.
- Higher education qualifications leading to a degree/diploma/certificate shall be described by the NHEQF in terms of such learning outcomes.
- The GEC shall set up facilitative norms for issues, such as credit transfer, equivalence, etc., through the NHEQF.
- The GEC will be mandated to identify specific skills that students must acquire during their academic programmes.

Professional Standard Setting Bodies (PSSBs)

The professional councils, such as the Indian Council for Agricultural Research (ICAR); Veterinary Council of India (VCI), National Council for Teacher Education (NCTE), Council of Architecture (CoA), National Council for Vocational Education and Training (NCVET) etc., will act as Professional Standard Setting Bodies (PSSBs).

They will play a key role in the higher education system and will be invited to be members of the GEC. These bodies, after restructuring as PSSBs, will continue to draw the curricula, lay down academic standards and coordinate between teaching, research and extension of their domain/ discipline, as members of the GEC.

RIGHT OF CHILDREN TO FREE AND COMPULSORY EDUCATION ACT, 2009

The passing of the Right of Children to Free and Compulsory Education (RTE) Act, 2009 marks a historic moment for the children of India. For the first time in India's history, children have been guaranteed their right to quality elementary education by the State with the help of families and communities.

RTE came into force on 1st April 2010. Under the provisions of this Act every child in the age group of 6-14 years will be provided eight years of elementary education in an age appropriate classroom in the vicinity of his/her neighborhood.

Provisions of the Act

Rights of Children

- To free and compulsory admission, attendance and completion of EE in a neighbourhood school is the right of every child in the age group of 06-14.

  (Free means removal by the state of any financial barrier that prevents a child from completing eight years of schooling; and compulsory means by. It ensures the State that no child has left to get elementary education. It is also parental duty to send children to school).
- Not enrolled/drop-out children be admitted to an age appropriate class after a period of Special Training.
- No child shall be failed or expelled from school up to class VIII (corresponds to the age group 6-14).

Protecting the Rights of the child in the School and the Classroom

- The onus is on teachers and school heads.
- Preparing them to embrace a new culture through appropriate programmes is a huge challenge.
- Banning corporal punishment, no detention policy, continuous and comprehensive evaluation, making schools and classrooms truly inclusive and so on.
- Protect the rights of the children to learn as per the curriculum through quality education.
- The issues are many and the task is stupendous with around 1.3 millions schools and 6 million teachers–NGO's could contribute-yet may not suffice.

Schools

- Norms and standards specified – applicable to all schools.
- Minimum infrastructure
- Teacher-Pupil Ratio of 1:30 (class I-V) and 1:35 (class VI-VIII)
- School days (200 to 220 days) and total instructional hours (800 to 1000 hours) for class I-V and VI-VIII accordingly
- Working days for teachers-weekly 45 working hours of work for teachers to be applied in every school.

Teachers

- Qualification for appointment of teachers laid down at national level
- Academic responsibility of the teachers specified
- No private tuition by fulltime school teachers

Bringing community and schools closer

- Community participation ensured through School Management Committee (SMC) comprising parents, teachers and elected representatives in which:
  - Three fourth members from among parents of children in the school
  - Proportionate representation to weaker and deprived sections
- Allocates major responsibility to the Local Authority-Panchayati Raj system
  - To proactively monitor the delivery of rights and entitlements of children

Protection of the Right

- Independent monitoring of the implementation of the Act is assigned to the National Council of Protection of Child Rights (NCPCR), the main responsibilities are:
  - examine and review safeguards for rights under this Act, and recommend measures for effective implementation;
  - inquire into complaints relating to child's right to free and compulsory education; and
  - conduct periodic social audit of the status of implementation and review.

Major Provision

1. The right of children to free and compulsory education till completion of elementary education in a neighborhood school.
2. It clarifies that 'compulsory education' means obligation of the appropriate government to provide free elementary education and ensure compulsory admission, attendance and completion of elementary education to every child in the six to fourteen age group.
3. It makes provisions for a non-admitted child to be admitted to an age appropriate class.
4. It specifies the duties and responsibilities of appropriate Governments, local authority and parents in providing free and compulsory education and sharing of financial and other responsibilities between the Central and State Governments.
5. It lays down the norms and standards relating to, inter alia, Pupil Teacher Ratios (PTRs) buildings and infrastructure, school working days, teacher working hours.
6. It provides for rational deployment of teachers by ensuring that the specified pupil teacher ratio is maintained for each school, rather than just as an average for the State or District or Block, thus ensuring that there is practically no urban-rural imbalance in teacher postings. It also prohibits deployment of teachers for non-educational work, other than decennial census, elections to local authority, state legislatures, parliament, and disaster relief.
7. It provides for appointment of appropriately trained teachers, i.e. teachers with the requisite training and academic qualifications.
8. For children in 6-14 age group it prohibits; (*i*) physical punishment and mental harassment, (*ii*) screening procedures for admission, (*iii*) capitation fees, (*iv*) private tuition by teachers, and (*v*) running of schools without recognition.
9. It provides for following penalties:

   (*a*) for charging capitation fee: fine up to 10 times the capitation fee charged;

(*b*) for resorting to screening during admission: ₹ 25,000 for first contravention ₹ 50,000 for each subsequent contravention; and

(*c*) for running a school without recognition: fine upto ₹ 1 lakh and in case of continuing contravention ₹ 10,000 for each day during which the contravention continues.

10. It provides for development of curriculum in consonance with the values enshrined in the Constitution and which would ensure the all round development of the child, building on the child's knowledge, potentiality and talent and making the child free from fear, trauma and anxiety through a system of child friendly and child-centered learning.
11. It provides for protection and monitoring of the child's right to free and compulsory education and redressal of grievances by the National and State Commissions for Protection of Child Rights, which shall have the powers of a civil court.
12. All private schools have to admit 25 per cent children from disadvantaged groups from their neighborhoods for free education, which can be extended if the number is not filled up with the customary one km radius-every year in the class in which they induct new children.

HISTORICALLY BACKGROUND OF NATIONAL POLICIES IN INDIA

Sargent Plan

One of first official attempts to plan a national system of education for India was made in 1944. It was most important plan of Post-War Educational Development in India prepared by the Central Advisory Board of Education (CABE). This is also called Sargent Plan or Report of 1944. The main object of the plan was to create in India, in a period of not less than forty years, the same standard of educational attainments as had already been admitted in England.

The main focus of this plan was on:

(*i*) Pre-primary education for children between 3 and 6 years of age;

(*ii*) Universal, compulsory, and free primary or basic education for all children between the ages of 6 and 14, divided into the junior basic (6-11) and senior basic (11-14);

(*iii*) High school education for six years for selected children between the ages of 11;

(*iv*) A university course of three years beginning after the Higher Secondary Education for selected students;

Secondary Education Commission (1952-53)

The need for the reorganization of secondary education with diversified courses had become urgent due to acceptance by the Government of India and the State Governments, of Basic Education as the pattern of education at the elementary stage. Therefore, the Central Advisory Board of Education in its meetings held in 1949 and 1951 recommended the appointment of a Commission for Secondary Education. The Government of India accordingly appointed the Secondary Education Commission under the Chairmanship of Dr. Lakshman Swami Mudaliar in 1952.

Major recommendations of Secondary Education Commission (1952-53)

The Commission expressed concern over the isolation of schools from the realities of life, over emphasis on academic instructions at the cost of holistic personality development, emphasis on English as medium of instruction and the examination oriented system of education. It gave following recommendations:

(*i*) The Commission propounded the aims and objectives of secondary education should be character building, developing democratic citizenship, economic and vocational efficiency, promoting leadership and prevention of our cultural heritage.

(*ii*) The Commission proposed a new organizational pattern for secondary education after completion of 4 or 5 years of primary or junior basic education. It is as follows:

- A Middle or Junior Secondary or Senior Basic Stage which should cover a period of 3 years;
- A Higher Secondary stage which should cover a period of 4 years.
- The commission also suggested abolition of the present intermediate classes. The 12th class should be attached to the university and the 11th class should be added to the high school.

(*iii*) The secondary education, which would be the end of all formal education for the majority of the citizens, must assume the responsibilities of providing necessary training for this purpose. The requisite in this connection is to develop the capacity for clear thinking and receptivity to new ideas.

Indian Education Commission (1964-66)

University Education Commission and Secondary Education Commission mainly focused on the particular stage of education for which they were set up, though they gave recommendations for other levels of education as well. While steps were taken to implement the recommendations of these commissions, the Constitution of Education Commission (1964-66) under the Chairmanship of **Prof. D. S. Kothari** was the first major attempt of the Government of India in the direction of educational reconstruction. The task of educational reconstruction was assigned to the Education Commission popularly known as **Kothari Commission**. The Education Commission was mandated to advise the Government on national pattern of education and on the general principles and policies for the development of education at all stages and in all aspects.

Major recommendations of Indian Education Commission (1964-66)

The Commission made several pathbreaking recommendations which were widely discussed throughout the country leading to a general consensus on national policy on education later on.

In the very first sentence the Commission recognized that "**the destiny of india is now being shaped in its classrooms**" which reflects the importance of education in the national development:

(*i*) In order to relate to the socio-economic needs and aspirations of the nation, the commission recommended the following objectives; Increase in productivity, promoting social and national integration, education and modernization and developing social, moral and spiritual values. The Commission thoroughly examined every aspect of the Indian education system and gave valuable suggestions to make education an instrument of national development.

(*ii*) Few measures were recommended by the Commission for linking education with productivity: introduction of science as basic component of school education; introduction of work experience as integral part of all education; vocationalization of secondary education; and emphasis on agriculture and allied sciences technology at the university stage.

(*iii*) A common school system of public education should be introduced. First ten years of schooling should cover a primary stage of seven or eight years and a lower secondary stage of three or two years providing a course of general education without any specialization.

(*iv*) At the school stage, the Government of India should lay down the minimum scales of pay for teachers. The State and Union Territories should then adopt equivalent or higher scales of pay to suit their local conditions. The minimum salaries of primary, secondary and university teachers should be in the ratio of 1 : 2 : 3.

(*v*) At the lower primary stage, only one language should be studied compulsorily, the mother tongue or the regional language should be taught at the option of the pupil. At the higher primary stage, only two languages should be taught on a compulsory basis; (i) mother tongue or the regional language, and (ii) the official or the associate official language of the Union. At the lower secondary stage (classes VIII-X), a study of three languages should be obligatory; and a student should be under an obligation to study either the official language of the Union or the associate official language which he / she had not elected at the higher primary stage.

National Policy on Education (1968)

The wide-ranging recommendations of the Education Commission of 1964-66 provided a basis for the Government of India to formulate the first ever National Policy on Education in 1968. The major aims of education as spelt out in the policy are:

- Promotion of national progress and security,
- Radical reconstruction of the education system to improve its quality at all stages,
- Greater attention to the development of science and technology,
- Cultivation of moral values and a closer relation between education and the life of the people,
- Development of a sense of common citizenship and culture,
- Strengthening of national integration,
- Equal opportunity to every child to help him develop his personality to the fullest,
- Provision of free and compulsory education for all children up to the age of 14 (Article 45 of the Constitution).

National Policy on Education (1986)

After the National Policy on Education (1968), the next important landmark pertaining to the national policy on education was the formulation of the National Policy on Education 1986. Prior to it, the Government of India circulated a document titled "Challenge of Education: A Policy Perspective" among the educationists of the country. Based on the wide ranging perceptions on various aspects of education given by them, the Government of India declared its new education policy under the title "National Policy on Education, 1986". Although most of the concerns expressed in the earlier policy were covered in this policy, one significant observation was made. It considered "education as a unique investment in the present and the future". This means that education system in our country should aim at not only catering to the needs of the present day Indian society but also fulfill the aspirations of the future society.

Acharya Rammurthy Committee

The next important document, which has deliberated deeply on aims of education, is the report of the Acharya Rammurthy Committee. The Acharya Rammurthy Committee was appointed by the Government of India to review National Policy on Education, 1986. The committee is known as the committee for Review of National Policy on Education, 1986. The committee submitted its report titled "Towards an Enlightened and Humane Society" in 1990. The committee spelt out long-term goals and aims for education. Broadly, it viewed the goal of education, as envisaged by the Father of the Nation, Gandhiji, *i.e.,* the goal of education is to establish a non-violent and non-exploiting social and economic order. This is the purpose of education in a modern, democratic society, its long-term goal. The committee held that education is a process, a long drawn out one, indeed a life long process of "learning to be, by learning to become". In order to qualify as an important first step of a process and of a life long process, it must equip the students with capabilities to continue to learn as well as to unlearn, seeing both learning and unlearning as important. According to the committee, education is a process of empowerment and an instrument for social change.

Policy Framework for Reforms in Education (2000)-(Ambani-Birla Report)

In September 1998, the Prime Minister's Council on Trade and Industry appointed six special subject groups to develop a policy framework for private investment in education, health and rural development. The group, which was responsible for developing a policy framework for reforms in education, was convened by Mukesh Ambani and its other member was Kumarmanglam Birla. The group submitted its report on April, 2000. The group set the following vision for education.

National Curriculum Framework for School Education-2000

The general objectives of education according to the National Curriculum Framework, 2000 are the following:

"Education liberates human beings from the shackles of ignorance, privation and misery. It must also lead to a non-violent and non-exploitative social system. School curriculum, therefore, has to aim at enabling learners to acquire knowledge, develop understanding and inculcate skills, positive attitudes, values and habits conducive to the all-round development of their personality. Young girls and boys are to be empowered through education to increase their capability. Paradigm shifts are therefore necessary to support a curriculum that values the interaction of the process and the content. Besides, the development of intrinsic values and the emotional intelligence of learners is crucial."

International Commission on Education (1972)

The UNESCO appointed an International Commission on education, under the chairmanship of Edgar Faure, which submitted its report named as 'Learning to be : The world of education today and tomorrow' in 1972.

The major goals of education as spelt out by the commission are:

- Towards a scientific humanism
- Development of creativity
- Towards social commitment
- Towards a complete man.

National Knowledge Commission (2005)

The ability of a nation to use and create knowledge capital determines its capacity to empower and enable its citizens by increasing human capabilities. The knowledge has been recognized as the key driving force in the 21st century and India's ability to emerge as a competitive player will substantially depend on its knowledge resources. To foster generational change, a systemic transformation is required that seeks to address the concerns of the entire knowledge spectrum. With this broad task in mind, the National Knowledge Commission (NKC) was constituted on 13th June, 2005 with a time-frame of three years, from 2nd October 2005 to 2nd October, 2008. As a high-level advisory body to the Prime Minister of India, the National Knowledge Commission was given a mandate to guide policy and direct reforms, focusing on certain key areas such as education, science and technology, agriculture, industry, e-governance etc. Easy access to knowledge, creation and preservation of knowledge systems, dissemination of knowledge and better knowledge services are core concerns of the commission.

Yashpal Committee Report

The 24 member committee chaired by Prof. Yashpal included amongst others the Chairpersons of UGC, AICTE, and NAAC, Vice Chancellors (current and former) of publicly funded universities, Directors of IIT (Madras), IIM (Bangalore) and NCERT, economists and bureaucrats from the Planning Commission, the Finance, Education and other ministries. Dr. Ramdas Pai, Chancellor of Manipal University, was the sole member on the committee from a private university. A few others from outside the education sector include Kiran Karnik (former President of NASSCOM) and legal expert N.R. Madhava Menon (a member of the Commission of Centre-State Relations).

Dr Anil Kakodkar Committee

The Ministry of Human Resource Development (MHRD) vide its order dated 3 February, 2010, constituted a Committee under the Chairmanship of Dr Anil Kakodkar, Chairman, BoG, IIT Bombay, to suggest a roadmap for strengthening the financial, administrative and academic autonomy of the IITs. The Committee includes eminent members like Shri T.V. Mohandas Pai, Member of the Board and Director, Human Resources, Infosys; Shri Hari Bhartia, Co-Chairman and MD of Jubilant Organosys; Prof. Ashok Jhunjhunwala, IIT Madras, Chennai; Dr. K. Mohandas, Vice-Chancellor, Kerala University of Health Sciences; Shri Ashok Thakur, Additional Secretary, MHRD.

*****

PLANNING AND ORGANIZATION OF TEACHING-LEARNING

CONCEPT OF SYLLABUS AND CURRICULUM

Education of individual takes place both in natural and contrived environments. Although, the learner is the key player in any kind of learning environment, the role of both the learner and the teacher assumes greater significance in a contrived environment.

Both the learner and the teacher act equally in the educational process to mediate their interaction with the help of certain pre-decided learning experiences. These learning experiences are usually the third dimension of the teaching-learning process and in pedagogic terms, is called curriculum.

We will try to understand curriculum through various definitions and also through its approaches, which reflect a person's viewpoint encompassing the foundations of curriculum.

MEANING OF CURRICULUM

According to Smith 'the idea of curriculum is hardly new-but the way we understand and theorize it has altered over the years - and there remains dispute as to meaning'.

The Latin meaning of the term 'curriculum' is a 'racecourse' used by chariots. Hence, it can be understood as any path or course of study which to be undertaken by an educational institution, to be covered in a specified timeframe.

The course of events can take place both inside and outside the school. Hence, while defining curriculum as 'course of events', one need to elaborate, 'which course of events'. It encompasses "the total experience provided to the learners in and out of school".

There are many definitions abound in the literature, which will help in broadening our understanding.

Marsh and Stafford highlight three dimensions of curriculum:

- curriculum includes not only list of contents but also the aims and objectives, learning experiences and evaluation;
- curriculum comprises of planning learning; and
- curriculum and instruction can not be separated.

Dewey defined Curriculum as a continuous reconstruction, moving from the child's present experience out into that represented by the organized bodies of truth that we call studies .... the various studies .... are themselves experience—they are that of the race.

Carter V. Good describes curriculum as "a systematic group of courses or sequences of subjects required for graduation or certification in a major field of study".

According to Wiles and Bondi, "a curriculum can be called as a plan for learning, which contain assumptions about the purpose of education in our society, it also has a definite structure through which the vision of the planners can be translated into learning experiences for the learner". Hence, any curriculum, comprises of two major dimensions: a vision and a structure. Tanner and Tanner define, "Curriculum is the reconstruction of knowledge and experience systematically developed under the auspices of the school (or university), to enable the learner to increase his other control of knowledge and experience". Doll, defined the curriculum of a school as the formal and informal content and process by which learners gain knowledge and understanding, develop skills, and alter attitudes, appreciations, and values under the auspices of that school.

According to Brown D.F, curriculum include all student school experiences relating to the improvement of skills and strategies in thinking critically and creatively, solving problems, working collaboratively with others, communicating well, writing more effectively, reading more analytically, and conducting research to solve problems.

Thus, a curriculum is neither a document nor a sequence of experiences. It is a plan of facilitating learning for the learner. This plan starts from where the learner is, enumerates all the aspects and dimensions of learning that are considered necessary, gives reasons why such learning is considered necessary, and what educational aims it would serve. The plan also defines stage-specific objectives, what content to teach, and how to organise it. It also recommends general principles of teaching methods and evaluation and criteria for good teaching–learning material. Such a plan, of course, is almost always set in a document or a set of documents and implemented through organised experiences for children under teachers' guidance; but perhaps conceptually the plan should remain in focus, while the document remains a contingent reality and the course of experiences as implementation of a plan.

Beane et al. have grouped most of these definitions under the following four categories, which clear indicate the nature of curriculum, which are as follows:

(*a*) **Curriculum as a Product:** The definition of curriculum as a product is derived from the idea that the school or university prepares a document which would consist of a list of courses and syllabi of those courses. These documents are the result of curriculum planning and development.

(*b*) **Curriculum as a Programme:** Here, a curriculum regent as to the courses of study offered by the school. It could also, mean a student's choice of courses within a given program of the school. Such a definition of curriculum is most widely accepted by schools. However, the broader interpretation of this definition relates to the broader purpose of the school i.e. learning and hence here, curriculum is the means of achieving that purpose and it will denote sources of learning other than just the courses the study. It acknowledges the learning that occurs in several school settings like cultural events, sports activities, in the cafeteria, in the bus, in the principal's office, etc. apart from the prescribed course of study that takes place through various activities.

(*c*) **Curriculum as Intended Learning Outcomes (ILOs):** Here, curriculum is defined as 'what is to be learned'. This definition of curriculum clearly demarcates what is to be learned from and how it is to be learned. The question of why something is to be learned is not considered. Curriculum in this context refers to knowledge of content, skills, attitudes and behaviour that learners are supposed to learn in school or college. Learners go through planned learning experiences by interacting with their peer group and teachers in the school environment, in general. However, proponents of this definition believe that such sources of learning then characterize "instruction". There is considerable debate over the meaning of the terms 'curriculum' and 'instruction'. Some curriculum designers see a distinct difference between what and how of learning. Their definition limits the idea of curriculum to the former. Curriculum as intended learning outcomes prescribes the result of instruction and not the means, i.e. the activities, material even the instructional content. The advantages of this definition are:

- Outcome is directly linked to the objectives, and
- The basic plans of learning and its implementation or transaction are kept as distinct entities.

The disadvantage of this definition is that it does not take a comprehensive view of learning. The what and how of learning are treated separately and this leads to fragmented planning.

(d) **Curriculum as Planned Learning Experiences:** The three definitions of curriculum discussed above have in common the idea that curriculum is something which is planned prior to the teaching-learning situations. The fourth category of definitions differs from the above as it refers to curriculum as experiences of the learners which is an outcome of the planned situations. The proponents of this group firmly believe that what happens is not always in accordance with what was planned. Hence the above definitions, in their opinion, constitute only the curriculum plans, whereas the actual curriculum is the learning that occurs in the students after going through different experiences.

In their opinion the outcomes of the planned situations of the course contents are more important than the course content itself. In other words, learning experiences must be well planned. A curriculum should include as analysis of the learner's learning experiences. To illustrate this definition, imagine that a teacher conducts a monthly project activity, with the goal of fostering team spirit and cooperation among the members. However, every month the teacher assigns poor grades to the shy and quiet members and high grades to the bold, talkative, and dominating members. As a result the former group would gradually get demotivated and resist any such activity. They will also learn that it is the high grades that matter and will not be able to include the intended qualities of team spirit and cooperation. Hence the course of events, which emerges, is different from what was intended. The advantages of this definition are:

- It is learner-centric and focuses more on learning than teaching.
- It imparts a complex and comprehensive meaning to the term 'curriculum'.

Difference Between Curriculum Framework, Curriculum, Syllabus and Textbooks

Most often, there is confusion in the terms curriculum framework, syllabus and curriculum itself. Let us try to understand the difference among these terms.

Curriculum Framework: It is a plan that interprets educational aims vis-avis both individual and society in order, to arrive at an understanding about the kinds of learning experiences to be given to the learner in the schools.

Curriculum: You have already studied various definitions as curriculum. It must be clear to you know that of Curriculum is planned activities which are designed to implement a particular educational aim includes the content to be taught and the knowledge, skills and attitudes which are to be deliberately fostered, together with statements of criteria for selection of content, and choices in methods, materials and evaluation.

Syllabus: Refers to the content of what is to be taught and the knowledge, skills and attitudes which are to be deliberately fostered; together with stage specific objectives.

Textbook: When as a teacher, you start working with children in classrooms; you have some 'content' that you have to teach, in other words, you have a syllabus. That syllabus is very often confined in the textbook. Thus, a textbook becomes an embodiment of syllabus—all that is in it has to be taught, and that is all that is to be taught. It becomes a methodological guide for all aspects of classroom practices —i.e. what has to be read, it also becomes the evaluation system—questions at the end of each chapter have to be answered orally and in writing, reproducing the text from the book itself. The possibility of providing enriched experiences to the children gets a little boost when teacher starts using textbooks as reflective guides.

TYPES OF CURRICULUM

Overt Curriculum

Overt curriculum is also known as explicit curriculum and intended curriculum. This includes all those curricular and co-curricular experiences, which are intentionally planned by the school, college or university organization to be provided to the learners. It consists of knowledge, skills, attitudes and values, which are overtly to be provided to the learners. Overt curriculum is designed keeping in mind the goals and objectives of the educational system. Thus, it is confined to those written understandings formally designed by curriculum designers and administrators.

Hidden Curriculum

Hidden Curriculum is unintended or unnoticed curriculum which is often unwritten. You know that curricular inputs are implicitly provided to the learner by the organization through various means. Learners learn a lot from the social environment of the classroom and the school. A teacher during her course of interaction with learners provide instructional inputs, which might not be planned and designed by her earlier. Through various non-verbal behaviour like gestures and postures, eye contact, appreciation of learner behaviour by nodding, the teacher conveys many things. A hidden curriculum also includes the value system of the school and its teachers. Hence, a hidden curriculum is as important as the overt curriculum. Learners learn 'appropriate' ways to act at school is the part of hidden curriculum.

Null Curriculum

It is physically not possible to teach everything in the schools, therefore many topics and subject areas are excluded intentionally. Eisner called them as 'Null Curriculum'; For example, life education, career planning, etc. are not fine part of overt curriculum but are important areas.

PREPARATION OF SCHOOL TIMETABLE

Timetabling is the method by which the curriculum is brought to the pupils in the school. The school timetable is a methodical and a pre-arranged scheme of studies and activities. It is a plan, showing the daily allotment of time among the various subjects, activities and classes. It shows the hours of schoolwork, the time allowed to different items of this work, the teaching load of each teacher, the length of each period and the time of interval. A timetable, in fact, is the second school clock, in the face of which are shown the intervals, the hours of the day between which lessons are given, the kind of activity in progress in each class, like recreation interval as well as the time for assembly and dismissal. It also shows art, craft, community, social service and sports activities which, though recurring regularly, do not rank as ordinary scholastic lessons in the classroom. The head of a school has a number of resources at his/her command - teachers, teaching areas, finance and time. A timetable is the means by which these resources are marshalled to provide the greatest possible educational opportunities and alternatives for pupils in the most cost-effective manner.

In the developing world the emphasis on cost-effectiveness cannot be overstated. The more efficiently resources are utilized the better the education for the greater number of children. Decisions expressed by the timetable affect the entire school population and reflect the educational programme and philosophy of the school.

NEED AND IMPORTANCE OF THE TIMETABLE

The timetable is a necessary tool for the efficient working of a school. It is really a mirror that reflects the entire educational programme of the school. "It is the timetable that supplies the framework within which the work of the school proceeds. It is the instrument through which the purpose of the school is to function". The values of the school timetable may be enumerated as follows:

- It ensures smooth and orderly working of the school
- It prevents wastage of time and energy
- It ensures equitable distribution of work among teachers
- It ensures equitable distribution of time to different subjects and activities
- It helps in adjusting schoolwork according to the needs of pupils
- It helps in the formulation of good habits
- It helps in school discipline

Thus a good timetable not only facilitates work, but also adds efficacy in various spheres. A timetable is, therefore, an absolute necessity for every type of school and its vital importance cannot be denied. Of course, there should be flexibility in the timetable; rigidity may cause problems. The time-table has to be relaxed at times as per needs and circumstances, e.g., absenteeism of teacher's.

While preparing a timetable certain aspects should be kept in mind to make a well balanced one. It should not be rigid and allow certain flexibility in it as well as in the mind of the teachers and Head. This is important if we want to achieve the aims and objectives, the vision that we have in mind for the school. The time-table should be prepared in such a manner that it can be moulded according to our needs and requirements without upsetting the other programmes. Teacher absenteeism is a common and recurring problem faced by all School Heads. This aspect should be kept in mind as substitute teachers are needed to work in place of absent teachers.

TYPES OF TIMETABLE

A good timetable clearly indicates what types of curricular and co-curricular activities are being carried on in the school at particular places and hours. It also shows under whose supervision and guidance those activities are being carried out. All this information may be contained in one timetable. But the more the number and variety of activities, the more the types of timetables. Only one timetable, with all types of information, does not serve the purpose. It is, therefore, desirable for the efficient working of the school programme to have the following types of timetable:

- Consolidated timetable for the whole school
- Class timetable
- Teacher's timetable
- Vacant periods timetable
- Games timetable
- Co-curricular activities timetable
- Homework timetable

PRINCIPLES OF TIMETABLE CONSTRUCTION

Preparing a good timetable is really a complicated piece of work because a number of factors and conditions that change from school to school determine it. Its construction, therefore, requires thorough concentration and perseverance of mind. While constructing a good timetable, the following important principles should always be kept in view:

- **Type of school:** Its type determines the nature of curricular and co-curricular activities to be organized in a school. Activities organized in a junior basic school will differ from those in a secondary or higher secondary school. Similarly rural schools will differ to a great extent from urban schools. Single teacher and double - shift schools have their own specific problems which must be solved through the timetable. It is, therefore, important that while constructing a timetable, the specific needs of the school for Which it is meant is always kept in mind.

- **Departmental regulations:** Generally, the State Department of Education prescribes the length of the school year, the duration of the school day, the duration of each of teaching periods and even the number of periods for each subject. It, therefore, becomes essential that the school timetable be in agreement with the government policy.
- **Amount of time available:** As we have stated above, the allotment of time to different Amount subjects of time and available. In some states, the duration of time to be allotted to each subject has been fixed by the Department of Education, both for summer as well as winter. The timetable will, therefore, be formed in accordance with departmental instructions. In the case of double-shift schools, the duration of the school day is shorter. It will, therefore, necessitate several changes in the school timetable.
- **Relative importance and difficulty of subjects:** The distribution of time and periods among the various school subjects is a matter of great importance. Each subject should be provided in the timetable according to its importance, which, of course, is determined by academic, social, economic and cultural considerations as well as by the future needs of the pupils.

  There is also the consideration of the relative difficulty of subjects. Thus, more time in secondary schools is given to Mathematics and English, not because they are more important but because they are considered more difficult. In junior basic schools, more time is devoted to reading, writing, Arithmetic and Craft because of their difficult nature, as compared to Social Studies and General Science.

  Similarly, the number of subjects, combination of subjects provided and the number of elective groups introduced in a particular higher secondary school must also be taken into consideration while framing a suitable timetable.
- **The element of fatigue:** Fatigue, in reality, is the state of inability to continue work after a prolonged activity of certain parts of the body. It is of two kinds: (*a*) Physical or muscular and (*b*) Mental or nervous.

  When any part of our body works for a long time, a sort of chemical action is produced with the blood in that part. As this action is too great, the waste product in the body is produced to such an extent that it too much to be carried easily by the blood. So, we feel a sort of loss of energy, which is called fatigue.

  Fatigue weakens attention and perception and diminished the power of insight and initiation. Hence the work rate is also diminished. In the school, some subjects are more fatiguing than others. They involve a heavy mental strain and effort. Such subjects should be taught during early hours when the brain is fresh.

  It has been noted psychologically that the second and the third periods on a school day are the best when the work curve reaches its highest point. Similarly the second and the third days of the week are the best, when momentum is the highest.

  Monday is only the warming up day and Saturday is perhaps the worst. So subjects like English, regional languages and Mathematics should be taught during the best periods of the day. Similarly subjects like arts, crafts, writing, science practical's and manual work, etc., that require less energy should be pursued in the last periods.

  Lastly, the duration of periods must change according to age, physical condition and season. In summer, periods should be of shorter duration as compared to winter. Similarly, in the case of primary classes, periods should not be very long. Small children get fatigued very soon and so they need frequent changes in activities and occupations.

- **Variety:** The timetable should be constructed in a manner that it allows frequent change of places and posture to pupils. The same subject should not be taught continuously for many periods, nor should the same class sit in a particular room for the whole day. Change of seat, room and posture is the best remedy against fatigue. Similarly, easy and difficult subjects and lessons should be provided alternatively in the timetable for the sake of variety. If a subject is to be taught for two or three periods in a week, it should not be provided on consecutive days. It should, rather, be fixed in the timetable after regular intervals.
- **Elasticity:** As already stated, the timetable is an instrument to help us in carrying out the schoolwork smoothly and efficiently. It should, therefore, be not rigid and fixed. It should rather be made as flexible and elastic as possible. However, it should be adhered to unless there are special situations. There must be ample scope for adjustments and changes to meet the specific needs of certain categories of pupils.

Change may also be necessary because of the transfer or absenteeism of some teachers. It should, however, be remembered that the timetable should not become our master because of its rigidity. It should always act as a faithful servant.

- **Staff, equipment and building:** While constructing a good timetable, the number and qualifications of teachers, and the number and size of classes and classrooms and equipment should always be kept in view. Again in case of a school where one room is used for two classes, the timetable will be arranged in a different manner as compared to a school having a spacious building. Equipment and furniture available in the school also determine the construction of the timetable to a certain extent.
- **Pupil-centred:** In essence a timetable should be pupil-centred to maximize learning opportunities, arranged with a variety of activities, with subjects spaced to sustain the children's interests and motivation, and taking into account age, concentration span, ability range, single grouping, class sizes and pupil career ambitions.
- **Vertical as well as horizontal deployment of teachers:** Staff should be deployed vertically and horizontally across the timetable. This means that teachers with different qualifications as well as experience should teach at different levels. Along with this, their interest should also be kept in mind as teachers like to teach those subjects that they find interesting and have studied.
- **Balance:** There should be a balance in the timetable in the sense that not too many double periods or practical subjects should follow one after the other.
- **Efficient deployment of teachers:** The best and most efficient deployment of teachers can be achieved if:
  - the teachers have been selected with proper qualifications and experience, *i.e.* if the teacher has to teach the senior class, then her/his qualification and experience must be according to that. If a teacher is a postgraduate in a subject and is sent to teach pupils of class I, then his/her qualification is wasted. It also does not benefit the class to which he/she is sent. However, if the postgraduate teacher is fond of younger children, let him teach lower classes too.
  - all the subjects are fully covered
  - there is a staffing equilibrium in terms of experience, sex and age
  - the frequency of transfer of teachers is minimized
  - teaching loads are balanced across the timetable.

- Allowance has to be made within the timetable organization, including non-teaching time for:
  - Pupil registration, assemblies, time between periods 10 change books and materials, pupil guidance and welfare
  - Staff development including departmental meetings, staff meetings and in-service workshops.

Case Study

As usual, the timetable for the whole school had been prepared. Three classes-one each from the Junior section, Middle section and the Senior section-were sent to the play field during a particular period. This created a problem on the field. A pupil of the Junior section got hit by a stray ball as the senior class was playing cricket. The child was badly hurt. The School Head had a problem facing the parents. She was thinking how to avoid such accidents. She analyzed the timetable bf all the three sections. She got them modified in such a manner that only one class could be on the play field in a particular period. But this was not possible for all the periods. Now she called the Physical Education teachers of all the three sections. She discussed the matter with them and it was decided that if more than one class is on the play field in a period, then the Physical Education teachers will co-ordinate and see to it that the three classes are in separate parts of the field, with one group practising Yoga or Aerobics, while another group is playing on the field; the third group, if any, may be involved in indoor games or some other activity. The School realized the importance of co-ordination between the three sections while preparing the timetable.

FOUNDATIONAL LITERACY AND NUMERACY: EARLY CHILDHOOD CARE AND EDUCATION

Early childhood (birth to 8 years) is a critical period of development and early literacy and early numeracy are two important skill areas that develop during this period. Literacy and numeracy development begins in the first three years of life and is closely linked with daily communications, actions, thoughts and drawings of young children. Parents and the home learning environment and interactions of young children with literacy materials as books, paper, and crayons are the building blocks for the development of language, reading, writing and numeracy. This understanding of early literacy development complements the current research supporting the critical role of early experiences in shaping brain development.

Education in the Early Years

Young children are active, energetic, curious and interested in people, objects and events around them. They actively seek to make meaning of their experiences and their capacities continuously evolve. Children learn by doing and actively use their sensory capacities to understand the world around them. They discover and construct knowledge through the activities they are involved in. To enable children to understand concepts and develop their abilities, adults need to provide them opportunities to explore their environment, manipulate objects, engage in experimentation and ask questions and search for answers. These hands-on experiences help them understand how things work and in this way each child re-constructs his/her own understanding of the world.

At the same time, children learn in context of relationships. Children also need guidance and instruction from teachers and more knowledgeable peers who can help the child to move from one developmental level to the next – they help the children to move through their zone of proximal development. Having identified concepts and tasks which are within the child's potential development level (*i.e.* what the child is capable of doing with help), the teacher needs to provide dynamic support, guidance and teaching so that the child reaches her potential and is able to do the task independently.

Definition of Literacy and Numeracy

UNESCO defines literacy as the 'ability to identify, understand, interpret, create, communicate, compute and use printed materials associated with varying contexts. Literacy is more than the ability to read and write. It involves the knowledge, skills and abilities—the competencies—that enable individuals to think critically, communicate effectively, deal with change and solve problems in a variety of contexts to achieve their personal goals, develop their knowledge and potential, and participate fully in society.

Numeracy encompasses the ability to use mathematical understanding and skills to solve problems and meet the demands of day-to-day living in complex social settings. To have this ability, a young person needs to be able to think and communicate quantitatively, to make sense of data, to have a spatial awareness, to understand patterns and sequences, and to recognise situations where mathematical reasoning can be applied to solve problems.

Why are Literacy and Numeracy Important?

Early literacy and numeracy skills are not only foundational for learning but are correlated with greater quality of life, personal well-being, national stability, prosperity and are critical for educational outcomes in later years. Strong literacy and numeracy helps children to learn, experiment, reason and create, to be active and informed citizens, and to contribute socially, culturally and economically. Lack of learning opportunities during the early stages of acquiring literacy and numeracy impede children's academic progress and motivation, resulting in further lack of achievement.

Vision

The vision for foundational literacy and numeracy therefore is to enable children to become independent and engaged readers and writers who are able to transition from 'learning to read' to 'reading to learn' and from 'learning to write' to 'writing for academic success and pleasure'. Children demonstrate an understanding of numbers and knowledge of mathematical concepts, make connections between related ideas and progressively apply their understanding in new and unfamiliar contexts. To achieve the vision it is important that we understand the present status of reading and writing among children in the country. Various researches conducted in the country point out that the children are facing a learning crisis.

The Learning Crisis

The National Policy on education (NEP, 2020) highlights that various governmental as well as non-governmental surveys clearly indicate that, at the current time, we are in a severe learning crisis with respect to these most basic skills: a large proportion of students (over 5 crore in number) currently in elementary school - have not attained foundational literacy and numeracy, *i.e.*, the ability to read and comprehend basic text and the ability to carry out basic addition and subtraction with Indian numerals. Numerous studies show that, in the current educational system, once students fall behind on foundational literacy and numeracy, they tend to maintain flat learning curves for years, perpetually unable to catch up. So many capable students have found themselves in this unfortunate black hole, unable to emerge. For many students, this has become a major reason for not attending school, or for dropping out altogether.

The NEP, 2020 further reiterates that it is imperative to address this crisis head on and immediately so that basic learning can be accomplished in schools and all students may thereby gain the opportunity to obtain an education of quality. Attaining foundational literacy and numeracy for all children must become an immediate national mission. Students, along with their schools, teachers, parents, and communities, must be urgently supported and encouraged in every way possible to help carry out this all-important target and mission, which indeed forms the basis of all future learning.

The NEP, 2020 has recommended that in order to avert the learning crisis there will be an increased focus on foundational literacy and numeracy—and generally, on reading, writing, speaking, counting, arithmetic, and mathematical thinking—throughout the preparatory and middle school curriculum, with a robust system of continuous formative/adaptive assessment to track and thereby individualize and ensure each student's learning. The aim of education will not only be cognitive development, but also building character and creating holistic and well-rounded individuals equipped with the key 21st century skills. For this assessment in our schooling system will shift from one that is summative and primarily tests rote memorization skills to one that ismore regular and formative. The system will be competency based, promote learning and development of children, and test higher-order skills, such as analysis, critical thinking, and conceptual clarity.

Way Forward

The Ministry of Education, Government of India has already launched the National Initiative for Proficiency in Reading with Understanding and Numeracy (NIPUN Bharat) mission along with a detailed implementation guideline for the states to ensure that every child in the country necessarily attains foundational literacy and numeracy (FLN) by the end of Grade 3, by 2026-27. For this, the learning outcomes have been defined for six years in a continuum in six levels from Pre-school to grade 3 (3-9 years). It has also set the 'Lakshya' (targets) for each class from Balvatika onwards. The mission guidelines recommend shifting towards competency based education and using school based assessment for providing continuous guidance to teachers.

In tune with the National Mission, the State Mission, District Mission and Block missions have to be chalked out by the states and ensure that the learning outcomes are achieved. Roles and responsibilities and functions of all the stakeholders involved in the mission at each level are defined in the NIPUN Guidelines.

A robust IT system is recommended to be used for FLN Mission for big data analytics at National, State and School level. The FLN Mission recommends leveraging DIKSHA (Digital Infrastructure for Knowledge Sharing) which is the national digital platform for school education in India, an initiative of National Council for Educational Research and Training (NCERT) and Ministry of Education. To empower the teachers, a capacity development programme for teachers and school heads, NISHTHA, FLN will be launched by the NCERT through DIKSHA online platform. A 3 Month School Preparatory Module—Vidya Pravesh has also been launched by the NCERT.

The FLN Guidelines also advocate engaging meaningfully with parents, families and community to create awareness among them also to engage them in the teaching learning process of their children.

COMPETENCY BASED LESSON PLANNING

When using the updated lesson plan teachers should consider the following points:

1. When teachers plan their lessons they should resort to "competences and curriculum standards" in the unit plans provided "for the first term and the one to be developed by Heads of department and supervisors in the second term". This means that they are going to write and develop the competences of the unit for instance, writing the competences of Unit ONE in the space provided for competences in day one "including the four skills" which may include any of the two ranges "range of attitudes and range of connections" and not only "reality and operations".

Specific Competence to be developed	Listening : ....
	Speaking : ....
	Reading : ....
	Writing : ....

2. Teachers should note that specific competences can be repeated in different days and in different units throughout the whole year because they are supposed to be developed over a long period of time and not in one teaching period like the learning objectives. Competences are different from

learning objectives. Competencies define the applied skills and knowledge that enable students to successfully perform their work over a long period of time, while learning objectives are specific to a certain course of instruction and they describe what the learner should be able to achieve at the end of a period of time "time bound" – 40 minutes. In short, objectives say what we want the learners to know and competencies say how we can be certain they know it.

3. In the rest of the days "days 2,3,4 till the last day of teaching a certain unit, teachers are going to write just the number of the competences" Listening 1.2 / Speaking 2.2 etc. In the procedure part they write the activities that develop the competences mentioned.
4. Teachers, with the help of the HODs, should know well which specific competences go with the lessons they are going to teach, they will choose from the competences written in the unit they are going to develop. They also can choose additional competences from the annual plan check the part of the annual plan entitled "competences : added by teachers" and in the unit plan "teacher's additions".
5. In part 4 of the lesson plan phonics - for both grades "1, 2" teachers write the main sounds they are going to introduce "f, h, ch, th, ou, oy…." etc.

Phonics (Sounds)	....

6. **Procedure and activities:** The main part of the lesson plan "Procedure and activities" focuses on teacher's regular procedure when dealing with a lesson and the suggested examples of learning activities the teacher will use to develop the competences. Teachers can use the provided activities and they may add their own creative ones.
7. **Assessment tools:** Refers to the tools of formative assessment which is considered the dominant assessment in competency based instructions that teachers utilize during teaching.

Assessment Tools	● Questions ● Oral response ● Worksheets ● Oral presentation ● Observation ● Quizzes ● Pair/Group wok ● Paper pencil tasks Other ....

8. **Feedback :** In all days except the last day of the learning unit, teachers should write what students learned by the end of that lesson and whether learners were responsive or not in addition to teacher's self evaluation.
9. **Reflection in relation to curriculum standards :** In the last day of teaching a unit the part entitled "Reflection in relation to curriculum standards", teachers should consult the unit plan and check the "Curriculum standards" to state whether competences are developed or not or partially developed. They need to specify the standards that go with the competences chosen.

   E.g. "Competency 2.1 and Standard 2.1". They should take into consideration the details of the curriculum standards and write the ones that were focused on in the unit :

   E.g. In Unit 2 the title of the unit is "My Body", so when copying the curriculum standard the focus should be on the following:

   "2.1. Use appropriate simple vocabulary to indicate/ name body parts and other things in small conversations or individual speech" no need to mention "classroom objects, people, places and food items" which will appear in other units, but by the end of grade 1 the curriculum standard should be written as it is written in the primary stage document:

   "2.1. Use appropriate simple vocabulary to indicate/name classroom objects, people and places, food items and other things in shortl conversations or individual speech".

(Reflection in relation to curriculum standards)	*By the end of this unit by students were able to:*	Developed	Partially developed	Not developed
	--			
	--			
	--			
	--			
	--			

COMPETENCY BASED ASSESSMENT

The Central Board of Secondary Education (CBSE) is set to implement competency based assessments as part of the 2025 curriculum reforms, ushering in a shift from rote learning to skills-focused education. This change is aligned with the National Education Policy (NEP) 2020, which prioritizes conceptual understanding, critical thinking, and real-world application. Competency based assessments emphasize a student's ability to apply knowledge and solve problems in practical contexts, rather than simply recalling information.

What are Competency Based Assessments?

Competency based assessments focus on testing students' understanding of key concepts and their ability to apply them practically. Unlike traditional exams, these assessments measure critical thinking, analytical skills, and problem-solving. Instead of requiring students to memorize content, Competency based questions often present real-life scenarios where students must use their knowledge to find solutions.

Key Features of Competency Based Assessments

Application-Focused: Students are tested on their ability to apply concepts in new or unfamiliar situations.

Skill-Based Evaluation: Emphasis is on critical thinking, problem-solving, and reasoning skills.

Real-World Relevance: Often involves case studies, practical examples, and real-life problems. By focusing on these aspects, competency based assessments aim to foster a deeper and more practical understanding of subjects, making learning more meaningful and relevant.

Impact on Student Learning

1. **Development of Critical Thinking and Problem-Solving Skills:** Competency based assessments encourage students to think deeply and critically, moving beyond surface-level learning.

   Higher-Order Thinking: Students are prompted to analyze, synthesize, and evaluate information.

   Real-Life Problem Solving: Practical application of knowledge enhances students' ability to handle real-world situations.

   Improved Learning Outcomes: As students engage with material in a meaningful way, they are likely to retain and understand it better.

2. **Encouragement of Conceptual Understanding:** With a focus on concepts rather than memorization, competency based assessments motivate students to build a solid understanding of each topic.

   Reduced Reliance on Rote Learning: Students learn concepts thoroughly rather than memorizing facts.

   Foundation for Lifelong Learning: A strong conceptual understanding is essential for higher education and career readiness.

Enhanced Retention: Concepts understood at a deeper level are remembered longer, helping students perform better.

3. **Reduced Exam-Related Stress:** By shifting away from high-stakes memorization, competency based assessments can help lower students' anxiety around exams.

   Less Emphasis on Cramming: Students focus on understanding, which reduces last-minute stress.

   Flexible Learning Approach: Skills-based learning is often more engaging and less overwhelming.

   Positive Exam Experience: Students may feel more confident tackling practical questions they've practiced throughout the year.

4. **Alignment with Global Education Standards:** Competency based assessments bring CBSE's approach closer to international education systems, preparing students for global academic and career opportunities.

   Increased Global Competitiveness: Students trained in Competency based learning are better prepared for international studies or job markets.

   Adaptability for Future Careers: Skills such as critical thinking and problem-solving are highly valued in modern workplaces.

   Preparation for Advanced Studies: Students familiar with practical assessments perform better in higher education environments that prioritize research and analysis.

Challenges of Competency Based Assessments

1. **Adjustment to New Learning Methods:** Shifting from memorization to skills-based learning requires a different approach from both students and teachers.

   Adaptation Period: Students accustomed to rote learning may initially struggle with the new format.

   Teacher Training Needs: Educators may need support and training to develop competency focused teaching methods.

   Learning Curve: Both students and teachers may face challenges as they adjust to new expectations and assessment styles.

2. **Increased Demands on Teachers:** Teachers will need to invest more time in preparing and grading competency based assessments, which may increase their workload.

   Complex Assessment Design: Creating assessments that accurately test competencies requires effort and planning.

   Ongoing Feedback Requirements: Teachers need to provide constructive feedback to support student growth in skills.

   Resource Requirements: Educators may need access to updated materials and training for effective implementation.

Strategies for Students to Succeed in Competency Based Assessments

1. **Prioritize Conceptual Clarity:** A solid understanding of core concepts is essential for answering Competency based questions effectively.

   Ask Questions: Students should ask questions in class to clarify any doubts about the topic.

   Use Visuals: Mind maps and diagrams help in organizing and connecting ideas.

   Connect to Real-Life Examples: Relating topics to real-life situations improves understanding and retention.

2. **Practice Critical Thinking and Analysis:** Developing analytical skills is key for Competency based assessments.

   Work with Case Studies: Practice with case studies and real-world examples to apply theoretical knowledge.

Participate in Group Discussions: Sharing ideas with peers helps in understanding different perspectives and strengthens critical thinking.

Challenge Assumptions: Students should regularly test and analyze their understanding by questioning their assumptions about topics.

3. **Engage in Active Learning Techniques:** Active learning can help reinforce knowledge and skills required for Competency based assessments.

   Think-Pair-Share: This method promotes individual thinking, collaborative discussion, and group sharing.

   Hands-On Projects: Projects and assignments that involve practical application help students engage with learning in a deeper way.

   Reflective Journals: Keeping a journal of daily learning can help students track their progress and reinforce what they've learned.

Role of Parents and Teachers in Supporting Competency Based Learning

1. **Create a Question-Friendly Environment at Home:** Parents can encourage children to ask questions and explore topics that interest them.

   Discuss Daily Concepts: Relate subjects like science, math, or language to daily life for more meaningful understanding.

   Use Educational Resources: Online videos, games, and interactive apps can help reinforce competencies.

   Support Inquiry-Based Learning: Encourage curiosity and exploration beyond the classroom.

2. **Emphasize Collaborative Learning in the Classroom:** Teachers can foster an environment where students work together to solve problems, building communication and teamwork skills.

   Group Activities: Group assignments and projects encourage collaboration and communication.

   Peer Teaching: Students explaining concepts to each other can strengthen their understanding and confidence.

   Debates and Discussions: Allow students to engage in discussions that require them to defend their viewpoints and critically assess information.

The new CBSE Competency based assessments mark a significant step toward developing critical thinking, problem-solving, and practical application skills in students. By moving beyond rote learning, CBSE aligns itself with global educational standards, preparing students for both higher education and the workforce.

Though the transition may bring challenges, the benefits for students, including reduced exam stress, better retention, and enhanced readiness for real-world challenges, make it a valuable shift in Indian education. With the support of teachers and parents, students can embrace this change and succeed in a more meaningful, skill-oriented learning environment.

INSTRUCTIONAL MATERIAL AND RESOURCES

Teaching Learning Materials (TLM), also known as instructional material and resources are essential tools that aid the teaching-learning process by making lessons more interactive, engaging, and effective. These materials include a variety of resources such as textbooks, workbooks, flashcards, digital media, and real-life objects, which help facilitate a better understanding of concepts. The primary purpose of TLM is to bridge the gap between theoretical knowledge and practical application, making learning more accessible and comprehensive for students.

In recent years, the accessibility and availability of teaching learning materials have escalated due to the revolution in technology. This has created new opportunities for teachers to access and use a broad range of resources to support their teaching. However, the sheer volume of materials can make it challenging to choose the most appropriate materials for a particular lesson or class. Therefore, it is important for teachers to ensure that they are using effective teaching learning materials to support student learning.

One of the key advantages of TLM is its ability to cater to different learning styles. Visual learners benefit from diagrams, charts, and illustrations, while auditory learners grasp concepts better through discussions, lectures, and recorded lessons. Similarly, kinesthetic learners thrive with hands-on activities, models, and interactive experiments. By incorporating diverse TLM into lesson plans, educators can create an inclusive learning environment that meets the needs of all students.

With advancements in technology, the accessibility of TLM has expanded significantly. Digital platforms now offer teachers a vast array of multimedia content, virtual simulations, and interactive resources. However, with an overwhelming volume of materials available, selecting the most suitable ones for a particular lesson is a challenge. To ensure effective learning outcomes, educators must carefully curate and integrate TLM that align with curriculum objectives and student needs.

TLM, or Teaching Learning Materials, refers to the instructional aids used by educators to enhance students' learning experiences. These materials serve as visual, auditory, or tactile learning aids, helping students grasp abstract concepts more easily. They play a crucial role in personalised learning, addressing diverse learning needs and styles.

Real-World Applications of TLM

- **Textbooks and Workbooks:** Standardised learning materials used across classrooms to provide a structured approach to education.
- **Visual Aids (Charts, Diagrams, Models):** Commonly used in subjects like science and mathematics to help students visualise complex concepts.
- **Digital Learning Tools (E-books, Online Simulations, Interactive Whiteboards):** These modern tools have revolutionised education by enabling remote learning and personalised instruction.
- **Experiential Learning Kits (STEM Kits, Virtual Labs):** Used to provide hands-on learning experiences, particularly in science, technology, engineering, and mathematics (STEM) education.
- **Storytelling & Role-Playing:** A technique widely used in language learning and history classes to make lessons more engaging.

The introduction of teaching learning materials is vital for any successful education system. These materials incorporate workbooks, textbooks, visual aids, and other resources that brace the teaching and learning process. The introduction of teaching learning materials has a significant impact on student achievement and teacher effectiveness.

Importance of Teaching-Learning Materials in Education

The introduction of teaching learning material is vital for effective education. Teachers and students use these materials to facilitate the learning process and improve their understanding of the subject matter. Here are some of the reasons why the introduction of teaching and learning materials is important:

- **Facilitate learning:** Learning materials equip students with vital resources to understand a concept or subject. These materials help students to visualise complex ideas, which makes learning easier and more enjoyable.
- **Enhance retention:** The use of audio materials, visual aids, and hands-on activities help students acquire information better and faster than just reading or listening to lectures.
- **Foster creativity:** Learning materials stimulate creativity & imagination, encouraging learners to think beyond the textbook

and come up with their own distinct ideas and solutions.

- **Cater to different learning styles:** Effective teaching learning materials cater to different learning styles, enabling students to engage with resources in ways that suit their individual requirements.
- **Save time:** Teaching learning materials save time for both teachers & students. Teachers use prepared materials to prepare their lessons, while students use them to reinforce and review what they have learned.

Types of Teaching-Learning Materials and Their Applications

Teaching-Learning Materials (TLM) come in various types, each serving a unique purpose in the classroom. These materials can help cater to different learning styles, making lessons more engaging and effective. Below are some common types of TLM and their uses:

Visual Aids: Charts, diagrams, and models are powerful tools for visualising abstract concepts. They help break down complex ideas into simpler, more digestible parts. For instance, a diagram of the water cycle can make it easier for students to understand the process of evaporation, condensation, and precipitation.

Audio Materials: Recordings and podcasts are excellent for enhancing listening skills and comprehension. They are especially useful in language learning, where hearing correct pronunciation and intonation is key. Audio materials can also bring stories and subjects to life, making learning more immersive.

Digital Resources: Interactive apps and online platforms make learning more dynamic and accessible. These digital tools provide interactive exercises, quizzes, and videos that can reinforce classroom teaching. They also allow for personalised learning, catering to the pace and style of each student.

Tangible Resources: Manipulatives and physical objects like blocks, counters, or scientific models enable hands-on learning. These resources are particularly effective in subjects like maths and science, where abstract ideas can be challenging to grasp without practical experience. They help students to explore concepts physically, aiding deeper understanding.

Printed Materials: Workbooks and textbooks provide a structured pathway for learning, offering foundational knowledge in an organised manner. They are essential for homework, revision, and practice, reinforcing what has been taught in class. Printed materials also serve as a reliable reference for students and teachers alike.

Objectives of Teaching and Learning Materials in the Classroom

The objectives of teaching learning materials are to improve the learning experience and facilitate the learning process. Here are some of the specific objectives of teaching-learning materials below:

- **Clarify concepts and information:** The introduction of teaching learning materials helps clarify composite concepts and information by representing them in an organized, clear & visual way. This helps learners to better understand and remember the material.
- **Engage students:** By using a range of TLM, teachers can engage learners and make learning more interesting and enjoyable. This enhances motivation and participation and leads to excellent overall learning outcomes.
- **Promote critical thinking:** TLMs can be used to promote critical thinking and problem-solving skills by presenting learners with real-world scenarios and asking them to implement their knowledge to solve problems.
- **Encourage active learning**: Teaching learning resources encourage active learning by equipping students with opportunities to engage in group work, hands-on activities, and discussions. This helps students retain information and develop a deeper understanding of the material.

- **Accommodate diverse learning styles:** Materials for teaching learning materials can be curated to accommodate diverse learning styles, enabling students to engage with resources in a way that best fits their individual needs and preferences.

Importance of TLM in the Teaching-Learning Process

Teaching Learning Materials (TLM) play a vital role in making the teaching-learning process more effective and engaging. For teachers, TLM serves as a structured aid that simplifies complex concepts, making lessons more interactive and comprehensible for students. By using visual aids, real-life objects, and digital tools, educators can cater to different learning styles, ensuring that no student is left behind.

How TLM Benefits Teachers?

1. **Enhances Lesson Delivery:** TLM provides teachers with structured resources that make lessons more interactive and engaging. Visual aids, models, and digital tools help explain complex topics clearly, making learning more accessible to students.
2. **Caters to Different Learning Styles:** Every student learns differently, some through visual representation, others through auditory or kinesthetic experiences. TLM helps teachers adapt their teaching methods to meet the needs of diverse learners, ensuring no student is left behind.
3. **Encourages Student Participation:** Interactive TLM, such as role-playing activities, flashcards, and group exercises, foster active learning, making students more involved in the lesson. This increased engagement leads to better retention and understanding.
4. **Saves Preparation Time for Teachers:** Pre-designed charts, models, and digital resources reduce the effort required for lesson planning, allowing teachers to focus more on student interaction and feedback.
5. **Supports Experiential Learning:** Practical, hands-on teaching materials help bridge the gap between theory and real-world application, making learning more meaningful for students.

   By incorporating TLM effectively, teachers can create a dynamic and engaging classroom environment, ensuring better comprehension, retention, and application of knowledge.

Understanding the Difference Between Teaching-Learning Materials and Teaching Aids

Teaching-Learning Materials (TLM) and Teaching Aids are both essential in the educational process, but they serve different purposes. Understanding these differences can help educators use them more effectively in the classroom.

Teaching-Learning Materials (TLM) Explained: Teaching-Learning Materials (TLM) encompass a broad range of resources used to support both teaching and learning processes. These materials include textbooks, workbooks, visual aids, digital content, and tangible objects that cater to facilitate deeper understanding, engagement, and active participation in the learning process.

The main goal of TLM is to enhance the educational experience by providing diverse tools that help students understand, retain, and apply knowledge. For instance, textbooks offer a structured way to present information, while online learning platforms and educational videos provide interactive content that can engage students more deeply.

Hands-on kits and models allow for experiential learning, making abstract concepts more tangible and easier to grasp. TLM is utilised across various stages of learning, from introducing new topics to revising and applying knowledge in practical scenarios.

Teaching Aids: Teaching Aids are a subset of TLM, specifically focused on tools that help teachers explain concepts or ideas more effectively in the classroom. These aids are particularly valuable for making lessons more interactive and understandable.

While TLM covers a wide spectrum, Teaching Aids are used mainly during the delivery of lessons to clarify or illustrate specific points. They assist teachers in conveying information in a way that captures students' attention and makes learning more engaging.

For example, charts can summarise information visually, flashcards can be used for quick reviews, models can provide a three-dimensional understanding of objects, and blackboards are useful for writing and drawing during the lesson. The purpose of Teaching Aids is to simplify complex ideas and enhance the effectiveness of teaching during instructional time.

Key Differences Between TLM & Teaching Aids

While TLM and Teaching Aids are often used interchangeably, they differ in their scope and usage. Understanding these distinctions can help educators choose the right tools for different stages of the learning process.

- **Functionality:** TLM encompasses a comprehensive range of resources that support the entire learning process, from introducing new concepts to reinforcing them through practice. In contrast, Teaching Aids are more focused on specific tools that facilitate the delivery of instruction, particularly during lessons.
- **Usage:** TLM is used throughout the learning process, including preparation, instruction, practice, and assessment. On the other hand, Teaching Aids are typically used during instructional time to support teaching, making complex ideas more accessible and engaging.

Why Both Matter in the Classroom

Both Teaching Learning Materials and Teaching Aids play crucial roles in the classroom. TLM provides a wide variety of resources that support different learning styles and help students engage with the material in multiple ways.

Teaching Aids, meanwhile, enhances the effectiveness of teaching by making lessons more interactive and understandable. Together, they create a more dynamic and supportive learning environment, ensuring that students not only learn but also retain and apply what they've learned.

DIGITAL TECHNOLOGY IN TEACHING-LEARNING

"Digital Technology" is a term that is not far away from becoming an integral part of anything and everything around us. Digital Technology, like wildfire, is sweeping across our modern landscape, igniting transformation in every sector, especially education. Its rapid expansion is reshaping the way we learn, connect, and access information, bringing new opportunities and challenges as it blazes a trail into the future. That all together is creating a greater scope every day for Digital Technology In Education where it works as a supplement to both teaching and learning.

Types of Digital Technology in Education

When we discuss the integration of digital technology in education, it's essential to define what we mean by "digital technology". Here's a closer look at the types of digital technology that are making a significant impact:

1. **Interactive Learning Software:** Being one of the most promising digital technologies in education, Interactive learning software includes educational applications, simulations, and games designed to engage students while teaching them essential concepts. These software solutions provide a dynamic and immersive learning experience, fostering curiosity and a deeper understanding of subjects.
2. **Learning Management Systems (LMS):** Learning Management Systems are again a prominent part of digital technology in education that has the power to supplement

learning and teaching at schools. These are digital platforms that streamline the management of educational content and resources. Further, they enable teachers to organize course materials, assessments, and communication with students in one place, making it easier to deliver and track learning outcomes.

3. **Smart Classroom Solutions:** Smart classrooms are equipped with digital technology as the devices that these smart classrooms can be based on involve - Interactive digital boards, Smart TVs, Digital White Boards, or smart projectors. All that to create an immersive learning environment. A Tools such as a Smart Class app facilitates real-time interaction and collaboration, making lessons more engaging and interactive.
4. **Educational Apps:** Educational apps encompass a wide variety of tools, from language learning apps to math practice apps, or to the one-stop learning apps that enable students to find everything they need to learn and grow in one single place such as the iPrep App. Further, these apps are accessible on tablets, smartphones, and computers, allowing students to learn on the go and personalize their educational journey.
5. **E-Books and Digital Textbook:** Digital textbooks provide students with a more interactive and portable alternative to traditional paper textbooks. Considered as the most convenient digital technology in education, these are mostly PDF versions of textbooks and one can have hundreds of these in one single device. Also, these do not get torn nor do they have any heavy weight for students and teachers to bear.
6. **Adaptive Learning Systems:** A highly promising and new-age digital technology in education is Adaptive learning systems. These use data and algorithms to personalize the learning experience for each student. They assess individuals' current learning levels, their strengths and weaknesses, and tailor content accordingly, ensuring that students receive the support they need to excel such as the "iPrep PAL" app where PAL stands for Personalized Adaptive Learning.
7. **Digital Libraries:** Digital libraries can digitize the way students learn and grow in classrooms, libraries, and labs in school. These are smart ICT labs based on tablets, notebooks, android laptops. These devices are usually preloaded with rich digital content for classes 1st to 12th. So teachers can make students use them to learn and grow whenever they see fit.
8. **Learning Analytics:** The most important digital technology is the one that proves the legitimacy and effectiveness of these digital technologies in education. And it is none other than Learning analytics. It involves the collection and analysis of data related to student performance and engagement. This information allows teachers to make data-driven decisions and identify areas for improvement in their teaching methods and curriculum.
9. **Digital Assessments:** Digital assessment tools, including practice sets, quizzes, and assessments with the use of digital tools such as tablets, mobile phones, or laptops, enable teachers to evaluate student performance efficiently. They offer immediate feedback, helping students understand their areas of improvement. Making them an integral part of digital technology in education.

By understanding the diverse range of digital technology used in education, we can appreciate the transformational potential of these tools in enabling universal access to learning and growth.

Advantages of Digital Technology in Education

Digital technology in education has significantly altered the methods of teaching and learning, presenting a multitude of benefits that possess the capacity to work as a strong supplement for the educational domain. Followings are the numerous advantages that arise from the incorporation of digital technology in education, with a specific emphasis on the types of digital technology mentioned earlier.

1. **Enhanced Interactivity and Engagement:** An essential benefit of incorporating digital technology in education and further in the classrooms is that it can increase student interaction and engagement. Smart classroom solutions, interactive learning software, and educational applications all contribute to a dynamic and immersive learning environment. Students transition from being passive recipients of information to becoming engaged participants in the educational process. These interactive and entertaining learning tools stimulate inquiry and promote a more profound comprehension of various subjects.
2. **Streamlined Management of Learning:** One of the most prominent uses of digital technology in education comes in the form of Learning Management Systems (LMS). These facilitate the administration of educational resources and content through a centralized platform. By implementing this approach, the teaching and learning process is optimized. This facilitates teachers' management of course materials, evaluations, and student correspondence. LMS enables teachers to more effectively deliver and monitor learning outcomes, which is ultimately advantageous for teachers and students.
3. **Personalized Education:** In the realm of education, digital technology enables individualized learning experiences. Utilizing data and algorithms, adaptive learning systems, such as the iPrep PAL app, customize material to the specific strengths and areas of improvement deficiencies of each student. This individualized approach guarantees that students obtain the necessary assistance to thrive, thereby enhancing the efficacy and efficiency of education.
4. **Adaptability and Accessibility:** The use of digital technology in education increases the adaptability and accessibility of education. Digital textbooks and educational applications are accessible on a wide range of devices, such as computers, tablets, and smartphones. This adaptability empowers students to engage in self-paced learning and personalize their academic trajectory. Moreover, the portability and sturdiness of digital textbooks obviate the necessity for burdensome luggage stuffed with conventional paper textbooks.
5. **Digitally Rich Content:** Smart ICT laboratories and digital libraries grant students access to a wealth of digital content, thereby enriching the educational experience. These educational materials provide students with an abundance of information and interactive components, enabling them to independently investigate and acquire knowledge. By utilizing digital libraries, teachers can supplement their teachings and captivate students with an assortment of multimedia materials.
6. **Constant Feedback:** Another added advantage of using digital technology in education is the digitization of assessments. Digital assessments and learning analytics provide teachers and students with

immediate feedback. Digital assessment tools, such as practice sets and exams, offer prompt and relevant evaluations of student performance.

This feedback enables teachers to better support their students' needs by enabling them to modify their teaching methods and curriculum and by assisting students in identifying areas for improvement. Not just that, with digital assessments, teachers can ensure accuracy in recording the learning progress of the students.

7. **Eco-friendly and economical:** The use of digital technology in education can be environmentally beneficial and cost-effective. Schools can achieve cost savings and environmental sustainability by decreasing their reliance on physical textbooks and paper assessments. In the long run, digital resources are frequently more cost-effective due to their capacity for effortless updating and sharing among students.

CLASSROOM OBSERVATION AND FEEDBACK ETC.

Effective instructional leaders work to guide and improve learning in schools through developing an understanding of teachers' and students' needs. Observing and coaching teachers is a common and useful way to determine these needs and identify possible areas for growth. However, these efforts are not always translated into improved practice, as teachers do not always make suggested changes to their instruction. Why do teachers sometimes fail to enact feedback they have been given? There might be many reasons, but instructional leaders have the power to encourage improvement in two important ways: by fostering a culture of professional growth and by providing high quality observation feedback.

Foster a Culture of Professional Growth

In many schools, teacher evaluation is a high-stakes process in which teachers are observed once a year and rated on their performance, with possible consequences for their job or their salary. In other schools, observation and evaluation is an afterthought, with overworked or under-engaged school leaders rarely stepping foot inside classrooms. Neither of these cases represents a culture of professional growth.

To ensure teachers are improving, leaders must first compel teacher buy-in for the process of improvement. Engaging teachers in meaningful discussions about the nitty-gritty details of planning, teaching, and assessing student learning sends the message that the leader cares about what is happening in these areas and models the need to be reflective about pedagogical decision making. Leaders can make classroom visits more frequent and lower stakes to diminish teacher anxiety or defensiveness related to the evaluation process.

Leaders can also encourage peer observation and collaborative professional development opportunities for teachers to normalize the practice of thinking and talking about ways to improve among the faculty. Veteran teachers should be encouraged to reflect on their strengths and share wisdom with others while also pushing themselves to try innovative approaches and continue to improve. Professional growth is more likely to occur in situations where teachers feel supported and able to take risks and positive relationships are a major contributor to those feelings.

In particular, the need for professional growth is evident for many teachers who are being forced to pivot from their traditional teaching methods to adapt to the realities of teaching with social distancing and supporting online learners. Effective leaders can help teachers see this as an opportunity for growth for everyone and not just a source of stress. Leaders can empathize with teachers' feelings of anxiety and hardship but then encourage a growth mindset and positive outlook, praising their efforts and recognizing innovative approaches to teaching.

Provide High-Quality Observation Feedback

Once a positive culture of professional growth has been established, teachers should be amenable to receiving feedback on their teaching. Effective leaders can observe their teachers in person in their classrooms or through videos or live streaming into classrooms. To ensure that observation feedback is transformative for teachers' practice, instructional leaders must give feedback that S.T.I.C.K.S.

Specific: A wealth of research indicates that both praise and constructive feedback should be as specific as possible. This does not mean presenting a laundry list of all detailed positive and negative observations, but rather, offering high-quality feedback focused on one or two specific points of emphasis during the observed lesson. Allowing the teachers to contribute to setting the goal of the observation invites more teacher buy-in and again fosters the culture of professional growth, as teachers feel less like they are being evaluated based on external criteria and more like they are getting feedback to help them grow.

Tied to Evidence: Instructional leaders are usually seasoned experts in teaching and can quickly and easily form impressions of other teachers' practice within minutes of being in a classroom. These impressions might be accurate, but they are not always communicated to teachers in a way that fosters growth. Instead of, "Your classroom was really noisy today," feedback tied to evidence might sound like, "I noticed students at the back table were not able to hear your instructions due to the talking on the side, and they lost time during the activity waiting for you to come over to re-explain it to them."

Includes Identified Action Steps: Together with the teacher, the instructional leader should seek to identify targeted action steps to be enacted following the observation. From the above example, this could be as simple as a direction like, "Next time you are going to give instructions, be sure to pause and wait for all side conversations to stop before speaking." More complex action plans could involve sharing resources with teachers, encouraging observations of other teachers skilled in particular areas, and co-planning or co-teaching lessons.

Checked for Follow-Up: Instructional leaders need to check back in with teachers on a timely basis to observe improvements and offer additional support. Ideally, the observer and the teacher will agree on a specific time in the near future when the observer can return to see the improvement in action. When this practice is regularly adhered to in schools, teachers know that their leaders will be coming back to check on their progress and feel compelled to enact the identified action steps because they know that is the expectation.

Kindly Delivered: Most teachers truly want to improve and are grateful for feedback. However, sometimes teachers might feel defensive when their practice is called into question. An instructional leader who can deliver constructive feedback gently, while still commanding high standards and continuous improvement, will find that teachers are more receptive to growth.

Student-Centred: Feedback is more likely to be translated into improved practice if the teacher can clearly see the ramifications for student learning. Observations can easily over-emphasize teacher actions by using checklists and rubrics solely focused on what the teacher says and does without analysis of student learning. Focusing on how students experience observed lessons rather than how the instructional leader views the lesson is important.

Instructional improvement is an ongoing process, and changes will not necessarily happen overnight. However, when leaders give feedback according to the S.T.I.C.K.S. method, teachers should be willing and able to incorporate that feedback into their practice in ways that will improve teaching and learning.

*****

Multiple Choice Questions

1. Mass media, cinema and library are passive agencies of education because
A. learner can not react to the feedback system of these agencies directly
B. they provide informal education
C. they can not come closer to the educant
D. all of these

2. Education of a child really begins
A. Once he takes birth
B. Once he attains the age of three
C. Once he is admitted to post nursery schools
D. Once he learns to speak

3. Family is the original social institution from which all other institutions emerged, who said this
A. Brown B. Ballard
C. Machiver D. None of them

4. Which of the following is not the primary function of schools
A. reorganization and reconstruction of Human experiences
B. all-round development of the child
C. to make the children self reliant
D. advancement of culture

5. In a democratic country, school should reflect
A. National aspirations
B. Community related local aspirations
C. Both of these
D. None of these

6. The best teacher in a village school is he who
A. carries community experiences to the class room
B. prepares instructional programmes in the interest of the community
C. carries classroom experiences to the community
D. All of these

7. Universalisation of education is the concept adopted by
A. modern state B. democratic state
C. totalitarian state D. religious state

8. Secular education in India means
A. an education opposed to religion
B. an education indifferent to religion
C. an education emphasizing equality of religions
D. none of these

9. School works as a social sub system for
A. transmission of culture
B. preservation of culture
C. advancement of culture
D. all of these

10. "Society is nothing but a process of interaction among people". Who said this?
A. Lapier B. Cuber
C. Reuter D. Payne

11. The best model of schooling is
A. Close interaction between education of society
B. Self reliant society by education
C. Reflection of openness by schools
D. All of these

12. Special provisions have been made for socially and educationally backward classes of the nation under article
A. 29 B. 31
C. 15 D. 19

13. Religious education is prohibited in government schools and colleges under Article
A. 29 B. 28 (1)
C. 39 (2) D. 15 (a)

14. Religious and linguistic minorities shall have the right to establish and administer their own educational institutions under Article

A. 30(1) B. 31(2)
C. 40 D. 41

15. Article 351 is about
A. education of tribals
B. promotion of Hindi
C. promotion of secularism
D. English as official language

16. Status of central university is given to any educational institution under union list of
A. Entry 65 B. Entry 63
C. Entry 66 D. None of these

17. Entry 25 of concurrent list states about
A. vocational and technical training of labour
B. the education of working class
C. the education of disabled
D. none of the above

18. Education in the mother tongue at primary stage to children belonging to linguistic minorities has been mentioned in Article
A. 250 B. 350
C. 349 D. 351

19. Educational and economic interests of SCs and STs have been safeguarded under Article
A. 46 B. 45(a)
C. 351 D. 52

20. Education of union territories is administered by the central government under Article
A. 350 B. 229
C. 239 D. 50

21. Education was transferred from state list of subjects to concurrent list in
A. 1976 B. 1972
C. 1980 D. 1950

22. Which of the following statements about growth and development is not correct?
A. Growth generally refers to quantitative changes while development refers to qualitative changes
B. Growth is a function of the environment
C. Growth is not possible without development and vice versa
D. Growth is determined by intrinsic and genetic factors of the organism

23. The limit of growth is fixed by
A. internal factors of the organism
B. nutrition and exercise
C. both of these
D. none of these

24. Development is
A. Maturation
B. Learning
C. Synthesis of abilities
D. All of these

25. Development takes place when
A. environmental forces work on the organism
B. environmental forces interact with the hereditary forces in an organism
C. both of these
D. none of these

26. Which of the following statements about development is correct?
A. Process of development can be improved by exercise and nutrition
B. Development may be positive and negative both
C. Development proceeds from general to specific
D. All of these

27. The son of a goldsmith becomes an expert goldsmith. It is an example of a
A. biological heredity
B. social heredity
C. transfer of instinct
D. none of these

28. All humans contain ______ chromosomes.
A. 26 B. 36
C. 46 D. 42

29. DNA test helps us to know
A. the genetic traits of a person
B. nature of personality and its composition
C. both of these
D. none of these

30. The law of inheritance was discovered by Gregor Mendel in
A. 1866 B. 1911
C. 1888 D. 1920

31. Which of the following statements regarding personality traits is correct?
 A. Traits of personality can not be developed in isolation without taking the help of environment
 B. Subjective traits of the individual are determined by genetic factors
 C. Bad environment can surpass good inheritance but good environment is not a substitute for poor heredity
 D. All of these

32. Which of the following characteristics denote infancy period?
 A. Physical growth is curvilinear
 B. Physical growth is rapid
 C. Head grows at relatively slower rate as compared to other parts of the body
 D. All of these

33. Which of the following is not the characteristic of infancy period?
 A. From bilateral to unilateral trend in motor organs
 B. From general to specific trend in motor organs
 C. Emotional/social development is not associated with motor development
 D. Steady mental development

34. Which of the following illustrates conceptual development?
 A. Perception is the beginning of concept formation
 B. Concept changes with changes in experiences
 C. Concept changes with age
 D. All of these

35. There is one thing common in language and physical development what is that?
 A. Spurts of development at different ages
 B. Dependence on experience
 C. Dependence on training
 D. None of these

36. Which of the following characteristics is not associated with emotional development?
 A. Emotion is accompanied by physiological changes
 B. Emotions start immediately after birth
 C. Intense form of emotions are seen during early childhood period
 D. Emotions are unrelated to physical development

37. The child acquires about three fourth of the brain weight by the age of
 A. 2½ years B. 2 years
 C. 6 years D. 8 years

38. Social development of an infant depends on
 A. his chance of interaction with others
 B. love and affection shown to the child
 C. the extent to which he is able to attract the attention of others
 D. all of the above

39. In which of the following stages the child looks self centred?
 A. Infancy B. Early childhood
 C. Adolescence D. Adulthood

40. In the period of infancy, emotions are
 A. intense, frequent and unstable
 B. like an open book(overt)
 C. need based
 D. all of these

41. Which of the following organs of the body shows rapid growth in infancy?
 A. growth of hands B. growth of head
 C. growth of legs D. growth of fingers

42. In normal learning environment, forgetting is caused
 A. due to lack of practice for a long time
 B. due to the interference of other learnt material
 C. due to lack of consolidation of memory traces
 D. all of these

43. Clear conception of size, weight, colour, time etc., is seen at the age of
 A. six B. four
 C. four and half D. five

44. Which of the following is not the characteristics of intellectual development of early childhood?
A. increased span of attention
B. exploration of the environment
C. ability to verbalize all known concepts
D. ability to distinguish past, present and future

45. Social development by the end of early childhood is marked by
A. the feeling of autonomy
B. the end of solitary plays
C. the temperament of co-operation and friendliness
D. all of these

46. Fictional world of the child starts at the age of
A. 5-6 B. 6-8
C. 3-4 D. 4-5

47. Girls are more dominating than boys in social situations in which of the following periods?
A. pre-adolescent period
B. early childhood period
C. both of these
D. none of these

48. In the period of early childhood, child is
A. helpless to hide his emotions
B. seen shifting his emotions very rapidly and frequently
C. guided by his innate tendencies and instincts
D. all of these

49. A nursery teacher should organize
A. group games in the school
B. those games which involve motor organs of the body
C. those games which help the child to manipulate the environment
D. all of these

50. Later childhood is called latency period because
A. creative potentials are dormant
B. sex remains dormant
C. it is a period of inactivity
D. all of these

51. Physical development of later childhood is marked by
A. Auscification of bones
B. Permanent teeth
C. Excessive motor activity
D. All of these

52. Girls surpass boys physically in
A. infancy B. later childhood
C. early childhood D. adolescence

53. The period of later childhood is marked by
A. intellectual maturity
B. high muscular energy
C. hero worship
D. all of these

54. Which of the following is not the characteristics of intellectual development of later childhood?
A. High interest in science fiction
B. Increased logical power
C. Careful for future
D. End of imaginary fears

55. Children are very much hateful or indifferent to opposite sex at the age of
A. 11-12 B. 13-14
C. 10-11 D. 15-16

56. Period of later childhood is marked by
A. slow and steady physical growth
B. stability in emotions
C. anger against injustice
D. all of these

57. At the end of later childhood period, the child
A. feels himself superior to girls
B. becomes independent of his family
C. wants to become hero
D. all of these

58. The best place of social development for a 12 years old child is
A. neighbourhood B. family
C. playground D. school

59. Group activities and group loyalties are at its peak at the age of
A. 10-12 B. 13-15
C. 8-10 D. 18-20

60. A teacher should not let a 12 years old child any time free because
A. child is always interested to get involve in physical or mental activities
B. spurts of creativity are seen at this age
C. child is frustrated
D. all of these

61. Elektra complex refers to
A. daughter comes closer to the father
B. son comes closer to the mother
C. inferiority complex in the presence of girls
D. none of these

62. According to Freud, super ego is properly developed during
A. latency period B. anal period
C. phallic period D. none of these

63. Development is a process of observable social interaction. This is the opinion of
A. Erikson B. Skinner
C. Robert Sears D. None of these

64. The secondary behaviour of the child according to Robert Sears starts with
A. reinforcement B. imitation
C. modelling D. none of these

65. The period of sensory motor adoptation of Piaget is
A. 0-2 years B. 1-3 years
C. 3-5 years D. 4-6 years

66. The child adopts the view points of others on the basis of consequences of these views in the
A. third stage of Kohlberg's theory
B. second stage of Kohlberg's theory
C. fourth stage of Kohlberg's theory
D. fifth stage of Kohlberg's theory

67. Which of the following is not the view point of cognitive theories of development?
A. moral principles are acquired automatically with age
B. super ego is formed during the period of adolescence
C. Moral values are determined by culture
D. Moral principles are universal

68. Organization of sensory experiences about a particular object is called
A. percepts B. reasoning
C. concept D. none of these

69. The concept building in a person depends on
A. the age and maturity of the person
B. past experiences of the learner
C. intelligence of the learner
D. all of these

70. Agreement on a concept is possible because
A. concepts are subjective
B. concepts are objective
C. concepts are hierarchical
D. B and C both

71. Which of the following statements about concepts is correct?
A. Some concepts are more powerful than others
B. All concepts are universal
C. Concepts are differentiated on the basis of their attributes
D. None of these

72. Which is the highest level of concept formation?
A. formal level B. sensory level
C. concrete level D. none of these

73. How many steps of problem solving has been given by Gates?
A. Six B. Seven
C. Five D. Ten

74. Freeman considers intelligence as an ability
A. to adjust in an adverse situation
B. to learn better and faster
C. to manipulate abstract materials
D. all of these

75. Single factor theory of intelligence was given by
A. Alfred Binet B. Thorndike
C. Freeman D. None of them

76. Which of the following is not the characteristics of 'S' factor according to Spearman ?
A. It is the acquired capacity of the individual
B. Specialization in only one trade is possible
C. It varies from activity to activity in the same individual
D. Individuals differ only in 'S' factor of intelligence

77. In multifactor theory, range is related to
A. Number of tasks that a person can do in a limited period of time
B. Difficulty level of items
C. General intelligence of learners
D. None of these

78. SI model of intelligence was given by J P Guilford in
A. 1911 B. 1904
C. 1967 D. 1975

79. Hierarchy theory of intelligence was given by
A. Jenson
B. Thorndike
C. Burt and Vernon
D. None of them

80. In the pre-Binet period, intelligence was considered as
A. Sensory acuity of the individual
B. Verbal ability of the individual
C. Associative ability of the individual
D. All of these

81. An age scale of intelligence was first developed by
A. Spearman B. Terman
C. Binet-Simon D. None of them

82. Binet-Simon scale of intelligence measures
A. General mental abilities not specific ones.
B. Mental growth of the individual over a period of time
C. The aptitude or level of an examinee not their speed
D. All of these

83. WAIS came into being in
A. 1939 B. 1955
C. 1960 D. 1964

84. Wechsler developed an intelligence test for children in
A. 1939 B. 1949
C. 1955 D. 1956

85. Catell's culture fair test of intelligence was developed in
A. 1960 B. 1961
C. 1965 D. 1955

86. Non-verbal test of intelligence is suitable for
A. deaf and dumb
B. illiterates
C. backward children
D. all of these

87. Intelligence testing is useful for knowing
A. individual difference
B. mental retardation
C. educational backwardness
D. all of these

88. Scores on intelligence tests can not be fully relied on because
A. fatigue level can influence the performance
B. cultural factors can influence the score
C. they generally do not reveal all the mental abilities of a person
D. all of these

89. Who among the following psychologists is of the view that a learner can be motivated by satisfying his needs?
A. Henry Murray B. Abraham Maslow
C. Both of these D. None of these

90. Permanent change in behaviour brought about by experience or training is called.
A. Learning B. Motivation
C. Assimilation D. None of these

91. The book "**A Theory of Motivation**" has been written by
A. Maslow B. K B Madson
C. Murray D. None of them

92. Motivated behaviour of a person is
A. Well directed and well guided towards the goal
B. Agitated until the goal is achieved
C. Both of these
D. None of these

93. Factors affecting motivations are
A. Physiological factors only
B. Psychological factors only
C. Psycho-social factors
D. All of these

94. Process of motivation is affected by all except
A. Habits
B. Mental sets and values
C. Physical factors
D. None of these

95. Which of the following does not come under the category of social motives?
A. Prestige and Status
B. Social approval
C. Personal goal
D. Money hoarding

96. Our action and behaviour is motivated by the desire for getting pleasure and avoiding pain. This is the opinion of
A. Thomas Hobbes B. Descartes
C. Kant D. John Locke

97. Fundamental instincts of humans are inherited rather than acquired. These instincts are the spring of human behaviour. The above opinion was held by
A. Charles Darwin B. Mc Dougall
C. Both of these D. None of these

98. Instinct theory of behaviour was rejected by psychologists on which of the following grounds?
A. Adult behaviour is guided by experience and learning also. It is not always guided by instinct
B. Human behaviour is affected by the cultural factors also
C. Human being is a rational animal. He is not supposed to be directed by instincts only
D. All of these

99. Central motive state was explained by
A. Morgan B. Mc Dougall
C. Murray D. None of them

100. Abraham Maslow was basically a
A. Pragmatist B. Humanist
C. Realist D. All of them

101. A self actualized person is one who
A. Does not accept restrictions imposed by the society
B. Always seeks perfection
C. Is very good in inter personal relationship with others
D. All of these

102. The theory of achievement motivation was developed by Mc Clelland of Harward University in
A. 1949 B. 1951
C. 1965 D. 1944

103. Achievement motive in a child can be developed by
A. Proper guidance and high expectation from the child
B. Telling the stories of great men to the child
C. Setting a realistic goal for the child
D. All of these

104. Which of the following is not a characteristic of learning?
A. Learning is a relatively permanent change in behaviour
B. Learning is a growth of the organism
C. Learning is directly observed
D. Learning is a goal directed process

105. In the beginning of life, the baby is guided by
A. maturation B. instincts
C. learning D. none of these

106. Accumulation of knowledge or facts becomes learning when
A. It is applied in real life situation
B. It is done by the learner himself
C. It is provided by the teacher
D. None of these

107. Dancing, driving, writing etc are the examples of

A. Mechanical learning
B. Perceptual motor learning
C. Psychomotor learning
D. both (B) and (C)

108. In Gagne's hierarchy, learning has been divided into

A. eight parts B. nine parts
C. seven parts D. none of the above

109. Match the following:

	(A)	(B)
(*i*)	Classical conditioning	1. Kohler
(*ii*)	Drive reduction	2. Hull
(*iii*)	Sign gestalt	3. Pavlov
(*iv*)	Learning by insight	4. Tolman

	(*i*)	(*ii*)	(*iii*)	(*iv*)
(*a*)	1	2	3	4
(*b*)	3	2	4	1
(*c*)	2	1	3	4
(*d*)	4	3	2	1

110. Reflexes are of two types according to Pavlov. They are physiological and

A. Psychic B. Neural
C. Mental D. None of these

111. In classical conditioning, extinction will take place when

A. Organism is poor in generalization
B. CS is given without UCS for a long time
C. CS > UCS
D. None of these

112. Backward conditioning will take place when

A. UCS is presented prior to CS
B. CS is presented prior to UCS
C. Reward is not given to the organism
D. None of these

113. When connection is not established between a CS and CR, due to any factor, that is called

A. Spontaneous recovery
B. Extinction
C. Inhibition
D. None of these

114. When a child responds to all women who wear black suit because of the black suit of her mother, it is the example of

A. internal inhibition
B. generalization
C. assimilation
D. all of these

115. Which of the following is not a behaviourist?

A. Watson B. Skinner
C. Pavlov D. Lewin

116. Learning according to Watson is

A. the shifting of old responses to the new stimuli
B. the result of connection between S-R formed in the brain
C. both of these
D. none of these

117. Which of the following points differentiates the theories of Watson and Guthrie?

A. law of contiguity
B. law of recency
C. generalization
D. law of frequency

118. In operant conditioning reward works as motives but in Guthrie's theory motives are

A. Stimuli given to the learner
B. Actions done by the learner
C. Both of these
D. None of these

119. We forget something not by disuse but by other learning. This is the theory of

A. contiguity
B. trial and error
C. learning by insight
D. perception

120. Which of the following is not an essential requirement for trial and error learning?

A. Drive
B. Barrier
C. Chance success
D. Selective movement of the organism

121. According to the law of trial and error, learning occurs when

A. it is satisfying for the learner
B. bond between S-R is strengthened by the repeated use
C. drive is there in the learner to act
D. all of these

122. Which of the following facilitates learning according to Thorndike?
A. Transfer of training
B. Mental set of the learner
C. Law of contiguity
D. All of these

123. In Hull's theory, for learning to occur, the S-R connection must be associated with the
A. cognitive field of the learner
B. diminution of the need
C. both of these
D. none of these

124. Reinforcement in Skinner's theory is similar to drive reduction in which theory
A. Hull's theory B. Guthrie's theory
C. Lewin's theory D. None of these

125. Which of the following theories is most quantitatively measurable?
A. Pavlov's B. Skinner's
C. Hull's D. None of these

126. In drive reduction theory, the effective stimulus in learning is the trace. It is formed
A. in the brain
B. by the bond of S-R
C. in the nervous system
D. none of these

127. In drive reduction theory, habit formation is a function of
A. stimulus potential
B. stimulus generalization
C. reaction potential
D. all of these

128. Hull may be considered superior to other S-R Theorists in the sense that he was able to measure
A. latency of response
B. reinforcement potential
C. both of these
D. none of these

129. Which of the following points differentiates Skinner from other S-R theorists?
A. His operant conditioning (type R learning)
B. His schedule of reinforcement
C. His way of shaping behaviour
D. All of these

130. Skinner's theory is more objective in nature than the others because
A. operant behaviour is external
B. reflexes never have zero strength
C. reinforcement is followed by responses
D. all of these

131. Aversive stimuli in operant conditioning means
A. individual will not do a particular act because of fear of such stimuli
B. individual will not do a particular act because of the disapproval from others
C. both of these
D. none of these

132. In Skinner's theory, reinforcement is given to the learner when
A. his response is 100% correct
B. his response is closer to the correct behaviour
C. both of these
D. none of these

133. Which of the following statements regarding S-R theories is not correct?
A. Man behaves like a machine
B. Behaviour is overt and can be objectively measured
C. Learning proceeds from simple to complex
D. Things are perceived in the context of figure ground *i.e.*, in relation to other things

134. Which of the following statements regarding field theories are correct?
A. Learning is not additive
B. Molar approach of behaviour is followed here
C. Interaction between organism and the environment is essential for learning
D. All of these

135. Operant conditioning is different from respondent conditioning in which of the following points
A. In OC reinforcement is given after the response is made
B. In operant conditioning, behaviour is controlled by central nervous system
C. A chain of responses is needed for shaping the behaviour (learning)
D. All of these

136. Thorndike and Skinner do not differ at all in
A. the law of effect
B. law of readiness
C. law of contiguity
D. all of these

137. According to gestalt psychologists, behaviour can not be quantified because
A. it is always changeable
B. it is governed by the configuration produced in the mind
C. it is rarely overt
D. all of these

138. Law of pragnanz is the other name of the law of
A. continuity B. closure
C. contiguity D. None of these

139. How does the law of similarity work according to field theorists?
A. Similar ideas and experiences get associated to form a whole
B. Similar objects or experiences are easily learnt
C. Both of these
D. None of these

140. Learning by insight looks similar to some extent to which of the following theories?
A. Need reduction theory
B. R type of learning
C. Trial and error theory
D. None of the above

141. The other name of conditioned reflexes is
A. psychic reflexes
B. motor reflexes
C. physiological reflexes
D. none of the above

142. According to Renzuli, a gifted child is one
A. Who possesses above average ability in almost every field
B. Who is committed to task and highly motivated
C. Who is definitely creative
D. All of these

143. Gifted and talented children must be identified as early as possible because
A. If their potentials are not developed by proper guidance of the teacher, it is a loss of the society
B. They are likely to create problems for others, if they are not given work according to their ability
C. Ordinary level of curriculum will not suit to these children
D. All of these

144. Achievement test can be a good indicator of intellectual power if
A. It is conducted immediately after the teaching is over
B. A student shows good performance consistently on different achievement test
C. Both of these
D. None of these

145. Which of the following skills does not require high intellectual ability?
A. Technical skills
B. Mechanical skills
C. Teaching skills
D. Management skills

146. Cognitive abilities related to giftedness are all except
A. High comprehensive and analytical abilities
B. High level of verbal intelligence
C. High retention power
D. None of these

147. A superior child is advanced to a normal child by at least
A. 2½ years B. Four years
C. 1 years D. 1½ years

148. A gifted child is
A. realistic in his approach
B. highly interested in solving social problems
C. more frequently chosen by his age mates and peers
D. all of these

149. Which of the following enrichment programmes is suitable for gifted children in the school?
A. Mathematics or Science Olympiad
B. Challenging home assignments
C. Map work during studies
D. All of these

150. Which of the following does not come under the category of acceleration for gifted children?
A. Skipping of classes
B. Early admission
C. Extra laboratory work
D. Organizing summer camps

151. Under achievers are those who
A. Score low on intelligence tests
B. Achieve low in the class consistently despite their superior intelligence
C. Are unable to correspond their achievement to the level of their innate abilities
D. Both (B) and (C)

152. Which of the following conditions must be satisfied in order to designate a person mentally retarded?
A. Sub-normal intellectual functioning
B. Very poor adaptive ability
C. Dependability on others
D. All of these

153. The best measure of identifying mildly mentally retarded is
A. Administration of standardized intelligence test
B. Administration of behaviour test
C. Administration of adjustment test
D. A combination of all

154. Physical trauma during pregnancy may cause
A. Mental retardation
B. Blindness
C. Deafness
D. All of these

155. All of the following may cause mental retardation except
A. Blood incompatibility
B. Action of toxic agent
C. Radio-activity
D. None of these

156. Which of the following is an important postnatal cause of mental retardation?
A. Brain injury
B. Infection
C. Severe malnutrition
D. All of these

157. Dullers do not differ from normal children in
A. Physical characteristics
B. Level of social expectancy
C. Both of these
D. None of these

158. Which of the following things is not required for educating mildly mentally retarded children?
A. Regular counseling
B. Remedial teaching
C. Modification in the curriculum
D. Regular evaluation

159. Teaching of which of the following skills is not suitable to borderline cases?
A. Electric fitting
B. Repairing of electric or electronic equipments
C. Oratory skills
D. Activity based skills

160. IQ range of morons are in the range of
A. 60-90 B. 50-75
C. 60-80 D. 30-50

161. Morons are slow in
A. Physical growth
B. Thinking and planning
C. Taking initiative
D. All of these

162. Unsatisfactory relation of a mentally retarded child with the environment is technically called

A. Autism
B. Maladjustment
C. Pseudo-dullness
D. None of these

163. All of the following are characteristics of morons except

A. They are restricted to unskilled or semi skilled occupations
B. They are likely to be delinquent more easily
C. They have stronger sex drives than the normals
D. They are educable upto normal level but at a slower rate

164. Which of the following modifications in the curriculum is needed for morons?

A. Activity based curriculum
B. Skill dominated curriculum
C. Emphasis on social training
D. All of these

165. Which of the following things can not be taught to Imbeciles?

A. Self help skills
B. Unskilled job to be performed under supervision
C. Writing skills
D. Social skills

166. In which of the following cases divergent thinking is required?

A. Attempting a multiple choice items
B. Writing an essay
C. Doing a research activity
D. Both (A) and (C)

167. Which of the following tests is similar to Guilford's test of cognitive abilities?

A. Word association test
B. Things test
C. Hidden shapes test
D. None of these

168. In Hidden shapes test of creativity, which of the following things is used?

A. Pictures
B. Words
C. Things
D. None of them

169. A creative child in the class can not be satisfied unless

A. He is given freedom to manipulate ideas or things
B. He is allowed to ask questions in his own way
C. Both of these
D. None of these

170. A creative child is one who

A. Is ideationally productive and unconventional
B. Does not stick to social and religious norms in a hard manner
C. Is all the time restless to do something uncommon and unique
D. All of these

171. For the development of creative potential of a child, the teacher should

A. Allow him to be critical to ideas and people
B. Give them chance of problem solving
C. Both of these
D. None of these

172. New ideas (Eureka) suddenly comes in the minds of the creative children in the stage of

A. Preparation
B. Illumination
C. Revision
D. Incubation

173. The technique to foster creativity in children is

A. Brain storming
B. Problem solving
C. Both of these
D. None of these

174. A teacher can foster creativity in children by

A. Developing confidence in them
B. Giving them opportunity to express
C. Both of these
D. None of these

175. Learning disabled children are

A. Deficient in using potentials
B. Low in intelligence
C. Slow in activity
D. None of these

176. Learning disabled children perform very poorly in

A. academic areas B. technical areas
C. both of these D. none of these

177. Problem of learning disability is more complex than that of other disabilities because
A. Its causes can not be easily ascertained by applying usual tests
B. It is associated to behaviour problems
C. Both of these
D. None of these

178. Educationally, learning disabled look similar to
A. dullers
B. backward children
C. both of these
D. none of these

179. In which of the following physical characteristics learning disabled children differ from the normal ones?
A. They are all the time clumsy and awkward
B. Poor coordination of motor abilities
C. Height, weight and health
D. All of these

180. Which of the following methods is most suitable for learning disabled children?
A. Behaviour guidance method
B. Remedial teaching
C. Brain storming
D. None of them

181. In order to improve work habits of learning disabled what should be done?
A. Unattending behaviour should be penalized
B. Close monitoring of the behaviour is needed
C. Cues and prompt should be given
D. All of these

182. Those who are normal in intelligence but slow in academic achievement due to psycho-social reasons are called
A. Backward children
B. Gifted under achievers
C. Both of these
D. None of these

183. Consistent low achievement leads to low intelligence because
A. 50% intellectual ability is expressed in verbal form
B. Learning develops thinking and reasoning power
C. Both of these
D. None of these

184. Which of the following situations may lead to educational backwardness?
A. Sensory impairment
B. Motor disability
C. Long diseases and health problems.
D. All of these

185. Emotional disturbances may lead to educational backwardness because
A. Proper emotional development is necessary for social interactions
B. Emotions will develop intellectual power, *i.e.*, emotional intelligence
C. Both of these
D. None of these

186. Which of the following factors will not lead to educational backwardness?
A. Poor socio economic status of the family
B. Poor educational environment of the school
C. Occupation of the family
D. Poor emotional climate of the family

187. Which of the following is an important cause of educational backwardness at primary level of education in India?
A. Poor school organisation
B. Lack of accountability
C. Attitude of the masses towards education
D. All of these

188. Which of the following measures should be adopted by the teacher to check educational backwardness?
A. Continuous evaluation and regular feedback
B. Remedial teaching
C. Adjustment and behaviour training
D. All of these

189. Teaching by small steps and frequent short assignment techniques are useful for
A. Slow learners
B. Learning disabled
C. Educationally backward children
D. Children of all types of disabilities

190. Special schools are required for backward children when
A. Backwardness is due to any serious physical handicap
B. The size of population of backward children in the society is very large as is the case of Gujarat where the achievement of students in mathematics is always seen very low
C. Both of these
D. None of these

191. Which of the following should be considered the most important quality of a teacher at primary level?
A. Patience and perseverance
B. Competence in methods of teaching and knowledge of subjects
C. Competence to teach in highly standardised language
D. Eagerness to teach

192. A teacher, because of his/her democratic nature, allows students to sit all over the class. Some sit together and discuss or do group reading. Some sit quietly and read themselves. A parent does not like it. Which of the following may be the best way to handle the situation?
A. Parents should request the principal to change the section of their ward
B. Parents should show trust in the teacher and discuss the problem with the teacher
C. Parents should take away the child from that school
D. Parents should complain against the teacher to the principal

193. The stage in which a child begins to think logically about objects and events is known as
A. Formal operational stage
B. Pre-operational stage
C. Concrete operational stage
D. Sensori-motor stage

194. 'Mind mapping' refers to
A. a plan of action for an adventure
B. drawing the picture of a mind
C. researching the functioning of the mind
D. a technique to enhance comprehension

195. The best way, specially at primary level, to address the learning difficulties of students is to use
A. expensive and glossy support material
B. easy and interesting textbooks
C. story-telling method
D. a variety of teaching methods suited to the disability

196. Which of the following will foster creativity among learners?
A. Providing opportunities to question and to nurture the innate talents of every learner
B. Emphasizing achievement goals from the beginning of school life
C. Coaching students for good marks in examination
D. Teaching the students the practical value of good education

197. According to Piaget, at which of the following stages does a child begin to think logically about abstract propositions?
A. Formal operational stage (11 years and up)
B. Sensori-motor stage (Birth–02 years)
C. Pre-operational stage (02–07 years)
D. Concrete operational stage (07–11 years)

198. Learning can be enriched if
A. more and more teaching aids are used in the class
B. teachers use different types of lectures and explanation
C. due attention is paid to periodic tests in the class
D. situations from the real world are brought into the class in which students interact with each other and the teacher facilitates

199. Which of the following statements ***cannot*** be considered as a feature of the process of learning?

A. Learning is a comprehensive process
B. Learning is goal-oriented
C. Unlearning is also a learning process
D. Educational institutions are the only place where learning takes place

200. A student of V-grade with 'visual deficiency' should be

A. helped with his/her routine-work by parents and friends
B. treated normally in the classroom and provided support through Audio CDs
C. given special treatment in the classroom
D. excused to do a lower level of work

201. Which of the following is a social characteristic of a leaner?

A. Power of sensory perception
B. Thinking ability
C. Power of synthetic imagination
D. Ability to relate oneself with others

202. Which is the characteristic of formative evaluation?

A. Evaluation occurs at the terminal point
B. Evaluation is used before programme design
C. Evaluation relates to indicating learning outcome of teaching
D. Evaluation is conducted during teaching

203. 'Cone of Experience' related to teaching-learning was suggested by:

A. John Dewey B. Kilpatrick
C. Froebel D. Edgar Dale

204. The field of study which uses role playing, simulation and self-evaluation as strategies for adult learners is known as:

A. Pedagogy B. Andragogy
C. Anthropology D. Psychology

205. Which among the following is a non-cognitive characteristic of learner?

A. Recalling
B. Problem solving
C. Identifying important sensory inputs
D. Believing what is true

206. Diagnostic Evaluation ascertains:

A. Students performance at the beginning of instructions
B. Causes and remedies of persistent learning problems during instructions
C. Degree of achievement of instructional objectives at the end
D. Learning progress and failure after instructions

207. Among the following which one is an example of instructional software?

A. Audio podcast
B. Printed material or book
C. Radio talk
D. Edusat

208. Which teaching aids enhance the skills like reading, listening and pronunciation?

A. Audio-lingual teaching aids
B. Scientific teaching aids
C. General knowledge teaching aids
D. Theoretical based teaching aids

209. As per the cognitive development theory of Jean Piaget, adolescent students are in which stage of development?

A. Sensory motor stage
B. Concrete operational stage
C. Operational stage
D. Formal operational stage

210. Which of the following statements is true in the case of a test prepared by you as a teacher?

A. If a test is reliable, it is objective
B. If a test is valid, it is reliable also
C. If a test is reliable, it is valid
D. If a test is valid and reliable, it is usable

211. Which of the following statements best explains the concept of team teaching?

A. More than two teachers teach
B. More than two teachers plan and teach together the same class
C. More than two teachers plan and teach the same class as per their expertise
D. A team of teachers who are ready and available to teach the students

212. Peer group interaction in a classroom helps in:
A. Concept understanding
B. Realization of One's misunderstanding
C. Rapport Building
D. Questioning

213. Reflective Practice implies use of one's:
A. Cognition
B. Metacognition
C. Metacognition on cognition
D. Reinforcement of learning

214. Inclusive education implies:
A. Ensuring learning outcome of every child to be the same
B. Including the disabled in the main stream
C. Provides compulsory education for children below 14 years
D. Ensuring that no child is left behind in education

215. Listening is important for a teacher to:
A. address the requirement of the learner
B. gain knowledge
C. keep the learner in good humour
D. evaluate the learner for the progress made

216. Which of the following is an example of higher order of cognitive learning outcome?
A. Learning of facts and their sequences
B. Learning roles and action sequences
C. Learning of concepts and abstractions
D. Learning of awareness and valuing

217. Which of the following is the key behaviour contributing to effective teaching?
A. Summarising what was told by a student
B. Encouraging students to elaborate on an answer
C. Using direct and indirect questioning
D. Explaining concepts in a logical step by step presentation

218. What are the elements of evaluation plane?
(*a*) Purpose (*b*) Resources
(*c*) Analysis (*d*) Authority

Select the correct answer from the options given below:
A. (*a*) and (*c*) B. (*b*) only
C. (*b*), (*c*) and (*d*) D. (*a*), (*b*) and (*c*)

219. Which of the following is an example of a maximum performance test?
A. Personality tests
B. Projective personality tests
C. Aptitude tests
D. Interest and attitude scales

220. Which of the learning outcomes are intended in teaching organized at understanding level?
A. Longer recall and retention of facts
B. Seeking of relationships and patterns among facts
C. Creative construction and critical interpretation of ideas
D. Mastery of facts and information

221. Who was the chairman of the NEP 2020 drafting committee?
A. Kailasavadivoo Sivan
B. Dr. K. Kasturirangan
C. Prof. Yaspal Sharma
D. Prof. G. RajaGopal

222. When did the Union Cabinet approved the new National Education Policy (NEP), 2020?
A. 29 June, 2020 B. 29 July, 2020
C. 29 August, 2020 D. 29 January, 2020

223. What is the guiding light for the National Education Policy 2020?
A. rich resources of ancient and modern India
B. rich heritage of Indian classical music and art
C. rich heritage of ancient and eternal Indian knowledge
D. rich heritage of Indian Sufi tradition

224. World-class Indian institutions set the highest standards of multidisciplinary teaching and research and hosted scholars and students from across backgrounds and countries. Find the name of the institution which is not in the list of NEP 2020.
A. Takshashila B. Nalanda
C. Osmania D. Valiabhi

225. According to NEP 2020 the Indian education system produced great scholars such as Charaka, Nagarjuna. Find out the odd one from the list.

A. Aryabhata B. Varahamihira
C. Xenocrates D. Bhaskaracharya

226. How many of the fundamental principles mentioned in National Education Policy 2020?
A. 5 B. 11
C. 22 D. 20

227. National Education Policy 2020 replaced by a new pedagogical and curricular structure. What is the new curricular structure according to NEP 2020?
A. "3 + 4 + 4 + 5" model
B. "5 + 3 + 3 + 4" model
C. "4 + 3 + 3 + 5" model
D. "5 + 4 + 3 + 3" model

228. What is the age group covered in school education according to NEP 2020 new curricular structure?
A. 16-18 B. 3-18
C. 6-18 D. 5-18

229. What are the classes which cover the "Secondary" stage according to NEP 2020 new curricular structure?
A. Class 6 to 9 B. Class 9 to 12
C. Class 6 to 8 D. Class 11 to 12

230. What are the classes which cover the "Middle" stage according to NEP 2020 new curricular structure?
A. Class 6 to 9 B. Class 9 to 12
C. Class 6 to 8 D. Class 11 to 12

231. What are the classes which cover the "Preparatory" stage according to NEP 2020 new curricular structure?
A. Class 6 to 9 B. Class 3 to 5
C. Class 6 to 8 D. Class 1 to 2

232. What are the classes which cover the "Foundational" stage according to NEP 2020 new curricular structure?
A. Covers only (Class 1 & 2)
B. Covers only (Anganwadi/pre-school/Balvatika)
C. Covers (Anganwadi/pre-school/Balvatika) and 2 years (Class 1 & 2)
D. Covers up to class 5

233. How much (per cent %) of a child's cumulative brain development occurs prior to the age of 6 according to NEP 2020?
A. Over 85% B. Over 95%
C. Over 75% D. Over 65%

234. NEP proposed that universal provisioning of quality early childhood development, care, and education must be achieved. What is the timeline for this?
A. 2030 B. 2035
C. 2040 D. 2050

235. What is the timeline to ensure that all students entering Grade 1 are school ready according to National Education Policy 2020?
A. 2035 B. 2040
C. 2025 D. 2030

236. Which educational organization will prepare NEP 2020 proposed pedagogical framework for Early Childhood Care and Education?
A. NCERT B. SCERT
C. SEDGC D. NTSC

237. National Education Policy 2020 proposed establishment of "Preparatory Class" or "Balavatika". What is the age limit for the "Preparatory Class" or "Balavatika"?
A. prior to the age of 6
B. prior to the age of 5
C. prior to the age of 4
D. prior to the age of 3

238. Ministry of Human Resources Development (MHRD) renamed as:
A. Ministry of Human Development
B. Ministry of Education
C. Ministry of Human Rights
D. Ministry of Human Capital

239. Consider the following statement regarding the foundational pillars in NEP 2020.
I. Accessibility II. Affordability
III. Accountability IV. Quality
V. Equity VI. Access
Select Correct answer given code below:
A. I, II, III Only
B. I, II, III, IV Only
C. I, II, III, IV, V Only
D. I, II, III, IV, V & VI

240. Under the chairmanship of whom 'Committee for Evolution of the New Education Policy' submitted its report in May 2016?
A. Late Shri T.S.R. Subramanian
B. Dr. K. Kasturirangan
C. Rina Ray
D. Shri Sanjay Dhotre

241. The Behavioural Approach focusses on the actual behaviour of .... in organisations.
A. Persons
B. Groups
C. Persons and groups
D. None of the above

242. ..... has/have been among the pioneer/pioneers fo the Behavioural Approach to the study of public administration.
A. Herbert A. Simon
B. Robert A. Dahl
C. Both A and B
D. Woodrow wilson

243. The greatest Limitation of which approach is that one cannot get a true picture of how an organization function in practice.
A. The Behavioural Approach
B. The Legal Approach
C. The Historical Approach
D. The Institution and Structural approach

244. What does 'Hierarchy of Authority' means?
1. The lower levels have to pursue the goals laid down by higher levels.
2. The upper levels of hierarchy set the goals to be pursued.
3. The upper levels can not take discipline action against subordinates.
4. The lower levels have the freedom to carry out the operations.

A. 1 and 2 B. 2 and 3
C. 3 and 4 D. 1 and 4

245. Authority and responsibility must go together. This is known as:
A. the principle of hierarchy
B. the principle of correspondence
C. the principle of span of control
D. the principle of centralization

246. According to Chester Barnard, orders are authoritative when they are:
A. issued by a superior
B. issued by the top executive
C. accepted by the subordinates
D. understood by the subordinates

247. The Greatman theory of leadership led to the rise of :
A. The Behavioural theory of leadership
B. The Trait theory of leadership
C. The situational theory of leadership
D. None of the above

248. The hollmark of leadership is :
A. Achievement of goals of the organisation
B. Settlement of disputes in the organisation
C. Capacity to influence others to follow
D. Maintaining the core values of the organisation and its distinctive identity

249. Assertion (A) : Functionally, a leader is partly a manager.
Reason (R) : A leader does all the management functions.

Codes :
A. A and R are true and R explains A
B. A and R are true but R does not explain A
C. A is true but R is false
D. A is false but R is true

250. Assertion (A) : The teams leader and manager are interchangeable.
Reason (R) : Leadership is a sub–class of management.

Codes :
A. A and R are true and R explains A
B. A and R are true but R does not explain A
C. A is true but R is false
D. A is false but R is true

251. Assertion (A) : The laissez–faire style of leadership depends on the leader to provide external motivation.
Reason (R) : The leader principally assumes the role of group member and supply materials when asked.

Codes :

A. A and R are true and R is the correct explanation of A

B. A and R are true but R is not the correct explanation of A

C. A is true but R is false

D. A is false but R is true

252. Assertion (A) : In contrast with trait theory, behavioural theory attempts to describe leadership in terms of what leaders do.

Reason (R) : Trait theory has failed to recognize the influence of situational factors on leadership

Codes :

A. A and R are true and R is the correct explanation of A

B. A and R are true but R is not the correct explanation of A

C. A is true but R is false

D. A is false but R is true

253. Match the following—

List I	List II
(*a*) Leadership is often made or broken by circumstance	1. Allen
(*b*) A person is born with the talent for personal leadership; he must learn management leadership	2. Follet
(*c*) We should think not only of what the leader does to the group, but also of what the group does to the leader.	3. Barnard
(*d*) Leadership depends upon the individual, the followers and the conditions.	4. Millet

Codes:

	(*a*)	(*b*)	(*c*)	(*d*)
A.	2	3	1	4
B.	2	4	3	1
C.	4	2	3	1
D.	4	1	2	3

254. Who has distinguished between leadership of position, leadership of personality and leadership of function?

A. Barnard B. Millet

C. Mooney D. Follet

255. Accoding to Barnard, which is not a function of leadership?

A. Manipulation of means

B. Stimulation of co-ordinated action

C. Defence of institutional integrity

D. Control of the instrumentality of action

256. The most important quality of leadership, according to Barnard is :

A. Persuasiveness

B. Decisiveness

C. Responsibility and Intellectual capacity

D. Vitality and Endurance

257. Who has analyses leadership in terms of circular response?

A. C.I. Barnard B. Mooney

C. M.P. Follet D. Millet

258. Match the following—

List I	List II
(*a*) Mooney	1. The essential circumstances of leadership are political and institutional
(*b*) Millet	2. Leadership is the form that authority assumes when it enters into process
(*c*) Follet	3. Leadership—goes beyond routine and taps bases of power beyond those that are organisationally decreed
(*d*) Katz & Kahn	4. We now think of the leader as being influenced by his group

Codes:

	(*a*)	(*b*)	(*c*)	(*d*)
A.	2	1	4	3
B.	2	4	3	1
C.	4	3	1	2
D.	3	4	2	1

259. Political responsiveness quality of leadership was highlighted by :

A. Terry B. Barnard
C. Appleby D. Millet

260. The democratic or participative style of leadership became popular during the era of:

A. Contingency model of leadership—Victor Vroom
B. Life cycle approach to leadership—Blake & Mounton
C. Path–Goal theory of leadership—Martin Evans and Robert House
D. Managerial Grid—Hersey & Blanchard

261. Which of the following pairs is correctly matched?

A. Contingency model of leadership → Victor Vroom
B. Life cycle approach of leadership → Blake & Mountan
C. Path–Goal theory of leadership → Mortin Evans and Robert House
D. Managerial Grid → Herrey & Blanchard

262. Match the following—

List I	*List II*
(*a*) Continuum of leadership styles	1. Phillip Yetton
(*b*) Three–dimensional model of leadership	2. Tonnenbaum
(*c*) Managerial Grid	3. W. Reddin
(*d*) Decision-participation model of leadership	4. Blake
	5. Kurt Lewin

Codes:

	(*a*)	(*b*)	(*c*)	(*d*)
A.	3	1	2	5
B.	5	3	1	4
C.	2	4	1	5
D.	2	3	4	1

263. Which of the following pairs is not correctly matched?

A. Michigan Leadership studies — Rensis Likert and others
B. Systems of management — Rensis Likert
C. Ohio state leadership studies — Fleishman and others
D. Iowa leadership studies — R. Tannenbaum

264. According to which theory, leadership is multidimensional?

A. Behavioural theory
B. Situational theory
C. Trait theory
D. None of the above

265. From which of the following can feed–back be obtained with in an organisation?

1. Vertical communication
2. Official records
3. Proceedings of the meetings
4. Horizontal communication

Codes :

A. 3 and 4 B. 1 and 3
C. 2 and 3 D. 1 and 4

266. Communication techniques, according to Barnard are important because through them:

A. the "Zone of Indifference" of the contributors is enlarged
B. the foundation for the formal authority structure is laid
C. the form and the internal economy of organisation is shaped
D. the different patterns of informal organisations are harmonised

267. Every organisation has an informal communication system which is commonly referred to as :

A. proper channel B. close circuit
C. grapevine D. circular

268. Which of the following are the correct pairs? Select the correct answer from the codes given below.

1. Authoritarian Leader — Recognition of individuality of the workers.
2. Democratic Leader — Participation and persuation oriented
3. Authoritarian Leadership style — Scientific Management School
4. Structure and consideration — Managerial grade.

Codes :

A. 1, 2 and 3 B. 2, 3 and 4
C. 1, 2, 3 and 4 D. 3 and 4

269. "The time has come to substitude word leadership for Management." This statement was made by :

A. Lawrence A Appley
B. Henry Mintzberg
C. Dr May Smith
D. Henry Fayol

270. Which of the following is the correct pair in the context of Leadership in different management systems I to IV as described by R. Likert Give the correct answer from the codes given below.

1. Exploitative, Authoritative System–1
2. Consultative System–2
3. Benenvolent Authoriative System–3
4. Participative group System–4

Codes :

A. 1, 2 and 4 B. 2, 3 and 4
C. 1, 2, 3 and 4 D. 1, 2 and 3

271. 3D theory of leadership styles was propounded by which of the following thinkers?

A. Fred E Fielder
B. William J Reddin
C. A Etzional
D. Robert R Blake and J.S. Monton.

272. 'Leadership' is one of the controlling functions of management, according to :

A. Prof. Munro B. Prof. Henri Fayol
C. Urwick D. Terry

273. Which are the qualities of a true leader according to Proff. Terry?

A. Energetic character, emotional stability and strength
B. Knowledge of human relations, personal motivation and capacity to communicate with skill
C. Teaching ability, social skill and technical competence
D. All of the above

274. Who formulated the leadership contigency model?

A. Fred E. Fiedler B. A.W. Falpin
C. Rensis Likert D. None of the above

275. Which of the following type of leaders were considered to be more effective by Likert?

A. People oriented
B. Task oriented
C. Production oriented
D. None of the above

276. Who said "Indeed, I have never observed any leader who was able to state adequately or intelligently, why he was able to be a leader, nor any statement of followers that acceptably expressed, why they followed."

A. Prof. Henri Fayol B. Prof. Barnard
C. Prof. Munro D. Terry

277. Prof. Allen has drown a line of distinction between personal leadership and:

A. management leadership
B. political leadership
C. social leadership
D. economic leadership

278. Who developed the path goal model of leadership behaviour?

A. L.P. Bradford B. R.J. House
C. F.E. Fiedler D. R. Likert

279. 'Task orientation' is associated with:

A. Tannenbaum and sachimdt
B. Cartwright and zander
C. Michigan studies
D. None of the above

280. The ultimate aim of all leadership theories and models is to build :

A. a leadeship model
B. a process that leads to optimisation of workers output
C. a cause and effect relationship
D. none of the above

281. Who emphasised that there is relationship between the nature of the job and the most desirable leadership–style for maximum leadership–effectiveness?

A. Leland P. Bradford
B. Victor H. Vroom
C. Robert J. House
D. Fred E. Fiedler

282. Who observed that there are almosts as many definitions of leadership as there are people who have tried to define it.
A. Stogdill B. Peter Druker
C. George R. Terry D. None of the above

283. Who defines leadership as the ability to secure desirable actions from a group of followings voluntarily with out the use of coercion?
A. Keith Davis B. Max Weber
C. Aford and Beatty D. Stogdill

284. According to whom leadership is the ability to persuade others to seek defined objectives, enthusiastically
A. Peter Druker B. Stogdill
C. Keith Davis D. None of the above

285. Which of the following is the approach to study leadership?
A. Traits approach
B. Situational approach
C. Group approach
D. All of the above

286. Functional of the leader in the setting and achieving of organisational goal is:
A. Policy-making B. Planning
C. Execution D. All of the above

287. According to George R. Terry traits generally associated with leadership are:
A. Mental and Physical energy
B. Emotional stability
C. Knwoledge of human relations
D. All of the above

288. Which type of leadership is more successful, especially in a crisis or emergency situation?
A. Democratic leadership
B. Autocratic leadership
C. Laissez–faire leadership
D. None of the above

289. In which type of leadership is the entire group involved in and accepts responsibility for goal setting and achievement?
A. Autocratic leadership
B. Democratic leadership
C. Laissez–faire leadeship
D. None of the above

290. In .... leadership the leader shows a greater concern for his people than for high production.
A. Autocratic B. Democratic
C. Laissez–faire D. None of the above

291. In which type of leadership does the leader only provide information, materials and facilities to his men to enable them to accomplish group objectives?
A. Free–rein or Laissez–faire
B. Democratic
C. Autocratic
D. None of the above

292. The University of Michigan Leadership studies, divided leadership into:
A. Employee – oriented
B. Production – oriented
C. Both the above
D. None of the above

293. In which type of leadership the leader alone determines policy and makes plans?
A. Autocratic leadership
B. Democratic leadership
C. Free–rein or Laissez fair leadership
D. None of the above

294. Which type of leadership can increase efficiency, save time and get quick results?
A. Autocratic leadership
B. Democratic leadership
C. Free–rein or Laissez leadership
D. None of the above

295. According to ...., a leader to be effective should be able to influence the followers perception of work goals, self–development goals and path of goal attainment.
A. Robert J. House B. Hersey
C. Blanchard D. Fiedler

296. According to ...., a leader's style is influenced by his views of man is work situations.
A. Max weber B. Taylor
C. Riggs D. Douglas McGregor

297. Who wrote the article, "The conditions of effective leadership in the Industrial organization"?

A. Douglas McGregor B. Sears
C. Woodward D. Riggs

298. The integrative of leadership should include the following variables :
A. Leader's awareness of self
B. Group's characteristics
C. Situatinal characteristics
D. All of the above

299. Who defined "Leadership is the activity of influencing people to strive willing for group objectives"?
A. G.R. Terry B. J.R. Weschler
C. Fred Massarik D. None of the above

300. George R. Terry's definition fo leadership laid emphasison.
A. Willingness to accept
B. Compulsion to influence people
C. Both of the above
D. None of the above

301. On which of the following approach the Michigan leadership studies are based?
A. Attitude criterion
B. Trait–approach
C. Behaviour approch
D. None of the above

302. Which theory is connected with the democratic leadership style?
A. Theory X B. Theory Z
C. Theory Y D. None of the above

303. Which according to Prof. Barnard are two essential qualities of leadership
A. Vitality, decisiveness
B. Power of endurance and foresight
C. Capacity to persuade others or persuesiveness
D. All of the above

304. If a student is not able to answer a question during the course of the lecture, then you will:
A. scold him and hence, insult him
B. tell him the correct answer yourself
C. try to understand why that student was not able to give correct answer
D. advise the student to study more carefully

305. Why do you like teaching work?
A. Children do not remain naughty in the presence of the teacher
B. Your parents had told you that it is a dignified profession
C. You have an interest in teaching
D. The person keeps on reading a lot in this profession

306. One solution to make class teaching more effective/meaningful is the following:
A. give home work in excess
B. stop the students after the school time and have discussions with them
C. immediately after the class lecture, ask questions related to the lecture
D. tell children that if they have not understood the lesson, you will teach the same once again

307. By which trait of the teacher, the students are generally impressed?
A. His knowledge/learning
B. His high moral character
C. His tough discipline
D. His relationship with the Principal

308. If, on a certain day, you are very tired and not in a mood to teach students in the class, then you will
A. Free children and send them home
B. Request your colleague (teacher) to teach children in your place
C. Tell children an ideal story
D. Tell children to go out and play

309. The best way to encourage a teacher, who works with complete dedication, is to:
A. give him a prize
B. give him an advance increment in his salary
C. arrange a felicitation function and felicitate him
D. praise his work from time to time

310. Whose behaviour affects students the most?
A. That of the Principal
B. That of a politician
C. That of a teacher
D. That of a tutor

311. If a student does not complete his home work on a regular basis, what will you do to rectify him?

A. You will complain to the Principal and get him punished

B. You will call the student in privacy and explain to him that (completion of) home work has many advantages

C. You would like to get the cooperation of the student in question

D. You will clearly tell the student that if he continues to ignore his home work, he would not be allowed to appear in the final examination

312. By which method, students learn to the maximum extent and with the utmost speed?

A. By seeing

B. By reading

C. By listening

D. By doing themselves

313. Which quality of the teacher is liked the most by students?

A. His punctuality

B. His impartiality

C. His love for discipline

D. His dominance

314. What should the teacher do to maintain the interest of students in class teaching?

A. Extensive use of examples from the practical life

B. Extensive use of teaching materials/aids

C. Giving ample opportunities to students for discussion/deliberations

D. All of these

315. Why would you like to take additional responsibilities as a teacher?

A. In order to gain new experiences

B. In order to please your Principal

C. In order to become popular among students

D. In order to cooperate

316. In your view, to win the confidence of the Principal, a teacher should:

A. keep on giving gifts to the Principal

B. keep on censuring and backbiting other teachers in collusion with the Principal

C. keep on executing his own teaching work in a satisfactory manner

D. gain popularity among students

317. You think that taking surprise tests is justified because:

A. students remain frightened due to these

B. you do not have to get yourself prepared at home for this purpose

C. you can escape the teaching session due to the alibi of taking a surprise test

D. the abilities and knowledge levels of students can be truly judged through such tests

318. If a student criticises another teacher in your presence, then you would:

A. punish him

B. inform that teacher about the critical remarks passed by that student

C. ignore his remarks/discussion

D. reprimand that student and spare him

319. A teacher should work according to:

A. his own liking/whims

B. the needs of the time

C. his capacity to work

D. his need

320. You are teaching in the class room and one student is busy reading a story book (instead of giving attention to the lecture). What would you do in such a situation?

A. You would reprimand that student and show him the way out of the class

B. You would tell the student to leave the story book and concentrate on the subject being taught

C. You would purposely ignore that student

D. You would wait for another student to complain about that student so that you may be able to file a complaint against him with the Principal

321. As a teacher, you would:

A. listen to the personal problems of the students only if they were special

B. always listen to the problems of students

C. never listen to the problems of students

D. listen to the problems of students and moderate them to the Principal

322. In order to participate in a conference or seminar, which is related to teaching, you would:
A. take leave from the school
B. get the permission of the Principal
C. not get the permission of the Principal
D. quietly leave the school and attend the conference or seminar

323. In your opinion, what should be the age for sending little children to school?
A. When the child starts speaking
B. When the child develops an interest in studies
C. When the child attains the age of plus five years
D. When the child attains the age of plus three years

324. Some students quietly run away from school. In order to check this habit of such students, you would:
A. try to know why they run away from school
B. inform the Principal about their habit of running away from school
C. inform the parents of such children about their habit of running away from school
D. try to make class teaching more interesting

325. Suppose that you give tuition to a student and he fails in the annual examination. In such a situation, you would:
A. request the Principal to help him get through
B. request other teachers to increase his marks
C. suggest the parent/guardian of the student that he/she should try to use references to contact other teachers so that they increase the marks of the student
D. teach that student with a renewed vigour and toil in future

326. As a teacher, where would you like to teach?
A. In the school of your own village
B. In the school of your district in which, children of the rich people study
C. In the school whose Principal is your acquaintance
D. In any school

327. Some teachers give tuitions. In your opinion, what is the reason for this?
A. They get ample opportunities to revise the subject matter being studied (when they give tuitions)
B. That is how they are able to keep themselves busy in quite a useful manner
C. They are always involved in earning (more) money
D. They nurture intense feelings of welfare of students

328. A superior teacher is one who:
A. gives his complete time to the school
B. strictly follows the norms of discipline
C. takes an interest in the all-round development of students
D. gives leadership to students

329. If a student misbehaves with you, then as a teacher, what would be your reaction?
A. You would file a complaint with the Principal
B. You would punish the student so that he pays evenly for his offense
C. You would pardon the student and forget the incident
D. You would complain to other teachers of the school and initiate a campaign to expel him from the school.

330. As a teacher, what type of behaviour of a student would be deemed serious by you?
A. Incomplete home work
B. Asking too many questions in the class
C. Talking to other students in the class during the course of a lecture
D. Slightly slow/weak in studies

331. Which method would you like to adopt to teach a new subject in the class?

A. You would tell children a day before the lecture that they should read the subject at their homes
B. You would tell students to write an article on that subject
C. You would discuss the subject with students in the light of their knowledge about it; then you would give new sets of information/data about that subject to students
D. You would give a small lecture to students regarding the importance of that (new) subject

332. A student is very weak in mathematics. What would you like to do to help him?
A. You would get an advice from the Principal in this context
B. You would give proper advice to the parents of the student in this context
C. You would talk to the student and find out what are his problems in mathematics; later you would remove those problems
D. You would order the most intelligent student in mathematics (of the class) to help the weak student

333. As a teacher, what would you like to do for your favourite student?
A. You would give him the maximum marks in the tests
B. You would make him the monitor of the class
C. You would not ask any difficult question from him in the class
D. You would adequately support him in his studies

334. The true objective of education is:
A. making students able so that they can earn a living
B. preparing students for jobs
C. helping students acquire knowledge
D. facilitating the all-round development of students

335. In order to raise the standards of education, which one of the following is vital?
A. High salaries of teachers
B. Continuous evaluation of students
C. Continuous evaluation of text books
D. Amendments in syllabi

336. Even after telling/explaining time and again in the class, a student is not able to understand a point. In such a situation, you would:
A. reprimand that student and show him the way out of the class
B. deem him incorrigible and stop paying attention to him
C. use another method/solution/material to explain the point/concept to him
D. call his parent/guardian and advise him to look for another arrangement for the study of their child/ward

337. Suppose that a person does not agree with your viewpoint. In such a situation, you would:
A. present the rationale of your view point before him
B. not like to talk to that person
C. consider him to be your opponent
D. behave with him in a rude manner

338. What suggestion would you like to give in order to stop the practice of copying in the examination hall?
A. All the examinees should be allowed to appear in the examination only after they are thoroughly searched
B. Those who are caught copying, should not be admitted to any school; they should also not be allowed to appear in any examination
C. Necessary improvements should be effected in the examination system
D. All the examinees should be given a free hand to copy during examinations

339. Some students of your class have weak eye sights. They are unable to clearly see whatever is written on the blackboard. What is your opinion about solving this problems?
A. Let these children sit in the front seats in the class

B. Call the parents/guardians of such children and advise them to arrange spectacles for their respective children/wards
C. Tell these children to get their eye sights rectified/corrected through suitable methods
D. All of these

340. Which teacher, in your view, is the best?
A. The one who deals with students only under the gamut of teaching
B. The one who is willing to get the maximum information related to the lives of children
C. The one who is popular among students due to his love for discipline
D. The one who is a well-wisher of students

341. Which method would you deem suitable for rectifying those students who interrupt the teaching process in the class?
A. They should be sent out of the class
B. They should be given harsh punishment in the class itself
C. They should be ignored
D. A complaint should be filed against them with the Principal

342. The job of the teacher is to generate:
A. affinity for studies among students
B. confidence in studies among students
C. a belief towards studies among students
D. affection/affiliation for studies among students

343. If a student asks an out of context question in your class, then, as a teacher, you would:
A. punish him
B. ignore his question
C. tell him that the question is out-of-context
D. tell the student that you would answer his question after the class

344. More indiscipline usually prevails in the class if:
A. the number of students is more than the specified norm
B. there is not enough work to keep children occupied
C. there are not enough playgrounds and other facilities for the children to play
D. the teacher is not able to make classroom teaching interesting enough

345. Which aspect would you like to emphasise upon while using visual aids during class teaching?
A. You would present such aids in a dramatic manner
B. They should be in accordance with the subject to be taught
C. They should be capable of taking children from the unknown to the known
D. You would tell children about them well in advance

346. If you find that many students take leave on the day of weekly test, then what solution would you like to devise to solve this problem?
A. You would stop taking weekly tests
B. You would inform the parents/guardians of the absent students in this context
C. You would take the test of the absent students the very next day
D. You would take weekly test on any day of the week

347. With the help of a cumulative records
A. the moral levels of children can be evaluated
B. the pace of educational progress of children can be known
C. children can be disciplined
D. the development of children can be gauged

348. If a student has asked you a question and you are not aware of its answer, then what would you like to do in such a situation?
A. You would tell that student that the question is illogical
B. You would not like to answer any question of that student
C. You would scold that student and discourage him to ask such questions
D. You would tell the student that you would find out the answer of that question and tell him about the same the next day

349. The use of audio-visual material/aids in the class is:
A. more useful for those students who are slow learners
B. more useful for those students who are intelligent
C. enhances the curiosity of children
D. takes the concentration of students away from the main subject

350. If you, as a teacher, have complete knowledge of your subject, then only:
A. you would be able to get respect from students
B. your students would pass with good marks
C. other teachers would also be impressed by you
D. you would be able to eliminate the doubts of your students

351. The curriculum can best be defined as:
A. A list of textbooks
B. A course outline
C. Total learning experiences provided by the school
D. Examination syllabus

352. Syllabus refers to:
A. Co-curricular activities
B. A detailed plan of all school activities
C. Prescribed content of a subject
D. Hidden learning experiences

353. Curriculum is broader than syllabus because it includes:
A. Only classroom teaching
B. Learning experiences inside and outside school
C. Only examinations
D. Only textbooks

354. Who is primarily responsible for curriculum development at the national level in India?
A. CBSE B. NCERT
C. SCERT D. School Principal

355. Syllabus is usually prepared for:
A. Whole school life
B. One subject
C. Co-curricular activities
D. School administration

356. Curriculum is considered dynamic because:
A. It never changes
B. It changes with societal needs
C. It is fixed by law
D. It depends on exams

357. Which of the following is NOT a component of curriculum?
A. Objectives
B. Content
C. Teaching strategies
D. School building

358. Overt curriculum refers to:
A. Unplanned learning
B. Informal learning
C. Explicitly taught subjects
D. Social values

359. Hidden curriculum includes:
A. Mathematics syllabus
B. Science textbook
C. Values and attitudes learned implicitly
D. Examination timetable

360. Discipline and punctuality are part of:
A. Overt curriculum
B. Hidden curriculum
C. Formal syllabus
D. Academic curriculum

361. Which of the following is an example of hidden curriculum?
A. History lesson
B. Moral values learned through school culture
C. English grammar
D. Science experiments

362. Hidden curriculum is:
A. Always planned
B. Written in syllabus
C. Unintentional learning
D. Examination-oriented

363. Teacher behaviour mainly influences:
A. Overt curriculum
B. Hidden curriculum

C. Academic syllabus
D. Time-table

364. Respect for authority is often learned through:
A. Textbooks
B. Timetable
C. Hidden curriculum
D. Lesson plans

365. A school timetable helps in:
A. Confusion
B. Wastage of time
C. Systematic use of time
D. Overburdening teachers

366. The main objective of a school timetable is:
A. Discipline only
B. Efficient organization of teaching-learning
C. Teacher convenience
D. Examination preparation

367. Which factor should be considered while preparing a timetable?
A. Teacher workload
B. Student age
C. Subject difficulty
D. All of the above

368. Subjects like Mathematics should be taught:
A. At the end of the day
B. During lunch break
C. When students are mentally fresh
D. Only twice a week

369. A good timetable avoids:
A. Flexibility
B. Teacher overload
C. Planning
D. Organization

370. Which timetable provides daily subject-wise distribution?
A. Master timetable
B. Class timetable
C. Teacher timetable
D. Examination timetable

371. Co-curricular activities should be placed:
A. Randomly
B. Only after exams
C. Properly within the timetable
D. Outside school hours only

372. Who usually prepares the school timetable?
A. Students
B. Parents
C. Headmaster/Principal
D. Education Minister

373. FLN focuses mainly on children of age:
A. 0–3 years B. 3–8 years
C. 8–12 years D. 12–16 years

374. Foundational Literacy refers to:
A. Writing essays
B. Reading with comprehension
C. Advanced grammar
D. Creative writing

375. Foundational Numeracy includes:
A. Algebra
B. Geometry
C. Basic number sense and operations
D. Trigonometry

376. FLN is emphasized in which policy?
A. RTE Act 2009 B. NEP 2020
C. NCF 2005 D. SSA

377. The goal of FLN is to:
A. Prepare for exams
B. Reduce dropout rates
C. Build strong learning foundation
D. Increase homework

378. Which skill is part of literacy?
A. Counting B. Measurement
C. Reading D. Estimation

379. Play-based learning is important for:
A. Secondary education
B. FLN
C. Higher education
D. Teacher training

380. ECCE covers children in the age group:
A. 0–6 years B. 6–12 years
C. 12–18 years D. 3–10 years

381. ECCE emphasizes:
A. Rote learning
B. Holistic development
C. Examinations
D. Memorization

382. Which of the following is a principle of ECCE?
A. Teacher-centred learning
B. Play and activity-based learning
C. Strict discipline
D. Formal exams

383. Anganwadi centers are related to:
A. Secondary education
B. ECCE
C. Higher education
D. Teacher training

384. ECCE focuses on development of:
A. Only cognitive skills
B. Only physical skills
C. Cognitive, social, emotional, physical skills
D. Academic skills only

385. Learning in ECCE should be:
A. Stressful
B. Child-centred
C. Exam-oriented
D. Teacher-dominated

386. Which activity is suitable for ECCE?
A. Lecture method
B. Worksheets only
C. Storytelling
D. Written exams

387. Language development in ECCE is promoted through:
A. Punishment
B. Story, rhyme, conversation
C. Homework
D. Tests

388. ECCE aims to prepare children for:
A. Competitive exams
B. Primary education
C. Higher education
D. Employment

389. Curriculum planning should be:
A. Rigid B. Flexible
C. Exam-centred D. Teacher-centred

390. Time-table reflects:
A. School discipline
B. Educational planning
C. Teacher interest
D. Student attendance

391. FLN success depends mainly on:
A. Textbooks
B. Teacher competence
C. Exams
D. Infrastructure only

392. Hidden curriculum is learned through:
A. School culture B. Syllabus
C. Lesson plans D. Textbooks

393. ECCE curriculum should be:
A. Academic-heavy
B. Developmentally appropriate
C. Exam-focused
D. Rigid

394. Which is NOT a feature of good timetable?
A. Balance of subjects
B. Flexibility
C. Overburden
D. Proper rest

395. Numeracy skills include:
A. Reading stories
B. Writing essays
C. Comparing quantities
D. Drawing pictures

396. Curriculum objectives should be:
A. Vague
B. Clear and achievable
C. Ignored
D. Only academic

397. The hidden curriculum mainly affects:
A. Academic achievement
B. Personality development
C. Examination scores
D. Memory

398. Play-way method is most suitable for:
A. Higher education
B. ECCE
C. Teacher training
D. Adult education

399. Literacy development begins best through:
A. Rote memorization
B. Meaningful interaction
C. Exams
D. Punishment

400. Effective teaching-learning requires:
A. Good curriculum planning
B. Proper timetable
C. Focus on FLN and ECCE
D. All of the above

401. Competency based lesson planning focuses primarily on:
A. Completion of syllabus
B. Time-bound teaching
C. Learner's ability to apply knowledge
D. Teacher-centred instruction

402. A competency is best defined as:
A. Subject knowledge only
B. Ability to recall facts
C. Combination of knowledge, skills, and attitudes
D. Teaching method

403. In competency based lesson planning, learning outcomes should be:
A. Vague
B. Content-focused
C. Measurable and observable
D. Exam-oriented

404. Which of the following best reflects a competency based objective?
A. Students will learn fractions
B. Students will understand fractions
C. Students will solve real-life fraction problems
D. Students will read about fractions

405. Teacher's role in competency based lesson planning is mainly:
A. Lecturer B. Facilitator
C. Controller D. Examiner

406. Competency based lesson plans emphasize:
A. Memorization
B. Application and performance
C. Textbook coverage
D. Rote learning

407. Which domain is emphasized most in competency based planning?
A. Cognitive only
B. Affective only
C. Psychomotor only
D. Integration of all domains

408. Learning activities in CBLP should be:
A. Teacher-directed
B. Lecture-based
C. Learner-centred
D. Exam-focused

409. Which method supports competency based learning best?
A. Dictation
B. Project method
C. Lecture method
D. Drill method

410. Competency based planning encourages:
A. Uniform pace for all learners
B. Mastery before progression
C. Fixed time schedules
D. Teaching to the test

411. Competency based assessment focuses on:
A. Marks and grades
B. Rank and comparison
C. Demonstration of skills
D. Written tests only

412. Which assessment tool best measures competency?
A. MCQ test
B. Essay test
C. Performance task
D. Memory-based test

413. In competency based assessment, assessment is:
A. Only at the end
B. Continuous and ongoing
C. Rare
D. Optional

414. Rubrics are used in competency based assessment to:
A. Assign grades only
B. Standardize evaluation criteria
C. Increase difficulty
D. Reduce feedback

415. Which is an example of competency based assessment?
A. Annual examination
B. Oral recall test
C. Practical demonstration
D. Objective test

416. Feedback in competency based assessment should be:
A. Delayed
B. Punitive
C. Specific and constructive
D. General

417. Portfolio assessment is useful because it:
A. Tests memorization
B. Shows learner progress over time
C. Saves teacher time
D. Focuses on exams

418. Self-assessment in CBA helps learners to:
A. Compete with others
B. Reflect on their learning
C. Memorize content
D. Avoid responsibility

419. Which principle underlies competency based assessment?
A. Time-bound testing
B. Norm-referenced evaluation
C. Criterion-referenced evaluation
D. Ranking system

420. Competency based assessment promotes:
A. Fear of exams
B. Rote learning
C. Mastery learning
D. Teaching to test

421. Instructional materials are mainly used to:
A. Replace the teacher
B. Support teaching-learning
C. Entertain students
D. Control discipline

422. Which is an example of instructional material?
A. School rules
B. Chalk and blackboard
C. Examination paper
D. Attendance register

423. Audio-visual aids help in:
A. Confusion
B. Increasing abstraction
C. Enhancing understanding
D. Reducing interest

424. Which instructional resource promotes experiential learning?
A. Textbook
B. Lecture notes
C. Laboratory equipment
D. Question bank

425. Teaching-learning materials should be:
A. Costly
B. Complex
C. Relevant and appropriate
D. Decorative

426. Digital resources in teaching include:
A. Chalk
B. Charts
C. Educational apps
D. Attendance sheets

427. Instructional materials are selected based on:
A. Teacher preference
B. Availability only
C. Learner needs and objectives
D. Cost only

428. Which is a print resource?
A. Video B. Audio recording
C. Textbook D. Smartboard

429. Use of teaching aids helps to:
A. Increase rote learning
B. Clarify concepts
C. Increase workload
D. Waste time

430. The most important criterion for selecting instructional material is:
A. Attractive appearance
B. Alignment with learning objectives
C. Cost
D. Size

431. Competency based lesson planning is aligned with:
A. Teacher-centred approach
B. Outcome-based education
C. Exam-oriented system
D. Rote learning

432. Which assessment technique best supports competency based learning?
A. Summative exam
B. Formative assessment
C. Annual test
D. Surprise test

433. Teaching aids in competency based learning mainly help in:
A. Memorization
B. Skill development
C. Exam preparation
D. Note writing

434. Real-life tasks in assessment help to measure:
A. Memory B. Understanding
C. Competency D. Speed

435. Which instructional resource supports collaborative learning?
A. Textbook
B. Worksheet
C. Group activity material
D. Question paper

436. Competency based assessment reduces emphasis on:
A. Feedback B. Application
C. Ranks and marks D. Skill mastery

437. A rubric mainly ensures:
A. Subjectivity
B. Bias
C. Transparency in assessment
D. Difficulty

438. Learning resources in competency based classrooms should be:
A. Limited
B. Flexible and diverse
C. Teacher-controlled
D. Exam-focused

439. Which instructional material best supports psychomotor skills?
A. Chart B. Model
C. Hands-on tools D. Textbook

440. Competency based learning allows learners to:
A. Progress without mastery
B. Learn at their own pace
C. Skip assessment
D. Focus only on theory

441. The main purpose of formative assessment is to:
A. Certify learning
B. Improve learning
C. Rank students
D. Promote competition

442. Instructional materials should be evaluated for:
A. Popularity
B. Learning effectiveness
C. Teacher comfort
D. Student marks

443. Which is NOT a characteristic of competency based assessment?
A. Performance-oriented
B. Criterion-referenced
C. Time-bound
D. Feedback-focused

444. Teaching-learning resources help to address:
A. Only fast learners
B. Individual differences
C. Only slow learners
D. Teacher workload

445. In competency based classrooms, assessment is:
A. Separate from teaching
B. Integrated with teaching
C. Ignored
D. Only summative

446. Which tool best documents learner competency over time?
A. Unit test B. Annual exam
C. Portfolio D. MCQ test

447. Instructional materials should encourage:
A. Passive learning
B. Active participation
C. Rote memorization
D. Silence

448. Competency based planning aligns teaching with:
A. Time limits
B. Textbook chapters
C. Learning outcomes
D. Examination pattern

449. Technology-based resources are most useful when they:
A. Replace teachers
B. Are used for entertainment
C. Support learning objectives
D. Are expensive

450. Effective teaching-learning occurs when lesson planning, assessment and resources are:
A. Independent B. Random
C. Integrated D. Ignored

451. Digital technology in education primarily aims to:
A. Replace teachers
B. Improve access and engagement
C. Increase screen time
D. Reduce interaction

452. Which is an example of a digital learning platform?
A. Chalkboard
B. LMS
C. Chart
D. Bulletin board

453. Smart classrooms mainly support:
A. One-way teaching
B. Interactive learning
C. Rote memorization
D. Discipline

454. Blended learning refers to:
A. Only online learning
B. Only face-to-face learning
C. Combination of online and offline learning
D. Distance education only

455. MOOCs are best described as:
A. Small private courses
B. Online courses open to many learners
C. Classroom tutorials
D. Teacher training workshops

456. Digital content enhances learning by:
A. Making students passive
B. Providing multimedia experiences
C. Eliminating teachers
D. Limiting collaboration

457. Which tool enables virtual collaboration?
A. Blackboard
B. Video conferencing app
C. Textbook
D. Notice board

458. E-learning supports:
A. Fixed pace learning
B. Self-paced learning
C. Teacher dominance
D. Rigid curriculum

459. Digital assessment tools mainly provide:
A. Delayed feedback
B. Immediate feedback
C. No feedback
D. Punishment

460. Which is a major challenge of digital learning?
A. Flexibility
B. Accessibility issues
C. Multimedia content
D. Interactive tools

461. Classroom observation is mainly used to:
A. Evaluate students only
B. Improve teaching practices
C. Punish teachers
D. Maintain discipline

462. Observation helps teachers to:
A. Ignore classroom realities
B. Reflect on teaching methods
C. Increase workload
D. Avoid feedback

463. Which is a tool for systematic observation?
A. Anecdotal record
B. Attendance register
C. Syllabus
D. Timetable

464. Peer observation focuses on:
A. Supervision
B. Collaborative professional learning
C. Inspection
D. Evaluation for promotion

465. Classroom observation should be:
A. Judgmental
B. Fear-inducing
C. Objective and supportive
D. Secret

466. Observation data is best used for:
A. Ranking teachers
B. Professional growth
C. Administrative punishment
D. Salary decisions

467. Which observation focuses on specific teaching behaviors?
A. Informal observation
B. Structured observation
C. Casual visit
D. Random observation

468. Effective feedback should be:
A. Vague
B. Delayed
C. Specific and timely
D. Punitive

469. Feedback in teaching-learning mainly aims to:
A. Find faults
B. Improve learning outcomes
C. Increase stress
D. Compare learners

470. Constructive feedback focuses on:
A. Past mistakes only
B. Improvement and guidance
C. Blame
D. Grades

471. Follow-up after feedback helps in:
A. Ignoring suggestions
B. Reinforcing improvement
C. Increasing workload
D. Stopping reflection

472. Peer feedback promotes:
A. Competition
B. Collaboration and reflection
C. Fear
D. Punishment

473. Feedback is most effective when it is:
A. Teacher-centred
B. Learner-centred
C. Authority-centred
D. Grade-centred

474. Digital tools enhance feedback by:
A. Delaying response
B. Providing real-time responses
C. Reducing interaction
D. Limiting access

475. Reflection in teaching refers to:
A. Memorizing lessons
B. Thinking critically about practice
C. Following routine
D. Avoiding change

476. Reflective teaching helps teachers to:
A. Repeat mistakes
B. Improve instructional strategies
C. Avoid innovation
D. Maintain status quo

477. Dialogue in constructivist classrooms promotes:
A. Passive listening
B. Shared meaning-making
C. Teacher dominance
D. Silence

478. Constructivist teaching emphasizes:
A. Transmission of knowledge
B. Learner-centred learning
C. Rote memorization
D. Examination focus

479. Reflection-in-action occurs:
A. After the lesson
B. Before teaching
C. During teaching
D. Only in training

480. Reflection-on-action occurs:
A. During teaching
B. After teaching
C. Before teaching
D. Never

481. Dialogic teaching encourages:
A. One-way communication
B. Questioning and discussion
C. Silence
D. Lecture only

482. Learner dialogue helps in:
A. Confusion
B. Constructing knowledge
C. Memorization
D. Discipline

483. Reflection journals are used to:
A. Record attendance
B. Document learning experiences
C. Evaluate exams
D. Punish learners

484. Digital technology supports constructivism by:
A. Promoting passive learning
B. Enabling exploration and collaboration
C. Limiting interaction
D. Emphasizing memorization

485. Classroom observation combined with reflection leads to:
A. Fear
B. Professional development
C. Punishment
D. Routine teaching

486. Feedback is considered formative when it:
A. Grades learners
B. Supports improvement
C. Ranks students
D. Certifies learning

487. Online discussion forums promote:
A. Monologue
B. Dialogue and reflection
C. Memorization
D. Teacher control

488. Which digital tool best supports reflective practice?
A. Calculator
B. E-portfolio
C. Chalk
D. Attendance register

489. Follow-up action after observation should focus on:
A. Fault-finding
B. Professional support
C. Punishment
D. Documentation only

490. Constructivist assessment emphasizes:
A. Recall
B. Understanding and application
C. Ranking
D. Speed

491. Digital feedback tools help teachers to:
A. Delay assessment
B. Track learner progress
C. Increase workload
D. Reduce interaction

492. Teacher reflection is most effective when it is:
A. Isolated
B. Collaborative
C. Ignored
D. Forced

493. Dialogue in classrooms should be:
A. Controlled strictly
B. Open and respectful
C. Avoided
D. One-sided

494. Observation-feedback cycle improves teaching by:
A. Repetition
B. Continuous improvement
C. Inspection
D. Control

495. Digital technology enhances observation through:
A. Surveillance
B. Video recording and analysis
C. Punishment
D. Monitoring only

496. Reflective practice mainly develops:
A. Rote skills
B. Professional judgment
C. Memorization
D. Examination skills

497. Constructivist classrooms encourage learners to:
A. Receive information
B. Co-construct knowledge
C. Memorize facts
D. Remain silent

498. Effective feedback should focus on:
A. Person
B. Task and process
C. Comparison
D. Marks

499. Use of digital dialogue tools supports:
A. Individual learning only
B. Collaborative learning
C. Isolation
D. Teacher monopoly

500. Integration of digital technology, feedback, and reflection leads to:
A. Mechanical teaching
B. Meaningful learning
C. Rote learning
D. Exam pressure

ANSWERS

1	2	3	4	5	6	7	8	9	10
A	A	B	D	C	D	A	C	D	C
11	**12**	**13**	**14**	**15**	**16**	**17**	**18**	**19**	**20**
A	C	B	A	B	B	A	B	A	C
21	**22**	**23**	**24**	**25**	**26**	**27**	**28**	**29**	**30**
A	B	A	D	C	D	B	C	C	A
31	**32**	**33**	**34**	**35**	**36**	**37**	**38**	**39**	**40**
D	D	C	D	A	D	B	D	A	D
41	**42**	**43**	**44**	**45**	**46**	**47**	**48**	**49**	**50**
C	D	A	C	D	A	C	D	D	B

51	**52**	**53**	**54**	**55**	**56**	**57**	**58**	**59**	**60**
D	B	D	C	A	D	D	C	A	A
61	**62**	**63**	**64**	**65**	**66**	**67**	**68**	**69**	**70**
A	A	C	B	A	A	C	A	D	D
71	**72**	**73**	**74**	**75**	**76**	**77**	**78**	**79**	**80**
B	A	C	D	A	D	A	C	C	A
81	**82**	**83**	**84**	**85**	**86**	**87**	**88**	**89**	**90**
C	D	B	B	B	D	D	D	C	A
91	**92**	**93**	**94**	**95**	**96**	**97**	**98**	**99**	**100**
A	C	D	D	C	A	C	D	A	B
101	**102**	**103**	**104**	**105**	**106**	**107**	**108**	**109**	**110**
D	B	D	C	B	A	D	A	B	A
111	**112**	**113**	**114**	**115**	**116**	**117**	**118**	**119**	**120**
B	A	C	B	D	C	D	A	A	D
121	**122**	**123**	**124**	**125**	**126**	**127**	**128**	**129**	**130**
D	D	B	A	C	C	A	A	D	A
131	**132**	**133**	**134**	**135**	**136**	**137**	**138**	**139**	**140**
A	C	D	D	D	A	B	B	A	C
141	**142**	**143**	**144**	**145**	**146**	**147**	**148**	**149**	**150**
A	D	D	C	A	D	A	D	D	C
151	**152**	**153**	**154**	**155**	**156**	**157**	**158**	**159**	**160**
D	D	D	D	D	D	C	C	C	B
161	**162**	**163**	**164**	**165**	**166**	**167**	**168**	**169**	**170**
D	A	D	D	D	D	B	A	C	A
171	**172**	**173**	**174**	**175**	**176**	**177**	**178**	**179**	**180**
C	B	C	C	D	A	A	B	B	A
181	**182**	**183**	**184**	**185**	**186**	**187**	**188**	**189**	**190**
D	A	C	D	C	C	D	D	D	C
191	**192**	**193**	**194**	**195**	**196**	**197**	**198**	**199**	**200**
A	B	C	C	D	A	D	D	D	B
201	**202**	**203**	**204**	**205**	**206**	**207**	**208**	**209**	**210**
D	D	D	B	D	B	C	A	D	B
211	**212**	**213**	**214**	**215**	**216**	**217**	**218**	**219**	**220**
C	A	B	D	A	C	D	D	C	B
221	**222**	**223**	**224**	**225**	**226**	**227**	**228**	**229**	**230**
B	B	C	C	C	C	B	B	B	C
231	**232**	**233**	**234**	**235**	**236**	**237**	**238**	**239**	**240**
B	B	A	A	D	A	B	B	D	A
241	**242**	**243**	**244**	**245**	**246**	**247**	**248**	**249**	**250**
C	C	D	A	B	C	B	C	C	D

251	252	253	254	255	256	257	258	259	260
D	B	D	D	C	D	C	A	C	D
261	262	263	264	265	266	267	268	269	270
C	D	D	B	B	C	C	B	A	C
271	272	273	274	275	276	277	278	279	280
B	B	D	A	A	A	A	B	A	C
281	282	283	284	285	286	287	288	289	290
A	A	C	C	D	D	D	B	B	B
291	292	293	294	295	296	297	298	299	300
A	C	A	A	A	D	A	D	A	A
301	302	303	304	305	306	307	308	309	310
A	C	D	C	C	C	A	C	C	C
311	312	313	314	315	316	317	318	319	320
B	D	B	D	A	C	D	D	C	B
321	322	323	324	325	326	327	328	329	330
B	B	D	A	D	D	C	C	C	C
331	332	333	334	335	336	337	338	339	340
C	C	D	D	B	C	A	C	D	D
341	342	343	344	345	346	347	348	349	350
A	D	C	D	B	D	D	D	A	D
351	352	353	354	355	356	357	358	359	360
C	C	B	B	B	B	D	C	C	B
361	362	363	364	365	366	367	368	369	370
B	C	B	C	C	B	D	C	B	B
371	372	373	374	375	376	377	378	379	380
C	C	B	B	C	B	C	C	B	A
381	382	383	384	385	386	387	388	389	390
B	B	B	C	B	C	B	B	B	B
391	392	393	394	395	396	397	398	399	400
B	A	B	C	C	B	B	B	B	D
401	402	403	404	405	406	407	408	409	410
C	C	C	C	B	B	D	C	B	B
411	412	413	414	415	416	417	418	419	420
C	C	B	B	C	C	B	B	C	C
421	422	423	424	425	426	427	428	429	430
B	B	C	C	C	C	C	C	B	B
431	432	433	434	435	436	437	438	439	440
B	B	B	C	C	C	C	B	C	B
441	442	443	444	445	446	447	448	449	450
B	B	C	B	B	C	B	C	C	C

451	**452**	**453**	**454**	**455**	**456**	**457**	**458**	**459**	**460**
B	B	B	C	B	B	B	B	B	B
461	**462**	**463**	**464**	**465**	**466**	**467**	**468**	**469**	**470**
B	B	A	B	C	B	B	C	B	B
471	**472**	**473**	**474**	**475**	**476**	**477**	**478**	**479**	**480**
B	B	B	B	B	B	B	B	C	B
481	**482**	**483**	**484**	**485**	**486**	**487**	**488**	**489**	**490**
B	B	B	B	B	B	B	B	B	B
491	**492**	**493**	**494**	**495**	**496**	**497**	**498**	**499**	**500**
B	B	B	B	B	B	B	B	B	B

*****

MANAGEMENT, SUPERVISION AND LEADERSHIP

1 MANAGEMENT

Management is an important factor for the success of any organized activity. Today management basically concern with changes and challenges, and it is difficult to manage.

Management is an art of getting things done through others. Management is to plan, organize, direct and control the resources of the organization for obtaining common objectives or goals. It is related with resources like material, money, machinery, methods, manufacturing and marketing.

Management principles are universal in nature. Management is necessary for all types of organization, such as public sector, private sector, govt. department, hotel, hospital, hostels, educational institutes, require management for several growth and expansion.

Definitions

1. **According to Taylor:** "Management is the art of knowing what you want to do and then seeing that it is done in the best and cheapest way."
2. **According to Lawrence:** "Management is the accomplishment of results through the efforts of other people."
3. **According to Henry Fayol:** "To manage is to forecast and to plan, to organize, to co-ordinate and to control."

NATURE OF MANAGEMENT

The essential features of management reveal its nature and importance. These are discussed below.

1. **Universality:** Management is an universal phenomenon in the sense that it is common and essential element in all enterprises. Managers perform more or less the same functions irrespective of their position or nature of the organisation. The basic principles of management can be applied in all managerial situations regardless of the size, nature and location of the organisation. Universality of managerial tasks andprinciples also implies that managerial skills are transferable and managers can be trained and developed.
2. **Purposeful:** Management is always aimed at achieving organisational goals and purposes. The success of management is measured by the extent to which the desired objectives are attained. In both economic and non-economic entetprises, the tasks of management are directed towards effectiveness (i.e., attainment of organisational goals), and efficiency (i.e., goal attainment with economy of resource use).
3. **Social process:** Management essentially invoives managing people organised in work groups: It includes retaining, developing and motivating people at work, as well as taking care of their satisfaction as social beings. All these interpersonal relations and interactions makes the management as a social process.
4. **Coordinating force:** Management co-ordinates the efforts of organisation

1973 (Mangement)—1

members through orderly arrangement of inter-related activities so as. to avoid duplication and overlapping. Management reconciles the individual goals with the organisational goals and integrates human and pllysical resources.

5. **Intangible:** Management is intangible. It is an unseen force. Its presence can be felt everywhere by the results of its effort which comes in the form of orderliness, adequate work output, satisfactory, working climate, employees satisfaction, etc.
6. **Continuous process:** Management is a dynamic and an on-going process. The cycle of management continues to operate so long as there is organised action for the achievement of group goals.
7. **Composite process:** Functions of management cannot be undertaken sequentially, independent of each other. Management is a composite process made up of individual ingredients. All the functions are perfomled by involving several ingredients. Therefore, the whole process is integrative and performed in a network fashion.
8. **Creative organ:** Management creates synergetic effect by producing results which are more than the sum of the individual efforts of the group members. It provides sequence to operations, matches jobs to goals, connects work to physical and financial resources. It provides creative ideas, new imaginations nnd visions to group efforts. It is not a passive force adopting to external environment but a dynamic life giving element in every organisation.

SCOPE OF MANAGEMENT

The scope of management is very large. The following activities are covered under the scope of management. Management Strives For: Low resource waste (high efficiency) High goal attainment (high effectiveness)

1. **Subject-matter of management:** It consists of the various functions like planning, organisation, staffing, directing and controlling.
2. **Principles of management have a universal application:** Every Organisation needs managers for managing business activities. The manager's job is basically the same at all levels. The managers at the higher levels have more important duties while managers at the lower levels have to perform routine functions i.e., duties. All the managers irrespective of their working place, make use of the management principles, and are universally applicable.
3. **Management is an interdisciplinary approach:** Management as a body of discipline takes the help of other disciplines like:
   - sociology,
   - psychology,
   - anthropology,
   - engineering,
   - economics, etc.

   Integration of the knowledge of the various subject is one of the important contributions of management.
4. **Functional areas of management:** It consists of the following functional areas or the various branches of management.

   (*a*) **Financial Management:** Financial Management means planning, organizing, directing and controlling the financial activities such as procurement and utilization of funds of the enterprise. It means applying general management principles to financial resources of the enterprise. It includes the followings:
   - Cost control,
   - Budgetary control,
   - Financial planning,
   - Management accounting,
   - Standard costing, etc.

(*b*) **Personnel Management:** Personnel management can be defined as obtaining, using and maintaining a satisfied workforce. It is a significant part of management concerned with employees at work and with their relationship within the organization. According to Brach, "Personnel Management is that part which is primarily concerned with human resources of organization." It includes the following:

- Manpower Planning,
- Recruitment,
- Selection,
- Training and development,
- Compensation Management,
- Promotions and transfers,
- Social Security, etc.

(*c*) **Production Management:** Production management means planning, organising, directing and controlling of production activities. Production management deals with converting raw materials into finished goods or products. It brings together the 6M's *i.e.*, men, money, machines, materials, methods and markets to satisfy the wants of the people. It includes the followings:

- Production Planning,
- Quality Control and inspection,
- Production control techniques, etc.

(*d*) **Marketing Management:** Marketing management is a business discipline which is focused on the practical application of marketing techniques and the management of a firm's marketing resources and activities. Rapidly emerging forces of globalization have led firms to market beyond the borders of their home countries, making international marketing highly significant and an integral part of a firm's marketing strategy. It includes the followings:

- Marketing of goods and services,
- Price Determination,
- Market Research,
- Sales Promotion,
- Advertisement,
- Publicity, etc.

Only few functional aspects are stated here. Manage-ment principles can be applied to any activity or event.

PROCESS OF MANAGEMENT

The study and application of management techniques in managing the affairs of the organization have changed its nature over the period of time.

1. **Multidisciplinary:** Management is basically multidisciplinary. This implies that, although management has been developed as a separate discipline, it draws knowledge and concepts from various disciplines. It draws freely ideas and concepts from disciplines such as psychology, sociology, anthropology, economics, ecology, statistics, operations research, etc. Management integrates the ideas and concepts taken from these disciplines and present newer concepts which can be put into practice for managing the organization.
2. **Dynamic nature of principle:** Based on integration and supported by practical evidences, management has formed certain principles. However, these principles are flexible in nature and change with the changes in the environment in which an organization exists.
3. **Relative, not absolute principles:** Management principles are relative, not absolute, and they should be applied according to the need of the organization. Each organization may be different from others. The difference may exist because of time, place, socio-cultural factors, etc.
4. **Management Science or Art:** There is a controversy whether management is science or art. However, management is both a science and art.

5. **Management as profession:** Management has been regarded as profession by many while many have suggested that it has not achieved the status of a profession.

FUNCTIONS OF MANAGEMENT

Managerial Functions: Various management scholars studied different organizations at different times; they identified the functions of management in their own ways. Henry Fayol, the father of functional or administrative management remarked: To manage is to forecast and plan, to organize, to command, to coordinate and to control.

Thus, Fayol classified management functions into five categories as follows:

(*i*) to forecast and plan,
(*ii*) to organize,
(*iii*) to command or to give orders,
(*iv*) to co-ordinate, and
(*v*) to control

Luther Gullick offered a list of administrative functions under the catchword **PODSCORB**. Each alphabet of this keyword – PODSCORB stands for the following activities: P for Planning, O for Organisation, D for Directing, S for Staffing, Co for Coordinating, R for Reporting, and B for Budgeting.

According to **Koontz and O'Donnell:** The most useful method of classifying managerial activities is to group them around the functions of planning, organizing, staffing, directing, and controlling. They think that coordination is not a separate function but is the essence of management. Thus, for the sake of analysis of their management process, we can classify the management functions into the following categories:

PLANNING

It is the basic function of management. It deals with chalking out a future course of action and deciding in advance the most appropriate course of action for achievement of pre-determined goals. According to KOONTZ – Planning is deciding in advance – what to do, when to do and how to do. It bridges the gap from where we are and where we want to be. A plan is a future course of actions. It is an exercise in problem solving and decision making. Planning is determination of courses of action to achieve desired goals. Thus, planning is a systematic thinking about ways and means for accomplishment of pre-determined goals. Planning is necessary to ensure proper utilization of human & non-human resources. It is all pervasive, it is an intellectual activity and it also helps in avoiding confusion, uncertainties, risks, wastages etc. Budgeting Planning involves the following steps.

(*i*) Determination of objectives;
(*ii*) Forecasting;
(*iii*) Formulation of policies and programmes;
(*iv*) Preparation of schedules.

Planning is a process of seeking answer to some of the following particular questions:

(*i*) What is to be done?
(*ii*) Why it is to be done?
(*iii*) How the work will be done?
(*iv*) Who will do the work?
(*v*) When the work will be done?
(*vi*) Where the work will be done?

Planning pervades at all the levels of organization. But the scope of planning is not the same at each level of organi- zation. Higher the level of organization, the broader the scope of planning. Planning may be long term and short term.

ORGANIZING

It is the process of bringing together physical, financial and human resources and developing productive relationship amongst them for achievement of organizational goals. According to Henry Fayol – To organize a business is to provide it with everything useful or its functioning *i.e.,* raw material, tools, capital and personnel's. To organize a business involves determining and providing human and non-human resources to the organizational structure. Organizing as a process involves:

(*i*) Identification of activities.

(*ii*) Classification of grouping of activities.

(*iii*) Assignment of duties.
(*iv*) Delegation of authority and creation of responsibility.
(*v*) Coordinating authority and responsibility relationships.

STAFFING

It is the function of manning the organization structure and keeping it manned. Staffing has assumed greater importance in the recent years due to advancement of technology, increase in size of business, complexity of human behaviour etc. The main purpose of staffing is to put right man on right job *i.e.*, square pegs in square holes and round pegs in round holes. According to Koontz & O'Donell –Managerial function of staffing involves manning the organization structure through proper and effective selection; appraisal & development of personnel to fill the roles designed the structure. Staffing involves:

(*i*) Manpower Planning (estimating man power in terms of searching, choose the person and giving the right place).
(*ii*) Recruitment, selection & placement.
(*iii*) Training & development.
(*iv*) Remuneration.
(*v*) Performance appraisal.
(*vi*) Promotions & transfer.

DIRECTING

It is that part of managerial function which actuates the organizational methods to work efficiently for achievement of organizational purposes. It is considered life-spark of the enterprise which sets it in motion the action of people because planning, organizing and staffing are the mere preparations for doing the work. Direction is that inert-personnel aspectof management which deals directly with influencing, guiding, supervising, motivating subordinate for the achievement of organizational goals. Direction has following elements:

(*i*) Supervision: It implies overseeing the work of subordinates by their superiors. It is the act of watching and directing work and workers.

(*ii*) Motivation: It means inspiring, stimulating or encouraging the subordinates with zeal to work. Positive, negative, monetary, non-monetary incentives may be used for this purpose.

(*iii*) Leadership: It may be defined as a process by which manager guides and influences the work of subordinates in desired direction.

(*iv*) Communications: It is the process of passing information, experience, opinion etc from one person to another. It is a bridge of understanding.

CONTROLLING

It implies measurement of accomplishment against the standards and correction of deviation if any to ensure achievement of organizational goals. The purpose of controlling is to ensure that everything occurs in conformities with the standards.

An efficient system of control helps to predict deviations before they actually occur.

According to *Theo Haimann* — Controlling is the process of checking whether or not proper progress is being made towards the objectives and goals and acting if necessary, to correct any deviation. According to **Koontz & O'Donell** – Controlling is the measurement & correction of performance activities of subordinates in order to make sure that the enterprise objectives and plans desired to obtain them as being accomplished. Therefore controlling has following steps:

(*i*) Establishment of standard performance.
(*ii*) Measurement of actual performance.
(*iii*) Comparison of actual performance with the standards and finding out deviation if any.
(*iv*) Corrective action.

THE ROLES OF MANAGER IN AN ORGANIZATION

A manager plays a crucial role in the success and smooth functioning of any organization. They are responsible for planning, organizing, leading and controlling serious activities to achieve organizational goals efficiently is multidimensional, involving both administrative and interpersonal responsibilities.

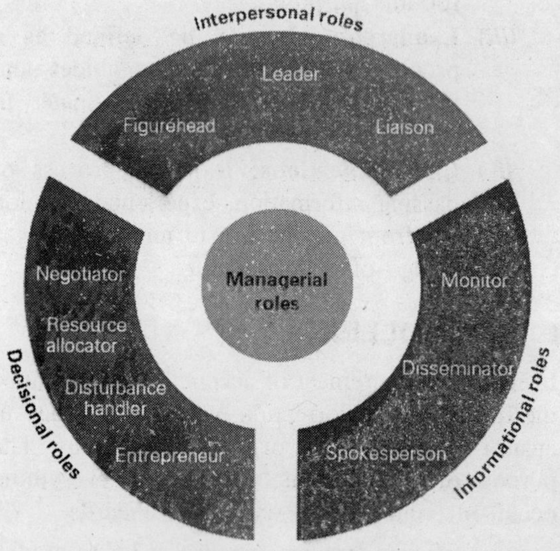

1. Interpersonal Roles

In the process of management needs to interact with subordinates to get things done by them, and also communicates with superiors, peers, trade union leaders, customers, government and other agencies whose interest is involved in the business. Its importance is evident from that a manager spends nearly 80 percent of his time, in interacting with these parties.

- **Figurehead role:** The manager works in a line of authority. His position is identified in terms of formal authority, responsibility, obligations and relationship. As a symbol of formal authority, he performs various ceremonial duties e.g. receiving visitors, attending weddings of subordinates, singing various documents, delivering speeches and lectures in important social gathering such as schools, clubs and other religious places.
- **Leadership role:** The most important role of the manager is to lead, guide and motivate subordinates and get work done properly. A manager is responsible not only for his own acts but for the activities performed by his subordinates. The leadership qualities of the manager help him in influencing the working behaviour of subordinates, contributing to a higher level of efficiency.
- **Liaison role:** A manager serves as connecting link, vertically with superiors and subordinates, and horizontally, with other managers at the same level. Outside the organization, the managers have to undertake liaison to assess the external environment to enable the organization to cope with it.

2. Informational Roles

To preserve and protect the identify of an organization and to secure its smooth functioning, the manager has to scan the external environment on a regular basis and to deal with outside parties, effectively for which he has to gather a lot relevant information on the various matters concerning the organizations.

The manager plays three important informational roles while managing the operations of an organization.

- **Role of monitor:** The managers interact and deal with insiders and outsiders and scan the external environmental constantly to get useful information. He collects information on the various aspects of the organization and its environment through reports, informal relations dealings and liaison work. He is the most well-informed member of his work group. While managing, he monitors every situation closely and minutely, collects information regarding it and finally, solves it effectively.
- **Role of disseminator:** The manager continuously transmits selected information which he has complied through the role of monitor to his subordinates. He keeps them well-informed regarding any change in the process, structure, policies and other plans of the organization. The needed information is disseminated among the subordinates by

him through formal and informal meetings, memorandums, orders and instructions issued from time to time.

- **Role of spokesperson:** A manager acts as a spokesperson of his group while supplying information to superiors and peers. Similarly, he keeps outside parties well-informed on behalf of the organization. He negotiates and enters into comprise with internal and external parties.

3. Decision-making Roles

By interacting with insiders and outsiders, the manager gets important information, which he can use or taking decisions and solving problems.

- **As an entrepreneur:** The managers have a primary responsibility of improving the overall functioning of their respective work units. They act as an entrepreneur; take bold decisions, seek better results from subordinates, initiate required changes, implementing them for the betterment of organization. To initiate and implement changes, managers have to be dynamic, innovative and creative.
- **As a disturbance or conflict handler:** An organization is a collective entity with diversity of interest and duality of roles for managers. For example, the owners group may be interested in high profits whereas the employees may seek more benefits in the form of higher wages and better working conditions. In such situations, it is only by applying managerial knowledge and playing the role of conflict handlers, thinking analytical and acting practically, that the managers can hope to effectively integrate the interest of employees with the organization. Similar conflicts may arise with outside parties which would have to be resolved through meetings, negotiations and compromise.
- **As a resource allocator:** To manage the organization, physical and human resources are mobilized and utilized efficiently by managers for the accomplishment of pre-determined objectives. They have to play the role of resources allocators. And, in the case of multiple objectives, they set priorities for allocation of resources.
- **As a negotiator:** Managers work on behalf of the organization or work unit, and subordinates, not only as a spokesperson but as negotiator. They enter into an agreement on behalf of the organization. For example, the personnel manager negotiates with trade unions and representatives of workers.

Multiple Choice Questions

1. Father of Modern Management theory is _____.
   A. Henry Fayol B. F.W. Taylor
   C. Henry Gantt D. None
2. Management can be considered as _______.
   A. Exact science B. Inexact science
   C. Psuedo science D. Either B or C
3. _______ has defined the basic problem of managing as the art of "knowing exactly what you want men to do and then see that they do it in the best and cheapest way".
   A. Henry Fayol
   B. F.W. Taylor
   C. Mary Parker Follett
   D. None of these
4. School of Management recognizes the existence of a centralized body of knowledge for the Management:
   A. System approach B. Empirical
   C. Contingency D. Operational
5. School of thought has developed ______ on the idea that there is no single best method to find solutions to Managerial problems.
   A. System approach B. Empirical
   C. Contingency D. Operational

6. Koontz and O'Donnel are the advocates of _______ approach to management.
A. System approach B. Empirical
C. Contingency D. Operational

7. According to ______ approach, management is a logical process and it can be expressed in terms of mathematical symbols and relationships.
A. Empirical
B. Management science
C. Contingency
D. Operational

8. Approach of management heavily concentrates on 'People' aspect of _______ management.
A. Human relations
B. System
C. Empirical
D. Management science

9. _______ is introduced to secure the benefits of division of labour or specialization at the supervising level under scientific management.
A. Operating management
B. Functional foremanship
C. Either A or B
D. None

10. The author of the famous book "General and Industrial Management" is _________.
A. Henry Fayol B. F.W. Taylor
C. Henry Gantt D. None

11. According to Fayol, the principles of Management are ________.
A. Rigid B. Flexible
C. Either A or B D. None

12. ____ principle states that an employee should receive orders form one superior only.
A. Unity of direction
B. Unity of command
C. Esprit de corps
D. None

13. According to ________ principle, there should always exist one head and one plan for a group of activities having the same objective.
A. Unity of direction
B. Unity of command
C. Esprit de corps
D. None

14. ______ highly suitable for large organizations having large number of managerial personnel at different levels.
A. Centralization
B. Decentralization
C. Departmentalization
D. All of these

15. _______ is the character of communication, in a formal organization by virtue of which it is accepted by a member of the organization as governing the action he contributes.
A. Responsibility B. Authority
C. Accountability D. Power

16. ________ developed the "Need Hierarchy Theory" to explain human behaviour within an organization.
A. A.H. Maslow B. Douglas McGregor
C. Herzberg D. Rensis Likert

17. ________ developed the concept of Management by Objectives.
A. A.H. Maslow B. Herbert Simon
C. Herzberg D. Peter F. Drucker

18. Management according to ______ Approach is the study of practical experience of Managers and hence such a study would provide a better understanding to the effective way of Managing an enterprise.
A. Empirical
B. Management science
C. Contingency
D. Operational

19. ______ approach is based on the idea that an organization is studied in detail and decisions are taken for each sub system, which in turn is in conformity with the total system.
A. Empirical
B. Management science
C. Contingency
D. System

20. _______ school of thought has developed on the idea that there is no single best method to find solutions to managerial problems.
A. Empirical
B. Management science
C. Contingency
D. Operational

21. _______ approach attempts to understand managerial problems and to provide suitable solutions by the application of scientific methodology.
A. Empirical
B. Management science
C. Contingency
D. Operational

22. _______ is considered as the primary function of management.
A. Organizing B. Planning
C. Staffing D. Controlling

23. MBO stands for:
A. Management of Business Objectives
B. Management By Objectives
C. Managing Business Operations
D. None of these

24. _______ is a sequence of activities to be undertaken for implementing the policies and achieving the objectives of an enterprise.
A. Procedures B. Programme
C. Rule D. Plans

25. _______ is an organizational structure which clearly defines duties, responsibilities, and authority.
A. Formal B. Informal
C. Natural D. None of these

26. _______ organization arises voluntarily or due to social interaction of people.
A. Formal
B. Informal
C. Line organization
D. All of these

27. _______ are certain assumptions about the future on the basis of which the plan will be formulated.
A. Programmes B. Planning premises
C. Planning issues D. Procedures

28. Concentration of authority of decision making at top levels of management is known as _______.
A. Concentration B. Decentralization
C. Centralization D. None of these

29. _________ is the process of searching for prospective employees and stimulating them to apply for the Job.
A. Selection B. Training
C. Recruitment D. Induction

30. ________ is the process of comparing actual performance with the standard and taking corrective Action.
A. Controlling B. Management
C. Planning D. Co-ordination

31. Value based management is essential to combine subjective and:
A. Normative phenomena
B. Objective phenomena
C. Power
D. Tangible items

32. _________ a process of integrating the interdepartmental activities as unified action towards the achievement of the common goal of the organization.
A. Controlling B. Directing
C. Co-ordination D. All of these

33. _______ refers to co-ordination between activities of a manager and his subordinates.
A. Vertical co-ordination
B. Horizontal co-ordinaiton
C. Diagonal co-ordination
D. None

34. ______ aims at visualizing and identifying deviation before they actually occur.
A. Predictive control
B. Concurrent control
C. Operational control
D. All of these

35. In ________ type of organization, workers receive instructions from various specialists.
A. Line B. Functional
C. Informal D. None

36. If duties and authority are shown in the organizational structure of the enterprise, then it is called ______.
A. Informal delegation
B. Formal delegation
C. Written delegation
D. None of these

37. ______ is the process of inducting an employee into the social set up of work.
A. Placement B. Induction
C. Absorption D. None of these

38. ________ is the activity of influencing people to strive willingly for group of objectives.
A. Motivation B. Leadership
C. Communication D. None of these

39. A leader should have ________.
A. Technical Knowledge
B. Empathy
C. Initiative
D. All of these

40. ________ is the act of recreating a core business process with the goal of improving product output, quality, or reducing costs.
A. Planning
B. CSR
C. Business process reengineering
D. None of these

41. The term "Open-Book Management" (OBM) was coined by ________ .
A. Henry Fayol B. Michael Hammer
C. Jack Stack D. None of these

42. ________ aims at making people work together for the common good of the organization.
A. communication B. conversation
C. combination D. connection

43. Consider the following basic steps involved in the process of control:
I. Identifying the strategic control points
II. Establish the standards
III. Measuring performance against standards.
IV. Correcting deviations from the standards.
The correct sequence of the above steps in the process of control is:
A. I, IV, III, II B. IV, III, II, I
C. II, I, IV, III D. II, III, I, IV

44. Match List-I with List-II and select the correct answer using the codes given below the lists:

List-I *(Management thinkers)*	**List-II** *(Contribution/work)*
I. Elton Mayo	A. Importance of integrating the company's and employee's goal
II. Frederic W. Taylor	B. Social problems of Industrial Civilisation
III. Henri Fayol	C. General and Industrial management.
IV. Many Parker Follet	D. Principles of Scientific Management

Codes:
A. I-A, II-D, III-C, IV-B
B. I-D, II-C, III-B, IV-A
C. I-B, II-D, III-C, IV-A
D. I-C, II-D, III-A, IV-B

45. An organisation structure is effective if it enables individuals to contribute to the objectives of the enterprise. This is known as:
A. Scalar Principle
B. Principle of functional definition
C. Principle of unity of objectives
D. None of these

46. Which one of the following orders indicates the correct logical order of managerial functions?
A. Organising, planning, directing, staffing, coordination and control
B. Planning, organising, staffing, directing, coordination and control
C. Planning, directing, organising, staffing, control and coordination
D. Organising, planning, staffing, directing, control and coordination

47. Effective direction does NOT depend on the:
A. Communication process
B. Forces at the subordinate level
C. Ability of the manager
D. Deployment of human resources

48. Planning refers to:
A. Looking backward
B. Looking forward
C. Looking forward and backward
D. Looking and actual performance to decide action to be taken

49. Management by exception introduces:
A. selective, responsibility oriented reporting
B. reporting of significant variances
C. requirement of full reports on performance
D. computation of actuals in different spheres of performance

50. Control refers to:
I. Establishment of standards
II. Measurement of actual performance against the set standards
III. Correction for deviation from standards

Of these statements:
A. I alone is correct
B. III alone is correct
C. I and II are correct
D. I, II, and III are correct

51. Match List-I with List-II and select the correct answer from the codes given below the lists:

List-I	**List-II**
I. Planning	A. Training
II. Staffing	B. Forecasting
III. Directing	C. Evaluating
IV. Controlling	D. Motivating
	E. Grouping

Codes :
A. I-C, II-A, III-D, IV-E
B. I-C, II-E, III-A, IV-B
C. I-B, II-A, III-D, IV-C
D. I-B, II-E, III-A, IV-C

52. In a functional organisation:
A. There are no advisors, the executives alone having the authority and competence
B. There are specialist advisors having no authority
C. The entire organisation is divided into functions with specific role for specialists
D. The organisation is divided into functions with specialists having authority

53. If a general manager asks the sales manager to recruit some sales men on his behalf, it is an instance of:
A. division of authority
B. decentralisation of authority
C. delegation of authority
D. delegation of responsibility

54. Which of the following management functions are closely related?
A. Planning and organising
B. Staffing and control
C. Planning and control
D. Planning and staffing

55. "Human Relating Approach" to management was origined by:
A. Henery Fayol B. Winslow Taylor
C. Elton Mayo D. Peter F. Drucker

56. The famous book "The Philosophy of Management" was written by:
A. Henery Fayol B. Oliver Sheldon
C. F. W. Taylor D. Urwick

57. Policy making is an important part of the process of:
A. Planning B. Co-ordinating
C. Organising D. Motivating

58. The managerial function of organising is:
A. To review and adjust plan in the light of changing conditions
B. To establish a programme for the accomplishment of objections
C. To create a structure of functions and duties to be performed by a group of people
D. To get things done through and with the help of people

59. Which of the following is the oldest type of organisation?
A. Functional organisation
B. Line organisation
C. Line and staff organisation
D. Committee organisation

60. The function of 'staff' in 'line and staff'organisation is to:
A. take advice from the line
B. advice the line
C. hold authority and responsibility
D. fix responsibility for performance of tasks in a definite manner upon certain individuals

61. Control function of management implies:
A. to bring harmony in various activities
B. to keep the work force content
C. taking corrective course of action
D. to provide sufficient finance

62. The main advantage of line and staff organisation is:
A. Simplicity
B. Specialisation
C. Availability of expert advice
D. Speedy decision making

63. General manager has delegated authority to production manager for achieving budgeted production. Who is responsible for low production to Board of Directors?
A. Production Supervisors
B. Production Manager
C. General Manager
D. None of these

64. Which of the following functions of management are more closely related?
I. Planning II. Co-ordination
III. Motivation IV. Control
A. I and II B. II and III
C. II, III, and IV D. I, II, and IV

65. Staffing includes:
I. Training II. Appraisal
III. Placement IV. Directing
A. I and III B. I, II and III
C. II and III D. I, II, III and IV

66. Match the following:

List-I	List-II
I. Need-Hierarchy Theory of Motivation	A. Taylor
II. M.B.O.	B. Maslow
III. Scientific Management	C. Herzberg
IV. Hygience Theory	D. Peter F. Drucker

Codes:
A. I-B, II-A, III-D, IV-C
B. I-C, II-B, III-D, IV-A
C. I-A, II-B, III-C, IV-D
D. I-B, II-D, III-A, IV-C

67. Span of control is narrow when the:
A. posts in the top management increases
B. posts in the middle management increases
C. posts in lower management increases
D. all of these

68. In Taylor's functional organisation there are eight foremen
I. Time and cost clerk
II. Route clerk
III. Speed boss
IV. Gang boss
V. Shop disciplinarian
VI. Instruction card clerk
VII. Repair boss
VIII. Inspector

Which of these foremen operate at the shop level?
A. I, II, III and IV
B. V, VI, VII, and VIII
C. III, IV, VII and VIII
D. IV, V, VI and VII

69. Match the following

List-I	List-II
I. Staff executives	A. Advisory function
II. Directing	B. Manpower development
III. Line executives	C. Guiding function
IV. Staffing	D. Management authority

Codes:
A. I-A, II-D, III-C, IV-B
B. I-A, II-C, III-D, IV-B
C. I-B, II-C, III-D, IV-A
D. I-B, II-A, III-C, IV-D

70. Which of the following constitute manpower planning?

I. Determining human resource requirements both quantitatively and qualitatively.
II. Finding the sources of talented individuals.
III. Planning for the human resource needs of an organisation.
IV. Reaching out to the right source for procuring the right people.

Select the correct answer using the codes given below:

Codes:

A. I, II and IV B. II and III
C. I and III D. I, II, III and IV

71. Understanding control does not signify under standing:

A. How one controls
B. What is meant by control
C. Who controls
D. What is controlled

72. Consider the following statements :
Strategic management process comprises

I. Goal setting, strategy formulation, administration and strategic control.
II. Setting courses of action attaining objective, process of seeking key areas and strategy formulation.
III. Integrating the organisation with culture.
IV. Strategic planning and acting on these plans.

Of these statements :

A. I, II and III are correct
B. II, III and IV are correct
C. I, II and IV are correct
D. I, III and IV are correct

73. Match List-I with List-II and select the correct answer using the codes given below the Lists:

List-I	**List-II**
I. Line authority	A. Some People in an organisation are vested with primary sources of authority
II. Staff authority	B. Some people in an organisation have legitimate right to expert influence on others.
III. Functional authority	C. Some people in an organisation lack independent.
IV. Formal	D. Some people have right to control activities of other departments as they relate to specific staff.

Codes :

A. I-A, II-B, III-C, IV-D
B. I-B, II-D, III-C, IV-A
C. I-A, II-C, III-D, IV-B
D. I-B, II-C, III-D, IV-A

74. Which is the most fundamental function of Management?

A. Planning B. Organising
C. Staffing D. Controlling

75. Consider the following statements:

I. MBO is a control technique in which managers devote time only on the areas of deviation.
II. MBO integrates the individual with the organisation and the organisation with the environment.
III. In MBO the control over people is Shifted to control over operations.
IV. The MBO Principle must be accompanied in practice by the principle of critical - point control.

Of these statements:

A. I and II are correct
B. II and III are correct
C. III and IV are correct
D. I and IV are correct

76. Which one of the following statements is correct?

A. Planning and controlling are essentially one and the same.
B. Controlling is a part of the planning process.

C. Controlling is a substitute for planning.
D. A control process is meaningless without pre-set goals.

77. Techniques of managerial control are useful in:
A. Selection of plant location
B. Identifying appropriate technology.
C. Profit planning
D. Conducting share holder's meetings.

78. Delegation of authority takes place when a manager thinks that:
A. The job is too difficult and hazardous
B. The job requires the high skill that he does not possess
C. He cannot look after all the demanding tasks by him self
D. He needs to punish his subordinate

79. According to the principle of "Span of control", there is:
A. A tendency to overload supervisors with too much of work
B. A limit to the number of subordinates a supervisor can effectively supervise
C. No limit to the number of subordinates a supervisor can supervise
D. A limit to delegation of authority to the subordinate

80. Establishment of management by objectives pre-supposes:
A. That limits of authority are not defined
B. That the employees are provided with result expected
C. Unlimited freedom to operate in the assigned task
D. Unlimited freedom to set goals

81. Which one of the following is the oldest form of organisation?
A. Functional organisation
B. Line organisation
C. Line and staff organisation
D. Departmentation

82. Which of the following pairs are correctly matched?

List-I	List-II
I. Planning	Sets out the objectives and complete set of policies.
II. Organisation	Enables the owner or top executive of a business to arrange, money, materials and methods.
III. Co–ordination	Orderly arrangement of group effort to provide unity of action.
IV. Control	Verifying whether everything occurs in conformity with the plan adopted, the instructions issued and principles established.

Select the correct answer using the codes given below:
Codes:
A. II, III and IV B. II and IV
C. I, III and IV D. I, II and III

83. Which one of the following monitors critical inputs and suggests preventive measures in the form of corrective action to correct inputs and processes?
A. Feed back control
B. Feed forward control
C. Budgetory control
D. Operational control

84. When management pays attention to more important areas and when the day-to-day routine problems are looked after by lower level management, it is known as:
A. Management by Objectives
B. Management by Exception
C. Participative Management
D. Critical Path Method

85. The following steps are involved in managing by objectives:
I. Preliminary setting of objectives at the top

II. Setting subordinates objectives
III. Tying resources with the goals
IV. Clarifying the organisational steps is
A. I, II, III, IV B. I, II, IV, III
C. I, III, II, IV D. I, IV, II, III

86. In management principles, grid refers to:
A. Diverse managerial styles
B. Coordination
C. Communication
D. Motivation

87. The process of determining how to pursue long term goals with the expected resources available to the organisation is called:
A. Operational planning
B. Strategic planning
C. Intermediate planning
D. Tactical planning

88. Which one of the following is the most appropriate management control technique for timely completion of a project?
A. Organisation chart
B. Management by objectives
C. PERT
D. Span of control

89. Hawthorne studies have underlined the significance of which of the following?
A. System approach to management
B. Contingency approach to management
C. Modern approach to management
D. Human relations approach to management

90. Is management by exception, one of the important principles of control?
A. Yes; because only the unusual deviations from standards should be brought to the notice of the management
B. No; because less significant deviations and the actual performance according to the standards are not brought to the notice of the management
C. Yes; because exception principle saves time of the subordinates staff
D. No; because the manager can attend too operative decisions, and the strategic problems can be left to the technocrats

91. The first step of the control process actually gets initiated in the managerial function of:
A. Staffing B. Planning
C. Communication D. Coordination

92. Consider the following.
I. Measurement
II. Projection
III. Selection
IV. Observation
V. Comparison
VI. Decision making

The correct sequence of the above ingredients of management by exceptions is:
A. I, II, III, IV, V, VI
B. I, II, III, V, IV, VI
C. I, II, III, VI, IV, V
D. I, II, III, IV, VI, V

93. Kurt Lewins' three phases of organizational change consist of:
A. Unfreezing, changing, feedback
B. Changing, refreezing, feedback
C. Unfreezing, evaluation, refreezing
D. Unfreezing, changing, refreezing

94. Which one of the following statements is not correct?
A. Management by objectives is a philosophy of management
B. Management by objectives is an approach of management
C. Management by objectives is a process of participative management
D. Management by objectives is a control technique

95. Which one of the following functions does not relate to O & M Division?
A. To enlarge the organisation
B. To improve organisation
C. To simplify methods
D. To create and maintain an efficient administrative machinery

96. Contingency school of management says that management is:
A. Practice - oriented
B. Principle - oriented
C. Result - oriented
D. Profit and loss - oriented

97. Which among the following is the oldest and simplest device for achieving coordination?
A. Hierarchy B. Planning
C. Incentives D. Rules

98. Which one among the following is an instance of participative management?
A. Board of Directors
B. Trade Unions
C. Work committees
D. Task force

99. Which one of the following is the correct sequence in terms of the four management functions, first identified by Henry Fayol?
A. Planning, organising, staffing and coordinating
B. Planning, organising, leading and controlling
C. Planning, motivating, directing and reporting
D. Planning, staffing, communicating and leading

100. According to behavioural scientists, organisation means the structure of:
A. Physical facilities
B. Tasks and relationships
C. Behaviour of the management with the working force
D. Attitude of workers with the management

Answers

1	2	3	4	5	6	7	8	9	10
A	D	B	D	C	D	B	A	B	A
11	12	13	14	15	16	17	18	19	20
B	B	A	B	B	A	B	D	D	C
21	22	23	24	25	26	27	28	29	30
B	A	B	B	A	B	B	C	C	A
31	32	33	34	35	36	37	38	39	40
B	B	D	B	A	A	A	B	D	C
41	42	43	44	45	46	47	48	49	50
C	A	B	D	C	B	C	D	B	D
51	52	53	54	55	56	57	58	59	60
C	D	C	C	C	B	A	C	B	B
61	62	63	64	65	66	67	68	69	70
A	C	C	D	B	D	B	C	B	C
71	72	73	74	75	76	77	78	79	80
A	C	C	A	B	D	C	C	B	B
81	82	83	84	85	86	87	88	89	90
B	C	B	B	A	C	A	C	D	A
91	92	93	94	95	96	97	98	99	100
B	A	D	C	A	C	B	C	A	B

◆◆◆◆◆

2 LEADERSHIP

Leadership is very essential for managing a country, organization and team. Leadership has been defined in different ways by different set of scholars. It is defined as the ability to influence a group towards the achievement of a vision or set of goals. Keith, Devis observe that, 'Without leadership, an organisation is but a middle of men and machines ..... leadership transforms potential into reality. It is the ultimate act which brings to success all the potential that is in an organization and its people.

In 1938, Chester Bernord gave a new definition of leadership and stated that, leadership is the ability of a superior to influence the behaviour of subordinates and persuade them to follow a particular course of action. A recent theorist on leadership, Williams states that, "Leadership is an interactive art in which the leader is dancing with the context, the problem, the faction and the objective.

A leader's actions significantly impact the followers daily life. Leadership impacts the individual followers as well as the team, department and entire organization. Leadership can be conceptualized in three different ways. Such as skill or ability, the second is the relationship between leader and follower and the third is a dynamic social process. An effective leader can guide their followers towards achieving specific goals in a manner aligned with their vision.

TASKS OF A LEADER

A leader plays a vital role in guiding individuals and groups toward the achievement of common goals. The effectiveness of an organization largely depends on how well a leader performs their tasks. The major tasks of a leader are discussed below.

1. **Setting Goals and Vision:** A leader sets clear goals and develops a vision for the future. This vision provides direction to the group and helps members understand what they are expected to achieve. Clear goals motivate people and align individual efforts with organizational objectives.
2. **Planning and Organizing:** Planning involves deciding in advance what actions need to be taken to achieve goals, while organizing involves arranging resources such as people, time, and materials. A leader assigns duties according to the skills and abilities of individuals to ensure efficient work performance.
3. **Decision Making:** Decision making is a crucial task of a leader. Leaders must evaluate different alternatives, assess risks, and choose the most suitable course of action. Effective decision making helps in solving problems and achieving organizational goals smoothly.
4. **Motivation:** Motivation is the process of encouraging employees to work willingly and enthusiastically. Leaders motivate subordinates through rewards, recognition, promotions, and positive feedback. Motivated employees show higher productivity and commitment.

5. **Communication:** A leader must communicate clearly and effectively. This includes giving instructions, explaining policies, and sharing information. Two-way communication allows leaders to receive feedback and understand employee concerns, which improves trust and cooperation.
6. **Supervision and Guidance:** Supervision ensures that work is performed as planned. Leaders guide employees by providing instructions, training, and support. They also correct mistakes and help employees improve their skills and performance.
7. **Maintaining Discipline:** Maintaining discipline involves ensuring that rules, regulations, and standards are followed. A leader must handle misconduct, resolve conflicts, and enforce discipline fairly to maintain order and harmony in the organization.
8. **Team Building:** A leader builds a strong and united team by encouraging cooperation, trust, and mutual respect among members. Team building helps reduce conflicts, improve communication, and increase overall efficiency.
9. **Developing Subordinates:** Leaders are responsible for the growth and development of their followers. They provide training, mentoring, and opportunities for learning. Developing subordinates improves their confidence and prepares them for future leadership roles.
10. **Coordination:** Coordination involves integrating the efforts of different individuals and departments. A leader ensures that everyone works together harmoniously toward common goals, avoiding duplication of work and confusion.
11. **Representation:** A leader represents the group or organization to higher authorities, customers, and external agencies. They communicate the needs and concerns of the group and protect its interests while maintaining a positive image of the organization.

LEADERSHIP STYLES

Leadership style refers to the way a leader provides direction, makes decisions, and motivates subordinates. Different situations require different leadership styles, and an effective leader knows how to adapt their style according to the needs of the organization and employees.

1. **Autocratic Leadership Style:** Autocratic leadership style is a leadership approach where the leader makes all decisions alone, exercises strict control, and expects subordinates to follow instructions without input. It is effective for quick decision-making and in situations requiring discipline.
2. **Democratic Leadership Style:** Democratic leadership style is a type of leadership in which the leader encourages participation and involvement of subordinates in decision making. The leader values employees' opinions, promotes open communication, and shares authority while taking final responsibility for decisions. This style improves motivation, teamwork, and job satisfaction.
3. **Laissez-Faire Leadership Style:** Laissez-Faire leadership style is a form of leadership in which the leader gives maximum freedom to subordinates to make decisions and carry out their work independently. The leader provides minimal supervision and control, making this style suitable for skilled and self-motivated employees.
4. **Transactional Leadership Style:** Transactional leadership style is a leadership approach where the leader focuses on performance, rewards, and punishments. It emphasizes clear roles, rules, and achieving short-term goals efficiently.
5. **Transformational Leadership Style:** Transformational leadership style is a leadership approach where the leader inspires and motivates followers to achieve more than expected, encourages innovation, and focuses on personal and organizational growth.

6. **Bureaucratic Leadership Style:** Bureaucratic leadership style is a leadership approach where the leader strictly follows rules, policies, and procedures, maintains formal authority, and ensures consistency and order in the organization.
7. **Situational Leadership Style:** Bureaucratic leadership style is a leadership approach where the leader strictly follows rules, policies, and procedures, maintains formal authority, and ensures consistency and order in the organization.

THEORIES OF LEADERSHIP

In influencing the people in the organization towards the goals of the organization, there have been various approaches adopted by different set of leaders, as one model may not be suitable for different organizations with different set of objectives. Moreover, such models or theories of leadership also depend on the qualities that a leader inherit or display in managing her/his team. Some of the theories of leadership ranging from conventional theories to contemporary theories have been dealt with over here, the chief of them being the following:

Great Man Theory: Great Man Theory suggests that leaders are born with natural qualities that make them capable of leading; leadership cannot be taught or developed.

Trait Theory: Trait Theory suggests that effective leaders are born with certain inherent qualities, such as intelligence, confidence, integrity, and communication skills. These traits distinguish leaders from non-leaders and increase the likelihood of success. However, the theory does not account for situational factors or the possibility of developing leadership through experience.

Behavioural Theories: Behavioral Theories focus on what leaders do rather than their personal traits. They emphasize that leadership can be learned and developed through actions and behaviors. Leaders may be task-oriented, focusing on goals, or people-oriented, focusing on relationships and employee welfare, depending on what is most effective in a given situation.

Situational Theories: Situational Theories suggest that there is no single best leadership style. Effective leadership depends on the situation and the readiness or maturity of followers. Leaders must adapt their style—such as directing, coaching, supporting, or delegating—based on the abilities, experience, and motivation of their team to achieve optimal results.

Transactional Theory of Leadership: Transactional Leadership Theory focuses on structured tasks, performance, and rewards or punishments. Leaders clarify roles and expectations, monitor performance, and use incentives to achieve short-term goals efficiently. It emphasizes discipline and routine management, ensuring tasks are completed correctly but offers limited scope for creativity or innovation.

Transformational Theory of Leadership: Transformational Leadership Theory emphasizes inspiring and motivating followers, encouraging innovation, and fostering personal and organizational growth beyond ordinary expectations.

SUCCESSFUL LEADER VS EFFECTIVE LEADER

Leadership is an essential aspect of organizational and social success. However, not all leaders are the same, and leadership can be evaluated in different ways. Two common concepts in leadership studies are successful leadership and effective leadership. While they may seem similar, there are significant differences between the two.

Successful Leader

A successful leader is primarily judged by the outcomes and achievements they attain. Success is often measured in terms of status, recognition, wealth, or the ability to achieve organizational or personal goals. A successful leader may achieve high results, gain popularity, or rise to a top position in an organization.

Characteristics of a Successful Leader:

- Focuses on results and achievements.
- Gains recognition and fame within and outside the organization.
- May use authority and power to reach objectives.
- Often driven by personal ambition or organizational targets.

Example: A leader who increases a company's profit significantly or leads a political movement to victory may be considered successful.

Limitation: Success does not always mean that the leader has built strong teams, developed followers, or ensured long-term sustainability. A successful leader may attain goals even by ignoring ethical or relational aspects.

Effective Leader

An effective leader is judged not only by results but also by how those results are achieved. Effectiveness emphasizes the leader's ability to influence, guide, and develop people, ensuring sustained performance and organizational growth. An effective leader balances results with people's development and long-term objectives.

Characteristics of an Effective Leader:

- Achieves goals while maintaining team morale and motivation.
- Builds trust, loyalty, and cooperation among followers.
- Communicates effectively and develops skills in others.
- Makes decisions ethically and considers long-term impact.

Example: A leader who successfully completes projects while empowering employees, promoting innovation, and creating a positive work culture is considered effective.

Strength: Effective leadership ensures both performance and sustainability, creating a positive impact on individuals and the organization.

Key Differences between Successful and Effective Leaders

Aspect	Successful Leader	Effective Leader
Focus	Achieving goals and personal success	Achieving goals and developing others
Measurement	Based on outcomes, status, or fame	Based on results, follower satisfaction, and sustainability
Relationship with Followers	May ignore follower' needs	Values and develops followers' potential
Approach	Results-oriented, sometimes authoritarian	Balanced, ethical, and participative
Impact	Short-term achievements	Long-term growth and positive culture

Multiple Choice Questions

1. Match :

List I

(*a*) A store clerk tells the top executive when to buy a commodity.

(*b*) A youth rushing to save life and property of a house on fire commands neighbours to collect water.

(*c*) A newly elected secretary advises members about their duties.

(*d*) A leader attempts to bend his followers to his will in most kind of work.

List II

1. Leadership by personality
2. Leadership by position

3. Leadership by function
4. Leadership by situation

Codes:

	(*a*)	(*b*)	(*c*)	(*d*)
A.	1	3	2	4
B.	2	4	3	1
C.	3	4	2	1
D.	3	2	4	1

2. The Greatman theory of leadership led to the rise of :

A. The Behavioural theory of leadership
B. The Trait theory of leadership
C. The situational theory of leadership
D. None of the above

3. The hollmark of leadership is :

A. Achievement of goals of the organisation
B. Settlement of disputes in the organisation
C. Capacity to influence others to follow
D. Maintaining the core values of the organisation and its distinctive identity

4. Assertion (A): Functionally, a leader is partly a manager.

Reason (R): A leader does all the management functions.

Codes:

A. A and R are true and R explains A
B. A and R are true but R does not explain A
C. A is true but R is false
D. A is false but R is true

5. Assertion (A): The terms leader and manager are interchangeable.

Reason (R): Leadership is a sub-class of management.

Codes:

A. A and R are true and R explains A
B. A and R are true but R does not explain A
C. A is true but R is false
D. A is false but R is true

6. Assertion (A): The laissez-faire style of leadership depends on the leader to provide external motivation.

Reason (R): The leader principally assumes the role of group member and supply materials when asked.

Codes:

A. A and R are true and R is the correct explanation of A
B. A and R are true but R is not the correct explanation of A
C. A is true but R is false
D. A is false but R is true

7. Assertion (A): In contrast with trait theory, behavioural theory attempts to describe leadership in terms of what leaders do.

Reason (R): Trait theory has failed to recognize the influence of situational factors on leadership:

Codes:

A. A and R are true and R is the correct explanation of A
B. A and R are true but R is not the correct explanation of A
C. A is true but R is false
D. A is false but R is true

8. Match the following.

List I

(*a*) Leadership is often made or broken by circumstance.
(*b*) A person is born with the talent for personal leadership; he must learn management leadership.
(*c*) We should think not only of what the leader does to the group, but also of what the group does to the leader.
(*d*) Leadership depends upon the individual, the followers and the conditions.

List II

1. Allen
2. Follet
3. Barnard
4. Millet

Codes:

	(*a*)	(*b*)	(*c*)	(*d*)
A.	2	3	1	4
B.	2	4	3	1
C.	4	2	3	1
D.	4	1	2	3

9. Who has distinguished between leadership of position, leadership of personality and leadership of function?

A. Barnard B. Millet
C. Mooney D. Follet

10. Acoding to Barnard, which is not a function of leadership?

A. Manipulation of means
B. Stimulation of co-ordinated action
C. Defence of institutional integrity
D. Control of the instrumentality of action

11. The most important quality of leadership, according to Barnard is:

A. Persuasiveness
B. Decisiveness
C. Responsibility and Intellectual capacity
D. Vitality and Endurance

12. Who has analyses leadership in terms of circular response?

A. C.I. Barnard B. Mooney
C. M.P. Follet D. Millet

13. Match the following.

List I	List II
(*a*) Mooney	1. The essential circumstances of leadership are political and institutional
(*b*) Millet	2. Leadership is the form that authority assumes when it enters into process
(*c*) Follet	3. Leadership—goes beyond routine and taps bases of power beyond those that are organisationally decreed
(*d*) Katz & kahn	4. We now think of the leader as being influenced by his group

Codes:

	(*a*)	(*b*)	(*c*)	(*d*)
A.	2	1	4	3
B.	2	4	3	1
C.	4	3	1	2
D.	3	4	2	1

14. Political responsiveness quality of leadership was highlighted by:

A. Terry B. Barnard
C. Appleby D. Millet

15. The democratic or participative style of leadership became popular during the era of:

A. Contingency model of leadership—Victor Vroom
B. Life cycle approach to leadership—Blake & Mounton
C. Path–Goal theory of leadership—Martin Evans and Robert House
D. Managerial Grid—Hersey & Blanchard

16. Which of the following pairs is correctly matched?

A. Contingency model of leadership → Victor Vroom
B. Life cycle approach of leadership → Blake & Mountan
C. Path–Goal theory of leadership → Mortin Evans and Robert House
D. Managerial Grid → Herrey & Blanchard

17. Match the following.

List I	List II
(*a*) Continuum of	1. Phillip Yetton leadership styles
(*b*) Three-dimensional	2. Tonnenbaum model of leadership
(*c*) Managerial Grid	3. W. Reddin
(*d*) Decision-participation model of leadership	4. Blake
	5. Kurt Lewin

Codes:

	(*a*)	(*b*)	(*c*)	(*d*)
A.	3	1	2	5
B.	5	3	1	4
C.	2	4	1	5
D.	2	3	4	1

18. Which of the following pairs is not correctly matched?

A. Michigan Leadership studies — Rensis Likert and others

B. Systems of management — Rensis Likert
C. Ohio state leadership studies — Fleishman and others
D. Iowa leadership studies — R. Tannenbaum

19. According to which theory, leadership is multidimensional?
A. Behavioural theory
B. Situational theory
C. Trait theory
D. None of the above

20. Which of the following is not an important variable in fielder's situational theory of leadership?
A. The leader and the subordinates
B. The goals of the organisation
C. The structure of organisation
D. The socio-economic and political conditions.

21. According to situational theory of leadership, which of the following statements is true?
A. It is possible to indicate a leadership style which is applicable to all organisations under all circumstances
B. The leader should always be considerate toward his subordinate
C. The leader should always keep strict control over his subordinates
D. The leader has to very is style of functioning according to the situation prevailing within the organisation

22. Which of the following style of leadership are generally considered effective in most of the organisations.
1. Autocratic 2. Democratic
3. Laissez-fair

Codes:
A. 1 and 2 only B. 1 and 3 only
C. 2 and 3 only D. 1, 2 and 3

23. According to Hersey and Blanchand's theory of leadership the immature subordinates need:
A. Hight task-low relationship style of leadership
B. A very high degree of consideration from the leader in task and relationship
C. Just a little guidance from the leader
D. Complete delegation of power

24. According to Hersey and Blanchard's theory of leadership fully mature subordinates need:
A. Low task-high relationship style of leadership
B. Low task-low relationship style of leadership
C. High task-high relationship style of leadership
D. High task-low relationship style of leadershp

25. Which of the following statements about the meaning of leadership is least applicable?
A. Leadership is the art of coordinating the work of individuals and groups to achieve desired ends.
B. Leadership is the art of influencing and persuading people to work together to achieve common objectives.
C. Leadrship is the exercise of authority and making of decision.
D. Leadership is the initiation of acts which result in a consistent pattern of group interaction directed towards the solution of a mutual problem.

26. Which of the following does not belong to the list of leadership traits given by various scholars?
A. Strict observance of rules and regulations under all circumstances
B. Willingness to assume responsibility
C. Emotional stability and maturity with capacity to use power with rostraint and wisdom
D. Persuasiveness and capacity to deal with subordinates

27. Trait theory indicates that:
1. There are no distinguishable traits that differentiate between leaders and non-leaders.
2. Some traits like human relations skills and high intellectual capacity are generally found in successful leaders.

3. There are distinguishable traits that can distinguish between successful and unsucessful leaders.

A. 1 and 2 B. only 2 and 3
C. 1 and 3 D. only 3

28. On which of the following theoretical grounds, trait theories of leadership have been questioned?

1. They merely describe the leadership traits.
2. They do not explain why any particular traits should make a successful leader.
3. They consider each trait separately; while in complex human personality all the traits act in combination.

Codes:

A. 1 and 2 only B. 2 and 3 only
C. 1 and 3 only D. 1, 2 and 3

29. With reference to comparison of trait theories and behavioural theories, which of the following statements is not true?

A. Both of theories has tried to match the leadership traits and the leadership behaviour.
B. Behavioural theories concentrated on the study of leadership behaviour, while trait theories studied leadership qualities.
C. Behavioural theories tried to find out what the leaders did; while the trait theories studied what the leaders were.
D. Behavioural theories tried to establish a relationship between leader behaviour and effectiveness; while trait theories only described leadership qualities.

30. The behaviouralists studied leadership behaviour in terms of:

1. Traits of leaders
2. Effectiveness of leadership
3. Leadership styles.

Codes:

A. 1 and 2 only B. 2 and 3 only
C. 1 and 3 only D. 1, 2 and 3

31. The functions of a leader according to behaviourablists are:

1. Problem solving functions.
2. Maintenance of good inter-personal relations.
3. Functions relating to strict maintenance of discipline in organisation.

Codes:

A. 1 and 2 only B. 2 and 3 only
C. 1 and 3 only D. 1, 2 and 3

32. Which of the following leadership styles were studied in behavioural theories?

1. Task oriented leadership style
2. Employee oriented leadership style
3. Charismatic leadership style

Code:

A. 1 and 2 only B. 2 and 3 only
C. 1 and 3 only D. 1, 2 and 3

33. Which of the following statements about the features of the-taskoriented leadership style is incorrect?

A. The leader closely supervises the work of the subordinates and directs them.
B. These is an atmosphere of complete trust and confidence between the leader and the subordinates.
C. The leader is very much concerned with getting the job done.
D. The leader is not very much concerned with the growth and development of the subordinates.

34. Which of the following statements about the employee-oriented style of leadership is not correct?

A. The leader tries to motivate the workers rather than control or direct them.
B. The leader tries for the welfare of the subordinates but does not trust them.
C. The leader resorts to group decision-making, rather than taking all the decisions himself.
D. The leader tries to develop the capabilities of his subordinates.

35. Studies of leadership behaviour by Blake and Moute describe different types of leadership. In this context which of the following categories is not correctly matched styles.

A. Impoverished little concern for people, as well as for production
B. Country club high concern for people, but lack production orientation
C. Team high concern for people, high concern for production
D. Middle of the road, Moderate concern for people

36. In likert's (Four Systems Approach) which of the following characteristics is not true system?
A. The leader defines the work in great detail
B. There is free communcation between the leader and the subordinate
C. The leader does not trust the subordinates and closely supervises them
D. Fear is the main motivator

37. The Likert's Four Systems Model, System IV has which of the following characteristics?
A. The leader cares for the subordinates, but does not trust them fully
B. The subordinates are not given freedom in the implementation of decision
C. The leader consults the subordinates and gives a lot of weight to their opinions
D. Communication within the organisation is based on complete trust.

38. The situational factor have been used in which of the following ways?
1. To identify which of the following factors are most important in a given set of circumstances.
2. To find out the leadership style that would be most effective in those circumstances.
3. To give the leaders warning signals in difficult organisational situation.

Codes:
A. 1 and 2 only B. 2 and 3 only
C. 1 and 3 only D. 1, 2 and 3

39. Which of the following statements about motivation is not correct?
A. Motivation means acting in particular manner with profit motive
B. Motivation refers to goal directed behaviour
C. Motivation results from some inner drive
D. Motivation results in improved performance

40. Match the following:

List I	List II
(*a*) Hygiene theory	1. Herzberg
(*b*) Theory X and Y	2. Paul Hersey
(*c*) Life cycle theory of leadership	3. Mclelland
(*d*) Achievement Motivation Theory	4. McGregor

Codes:

	(*a*)	(*b*)	(*c*)	(*d*)
A.	1	2	3	4
B.	2	1	4	3
C.	4	3	2	1
D.	1	4	2	3

41. Match List I with List II.

List I	List II
(*a*) Job enrichment	1. Maslow
(*b*) Transactional analysis	2. Herzberg
(*c*) Hierarchy of needs	3. Berne
(*d*) Situational leadership	4. Fiedler

Codes:

	(*a*)	(*b*)	(*c*)	(*d*)
A.	2	3	1	4
B.	3	4	1	2
C.	2	3	4	1
D.	1	2	4	3

42. Assertion (A): Clarity of goals in an organisation an wellstructured organisation result in effectiveness of the leader.

Reason (R): A leader in such a situation has personal qualities and traits.

Codes:
A. A and R are true and R is the correct explanation of A
B. A and R are true but R is not the correct explanation of A
C. A is true but R is false
D. A is false but R is true

43. Assertion (A): Orders issued in general terms encounter problems of interpretation and implementation.

Reason (R): Most of the time is consumed in the organisations by interpretations and re-interpretation of orders to concrete situation.

Codes:

A. A and R are true and R is the correct explanation of A
B. A and R are true but R is not the correct explanation of A
C. A is true but R s false
D. A is false but R is true

44. Match the following:

List I	List II
(*a*) RJS Baker	1. Leadership and Administration
(*b*) Herbert A. Simon	2. Administration theory and Public Administration
(*c*) Phillip Selznik	3. Motivation and Personality
(*d*) A.H. Maslow	4. The New Science of Management Decision

Codes:

	(*a*)	(*b*)	(*c*)	(*d*)
A.	1	2	4	3
B.	2	3	1	4
C.	2	4	1	3
D.	4	1	2	3

45. Which of the following are the correct pairs? Select the correct answer from the codes given below.

1. Authoritarian Leader — Recognition of individuality of the workers.
2. Democratic Leader — Participation and persuation oriented
3. Authoritarian Leadership style — Scientific Management School
4. Structure and consideration — Managerial grade.

Codes:

A. 1, 2 and 3 B. 2, 3 and 4
C. 1, 2, 3 and 4 D. 3 and 4

46. "The time has come to substitude word leadership for Management." This statement was made by:

A. Lawrence A Appley
B. Henry Mintzberg
C. Dr May Smith
D. Henry Fayol

47. Which of the following is the correct pair in the context of Leadership in different management systems I to IV as described by R. Likert Give the correct answer from the codes given below?

1. Exploitative, Authoritative System–1
2. Consultative System–2
3. Benenvolent Authoriative System–3
4. Participative group System–4

Codes:

A. 1, 2 and 4 B. 2, 3 and 4
C. 1, 2, 3 and 4 D. 1, 2 and 3

48. 3D theory of leadership styles was propounded by which of the following thinkers?

A. Fred E Fielder
B. William J Reddin
C. A Etzional
D. Robert R Blake and J.S. Monton.

49. 'Leadership' is one of the controlling functions of management, according to :

A. Prof. Munro B. Prof. Henri Fayol
C. Urwick D. Terry

50. Which are the qualities of a true leader according to Proff. Terry?

A. Energetic character, emotional stability and strength
B. Knowledge of human relations, personal motivation and capacity to communicate with skill
C. Teaching ability, social skill and technical competence
D. All of the above

51. Who formulated the leadership contigency model?

A. Fred E. Fiedler B. A.W. Falpin
C. Rensis Likert D. None of the above

52. Prof. Allen has drown a line of distinction between personal leadership and:
A. management leadership
B. political leadership
C. social leadership
D. economic leadership

53. Who emphasised that there is relationship between the nature of the job and the most desirable leadership-style for maximum leadership-effectiveness?
A. Leland P. Bradford
B. Victor H. Vroom
C. Robert J. House
D. Fred E. Fiedler

54. Who observed that there are almosts as many definitions of leadership as there are people who have tried to define it.
A. Stogdill B. Peter Druker
C. George R. Terry D. None of the above

55. Who defines leadership as the ability to secure desirable actions from a group of followings voluntarily with out the use of coercion?
A. Keith Davis B. Max Weber
C. Aford and Beatty D. Stogdill

56. According to whom leadership is the ability to persuade others to seek defined objectives, enthusiastically.
A. Peter Druker B. Stogdill
C. Keith Davis D. None of the above

57. Which type of leadership is more successful, especially in a crisis or emergency situation?
A. Democratic leadership
B. Autocratic leadership
C. Laissez-faire leadership
D. None of the above

58. In which type of leadership is the entire group involved in and accepts responsibility for goal setting and achievement?
A. Autocratic leadership
B. Democratic leadership
C. Laissez-faire leadeship
D. None of the above

59. In .... leadership the leader shows a greater concern for his people than for high production.
A. Autocratic B. Democratic
C. Laissez-faire D. None of the above

60. In which type of leadership does the leader only provide information, materials and facilities to his men to enable them to accomplish group objectives?
A. Free-rein or Laissez-faire
B. Democratic
C. Autocratic
D. None of the above

61. The University of Michigan Leadership studies, divided leadership into:
A. Employee - oriented
B. Production - oriented
C. Both the above
D. None of the above

62. In which type of leadership the leader alone etermines policy and makes plans?
A. Autocratic leadership
B. Democratic leadership
C. Free-rein or Laissez fair leadership
D. None of the above

63. Which type of leadership can increase efficiency, save time and get quick results?
A. Autocratic leadership
B. Democratic leadership
C. Free-rein or Laissez leadership
D. None of the above

64. According to ...., a leader's style is influenced by his views of man is work situations.
A. Max weber B. Taylor
C. Riggs D. Douglas McGregor

65. Who wrote the article, "The conditions of effective leadership in the Industrial organization"?
A. Douglas McGregor
B. Sears
C. Woodward
D. Riggs

66. The integrative of leadership should include the following variables:

A. Leader's awareness of self
B. Group's characteristics
C. Situatinal characteristics
D. All of the above

67. .... emphasised that leadership effectiveness is strongly influence by the follower's style and expectation.

A. Victor H. Vroom
B. Leland D. Benne
C. Renold Lippet
D. None of the above

68. .... stressed that there is relationship between the nature of the job and the most desirable leadership style or maximum leadership effectiveness.

A. V.H. Vroom B. F.E. Fiedler
C. D. Benne D. L.P. Bradford

69. .... of motivation are those which explain how behaviour is energised and directed.

A. The content theories
B. The reinforcement theories
C. The process theories
D. None of the above

70. Who defined "Leadership is the activity of influencing people to strive willing for group objectives"?

A. G.R. Terry B. J.R. Weschler
C. Fred Massarik D. None of the above

71. George R. Terry's definition fo leadership laid emphasison.

A. Willingness to accept
B. Compulsion to influence people
C. Both of the above
D. None of the above

72. On which of the following approach the Michigan leadership studies are based?

A. Attitude criterion
B. Trait–approach
C. Behaviour approch
D. None of the above

73. Which theory is connected with the democratic leadership style?

A. Theory X B. Theory Z
C. Theory Y D. None of the above

74. A leader's primary responsibility is to ________ the vision and direction of the organization.

A. create B. maintain
C. delegate D. communicate

75. Effective leadership requires the ability to ________ and inspire others towards a common goal.

A. discourage B. direct
C. empower D. force

76. The task of a leader often includes ________ challenges that arise within a team or organization.

A. ignoring B. solving
C. avoiding D. creating

77. A key aspect of leadership is the ability to ________ decisions that align with the organization's values.

A. reverse B. delay
C. make D. reject

78. Leaders are expected to ________ team members, helping them to grow both personally and professionally.

A. criticize B. support
C. dismiss D. control

79. One of the tasks of a leader is to ensure that there is ________ within the team.

A. conflict B. clarity
C. confusion D. frustration

80. A leader must be able to ________ resources efficiently to meet organizational objectives.

A. waste B. ignore
C. allocate D. hide

81. In times of crisis, the leader's role is to ________ the team and maintain focus on the mission.

A. panic B. demotivate
C. guide D. criticize

82. A leader's success is often measured by their ability to ________ others to achieve collective goals.

A. control B. manipulate
C. inspire D. ignore

83. Leaders must be skilled at ________ and resolving conflicts that arise within their team.

A. avoiding B. encouraging
C. escalating D. managing

84. The task of a leader includes creating an environment where ________ can thrive.

A. failure B. creativity
C. resistance D. isolation

85. An effective leader is expected to ________ their team's strengths and weaknesses.

A. ignore B. recognize
C. hide D. challenge

86. A leader must be able to ________ under pressure while making decisions for the team.

A. panic B. lead
C. fail D. hide

87. Leaders should ________ a culture of continuous improvement and learning within their team.

A. discourage B. maintain
C. enforce D. foster

88. The leader's task is to establish ________ that guide the team towards success.

A. obstacles B. rules
C. rewards D. visions

89. Match the leadership style with its primary characteristic:

Leadership Style	Characteristic
(*a*) Autocratic Leadership	1. Emphasizes inspiring and motivating followers.
(*b*) Transformational Leadership	2. Focuses on strict rules and obedience.
(*c*) Laissez-Faire Leadership	3. Delegates decision making to employees.
(*d*) Transactional Leadership	4. Focuses on rewards and punishments based on performance.

	(*a*)	(*b*)	(*c*)	(*d*)
A.	2	1	3	4
B.	2	1	4	3
C.	1	2	3	4
D.	1	2	4	3

90. Match the leadership style with the typical behavior of the leader:

Leadership Style	Leader's Behavior
(*a*) Democratic Leadership	1. Leader provides clear directives without feedback.
(*b*) Charismatic Leadership	2. Leader seeks input from team members and encourages participation.
(*c*) Servant Leadership	3. Leader focuses on serving the team and empowering them.
(*d*) Bureaucratic	4. Leader follows strict rules and procedures in decision-making.

	(*a*)	(*b*)	(*c*)	(*d*)
A.	1	2	3	4
B.	1	2	4	3
C.	2	1	3	4
D.	2	1	4	3

91. Match the leadership style with its typical decision-making process:

Leadership Style	Decision-Making Process
(*a*) Paternalistic Leadership	1. The leader makes decisions without consulting others.
(*b*) Coaching Leadership	2. The leader uses coaching to help team members make decisions.
(*c*) Autocratic Leadership	3. The leader provides guidance but gives employees some

decision-making authority.

(*d*) Democratic Leadership — 4. The leader encourages team input and makes decisions collaboratively.

	(*a*)	(*b*)	(*c*)	(*d*)
A.	2	1	3	4
B.	2	1	4	3
C.	3	2	4	1
D.	3	2	1	4

92. Match the leadership style with the primary focus of the leader:

Leadership Style	**Primary Focus of the Leader**
(*a*) Transactional Leadership	1. Focuses on long term goals and vision.
(*b*) Laissez-Faire Leadership	2. Focuses on clear rules and structured goals.
(*c*) Visionary Leadership	3. Focuses on motivation and rewards for performance.
(*d*) Servant Leadership	4. Focuses on empowering and helping employees grow.

	(*a*)	(*b*)	(*c*)	(*d*)
A.	4	3	2	1
B.	1	2	3	4
C.	3	2	4	1
D.	3	2	1	4

93. Match the leadership style with its impact on employee autonomy:

Leadership Style	**Impact on Employee Autonomy**
(*a*) Autocratic Leadership	1. Provides limited autonomy to employees.
(*b*) Laissez-Faire Leadership	2. Employees are given high levels of autonomy.
(*c*) Coaching Leadership	3. Encourages independence but with guidance.
(*d*) Democratic Leadership	4. Involves employees in decision-making and gives them some autonomy.

	(*a*)	(*b*)	(*c*)	(*d*)
A.	2	3	1	4
B.	2	3	4	1
C.	1	2	3	4
D.	1	2	4	3

94. Match the leadership style with its approach to motivation:

Leadership Style	**Approach to Motivation**
(*a*) Transactional Leadership	1. Motivation based on intrinsic rewards and personal development.
(*b*) Charismatic Leadership	2. Motivation based on recognition and tangible rewards.
(*c*) Visionary Leadership	3. Motivation based on the leader's enthusiasm and vision.
(*d*) Democratic Leadership	4. Motivation based on collaborative decision-making.

	(*a*)	(*b*)	(*c*)	(*d*)
A.	2	3	1	4
B.	2	3	4	1
C.	1	2	3	4
D.	1	2	4	3

95. Match the leadership style with the typical leadership actions:

Leadership Style	**Typical Leadership Actions**
(*a*) Bureaucratic Leadership	1. Encourages creativity and innovation.
(*b*) Autocratic Leadership	2. Focuses on managing people through strict policies.

(*c*) Transformational Leadership — 3. Provides inspiration and motivation to employees to go beyond their self-interest.

(*d*) Servant Leadership — 4. Puts the needs of the employees first and helps them grow.

	(*a*)	(*b*)	(*c*)	(*d*)
A.	2	1	3	4
B.	2	1	4	3
C.	1	2	3	4
D.	1	2	4	3

96. Match the leadership style with its view of authority:

Leadership Style	View of Authority
(*a*) Paternalistic Leadership	1. Authority is used in a parent-like way for the well-being of employees.
(*b*) Democratic Leadership	2. Authority is shared and input is encouraged from the team.
(*c*) Laissez-Faire Leadership	3. Authority is minimal, allowing employees to self-manage.
(*d*) Autocratic Leadership	4. Authority is centralized in the leader, and decision-making is done alone.

	(*a*)	(*b*)	(*c*)	(*d*)
A.	2	1	4	3
B.	2	1	3	4
C.	1	2	4	3
D.	1	2	3	4

97. Match the leadership style with its typical follower behavior:

Leadership Style	Follower Behavior
(*a*) Charismatic Leadership	1. Followers are highly motivated by the leader's personal qualities.
(*b*) Transactional Leadership	2. Followers comply based on rewards and punishments.
(*c*) Laissez-Faire Leadership	3. Followers have high autonomy and self-direction.
(*d*) Democratic Leadership	4. Followers collaborate and contribute to decision-making.

	(*a*)	(*b*)	(*c*)	(*d*)
A.	1	2	4	3
B.	1	2	3	4
C.	3	4	1	2
D.	4	3	1	2

98. Match the leadership style with the typical feedback approach:

Leadership Style	Feedback Approach
(*a*) Coaching Leadership	1. Provides feedback to improve performance and foster development.
(*b*) Transactional Leadership	2. Focuses on regular performance evaluations based on targets.
(*c*) Transformational Leadership	3. Provides feedback that motivates and encourages innovation.
(*d*) Autocratic Leadership	4. Provides little feedback, focusing on top-down control.

	(*a*)	(*b*)	(*c*)	(*d*)
A.	1	2	3	4
B.	2	1	3	4
C.	3	4	1	2
D.	3	4	2	1

99. Consider the following statements about Trait Theory:

1. It assumes leaders are born with certain qualities.
2. It emphasizes leadership behavior rather than characteristics.

Which of the above statements is/are correct?

A. 1 only B. 2 only

C. Both 1 and 2 D. Neither 1 nor 2

100. With reference to Behavioral Leadership Theory:

1. It focuses on observable actions of leaders.
2. It suggests leadership skills can be learned.

Which of the statements is/are correct?

A. 1 only B. 2 only

C. Both 1 and 2 D. Neither 1 nor 2

Answers

1	2	3	4	5	6	7	8	9	10
C	B	C	C	D	D	B	D	D	C
11	**12**	**13**	**14**	**15**	**16**	**17**	**18**	**19**	**20**
D	C	A	C	D	C	D	D	B	D
21	**22**	**23**	**24**	**25**	**26**	**27**	**28**	**29**	**30**
D	A	A	B	C	A	B	D	A	B
31	**32**	**33**	**34**	**35**	**36**	**37**	**38**	**39**	**40**
A	A	B	B	D	B	D	A	A	D
41	**42**	**43**	**44**	**45**	**46**	**47**	**48**	**49**	**50**
A	C	A	C	B	A	C	B	B	D
51	**52**	**53**	**54**	**55**	**56**	**57**	**58**	**59**	**60**
A	A	A	A	C	C	B	B	B	A
61	**62**	**63**	**64**	**65**	**66**	**67**	**68**	**69**	**70**
C	A	A	D	A	D	A	B	C	A
71	**72**	**73**	**74**	**75**	**76**	**77**	**78**	**79**	**80**
A	A	C	D	C	B	C	B	B	C
81	**82**	**83**	**84**	**85**	**86**	**87**	**88**	**89**	**90**
C	C	D	B	B	B	D	B	A	C
91	**92**	**93**	**94**	**95**	**96**	**97**	**98**	**99**	**100**
D	D	C	A	A	D	B	A	A	C

◆◆◆◆◆

3

HUMAN RESOURCE DEVELOPMENT

MEANING OF HRD

In simple words, HRD is an organised learning experience aimed at matching the organisational need for human resource with the individual need for career growth and development. It is a system and process involving organised series of learning activities designed to produce behavioural changes in human beings in such a way that they acquire desired level of competence for present or future role.

According to Prof. T.V. Rao the best known Indian HRD expert: HRD is a process in which the employees of an organisation are continually helped in a planned way to:

(*a*) acquire or sharpen capabilities required to perform various functions associated with their present or expected future roles.

(*b*) develop their general capabilities so that they may be able to discover their own inner potentialities and exploit them to full for their own and organisational development purpose, and

(*c*) to develop an organisational culture where superior- subordinate relationships, teamwork and collaboration among different sub-units are strong and contribute to organisational wealth (or professional well-being) and motivation and pride of the employees'.

On the basis of these definitions the following features of HRD may be identified.

(*i*) Human resource development is a planned and systematic approach to the development of people. It is not a fragmented of piece-meal approach but a total system of interacting elements designed to improve the total personality.

(*ii*) Human resource development is a continuous process of developing the competencies, motivation, dynamism and effectiveness of employees. It is based on the belief that there is no end to the development of an individual and learning continues throughout life.

(*iii*) Human resource development is an interdisciplinary concept. Experts belonging to different disciplines tend to adopt a compartmentalized approach to HRD. But HRD involves confluence of ideas from many sciences. Sociology provides new insights in the growth and development of human systems through the study of families, communities and other groups. Psychology provides explanation of human behaviour in terms of perception, motivation, morale etc. It provides instruments for use in selection, induction, training, counseling, etc. of employees. Anthropology focuses on traditions, kinship, culture, etc., which is helpful in conflict management, intercultural relationships etc. Political science provides conceptual base for power, status, politics etc. Economic and management also contribute to HRD in their own ways.

(*iv*) Human resource development has both micro and macro aspects. At the micro level HRD is concerned with improving the skills, attitudes and behaviour of employees in organisational settings for the benefit of both the individual and the organisation. At the macro level, HRD involves improving the quality of life of people in a country. Development of people is done by providing the right environment wherein the individual may grow to his fullest stature and realise his fullest potential. HRD is a part of educational and developmental planning for nation's welfare.

(*v*) HRD is a process not merely a set of mechanisms and techniques. The techniques like performance appraisal, counseling, training and organisation development are used to initiate, facilitate and promote this process. The process has no limit and, therefore, the techniques have to be reviewed and revised periodically.

CONCEPT OF HUMAN RESOURCE DEVELOPMENT (HRD)

Human Resource Development is to bring the best in man. HRD is the process of increasing the capacities of human resources through development. HRD is a process of adding value to individuals, teams, organisation as human system. HRD includes development of people, organisation and society. HRD concept is concerned in developing:

(*i*) Knowledge—technical, management

(*ii*) Skills (abilities)

(*iii*) Attitudes

(*iv*) Build values/beliefs

More focus on items 3 and 4, HRD is latest innovation in management. HRD is most vital for success of an organisation through well developed and committed people.

HRD INSTRUMENTS/MECHANISMS

Any systematic or formal way of developing the competencies and motivation of individuals in an organisation and building the organisation's climate can be called as HRD method. As such there can be many HRD methods available for organisations. However, the most frequently used methods are as follows:

(*i*) **Manpower planning:** Manpower planning is the sheet anchor of all HRD efforts. It is concerned with the following:

(*a*) Assessment of manpower needs, including forecasting such needs based on the analysis of the policies of the company, trends of its development, plans for diversification, etc.

(*b*) Manpower audit, *i.e.*, examining whether manpower strength for various jobs is inadequate or more than what should be employed. Both understaffing and overstaffing may be highly demotivating in the company.

Thus, manpower planning is linked with corporate plans and strategies on one hand and the job analysis on the other.

(*ii*) **Performance Appraisal and Feedback:** It is a very critical HRD mechanism under which the performance of an employee is periodically appraised by the employee himself in collaboration with his boss. In the light of the difficulties faced by the employee he redefines his future goals. The mechanism emphasises the development of the employees (by identifying their growth needs) rather than their evaluation. Open, objective and participative appraisal and feedback develop better superior-subordinate relations. During the appraisal interview the superior shares the concerns of the subordinate and even guides him to achieve his targets.

(*iii*) **Training, Education and Development:** There are 3 different HRD mechanisms with different focus and purpose as shown in the following table:

Activity	Focus	Purpose
Training	Learning of present job	Improved performance on the present job of the employee
Education	Learning of the other related jobs	Preparation of the employee for related jobs in not too distant a future
Development	Learning not related to any specific present or future job	General growth of the employee

Three broad areas in which training may be imparted are technical, behavioural and conceptual. It is commonly believed that the rank and file workers need training in the Technical area only. Training in the other two areas is not very useful for them. But recent experiences of many Indian companies, such as Petrifies (Baroda), have shown that behavioural training to workers produces several useful results.

(iv) **Potential Appraisal and Promotion:** It is another important HRD mechanism which is concerned with identifying the potential of an employee for future development and promotion in the company. This focuses on finding out periodically the extent to which a given individual possesses the critical attributes required to handle higher level responsibilities. Thus it is linked with job and role analysis. In HRD promotion is not considered to be a reward. This is because it is not based on performance, but it is based on the potential of an employee.

(v) **Career Development and Career Planning:** It may be useful to help new employees become aware of the various phases of development in the company, and plan with senior employees their specific career path. Necessary help may also be given to employees with limited potential to cope with reality. In the HRD system, corporate growth plans are not kept secret. They are made known to the employees to plan their career.

(vi) **Compensation and Reward:** These are common positive reinforces. They should be clearly related to the performance and behaviour of employees. Failure to reward employees properly or over rewarding undeserving employees reduces the reinforcing effect of rewards. Under HRD while salary structure is based on job analysis, salary increase is linked with performance.

(vii) **O.D. Techniques:** Many organisations make use of several O.D. techniques for the development of their human resource. These include team-building, organisational mirroring, T-group, etc. In team-building people learn how to work in collaboration with each other. Under organisational mirroring, the host group gets feedback from representatives from several other organisational groups about how it is perceived and regarded. The intervention is designed to improve the relationships between groups and increase the inter-group effectiveness. In T-group participants learn to be more competent in inter-personal relationships. They learn about themselves, how others react to their behaviour and about the dynamics of group formation, group norms and group growth.

(viii) **Role Analysis and Role Development:** This is an extremely important technique of HRD. Under it the job of an individual in the organisation is analysed and enriched in terms of his role and not in terms of his job. He, his immediate superior and subordinates sit together to discuss their expectations about the job from each other. They then arrive at a consensus about the individual's role and prepare his role description. It is always ensured that a role is sufficiently challenging for the individual, provides him

adequate autonomy for taking initiative and is linked with other organisational roles to avoid a feeling of isolation. Whereas role analysis, role development and role description are usually related to managerial jobs, job analysis, job enrichment and job description are related to workers' jobs. Job analysis of a worker's job is done to know its critical attributes which ultimately determine all those job qualities or attributes which a jobholder should possess. Job descriptions describe these qualities. Job enrichment signifies efforts to make a job more motivating.

(*ix*) **Quality of Work Life:** For overall development of workers, only good wages are not enough. They also need to be provided with good physical conditions and motivating work. If the work is monotonous or boring it must be redesigned. Several Indian organisations are taking initiative in improving quality of work life of their workers. Bharat Heavy Electricals (BHEL) is one such organisation, which took up job redesign as an O.D. intervention as early as 1975. In an HRD system there is always a focus on employee welfare and quality of work life.

(*x*) **Participative Devices:** Following are some important participative devices:

Bi-partite Meetings (between management and workers):

(*a*) To arrive at settlements concerning worker's wages and service conditions.

(*b*) To review the working of existing settlements and examine their impact on workplace discipline, work ethics, customer service, etc.

Information Sharing: To share information about the business profitability, performance of the company, competition, marketing, etc.

Joint Surveys: Management and union to undertake joint surveys on the state of morale, motivation, grievances of workers, etc., and to jointly plan ways of dealing with these problems.

Task forces: To undertake study of problems like 'Absenteeism', 'Indiscipline', etc., and suggest ways to solve the problem.

Collaborative projects: To undertake jointly certain projects, e.g., a project on employee welfare or workers' education.

Quality Circles: To involve workers at the grass root level for periodically discussing work related problems. Quality circles are small groups of employees which are formed voluntarily. They work on the simple premise that the people who do a job every day know more about it than anyone else, particularly when quality or productivity is involved. In the last few years, many companies, both in the private and public sector (such as J.K. Jute, Bharat Electronics, BHEL, HMT, etc.) have recorded substantial gains by implementing the suggestions given by quality circles in their organisation.

(*xi*) **Communication:** This process is fundamental to all aspects of life and is vital to the function of integration. Real communication takes place when the listener truly hears and understands the position and intent of the speaker. This requires a type of listening which is called projective. While hearing the remarks of the speaker the listener must project himself into the mind of the speaker in order to understand the speaker's viewpoint.

(*xii*) **Counseling:** It is an important HRD mechanism to provide timely guidance to workers on problems relating to hand and heart. Many Indian companies employ trained counselors for this purpose.

(*xiii*) **Grievance Redressal:** A grievance redressal procedure is vital to all organizations big or small. The mere fact that an employee has access to a judicial type of justice is satisfying eventhough he never has an occasion to use it.

(*xiv*) **Data Storage and Research:** This also is a very important HRD mechanism. It is very essential to preserve systematic information about every individual employee on various topics such as the employee's personal characteristics, performance-potential, promotions, salary, etc. so that this may be used for counseling, career planning, training, promotion, etc. Moreover, this information also serves as a base for research on employee problems. Sometimes fresh data may be needed for identifying appropriate interventions for improving the utilization of human resources.

(*xv*) **Industrial relations:** Last though not the least important subsystem of HRD is industrial relations. Good industrial relations based on mutual trust and goodwill make the execution of HRD programmes easy. Poor industrial relations based on mutual distrust and fear make execution difficult. Historically, unions in our country have been playing the role of agitators and bargainers. The thrust of their activities has been towards the economic wellbeing of the workers. In HRD unions are encouraged to make a thrust towards the psychological and social wellbeing of workers. Some important areas in which they are asked to participate are as follows:

(*a*) **Communication:** Unions can pass on greater and more varied information to workers about themselves and the organisation. At present they only communicate on service conditions and related issues under this belief that workers are not interested in receiving information on any other issues. This is wrong.

(*b*) **Counseling:** Unions can play a very positive role in providing counseling services to employees. Cases of excessive drinking, smoking, drug addiction, indebtedness, etc., are not infrequent and need to be attended to by the unions. Defending a workman during departmental enquiry for these misconducts in not enough.

(*c*) **Education and training:** Another important area in which unions can play a development role is education of workers. Unions can help them acquire new human relations and work related skills. The former would include skills of collaboration, empathy, collective action, etc. The latter would include skills to do new jobs and new projects.

(*d*) **Welfare:** Unions can help management in developing innovative welfare schemes for employees such as workers' cooperatives, workers' banks, nursery schools, etc.

(*e*) **Family and vocational guidance:** Unions can help workers' families in several ways. For example, they can provide guidance in respect of the education and career of workers' children. They can provide conciliation services in settling family quarrels. They can help in creating jobs for the wives of workers and so on.

(*f*) **Research:** Unions can play a very significant role in generating data on various dimensions of workers' needs, aspirations, standard of living, etc. For this purpose they can launch research projects either independently or in collaboration with academic institutions.

Multiple Choice Questions

1. Human Resource Development (HRD) is best described as:
Statements:
1. A continuous process
2. Focused only on employee training
3. Concerned with developing competencies
4. Aimed at organizational effectiveness

Choose the correct option:
A. 1, 3 and 4 B. 1 and 2
C. 2 and 3 D. All of the above

2. According to Leonard Nadler, HRD includes:
Statements:
1. Training
2. Education
3. Development
4. Performance appraisal only

Choose the correct option:
A. 1, 2 and 3 B. 2 and 4
C. 1 and 4 D. All of the above

3. HRD differs from traditional HRM because HRD:

Statements:
1. Emphasizes long-term development
2. Focuses on human potential
3. Is reactive in nature
4. Is proactive and future-oriented

Choose the correct option:
A. 1 and 3 B. 2 and 4
C. 1, 2 and 4 D. All of the above

4. HRD is considered a system because:
Statements:
1. It has interrelated subsystems
2. It interacts with the external environment
3. It operates in isolation
4. It has feedback mechanisms

Choose the correct option:
A. 1, 2 and 4 B. 1 and 3
C. 2 and 3 D. All of the above

5. Which of the following are core components of HRD?
Statements:
1. Training and Development
2. Career Planning
3. Organizational Development
4. Wage and Salary Administration

Choose the correct option:
A. 1, 2 and 3 B. 2 and 4
C. 1 and 4 D. All of the above

6. HRD focuses on:
Statements:
1. Skill enhancement
2. Attitude development
3. Knowledge acquisition
4. Punitive control mechanisms

Choose the correct option:
A. 1, 2 and 3 B. 2 and 4
C. 1 and 4 D. All of the above

7. The concept of HRD emerged mainly due to:
Statements:
1. Technological changes
2. Global competition
3. Human relations movement
4. Decline of labor unions

Choose the correct option:
A. 1, 2 and 3 B. 2 and 4
C. 1 and 4 D. All of the above

8. HRD aims at developing:
Statements:
1. Individual capabilities
2. Team effectiveness
3. Organizational culture
4. Only managerial staff

Choose the correct option:
A. 1, 2 and 3 B. 1 and 4
C. 2 and 4 D. All of the above

9. Which statements reflect a modern view of HRD?

Statements:

1. Employees are assets
2. Learning is continuous
3. People are replaceable costs
4. Growth of individuals benefits organizations

Choose the correct option:

A. 1, 2 and 4 B. 2 and 3
C. 1 and 3 D. All of the above

10. HRD is future-oriented because it:

Statements:

1. Prepares employees for future roles
2. Enhances adaptability
3. Focuses only on present performance
4. Builds learning organizations

Choose the correct option:

A. 1, 2 and 4 B. 2 and 3
C. 1 and 3 D. All of the above

11. The primary goal of HRD is to:

Statements:

1. Improve employee competence
2. Enhance organizational effectiveness
3. Increase job satisfaction
4. Reduce employee autonomy

Choose the correct option:

A. 1, 2 and 3 B. 2 and 4
C. 1 and 4 D. All of the above

12. HRD aims to create:

Statements:

1. A learning culture
2. Employee commitment
3. Resistance to change
4. High trust climate

Choose the correct option:

A. 1, 2 and 4 B. 1 and 3
C. 2 and 3 D. All of the above

13. One of the goals of HRD is to:

Statements:

1. Develop problem-solving skills
2. Encourage innovation
3. Maintain status quo
4. Promote leadership qualities

Choose the correct option:

A. 1, 2 and 4 B. 2 and 3
C. 1 and 3 D. All of the above

14. HRD contributes to organizational growth by:

Statements:

1. Improving productivity
2. Enhancing employee motivation
3. Reducing learning opportunities
4. Aligning individual and organizational goals

Choose the correct option:

A. 1, 2 and 4 B. 1 and 3
C. 2 and 3 D. All of the above

15. Which of the following are long-term goals of HRD?

Statements:

1. Talent development
2. Succession planning
3. Immediate cost cutting
4. Organizational sustainability

Choose the correct option:

A. 1, 2 and 4 B. 2 and 3
C. 1 and 3 D. All of the above

16. HRD seeks to balance:

Statements:

1. Individual goals
2. Organizational goals
3. Societal goals
4. Personal conflicts

Choose the correct option:

A. 1, 2 and 3 B. 1 and 4
C. 2 and 4 D. All of the above

17. A key goal of HRD is to:

Statements:

1. Enhance employability
2. Improve adaptability to change Promote rigid job roles
3. Develop interpersonal skills

Choose the correct option:

A. 1, 2 and 4 B. 2 and 3
C. 1 and 3 D. All of the above

18. HRD aims at:

Statements:

1. Building competencies
2. Encouraging participation
3. Discouraging creativity
4. Improving quality of work life

Choose the correct option:

A. 1, 2 and 4 B. 1 and 3
C. 2 and 3 D. All of the above

19. Which of the following reflect strategic goals of HRD?

Statements:

1. Competitive advantage
2. Leadership pipeline
3. Employee dependency
4. Organizational agility

Choose the correct option:

A. 1, 2 and 4 B. 2 and 3
C. 1 and 3 D. All of the above

20. HRD supports organizational change by:

Statements:

1. Developing change agents
2. Enhancing learning capability
3. Creating fear of failure
4. Encouraging flexibility

Choose the correct option:

A. 1, 2 and 4 B. 2 and 3
C. 1 and 3 D. All of the above

21. Assertion (A): Performance appraisal is a systematic evaluation of an employee's job performance.

Reason (B): It assesses how well an employee performs tasks assigned against predetermined standards.

Choose the correct answer:

A. Both A and R are true, and R is the correct explanation of A
B. Both A and R are true, but R is not the correct explanation of A
C. A is true, but R is false
D. A is false, but R is true

22. Assertion (A): Performance appraisal focuses only on past performance.

Reason (B): It ignores future potential and developmental needs.

Choose the correct answer:

A. Both A and R are true, and R is the correct explanation of A
B. Both A and R are true, but R is not the correct explanation of A
C. A is true, but R is false
D. A is false, but R is true

23. Assertion (A): Objective appraisal methods reduce subjectivity in performance evaluation.

Reason (B): They rely on measurable and quantifiable performance criteria.

Choose the correct answer:

A. Both A and R are true, and R is the correct explanation of A
B. Both A and R are true, but R is not the correct explanation of A
C. A is true, but R is false
D. A is false, but R is true

24. Assertion (A): Performance appraisal is an essential input for HRD interventions.

Reason (B): Appraisal identifies training and develop-ment needs of employees.

Choose the correct answer:

A. Both A and R are true, and R is the correct explanation of A
B. Both A and R are true, but R is not the correct explanation of A
C. A is true, but R is false
D. A is false, but R is true

25. Assertion (A): 360-degree appraisal improves the accuracy of performance assessment.

Reason (B): Feedback is obtained from multiple sources such as peers, subordinates, and superiors.

Choose the correct answer:

A. Both A and R are true, and R is the correct explanation of A
B. Both A and R are true, but R is not the correct explanation of A
C. A is true, but R is false
D. A is false, but R is true

26. Assertion (A): Performance appraisal is primarily a control mechanism.

Reason (B): Its main objective is to punish poor performers.

Choose the correct answer:

A. Both A and R are true, and R is the correct explanation of A
B. Both A and R are true, but R is not the correct explanation of A
C. A is true, but R is false
D. A is false, but R is true

27. Assertion (A): Biases in appraisal reduce its effectiveness.

Reason (B): Appraiser perceptions and errors affect objectivity.

Choose the correct answer:

A. Both A and R are true, and R is the correct explanation of A
B. Both A and R are true, but R is not the correct explanation of A
C. A is true, but R is false
D. A is false, but R is true

28. Assertion (A): Potential appraisal focuses on an employee's future roles.

Reason (B): It evaluates the ability of employees to handle higher responsibilities.

Choose the correct answer:

A. Both A and R are true, and R is the correct explanation of A
B. Both A and R are true, but R is not the correct explanation of A
C. A is true, but R is false
D. A is false, but R is true

29. Assertion (A): Potential appraisal and performance appraisal are identical.

Reason (B): Both assess current job effectiveness.

Choose the correct answer:

A. Both A and R are true, and R is the correct explanation of A
B. Both A and R are true, but R is not the correct explanation of A
C. A is true, but R is false
D. A is false, but R is true

30. Assertion (A): Potential appraisal is more developmental in nature than performance appraisal.

Reason (B): It emphasizes future growth and capability building.

Choose the correct answer:

A. Both A and R are true, and R is the correct explanation of A
B. Both A and R are true, but R is not the correct explanation of A
C. A is true, but R is false
D. A is false, but R is true

31. HRD helps in knowledge management by:

Statements:

1. Creating knowledge
2. Sharing knowledge

3. Hoarding information
4. Applying knowledge

Choose the correct answer:

A. 1, 2 and 4 B. 2 and 3
C. 1 and 3 D. All of the above

32. Which statements are true about HRD philosophy?

Statements:

1. People have unlimited potential
2. Development benefits both individual and organization
3. Learning is episodic
4. Participation enhances effectiveness

Choose the correct answer:

A. 1, 2 and 4 B. 2 and 3
C. 1 and 3 D. All of the above

33. HRD ultimately aims to achieve:

Statements:

1. Individual excellence
2. Organizational excellence
3. Social well-being
4. Employee exploitation

Choose the correct answer:

A. 1, 2 and 3 B. 1 and 4
C. 2 and 4 D. All of the above

34. HRD helps in knowledge management by:

Statements:

1. Creating knowledge
2. Sharing knowledge
3. Hoarding information
4. Applying knowledge

Choose the correct answer:

A. 1, 2 and 4 B. 2 and 3
C. 1 and 3 D. All of the above

35. Which of the following is an off-the-job training method?

A. Job rotation
B. Coaching
C. Vestibule training
D. Apprenticeship

36. Training needs analysis is conducted to:

A. Increase wages
B. Identify skill gaps
C. Reduce labor turnover
D. Improve industrial relations

37. Which level of analysis identifies organizational goals and strategies?

A. Task analysis
B. Individual analysis
C. Organizational analysis
D. Performance analysis

38. Which method develops decision-making skills?

A. Lecture method
B. Case study method
C. Job instruction training
D. Induction training

39. Evaluation of training effectiveness is important to:

A. Increase training hours
B. Justify training investment
C. Reduce employee benefits
D. Promote unions

40. Kirkpatrick's four-level model evaluates:

A. Cost, benefit, profit, loss
B. Reaction, learning, behavior, results
C. Skill, attitude, knowledge, ability
D. Input, process, output, outcome

41. Which training method is most suitable for shop-floor workers?

A. Role play
B. Apprenticeship
C. Management games
D. Conference method

42. The area from which applicants can be recruited is ....

A. Job agencies
B. Labour markets
C. Employment lines
D. Labour unions

43. Coaching as a training method involves:
A. Group learning
B. Classroom teaching
C. One-to-one guidance
D. Self-learning only

44. Training is considered an investment because it:
A. Increases fixed costs
B. Yields long-term benefits
C. Reduces employee autonomy
D. Guarantees promotion

45. Which of the following is a statutory welfare facility in India?
A. Canteen
B. Housing allowance
C. Bonus
D. Profit sharing

46. Non-statutory welfare measures include:
A. Drinking water
B. Safety provisions
C. Recreational facilities
D. First-aid appliances

47. The main objective of employee welfare is to:
A. Control workers
B. Improve quality of work life
C. Increase supervision
D. Reduce training needs

48. Welfare measures contribute to industrial relations by:
A. Encouraging conflict
B. Enhancing employee satisfaction
C. Reducing management authority
D. Promoting strikes

49. Employee welfare is important because:
A. Employees are organizational liabilities
B. It increases employee exploitation
C. Healthy employees are more productive
D. It replaces training

50. Which welfare measure improves work–life balance?
A. Overtime work
B. Flexible working hours
C. Strict supervision
D. Wage cut

51. The responsibility of employee welfare primarily lies with:
A. Trade unions only
B. Government only
C. Employer
D. Customers

52. Welfare facilities are considered a part of:
A. Human resource development
B. Production management
C. Financial management
D. Marketing management

53. Which statements are true about HRD philosophy?

Statements:
1. People have unlimited potential
2. Development benefits both individual and organization
3. Learning is episodic
4. Participation enhances effectiveness

A. 1, 2 and 4
B. 2 and 3
C. 1 and 3
D. All of the above

54. Which of the following statements about motivation are correct?
1. Motivation is an internal psychological process
2. Motivation can be directly observed
3. Motivation influences direction, intensity, and persistence of behavior
4. Motivation is independent of individual needs

A. 1 and 3 B. 1, 2 and 3
C. 2 and 4 D. All of the above

55. According to Maslow's hierarchy of needs, which need becomes dominant once lower-level needs are satisfied?

A. Physiological
B. Safety
C. Esteem
D. Self-actualization

56. Herzberg's two-factor theory suggests that:

1. Hygiene factors prevent dissatisfaction
2. Motivators create job satisfaction
3. Absence of motivators causes dissatisfaction
4. Hygiene factors lead to motivation

A. 1 and 2 B. 1, 2 and 3
C. 2 and 4 D. All of the above

57. Which of the following are motivators according to Herzberg?

A. Salary and company policy
B. Working conditions and supervision
C. Achievement and recognition
D. Job security and interpersonal relations

58. McClelland's theory of needs emphasizes:

A. Hierarchy of needs
B. Equity and fairness
C. Achievement, power, and affiliation
D. Expectancy and valence

59. In Vroom's expectancy theory, motivation is a function of:

1. Expectancy
2. Instrumentality
3. Valence
4. Reinforcement

A. 1, 2 and 3 B. 2 and 4
C. 1 and 4 D. All of the above

60. Which of the following theories is classified as a process theory of motivation?

A. Maslow's theory
B. Herzberg's theory
C. McClelland's theory
D. Equity theory

61. Which of the following statements about intrinsic motivation are correct?

1. It arises from the work itself
2. It is driven by external rewards
3. It leads to higher job satisfaction
4. It is short-term in nature

A. 1 and 3
B. 2 and 4
C. 1, 2 and 3
D. All of the above

62. Which of the following are objectives of career planning?

1. Optimal utilization of human resources
2. Employee motivation and retention
3. Reduction of employee aspirations
4. Alignment of individual and organizational goals

A. 1, 2 and 4
B. 1 and 3
C. 2 and 3
D. All of the above

63. Career planning is primarily the responsibility of:

A. Employee only
B. Organization only
C. Both employee and organization
D. Trade unions

64. Which stage of career involves exploration and self-assessment?

A. Establishment stage
B. Maintenance stage
C. Decline stage
D. Exploration stage

65. Career development differs from career planning because career development:

A. Is an individual activity
B. Is organization-initiated
C. Focuses on implementation of career plans
D. Ends with promotion

66. Which of the following are career development activities?

1. Training and development
2. Mentoring
3. Succession planning
4. Wage fixation

A. 1, 2 and 3
B. 2 and 4
C. 1 and 4
D. All of the above

67. Dual career paths in organizations are designed to:

A. Reduce employee costs
B. Promote only managers
C. Provide growth for technical specialists
D. Eliminate promotions

68. Which of the following enhances career motivation?

A. Lack of feedback
B. Clear career goals
C. Job insecurity
D. Role ambiguity

69. Career planning contributes to organizational effectiveness by:

1. Reducing turnover
2. Improving employee commitment
3. Increasing career frustration
4. Developing future talent

A. 1, 2 and 4 B. 1 and 3
C. 2 and 3 D. All of the above

70. HRD is related to:

A. Work improvement
B. Error
C. Profit
D. Pricing

71. In a 360 degree of appraisal of the employee, his performance is rated by:

A. superiors only
B. superiors and subordinates
C. superiors and peers
D. superiors, peers and subordinates

72. In a wage system where employee is paid a fixed amount irrespective of output is called:

A. Time rate system
B. Piece rate system
C. Time cum bonus system
D. Piece cum bonus rate system

73. The selection method is considered to be reliable if it ....

A. Produces consistent results across different situations and times
B. Is not challenged in a court of law
C. Is administered by the same manager, every time.
D. Is managed by qualified personnel

74. HRM involves:

A. Employee training
B. Industrial relation
C. Remuneration
D. All of these

75. Work participation in management means:

A. duty
B. employee involvement
C. security
D. risk

76. Most organizations use interviews as an essential step in the selection process. Interviews may be categorized into three broad types. .... is not a type of interview in the selection process.

A. Preliminary interview
B. Decision making interview
C. Exit interview
D. Selection interview

77. .... it is concerned with the determination of the number of personnel required in an organization.

A. Human resource planning
B. Job analysis
C. Motivation
D. Human welfare

78. …………… is a welcoming process through which the employee feels at home.

A. Recruitment B. Selection
C. Appointment D. Induction

79. It helps the employees acquainted with jobs and also to increase their aptitudes and skills and knowledge:

A. Training B. Orientation
C. Eliminating D. Recruiting

80. …………… management is concerned worth the peoples dimension in organizations.

A. Human resource
B. Business
C. Banking
D. None of these

81. The results of the job analysis are written in a statement known as ……………

A. job evaluation
B. job description
C. job specification
D. None of these

82. HRM includes:

A. Judgement B. Job description
C. Cost D. Action

83. What are the ideas underpinning 'soft, commitment' or high-road HRM practices?

A. Labour needs to be treated as assets to be invested in
B. Employees are a cost which should be minimized
C. A lack of mutuality existing between employee and employer
D. A disregard for unlocking discretionary effort

84. Firing the non-performing employees, HR manager is said to perform the:

A. Interpersonal role
B. Informational role
C. Supportive role
D. Decisional role

85. Which of the following is not a function normally performed by the HR department?

A. Employee relation
B. Training and Development
C. Accounting
D. Recruitment and Selection

86. Which of the following statements most accurately defines human resource management?

A. Human resource management contributes to business strategy and plays an important role in the implementation of business strategy
B. Human resource management is an approach to managing people
C. Human resource management seeks to achieve competitive advantage through the strategic deployment of a highly committed and capable workforce, using an integrated array of cultural, structural and personnel techniques
D. Human resource management focuses on people as the source of competitive advantage

87. Which of the following is a key HR role?

A. Personnel administrator
B. Business ally
C. Payroll advisor
D. Organisational geographer

88. In strategic human resource management, HR strategies are generally aligned with:

A. Business strategy
B. Marketing strategy
C. Finance strategy
D. Economic strategy

89. The focus of Human Resource Management revolves around:

A. Machine B. Motivation
C. Money D. Men

90. Strategic management process usually consists of …………… steps.

A. Four B. Five
C. Six D. Seven

91. Treating employees as precious human resources is the basis of the .... approach.

A. Hard HRM
B. Soft HRM
C. Medium HRM
D. Utiliarian approach

92. HRM typically provides which of these types of training to temporary employees?

A. Retirement planning
B. Benefits options
C. Orientation
D. Career planning and management

93. HR's basic challenges in formulating strategies include(s):

A. Need to support corporate productivity and performance improvement efforts
B. Employees not play any role in performance improvement efforts
C. Not being involved in designing the company's strategic plan
D. Management agenda's

94. The biggest problem facing e-HR is the:

A. rarity of HR
B. diversity of HR
C. security of HR data
D. substitutability of HR

95. In which stage of HR intranet site development are multiple sites linked together to create a seamless experience for the individual?

A. Personalised
B. Integrated
C. Transactional
D. Brochureware

96. Formulating and executing HR systems that produce employee competencies and behaviours needed to achieve the company's strategic aims is (are):

A. Strategic HR Management
B. Strategy execution
C. HR strategies
D. Strategic implementation

97. Which approach that seeks to the link strategy, business, performance and HRM policies and practices, assumes that there are a number of HRM practices that are suitable for all organisations?

A. Best practice
B. Best fit
C. Resource-based view
D. Life cycle models

98. Relationship between HRM & Management?

A. Both are same
B. Management is one aspect of HRM
C. HRM is one aspect of Management
D. No relationship exists

99. Why might there be some difficulty in identifying and applying the best-practice approach to HRM in organisations?

A. Because the best-practice approach tends to be resource-intensive
B. Because there is much variation in the literature and empirical research as to what constitutes best-practice
C. Because the best-practice approach would not fit the cost-reduction driven strategies favoured by many in short-termist economies
D. Because the best-practice approach does not emphasize the individual business context

100. Which of the following is NOT a goal of HRM?

A. Integration of HRM with the corporate strategy of the organisation
B. Producing the desired human behaviour that helps to achieve organisations goals
C. Creation of a flexible environment that can easily adopt change
D. To endure proper delivery of products

Answers

1	2	3	4	5	6	7	8	9	10
A	A	C	A	A	A	A	A	A	A
11	**12**	**13**	**14**	**15**	**16**	**17**	**18**	**19**	**20**
A	A	A	A	A	A	A	A	A	A
21	**22**	**23**	**24**	**25**	**26**	**27**	**28**	**29**	**30**
A	C	A	A	A	C	A	A	D	A
31	**32**	**33**	**34**	**35**	**36**	**37**	**38**	**39**	**40**
A	A	A	A	C	B	C	B	B	B
41	**42**	**43**	**44**	**45**	**46**	**47**	**48**	**49**	**50**
B	B	C	B	A	C	B	B	C	B
51	**52**	**53**	**54**	**55**	**56**	**57**	**58**	**59**	**60**
C	A	A	A	D	A	C	C	A	D
61	**62**	**63**	**64**	**65**	**66**	**67**	**68**	**69**	**70**
A	A	C	D	C	A	C	B	A	A
71	**72**	**73**	**74**	**75**	**76**	**77**	**78**	**79**	**80**
D	A	A	D	B	C	A	D	A	A
81	**82**	**83**	**84**	**85**	**86**	**87**	**88**	**89**	**90**
B	B	A	D	C	C	B	A	D	B
91	**92**	**93**	**94**	**95**	**96**	**97**	**98**	**99**	**100**
B	C	A	C	B	A	A	C	A	D

◆◆◆◆◆

4

MORAL AND INCENTIVES

Morals and incentives play a crucial role in shaping human behavior and decision-making. While morals guide individuals toward ethical actions based on values and principles, incentives motivate behavior through rewards or consequences. Understanding their interaction helps explain choices in personal, social, and economic contexts.

TYPES OF INCENTIVES PLAN

Wage Incentives Plan

Wage Incentive Plans may be broadly classified into two broad categories:

(*a*) Individual incentive plans

(*b*) Group incentive plans

(a) Individual Incentive Plans

Under individual incentive plans, earnings are related directly to the performance of the individual worker. In case of group incentive schemes, earnings of a group are related to the performance of the group as a whole. In plant wide schemes, performance of the factory as whole is used as the basis for calculating earnings of workers.

Individual incentives may be based on time or output. Under time based plans, a standard time is determined and bonus is given if a worker completes the job in less than standard time. Under output based plans, a standard of output is determined and workers producing more than the standard output are given bonus.

Individual incentives are of various types:

1. **Halsey Premium Plan or Weir Plan:** This plan was developed by F.A. Halsey and was first introduced in the Weir Engineering Works, England. Under this plan, the average time required for every activity is calculated on the basis of average efficiency of average worker, known as standard time. Workers completing their work within standard time are paid incentive at a standard rate. The workers completing their works in less than standard time are paid the incentive according to the standard rate and bonus on the basis of time saved by them.

   For example: Considering that the employer shares with the employee 50% of the wages saved on account of time saved by the worker. Earning is calculated as under:

   Earning = Hours worked × Rate per hour + (50% of time saved × rate per hour)

   Here, Time saved = Standard time – Time worked

   Standard Time (S) = 10 hrs

   Time Taken (T) = 8 hrs

   Rate of Wages (R) = ₹ 20 per hr.

   Bonus (P) = 50%

   Total Wages (W) = $T \times R + 50\% (S - T) \times R$

   $= 8 \times 20 + 50/100 \times (10 - 8) \times 20$

   $= 160 + 20 =$ ₹ 180

2. Rowan Plan: The Rowan plan is a modification of Halsey plan. James Rowan devised this plan. Under this plan, workers are paid over and above the wages for the hours they put in, an extra payment for hours worked in proportion to time saved and standard time. Standard time is determined in the same manner as in Halsey.

Earnings = Hours × Rate per hour + (Time saved/ Standard time × Hours worked × Rate per hour).

Using the data given under Halsey Plan

= 8 × 20 + (8 × 20 × 2/10) = ₹ 192

3. Emerson Efficiency Plan: Herrington Emerson devised this plan. Under this plan time for the job is determined scientifically and a minimum time wage is guaranteed to all the workers. The efficiency of the worker is determined in the ratio of actual time taken by the worker with the standard time of the work. Emerson believed that generally, worker produces only 67% of the standard output, therefore Bonus is paid at an increasing percentage beyond the prescribed level of efficiency *i.e.,* 67%.

Earnings = Time taken × Rate per hour + % of Bonus × Time taken × Rate per hour.

For example:

Standard Time (S) = 10 hrs

Time Taken (T) = 8 hrs

Time Wage = ₹ 20 per hr

Bonus = 10% upto 75% efficiency
= 20% for 75% – 100%
= 30% beyond 100%

Total Wages = (T × R) + (Percentage of bonus × T × R)

In this case, the efficiency level is = 10/8 × 100 = 125% and therefore, bonus at 30% is payable

Total Wages = 8 × 20 + 30/100 (8 × 20)
= 160 + 48 = ₹ 208

Worker A : Time taken 16 hrs, Bonus = NIL

Worker B : Time taken 14 hrs, Bonus
= 1/10 × 14 × 20

Worker C : Time taken 10 hrs, Bonus
= 2/10 × 10 × 20

Worker D : Time taken 8 hrs, Bonus
= 3/10 × 8 × 20

4. Bedeaux Point Plan: Charles Bedeaux devised this plan. Under his plan, standard time for every work is determined scientifically and is expressed in terms of B. For instance, a standard time of 240 B means the job should be completed within 240 minutes. In determining the Bs, the time of operation and the rest time both are taken into account. Minimum time wage is guaranteed to all workers. The workers who complete the job within or more than the standard time are paid at the normal time rate. Those who complete the job in less than the standard time are paid bonus for the time saved. Generally, 75% of the wages for the time saved are paid as bonus to the worker and 25% of the foreman:

Total Wages = S × R + 75% of ₹ (S – T)

For example:

Standard Time (S) = 240 Bs (4 hrs)

Actual Time Taken (T) = 180 Bs (3 hrs)

Rate of Wages (R) = ₹ 0.50 per B

Total Wages = 240 × 0.50
+ 75/100 × 0.50 (240 – 180)
= 120 + 75 × 30/100
= ₹ 142.50

5. Talyor's Differential Piece Rate Plan: F.W. Taylor suggested differential piece rate plan as an alternative to time rate system which he considered as unscientific and lacks incentive elements. In this plan, Taylor did not provide for minimum guarantee wage payment to each worker. According to him, it is possible to calculate standard workload for every worker on the basis of time and motion studies. In his plan, he suggested two piece rates for workers. The lower rate to those who are average or less efficient and give production below the standard workload fixed. The higher piece rate is suggested for those who are above average or efficient and give production over and above the standard workload fixed. Naturally, an efficient worker will be paid at a higher rate and an inefficient worker will be paid at a lower rate.

For Example: Suppose the standard output is 50 units per day. The piece rates fixed are ₹ 4.00 and ₹ 3.00 per unit. Three workers A, B and C produce 40, 50 and 60 units respectively during a day. Their total wages will be as follows:

Worker A : 40 × ₹ 3.00 = ₹ 120

Worker B : 50 × ₹ 4.00 = ₹ 200

Worker C : 60 × ₹ 4.00 = ₹ 240

6. **Merrick's Multiple Piece Rate Plan:** This plan was developed to overcome a drawback in Taylor's plan. This drawback related to an abrupt change in piece rate. Under it, three graded piece rates are prescribed. The workers who produce less than 83% of standard output are paid at a basic piece rate. Those producing from 83% to 100% of the standard output are paid 110% of basic piece rate. Lastly, the workers producing more than 110% of standard output are paid 120% of basic piece rate. Thus, this system is an improvement over the Taylor's plan as it reduces the severity of the Taylor's plan.
7. **Gantt's Task and Bonus Plan:** Unlike Taylor's and Merrick's plans, minimum time wage is guaranteed to every worker under Gantt's task and bonus wage plan. A definite task representing first class performance is fixed as a standard after careful time and motion studies. If a worker achieves or excels it, he gets extra wages varying between 25% to 50% of the hourly rate for the time allowed for the task. But if a worker fails to complete the task within the standard time, he receives only the wages for actual time spent at the specified rate.

For example: Suppose the standard time fixed for the job is 8 hours and the time rate is ₹ 20 per hour and the rate of bonus is 25 percent. A worker, who completed the task in 10 hours, will be paid 160 (8 × ₹ 20) only. On the other hand, the worker who completes the task in 6 hours will receive ₹ 200 (₹ 160 + 25% of ₹ 160).

(b) Group Incentive Plans

Under this plan, earnings of a team (group) are directly related to the performance of the team as a whole. Under this scheme, the bonus is calculated for a group of workers and the total amount is distributed among the group members in preparation to the wages earned by each.

There are three main types of group incentives:

1. **Priestman Bonus Plan:** Under this plan a committee of workers and management sets the standards of performance. A minimum wage is guaranteed to each worker.

   The group gets bonus when actual output exceeds the standard. The group supervisor also gets a share in the group bonus. The plan is easy and promotes team spirit among employees. But it makes no distinction between efficient and inefficient workers.
2. **Scanlon plan:** It is a plant wide scheme designed to involve workers in making suggestions for reducing the cost of operations and improving work methods by showing the gains of increased productivity. It has two basic features:
   (*i*) Financial incentives are used to increase productivity and to reduce costs.
   (*ii*) Departmental/plant screening committees are set up to evaluate employee suggestions. The plan is based on the belief that plant wide cooperation is essential for increasing productivity.
3. **Towne's gain sharing plan:** Towne's gain sharing plan is another system of group incentive. Under this plan half of the savings in labour cost as a result of output in excess of standard is distributed among workers

and the foreman. The foreman gets a certain percentages as fixed in advance. The bonus is paid half yearly.

Theories of Motivation

1. **Maslow's Hierarchy of Needs:** Motivation is based on fulfilling needs in stages, from basic needs (food, safety) to higher needs (self-esteem and self-actualization).
2. **Herzberg's Two-Factor Theory:** Motivation depends on hygiene factors (salary, work conditions) and motivators (achievement, recognition).
3. **McClelland's Theory of Needs:** People are motivated by three needs: achievement, power, and affiliation.
4. **Expectancy Theory (Vroom):** Motivation depends on believing that effort leads to performance and rewards.
5. **Self-Determination Theory:** Motivation comes from fulfilling needs for autonomy, competence, and relatedness.
6. **Incentive Theory:** Behavior is motivated by rewards and incentives.

How Managers Motivate Employees

1. **Clear Goals:** Managers set clear and achievable goals to give direction and purpose.
2. **Rewards and Incentives:** Use of bonuses, promotions, and recognition to encourage performance.
3. **Positive Work Environment:** Creating a supportive, safe, and respectful workplace.
4. **Feedback and Communication:** Regular feedback helps employees improve and stay motivated.
5. **Participation in Decisions:** Involving employees increases commitment and responsibility.
6. **Training and Development:** Providing learning opportunities helps personal and professional growth.
7. **Recognition and Appreciation:** Praising good work boosts confidence and morale.

CONCEPT OF MORALS

Morals are the standards or principles that guide human behavior in distinguishing right from wrong. They influence how individuals act, make decisions, and interact with others in personal, social, and professional life. Morals are shaped by various factors, including culture, religion, family upbringing, and societal norms. They help maintain harmony, fairness, honesty, and respect within a community. Following moral principles encourages ethical behavior and accountability, while neglecting them can lead to conflicts and distrust. Understanding and practicing morals is essential for building character, maintaining social order, and fostering positive relationships.

Multiple Choice Questions

1. According to Maslow's hierarchy of needs, which of the following scenarios best illustrates self-actualization in an employee?
   A. An employee works overtime to earn a higher salary.
   B. An employee takes on challenging projects to realize their full potential.
   C. An employee seeks health benefits provided by the company.
   D. An employee seeks recognition from peers for completed work.
2. Herzberg's two-factor theory divides workplace factors into hygiene factors and motivators. Which of the following combinations correctly represents a hygiene factor and a motivator?
   A. Salary – Achievement
   B. Recognition – Work environment

C. Job security - Promotion
D. Achievement - Respect

3. In expectancy theory, motivation is highest when an employee:
A. Believes effort will lead to good performance and performance will lead to rewards.
B. Works hard without expecting any reward.
C. Observes others working hard and copying them.
D. Focuses solely on monetary incentives.

4. Which of the following best demonstrates moral behavior in a corporate setting?
A. Reporting a colleague's minor mistakes publicly
B. Following company policies even when no one is watching
C. Taking shortcuts to meet deadlines
D. Ignoring ethical concerns if profits are high

5. McClelland's need for affiliation is best demonstrated when an employee:
A. Seeks leadership positions to influence others
B. Desires strong social bonds and harmonious relationships at work
C. Aims to outperform colleagues at all costs
D. Prefers working alone to achieve personal goals

6. Which of the following managerial practices aligns most closely with motivating employees through intrinsic motivation rather than extrinsic rewards?
A. Providing yearly bonuses for high performers
B. Giving employees challenging tasks that allow skill development
C. Increasing salary for meeting targets
D. Punishing employees for missing deadlines

7. Which statement reflects the interplay of morals and incentives in workplace decision-making?
A. Incentives always lead employees to act ethically.
B. Strong moral principles can prevent unethical behavior even when incentives encourage shortcuts.
C. Morals are irrelevant if incentives are high.
D. Incentives and morals function independently in every workplace.

8. A manager wants to increase team motivation while maintaining ethical standards. Which approach is most effective?
A. Offering excessive bonuses without setting clear ethical guidelines
B. Encouraging collaboration, providing recognition, and reinforcing ethical behavior
C. Ignoring team conflicts as long as targets are met
D. Rewarding only the top performer and ignoring team effort

9. Self-determination theory emphasizes autonomy, competence, and relatedness. Which scenario best reflects this theory?
A. Employees are forced to follow strict instructions without choice
B. Employees choose their tasks, receive skill-building opportunities, and collaborate with supportive peers
C. Employees are motivated purely by monetary rewards
D. Employees are only evaluated on attendance

10. Which of the following is NOT a typical outcome of neglecting moral principles in an organization?
A. Reduced trust among employees
B. Ethical conflicts and fraud
C. Enhanced teamwork and cooperation
D. Negative reputation

11. Incentive theory of motivation suggests that behavior is largely influenced by external rewards. Which example illustrates this principle most clearly?

A. An employee volunteers to mentor colleagues without reward
B. An employee works extra hours to receive a year-end bonus
C. An employee studies new skills for personal satisfaction
D. An employee collaborates to maintain harmony at work

12. Which combination reflects both hygiene factors and motivators according to Herzberg, and their effect on job satisfaction?

A. Salary and work environment prevent dissatisfaction, recognition and achievement increase satisfaction
B. Recognition and promotions prevent dissatisfaction, salary increases satisfaction
C. Punishments prevent dissatisfaction, bonuses increase dissatisfaction
D. Workload and pressure increase satisfaction, training prevents dissatisfaction

13. Which of the following actions best demonstrates an employee following moral principles despite a tempting incentive?

A. Reporting an error in financial accounts despite a bonus being offered for hiding it
B. Completing tasks faster to receive a reward without regard to quality
C. Copying work from a colleague to meet deadlines
D. Ignoring company rules to maximize personal gain

14. According to McClelland's theory, employees with a high need for power are likely to:

A. Seek opportunities to influence or lead others in decision-making
B. Avoid leadership roles and prefer independent work
C. Focus only on social relationships with peers
D. Work solely for monetary rewards

15. Which managerial action is most likely to enhance intrinsic motivation among employees?

A. Offering cash incentives for every task completed
B. Assigning tasks that match employees' skills and provide growth opportunities
C. Strictly monitoring employees with penalties for errors
D. Rotating employees randomly to avoid favoritism

16. Which statement best explains the relationship between morals and social harmony?

A. Morals are optional guidelines for personal benefit
B. Morals help establish trust, fairness, and cooperation in society
C. Morals only matter in religious contexts
D. Social harmony is independent of individual moral behavior

17. An organization wants to motivate employees while fostering ethical behavior. Which strategy aligns with both goals?

A. Implementing a reward system for productivity while promoting ethical training
B. Focusing solely on monetary incentives without guidelines
C. Encouraging competition without ethical oversight
D. Ignoring employee input on ethical concerns

18. Which scenario best illustrates the effect of intrinsic motivation according to self-determination theory?

A. An employee voluntarily leads a challenging project because it aligns with personal growth goals
B. An employee works overtime only to earn a bonus

C. An employee attends training to avoid penalties
D. An employee completes tasks solely for recognition

19. Which of the following is a likely consequence of failing to provide recognition and appreciation in a workplace?
A. Increased morale and engagement
B. Reduced motivation and job satisfaction
C. Enhanced teamwork
D. Greater ethical adherence

20. Which of the following statements best explains the difference between morals and incentives?
A. Morals guide behavior based on ethical principles, while incentives motivate behavior through rewards or consequences
B. Morals are always financial, while incentives are always ethical
C. Both morals and incentives are only extrinsic motivators
D. Morals and incentives are unrelated to behavior

21. Which of the following demonstrates a manager using both intrinsic and extrinsic motivation effectively?
A. Giving employees bonuses for completing tasks while providing opportunities to develop new skills
B. Giving bonuses only without training
C. Assigning tasks randomly
D. Ignoring ethical behavior

22. A moral dilemma occurs when:
A. There is a conflict between personal gain and ethical standards
B. Employees work overtime voluntarily
C. A team receives incentives for good performance
D. Rules are clear and easy to follow

23. Which of the following is an example of a hygiene factor according to Herzberg?
A. Recognition B. Achievement
C. Salary D. Responsibility

24. Which of the following best shows an employee with a high need for achievement?
A. Preferring routine tasks
B. Setting challenging goals and striving to accomplish them
C. Avoiding feedback
D. Seeking only social approval

25. Which of the following practices helps managers maintain ethical standards while motivating employees?
A. Encouraging shortcuts to meet targets
B. Implementing a clear code of conduct along with incentives
C. Ignoring employee complaints
D. Rewarding only financial performance

26. According to self-determination theory, a lack of autonomy is likely to result in:
A. Increased intrinsic motivation
B. Reduced motivation and engagement
C. Greater financial incentives
D. Improved social harmony

27. Which of the following best illustrates the use of extrinsic motivation in a workplace?
A. Assigning meaningful work
B. Offering a promotion for exceeding targets
C. Providing training for personal growth
D. Allowing flexible work hours

28. Which factor is least likely to shape an individual's moral values?
A. Family B. Religion
C. Technology D. Culture

29. An organization encourages ethical behavior by rewarding employees for reporting violations. This reflects:
A. Pure intrinsic motivation
B. Combination of incentives and moral reinforcement
C. Only extrinsic punishment
D. Ignoring ethical standards

30. Which statement reflects Herzberg's theory regarding dissatisfaction?

A. Hygiene factors prevent dissatisfaction but do not create motivation
B. Hygiene factors increase satisfaction directly
C. Motivators prevent dissatisfaction only
D. Both hygiene factors and motivators reduce dissatisfaction equally

31. Which of the following scenarios best illustrates moral courage?

A. Ignoring workplace harassment
B. Reporting unethical practices despite personal risk
C. Following unethical orders for personal gain
D. Complaining only to peers

32. In expectancy theory, "valence" refers to:

A. Effort put into work
B. Value an individual places on the expected reward
C. Level of supervision
D. Company policies

33. Which of the following is an example of a manager fostering intrinsic motivation?

A. Assigning repetitive tasks for a reward
B. Providing challenging projects that develop skills
C. Giving cash bonuses for attendance
D. Enforcing strict rules

34. Which of the following best illustrates the importance of morals in business?

A. Increasing profits at all costs
B. Building trust, long-term relationships, and reputation
C. Ignoring ethical concerns
D. Reducing employee engagement

35. Which of the following best reflects the effect of recognition on employees?

A. Reduces motivation
B. Increases satisfaction and performance
C. Creates conflicts
D. Encourages unethical behavior

36. Which of the following is a key difference between Maslow and Herzberg theories?

A. Maslow focuses on a hierarchy of needs; Herzberg separates hygiene and motivators
B. Maslow focuses on financial incentives; Herzberg focuses on morals
C. Maslow focuses on ethics; Herzberg focuses on punishments
D. Both are identical

37. Which scenario reflects high ethical standards in leadership?

A. Leaders ignoring misconduct for profit
B. Leaders promoting transparency and fairness
C. Leaders rewarding only top performers
D. Leaders favoring friends

38. Which of the following is a primary goal of using incentives in organizations?

A. Punish employees
B. Motivate desired behavior and performance
C. Ignore underperformance
D. Reduce ethical standards

39. Which is an example of intrinsic motivation?

A. Working hard to earn a bonus
B. Solving a problem because it is personally rewarding
C. Completing tasks to avoid punishment
D. Following orders only for recognition

40. Which of the following is a key feature of moral principles?

A. They are optional guidelines
B. They distinguish right from wrong
C. They guarantee financial success
D. They are always externally enforced

41. Which of the following is NOT an outcome of effective managerial motivation?

A. Increased productivity
B. Improved employee satisfaction
C. Reduced morale
D. Higher engagement

42. A manager rewards both teamwork and individual achievement. This strategy is most aligned with:

A. Extrinsic motivation only
B. Balancing extrinsic and intrinsic motivation
C. Punishment-based motivation
D. Ignoring employee growth

43. Which of the following best demonstrates an ethical decision influenced by strong moral values?

A. Cutting corners to save costs
B. Refusing to manipulate reports despite pressure
C. Ignoring rules for personal gain
D. Copying others' work to succeed

44. Which of the following is most likely to motivate employees according to McClelland's theory?

A. Assigning routine work
B. Opportunities for achievement, power, and affiliation
C. Providing fixed salary only
D. Ignoring employee goals

45. A positive work environment contributes to motivation because it:

A. Reduces stress, encourages collaboration, and boosts engagement
B. Focuses only on competition
C. Increases dissatisfaction
D. Promotes unethical behavior

46. Which of the following best illustrates the role of ethics in managerial decision-making?

A. Choosing actions based solely on profit
B. Balancing organizational goals with fairness, integrity, and social responsibility
C. Ignoring employee input
D. Prioritizing speed over accuracy

47. Which scenario reflects the combination of moral guidance and incentive motivation?

A. Rewarding employees for meeting targets and reinforcing honesty in reporting
B. Offering cash only without guidance
C. Ignoring ethical concerns for efficiency
D. Motivating employees randomly

48. Which of the following best reflects the relationship between recognition and intrinsic motivation?

A. Recognition undermines intrinsic motivation
B. Recognition enhances feelings of competence and satisfaction
C. Recognition is irrelevant
D. Recognition only affects extrinsic rewards

49. According to self-determination theory, which of the following is necessary for sustainable motivation?

A. Autonomy, competence, and relatedness
B. Punishment only
C. Rewards only
D. Peer pressure

50. Which of the following statements best summarizes the combined role of morals and incentives in organizational behavior?

A. Morals guide ethical choices; incentives encourage desired behavior, and together they enhance productivity and trust
B. Incentives always replace morals
C. Morals and incentives conflict and cannot coexist
D. Morals are irrelevant if incentives exist

51. Which of the following statements are correct about Maslow's hierarchy of needs?

1. Physiological needs are the most basic level of needs.
2. Self-actualization is achieved only after all lower needs are satisfied.
3. Esteem needs are less important than physiological needs.

Options:

A. 1 and 2
B. 2 and 3
C. 1 and 3
D. All three

52. Regarding Herzberg's two-factor theory:

1. Motivators lead to job satisfaction.
2. Hygiene factors prevent dissatisfaction but do not motivate.
3. Hygiene factors include recognition and achievement.

Options:

A. 1 and 2 B. 2 and 3
C. 1 and 3 D. All three

53. Which statements are true about McClelland's theory of needs?

1. Need for achievement drives individuals to excel in challenging tasks.
2. Need for power focuses on social relationships rather than leadership.
3. Need for affiliation emphasizes harmonious interactions with others.

Options:

A. 1 and 3 B. 1 and 2
C. 2 and 3 D. All three

54. Which of the following statements correctly describe intrinsic motivation?

1. It comes from personal satisfaction or enjoyment of the task.
2. It is driven solely by financial rewards.
3. Self-determination theory focuses on autonomy, competence, and relatedness to explain intrinsic motivation.

Options:

A. 1 and 3 B. 2 only
C. 1 and 2 D. All three

55. About the relationship between morals and incentives:

1. Morals guide ethical decision-making.
2. Incentives always ensure ethical behavior.
3. Combining morals and incentives can enhance productivity and trust.

Options:

A. 1 and 3 B. 1 and 2
C. 2 and 3 D. All three

56. Which statements about expectancy theory are correct?

1. Motivation depends on the belief that effort leads to performance.
2. Valence refers to the value of the expected reward.
3. Expectancy theory ignores the link between effort and outcome.

Options:

A. 1 and 2 B. 2 and 3
C. 1 and 3 D. All three

57. About incentives in organizations:

1. Incentives can be financial or non-financial.
2. Extrinsic incentives include recognition, bonuses, and promotions.
3. Intrinsic incentives include personal satisfaction and skill development.

Options:

A. 1, 2, and 3 B. 1 and 2 only
C. 2 and 3 only D. 1 and 3 only

58. Which statements are true about moral behavior in the workplace?

1. It includes honesty, integrity, and fairness.
2. It is influenced only by personal interest, not societal norms.
3. Strong moral values help in building trust and social harmony.

Options:

A. 1 and 3 B. 1 and 2
C. 2 and 3 D. All three

59. Regarding managerial motivation:

1. Recognition and praise increase employee engagement.
2. Punishment alone is an effective long-term motivator.
3. Employee participation in decision-making enhances commitment.

Options:

A. 1 and 3 B. 2 only
C. 1 and 2 D. All three

60. About self-determination theory:

1. Autonomy is the ability to make choices about one's work.
2. Competence refers to feeling effective and capable.
3. Relatedness emphasizes working in isolation to achieve goals.

Options:

A. 1 and 2 B. 1 and 3
C. 2 and 3 D. All three

61. Assertion (A): Maslow's hierarchy of needs suggests that unmet higher-level needs do not affect motivation.

Reason (R): Self-actualization is achieved only after lower-level needs are fully satisfied.

A. Both A and R are true, and R is the correct explanation of A
B. Both A and R are true, but R is not the correct explanation of A
C. A is true, R is false
D. A is false, R is true

62. Assertion (A): Herzberg's hygiene factors do not directly motivate employees.

Reason (R): Salary, job security, and working conditions are considered hygiene factors.

A. Both A and R are true, and R correctly explains A
B. Both A and R are true, but R does not explain A
C. A is true, R is false
D. A is false, R is true

63. Assertion (A): Intrinsic motivation is more sustainable than extrinsic motivation.

Reason (R): Intrinsic motivation comes from personal satisfaction rather than external rewards.

A. Both A and R are true, and R correctly explains A
B. Both A and R are true, but R does not explain A
C. A is true, R is false
D. A is false, R is true

64. Assertion (A): Incentives always ensure ethical behavior in organizations.

Reason (R): Employees may prioritize rewards over moral standards.

A. Both A and R are true, and R correctly explains A
B. Both A and R are true, but R does not explain A
C. A is false, R is true
D. A is true, R is false

65. Assertion (A): Recognition and praise increase employee motivation.

Reason (R): Employees feel competent and valued when their efforts are acknowledged.

A. Both A and R are true, and R correctly explains A
B. Both A and R are true, but R does not explain A
C. A is true, R is false
D. A is false, R is true

66. Assertion (A): McClelland's theory emphasizes three basic human needs: achievement, power, and affiliation.

Reason (R): Employees motivated by achievement prefer easy tasks to avoid risk.

A. Both A and R are true, and R correctly explains A
B. Both A and R are true, but R does not explain A
C. A is true, R is false
D. A is false, R is true

67. Assertion (A): Hygiene factors can prevent dissatisfaction but cannot create job satisfaction.

Reason (R): Recognition, responsibility, and advancement are motivators that increase satisfaction.

A. Both A and R are true, and R correctly explains A

B. Both A and R are true, but R does not explain A
C. A is true, R is false
D. A is false, R is true

68. Assertion (A): Morals are always shaped entirely by personal choice.

Reason (R): Culture, religion, and society influence moral development.

A. Both A and R are true, and R correctly explains A
B. Both A and R are true, but R does not explain A
C. A is false, R is true
D. A is true, R is false

69. Assertion (A): Expectancy theory states that motivation depends on the perceived link between effort and reward.

Reason (R): Employees are motivated if they believe their performance will lead to valued outcomes.

A. Both A and R are true, and R correctly explains A
B. Both A and R are true, but R does not explain A
C. A is true, R is false
D. A is false, R is true

70. Assertion (A): Self-determination theory emphasizes autonomy, competence, and relatedness.

Reason (R): Autonomy allows employees to make choices about how to perform tasks.

A. Both A and R are true, and R correctly explains A
B. Both A and R are true, but R does not explain A
C. A is true, R is false
D. A is false, R is true

71. Assertion (A): Extrinsic incentives include bonuses and promotions.

Reason (R): Extrinsic incentives directly increase intrinsic satisfaction.

A. Both A and R are true, and R correctly explains A
B. Both A and R are true, but R does not explain A
C. A is true, R is false
D. A is false, R is true

72. Assertion (A): Ethical behavior in the workplace improves social harmony and trust.

Reason (R): Employees with strong moral values are less likely to engage in fraud or misconduct.

A. Both A and R are true, and R correctly explains A
B. Both A and R are true, but R does not explain A
C. A is true, R is false
D. A is false, R is true

73. Assertion (A): Employees motivated by achievement tend to avoid challenging tasks.

Reason (R): High-need achievers set challenging goals and seek personal accomplishment.

A. Both A and R are true, and R correctly explains A
B. Both A and R are true, but R does not explain A
C. A is false, R is true
D. A is true, R is false

74. Assertion (A): Incentives and moral principles are independent and do not influence each other.

Reason (R): Strong moral values can prevent unethical behavior even when incentives encourage shortcuts.

A. Both A and R are true, and R correctly explains A
B. Both A and R are true, but R does not explain A
C. A is false, R is true
D. A is true, R is false

75. Assertion (A): Recognition, praise, and positive feedback enhance intrinsic motivation.

Reason (R): Positive reinforcement improves employees' feelings of competence and belonging.

A. Both A and R are true, and R correctly explains A
B. Both A and R are true, but R does not explain A
C. A is true, R is false
D. A is false, R is true

76. According to Maslow, the highest level of human needs is ________.

A. Physiological B. Safety
C. Self-actualization D. Esteem

77. Herzberg classified factors that prevent dissatisfaction but do not motivate employees as ________.

A. Motivators B. Hygiene factors
C. Extrinsic rewards D. Intrinsic factors

78. In McClelland's theory, the need for _____ drives individuals to excel in challenging tasks.

A. Power B. Affiliation
C. Achievement D. Recognition

79. ________ motivation comes from internal satisfaction or personal growth rather than external rewards.

A. Extrinsic B. Intrinsic
C. Hygiene D. Incentive

80. According to expectancy theory, ________ refers to the value an individual places on the expected reward.

A. Effort B. Valence
C. Hygiene D. Motivation

81. Managers can motivate employees by providing recognition, praise, and ________ to boost morale.

A. Punishments B. Feedback
C. Ignorance D. Isolation

82. Morals are principles that help individuals distinguish ________ from ________.

A. Success, failure
B. Right, wrong
C. Good, bad only in law
D. Reward, punishment

83. Self-determination theory emphasizes three key factors: autonomy, competence, and ________.

A. Incentives B. Recognition
C. Relatedness D. Hygiene

84. Extrinsic incentives include ________, promotions, and other rewards given by the organization.

A. Recognition
B. Personal satisfaction
C. Autonomy
D. Morals

85. According to Herzberg, motivators that increase job satisfaction include achievement, responsibility, and ________.

A. Salary
B. Promotion
C. Working conditions
D. Job security

86. A positive work environment increases employee motivation by reducing stress and encouraging ________.

A. Conflict B. Collaboration
C. Isolation D. Punishment

87. Ethical behavior in organizations promotes trust, fairness, and ______ among employees.

A. Competition B. Social harmony
C. Laziness D. Isolation

88. In motivation theory, an incentive is anything that encourages a person to act in a desired ________.

A. Behavior B. Thought
C. Mood D. Punishment

89. Hygiene factors include salary, job security, and ________, which prevent dissatisfaction.

A. Recognition B. Working conditions
C. Achievement D. Autonomy

90. Employees with a high need for ________ prefer social interaction and maintaining harmonious relationships.

A. Achievement B. Affiliation
C. Power D. Recognition

91. Which of the following is considered a hygiene factor in Herzberg's two-factor theory?

A. Achievement B. Responsibility
C. Salary D. Recognition

92. Employees motivated by the need for power are primarily driven by:

A. Social relationships
B. Influence and control over others
C. Personal achievement
D. Job security

93. Which of the following is an example of intrinsic motivation?

A. Completing a project for a cash bonus
B. Solving a problem for personal satisfaction
C. Attending training to avoid penalties
D. Meeting targets for recognition

94. According to Maslow, which need comes immediately after safety needs?

A. Esteem
B. Social/Belonging
C. Self-actualization
D. Physiological

95. Which of the following statements is true about extrinsic motivation?

A. It arises from personal satisfaction
B. It comes from rewards or recognition provided by others
C. It is always more sustainable than intrinsic motivation
D. It cannot be measured

96. Which managerial action best promotes ethical behavior among employees?

A. Offering bonuses without ethical guidelines
B. Promoting transparency and accountability
C. Ignoring minor violations for efficiency
D. Encouraging competition without rules

97. Which of the following is NOT a principle of moral behavior in the workplace?

A. Honesty
B. Integrity
C. Exploitation of loopholes
D. Fairness

98. According to self-determination theory, relatedness refers to:

A. Employee autonomy in decision-making
B. Positive social relationships and sense of belonging
C. Skill development
D. Financial incentives

99. Which of the following statements correctly describes expectancy theory?

A. Motivation depends solely on intrinsic satisfaction
B. Employees are motivated if they believe effort leads to performance and performance leads to valued outcomes
C. Motivation arises only from monetary rewards
D. Effort and outcome are unrelated

100. Which of the following is an example of combining morals and incentives effectively in management?

A. Rewarding employees for achieving targets while encouraging ethical behavior
B. Ignoring ethics as long as targets are met
C. Giving bonuses for shortcuts that increase efficiency
D. Focusing solely on punishment for mistakes

Answers

1	**2**	**3**	**4**	**5**	**6**	**7**	**8**	**9**	**10**
B	A	A	B	B	B	B	B	B	C
11	**12**	**13**	**14**	**15**	**16**	**17**	**18**	**19**	**20**
B	A	A	A	B	B	A	A	B	A
21	**22**	**23**	**24**	**25**	**26**	**27**	**28**	**29**	**30**
A	A	C	B	B	B	B	C	B	A
31	**32**	**33**	**34**	**35**	**36**	**37**	**38**	**39**	**40**
B	B	B	B	B	A	B	B	B	B
41	**42**	**43**	**44**	**45**	**46**	**47**	**48**	**49**	**50**
C	B	B	B	A	B	A	B	A	A
51	**52**	**53**	**54**	**55**	**56**	**57**	**58**	**59**	**60**
A	A	A	A	A	A	A	A	A	A
61	**62**	**63**	**64**	**65**	**66**	**67**	**68**	**69**	**70**
A	A	A	C	A	B	B	C	A	A
71	**72**	**73**	**74**	**75**	**76**	**77**	**78**	**79**	**80**
B	A	C	C	A	C	B	C	B	B
81	**82**	**83**	**84**	**85**	**86**	**87**	**88**	**89**	**90**
B	B	C	A	B	B	B	A	B	B
91	**92**	**93**	**94**	**95**	**96**	**97**	**98**	**99**	**100**
C	B	B	B	B	B	C	B	B	A

◆◆◆◆◆

5 COMMUNICATION

It's nearly impossible to go through a day without the use of communication. Communication is sending and receiving information between two or more people. The person sending the message is referred to as the sender, while the person receiving the information is called the receiver. The information conveyed can include facts, ideas, concepts, opinions, beliefs, attitudes, instructions and even emotions. Even animals also communicate.

Usually, they communicate, through non-verbal means, they express their feelings, pain, pleasure, joy, sorrow, anger, pity and other emotions. But their language is silent. Besides silent languages, there is a special kind of language - verbal language.

Verbal languages can be used by those who are able to form all sorts of concepts. Since only human beings are able to form all sorts of concepts, therefore verbal languages have been evolved from and confined only to humans.

COMMUNICATION PROCESS

Models of communication are conceptual models used to explain the human communication process. In this section, you will learn about three models of communication:

I. Linear model
II. Interactive model
III. Transactional model

I. Linear Model

It is a simple one way communication model. The message flows in a straight line from sender to the receiver. There is no concept of feedback. The only task that a receiver does here is to receive the message. Different models that follow linear model of communication are:

1. Lasswell's Model
2. Aristotle's Model
3. Shannon Weaver Model
4. Berlo's S-M-C-R Model

II. Interactive Model

The main flaw in the linear model is that it depicts communication as a one-way process where speakers only speak and never listen. It also implies that listeners listen and never speak or send messages. Schramm came out with a more interactive model that saw the receiver or listener providing feedback to the sender or speaker. The speaker or sender of the message also listens to the feedback given by the receiver or listener. Both the speaker and the listener take turns to speak and listen to each other. Feedback is given either verbally or non-verbally, or in both ways. This model also indicates that the speaker and listener communicate better if they have common fields of experience, or fields which overlap. This model is described in Schramm's book "The Process and Effects of Communication".

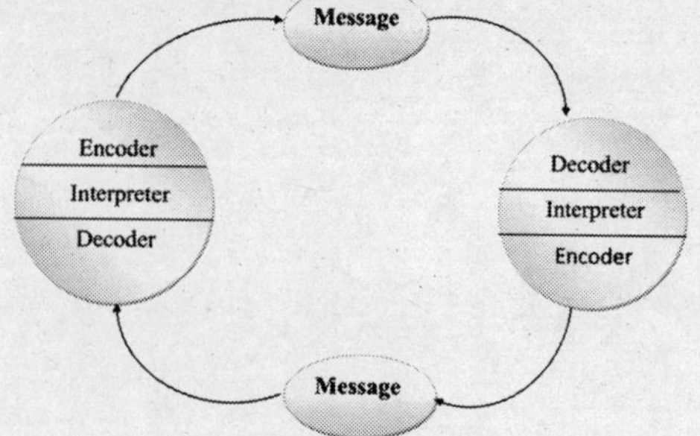

Fig. Interactive Model

III. Transactional Model

The main drawback in the interactive model is that it does not indicate that communicators can both send and receive messages simultaneously. This model also fails to show that communication is a dynamic process which changes over time. The transactional model shows that the elements in communication are interdependent. In transactional model, senders and receivers both are known as communicators and both play equally important role in communication.

There are three implications in the transactional model:

(*i*) "Transactional" means that communication is an ongoing and continuously changing process. You are changing, the people with whom you are communicating are changing, and your environment is also continually changing as well.

(*ii*) In any transactional process, each element exists in relation to all the other elements. There is this interdependence where there can be no source without a receiver and no message without a source.

(*iii*) Each person in the communication process reacts depending on factors such as their background, prior experiences, attitudes, cultural beliefs and self-esteem.

Transactional model relates communication with social reality, cultural up-bringing and relational context (relationships). Non-verbal feedback like gestures, body language, is also considered as feedback in this model.

VERBAL AND NON-VERBAL COMMUNICATIONS

We communicate by exchanging symbols to describe our ideas and experiences. Language is a common symbol system which we use for sharing our experiences with others. We can also use symbols like pictures, colours, signs and sounds to communicate. We do communicate a number of things, by our facial expressions, movements, clothing and so on, irrespective of whether we speak or not.

Communication may be Verbal or Non-verbal. Verbal communication means "that includes words" and communication without words is known as Non-verbal communication. Verbal Communication is further of two types Oral or Written.

Verbal Communication

Verbal communication is any communication that uses words to share information with others. These words may be both spoken and written. Here the sender gives words to his feelings, thoughts, ideas and opinions and expresses them in the form of speeches, discussions, presentations, and conversations.

Types of Verbal Communication

1. **Oral Communication**: Words are the most common symbols of communication and that too in oral form both in organizational and non-organizational context. Man is the only species gifted with language and the use of language is primarily in speech for writing comes afterwards. It is primarily oral communication that brings members of a family, neighbours, friends and colleagues together.
2. **Written Communication:** Written communication include memos, letters, fax transmissions, electronic mail, instant messaging, periodicals, notices placed on bulletin boards, quotations, reports, forms, agenda, diaries, house magazines, manuals or any other device that is transmitted via written words or symbols.

Non-verbal Communication

Every time we verbally give a message to someone, we also impact a non-verbal message. Besides words in oral or written form, message can be transmitted without using words which includes body movements, posture and gestures. Body movements are strong indicators of how you feel. Leaning forward usually conveys a positive attitude towards the other person, while leaning backwards could be interpreted negatively. Posture also communicates a great deal of information about you. The way you sit, stand, slump or slouch provides information about your sex, status, self-image, attitudes and emotional state. Slouching or sitting with your head in your hands often indicates that you are feeling low, whereas sitting with your feet on the desk may be interpreted by others as a sign of your feeling of superiority.

Gestures are movements of hands, legs, arms and feet. People vary in the amount of gesturing they use. Hand gestures are commonly used to describe or emphasize a verbal description or to communicate attitudes. For example, in a conversation, crossing your arms generally conveys a less aggressive attitude than putting your hands on your hips. We lift one eyebrow for disbelief. We rub our noses for puzzlement. We clasp our arms to isolate ourselves or to protect ourselves. We shrug our shoulders for indifference, wink one eye for intimacy, tap our fingers for impatience, and slap our forehead for forgetfulness.

On the basis of Direction of Communication

(*i*) **Downward Communication:** Downward communication occurs when information and messages flow down through an organization's formal chain of command or hierarchical structure. In other words, messages and orders start at the upper levels of the organizational hierarchy and move down toward the bottom levels. Responses to downward communications move up along the same path.

(*ii*) **Upward Communication:** Communication is a very important part of working in the business environment. Managers must be able to communicate with employees and employees must be able to communicate with managers in order to have a profitable business. Upward communication is the flow of information from front line employees to managers, supervisors, and directors.

(*iii*) **Horizontal or Lateral Communication:** Horizontal communication is the transmission of information between people, divisions, dep artments or units within the same level of organizational hierarchy. You can distinguish it from vertical communication, which is the transmission of information between different levels of the organizational hierarchy. Horizontal communication is often referred to as 'lateral communication'.

BARRIERS TO COMMUNICATION

Barriers to communication are those factors which produce obstacles in the way of reaching message to the receiver. There are five kinds of barriers to communication:

1. **Personal Barriers:** Human beings differ from one another because of different geographical, economic, social, educational or occupational backgrounds. Some characteristics are inherited by them due to their birth, family backgrounds, upbringing or social events that are unique to them. These include:
   (*a*) personal emotions;
   (*b*) biases;
   (*c*) perceptual variations;
   (*d*) competencies;
   (*e*) mental faculties;
   (*f*) five senses and
   (*g*) psychological problems.
2. **Semantic Barriers:** Semantic is the science of meanings. A word can carry as many as five hundred meanings. Semantic barriers arise due to differences in meanings, which people attach to the different words. The meanings of the words are not in the words; these are with us. A poor choice of symbols or their confused meanings could distort communi-cation. Semantic barriers can be subdivided into:

(*a*) word interpretations;
(*b*) gestures (handshakes and frowns);
(*c*) language translations;
(*d*) signs and symbols; and
(*e*) cue meanings.

3. **Organisational Climatic Barriers:** These are the barriers that are created due to problems in the culture of the organisation and also, due to lack of proper directions of the managers or top brass!

These are as follows:

(*a*) Fears
(*b*) Fears of being misinterpreted
(*c*) Fear of distortion by grapevine
(*d*) Fear of exposing oneself to criticism
(*e*) Fear of getting fired.
(*f*) Poor or Ego-centered Supervision: Poor super-vision may create obstacles in the communi-cation process. Typically, the person may think that he is being ignored or dominated.
(*h*) Insincerity and Lack of Confidence: Insincerity means that communication is superficial. Lack of confidence means that the message or the communicator of the message is not trustworthy.

4. **Organisational Structure Barriers:** When the organizational structure is not properly defined, the responsibility and authority are not assigned and channels are also not clear. Thus, communication is likely to be ineffective and even harmful. These barriers are as follows:

(*a*) Lack of chain of command
(*b*) Bureaucratic
(*c*) Political manipulations.
(*d*) Class conflicts

5. **Technical Barriers:** These are the barriers that arise due to

(*a*) Space or geographical distance;
(*b*) Mechanical failures and disturbances;
(*c*) Physical obstructions (too much emphasis on the Organisation structure);
(*d*) Technological malfunctions (like bad telephone lines, poor printouts from the printer etc);
(*e*) Improper time of communication; and
(*f*) Wrong time of communication

Multiple Choice Questions

1. _______ means communication without words.

A. Object communication
B. Written communication
C. Oral communication
D. Non-verbal communication

2. The person who transmits the message is called _______.

A. channel B. sender
C. receiver D. response

3. At each stage in the process of communication, there is a possibility of interference which may hinder the process. Such interference is known as ________.

A. sender B. receiver
C. barrier D. none of them

4. _______ describes all forms of human communication that are not verbal.

A. prosody B. vocalics
C. haptics D. para language

5. Normally communication is _______, wherein the information or message is transferred from one person to other.

A. impersonal B. interpersonal
C. personal D. important

6. A _____ connects the sender to the receiver.

A. Channel B. Noise
C. Communication D. Feedback

7. The _______ in the usage of words may be a serious barrier to effective communication.
A. disturbance B. discrimination
C. disorder D. distortion

8. Most of us use _____ and ______ in addition to words, when we speak.
A. words and gestures
B. gestures and body language
C. body language and posture
D. posture and eye gazing

9. ______ refers to pitch, loudness, duration, intonation and tempo.
A. touches B. prosody
C. gestures D. haptics

10. Communication that takes place between the members of an organization – within themselves is_____.
A. external B. formal
C. informal D. internal

11. Informal meetings mark the ______ of the problem.
A. immediately B. immediacy
C. importance D. improvement

12. The problem with proofreading is that you will have to be good at ______ and ______.
A. spelling, punctuation
B. pronunciation, spelling
C. punctuation, pronunciation
D. para phrasing, spelling

13. Every sentence has two essential parts a ______ and a ______.
A. clause, predicate B. subject, phrase
C. predicate, subject D. subject, clause

14. Oral communication ensures ____ and ___.
A. fluency; speed
B. adequate attention; immediate response
C. speedy interaction; immediate response
D. speed; attention

15. As a means of communication, e-mails have features of immediacy of both _____ and ______.
A. reading, receiving
B. writing, sending
C. calling, receiving
D. receiving, sending

16. Unclarified assumptions in a communication can lead to________ and ________.
A. premature evaluation, poor listening
B. lack of planning, physical barriers
C. information overload, selective perception
D. confusion, misunderstanding

17. A resume needs conceptualization of your _____ and ______ all into one document.
A. objectives, experiences
B. projects, skills
C. accomplishments, experiences
D. skills, aims

18. ________ and ________ are act as barriers to communication.
A. semantic distortions, lack of planning
B. sender, receiver
C. the channel, message
D. feedback, sender

19. The primary goal of communication is to _______.
A. to create barriers
B. to create noises
C. to effect a change
D. none of these

20. Communication through ________ and ________ is called verbal communication.
A. written material and gestures
B. gestures and spoken words
C. spoken words and written material
D. body language and gestures

21. ____ is an exchange of facts, ideas, opinions or emotions by two or more persons.
A. communication B. combination
C. conversation D. connection

22. _________ is the study of touches as non-verbal communication.
A. haptics B. body language
C. gestures D. prosody

23. ______ and ______ as visual aids should contain the minimum information necessary.

A. flip charts, slide
B. PowerPoint, overhead projects
C. video, film
D. overhead projects, slides

24. Too much of ________ communication in the workspace may also prove ________. It may lead to negligence of work.

A. formal, positive
B. informal, negative
C. verbal, positive
D. non-verbal, negative

25. Communication helps managers utilize ________ and _____ in the most effective and efficient manner.

A. employees, organization
B. control, evaluation of performance
C. plans, goals
D. manpower, resources

26. In large organizations, upward communication often becomes distorted primarily due to:

A. Excessive formalization of communication channels
B. Power distance and fear of negative consequences
C. Lack of technological support systems
D. Overemphasis on written communication

27. Which of the following BEST explains why downward communication may fail even when messages are clear and well-structured?

A. Employees lack technical competence
B. The informal communication network overrides formal messages
C. Psychological resistance and perceptual differences among subordinates
D. Messages are transmitted too quickly

28. When middle management acts as a "communication bottleneck", the organization is MOST likely experiencing:

A. Breakdown of lateral communication
B. Over-centralization affecting upward and downward communication
C. Excessive informal communication
D. Semantic barriers in message encoding

29. Which condition MOST enhances the effectiveness of lateral communication in a matrix organization?

A. Strong vertical authority and strict hierarchy
B. Clearly defined performance appraisal systems
C. Shared goals and mutual interdependence among units
D. Formal reporting relationships

30. A manager who selectively passes only positive feedback to top management is contributing to:

A. Information overload in downward communication
B. Filtering in upward communication
C. Role ambiguity in lateral communication
D. Redundancy in formal communication

31. Which of the following scenarios BEST demonstrates the strategic role of downward communication?

A. Employees negotiating task responsibilities across departments
B. Senior management translating organizational vision into operational objectives
C. Employees reporting operational problems to supervisors
D. Informal peer discussions on workflow improvements

32. Excessive reliance on lateral communication without adequate downward guidance is MOST likely to result in:

A. Improved innovation and collaboration
B. Faster decision-making
C. Role confusion and authority dilution
D. Strong organizational culture

33. In knowledge-based organizations, upward communication becomes critical primarily because it:

A. Reinforces managerial authority
B. Facilitates employee compliance

C. Enables strategic decision-making through ground-level insights
D. Reduces the need for formal controls

34. Which factor MOST differentiates lateral communication from informal communication?
A. Speed of message transmission
B. Absence of hierarchy
C. Purposeful coordination across equivalent organizational levels
D. Use of non-verbal cues

35. Downward communication is MOST effective when it is:
A. Highly centralized and tightly controlled
B. Limited to written instructions
C. Supported by feedback mechanisms and clarification channels
D. Delivered only through formal authority

36. In multinational corporations, which challenge MOST complicates downward communication?
A. Time zone differences
B. Cultural differences affecting interpretation and acceptance of messages
C. Overuse of digital platforms
D. Excessive lateral communication

37. Which statement BEST captures the relationship between communication direction and organizational effectiveness?
A. Strong downward communication alone ensures control and efficiency
B. Effective lateral communication can substitute vertical communication
C. Balanced integration of upward, downward, and lateral communication enhances adaptability
D. Upward communication is less critical in stable environments

38. Which communication channel is MOST appropriate for conveying ambiguous and emotionally sensitive information?
A. Formal written report
B. Email
C. Face-to-face communication
D. Notice board announcement

39. According to Media Richness Theory, which channel is considered the richest?
A. Video conferencing
B. Telephone
C. Email
D. Face-to-face interaction

40. Which factor MOST influences the selection of a communication channel in organizations?
A. Cost of the channel
B. Organizational size
C. Nature and complexity of the message
D. Sender's personal preference

41. Which of the following is a limitation of written communication channels?
A. Lack of legal validity
B. Absence of feedback and emotional cues
C. High cost
D. Time inefficiency

42. In virtual teams, which communication channel MOST reduces misunderstandings?
A. Text messages
B. Emails
C. Video conferencing
D. Online notice boards

43. When speed is critical and record-keeping is not required, the BEST communication channel is:
A. Formal memo B. Email
C. Telephone call D. Circular

44. Which channel is MOST suitable for standardized and routine communication?
A. Face-to-face discussion
B. Informal conversation
C. Written manuals and reports
D. Video meetings

45. Excessive reliance on digital communication channels can lead to:
A. Improved message clarity
B. Reduced information overload

C. Communication fatigue and misinterpretation
D. Stronger interpersonal relationships

46. Which communication channel BEST supports two-way feedback in real time?
A. Written report B. Email
C. Video conference D. Circular

47. Formal communication channels are primarily designed to:
A. Encourage social interaction
B. Support organizational authority and accountability
C. Replace informal networks
D. Increase speed of communication

48. Which of the following channels is MOST prone to message distortion?
A. Written communication
B. Face-to-face communication
C. Informal grapevine
D. Official circulars

49. In cross-cultural communication, which channel minimizes cultural misunderstanding?
A. Email
B. Written notice
C. Face-to-face communication
D. Text messaging

50. Which communication channel is MOST effective for persuasion at senior management level?
A. Email
B. Detailed written report
C. Face-to-face presentation
D. Informal discussion

51. The use of multiple communication channels for the same message is known as:
A. Channel redundancy
B. Channel filtering
C. Media displacement
D. Communication overload

52. Which situation BEST justifies the use of a written communication channel?
A. Resolving interpersonal conflict
B. Conveying policy changes requiring legal documentation
C. Motivating employees
D. Brainstorming ideas

53. Which channel MOST supports knowledge sharing in learning organizations?
A. Formal circulars
B. Informal communities of practice
C. Notice boards
D. Policy manuals

54. Communication channels that follow the chain of command are known as:
A. Informal channels
B. External channels
C. Formal channels
D. Horizontal channels

55. **Assertion (A):** Face-to-face communication is considered the richest communication channel.

Reason (R): It allows immediate feedback, multiple cues, and personal focus.

A. Both Assertion (A) and Reason (R) are true, and R is the correct explanation of A
B. Both A and R are true, but R is NOT the correct explanation of A
C. A is true, but R is false
D. A is false, but R is true

56. **Assertion (A):** Over-reliance on email can reduce communication effectiveness in organizations.

Reason (R): Email lacks non-verbal cues and emotional context.

A. Both Assertion (A) and Reason (R) are true, and R is the correct explanation of A
B. Both A and R are true, but R is NOT the correct explanation of A
C. A is true, but R is false
D. A is false, but R is true

57. Assertion (A): Informal communication channels should be completely eliminated from organizations.

Reason (R): Informal channels always spread inaccurate information.

A. Both Assertion (A) and Reason (R) are true, and R is the correct explanation of A
B. Both A and R are true, but R is NOT the correct explanation of A
C. A is true, but R is false
D. A is false, but R is true

58. Assertion (A): Channel redundancy improves communication effectiveness.

Reason (R): Using multiple channels reduces the risk of message distortion.

A. Both Assertion (A) and Reason (R) are true, and R is the correct explanation of A
B. Both A and R are true, but R is NOT the correct explanation of A
C. A is true, but R is false
D. A is false, but R is true

59. Assertion (A): Communication channel selection influences managerial credibility.

Reason (R): Inappropriate channel choice can signal poor leadership judgment.

A. Both Assertion (A) and Reason (R) are true, and R is the correct explanation of A
B. Both A and R are true, but R is NOT the correct explanation of A
C. A is true, but R is false
D. A is false, but R is true

60. Assertion (A): Lateral communication reduces dependence on hierarchical channels.

Reason (R): It enables coordination among employees at the same organizational level.

A. Both Assertion (A) and Reason (R) are true, and R is the correct explanation of A
B. Both A and R are true, but R is NOT the correct explanation of A
C. A is true, but R is false
D. A is false, but R is true

61. Assertion (A): Digital communication channels always improve organizational efficiency.

Reason (R): They are faster and cheaper than traditional channels.

A. Both Assertion (A) and Reason (R) are true, and R is the correct explanation of A
B. Both A and R are true, but R is NOT the correct explanation of A
C. A is true, but R is false
D. A is false, but R is true

62. Assertion (A): Communication noise can exist even when advanced technology is used.

Reason (R): Psychological and semantic barriers affect message interpretation.

A. Both Assertion (A) and Reason (R) are true, and R is the correct explanation of A
B. Both A and R are true, but R is NOT the correct explanation of A
C. A is true, but R is false
D. A is false, but R is true

63. Assertion (A): Managers should avoid face-to-face communication for conflict resolution.

Reason (R): Direct interaction may increase emotional intensity.

A. Both Assertion (A) and Reason (R) are true, and R is the correct explanation of A
B. Both A and R are true, but R is NOT the correct explanation of A
C. A is true, but R is false
D. A is false, but R is true

64. The PRIMARY reason for the communication failure is:

A. Lack of formal authority

B. Inappropriate choice of communication channel

C. Employee incompetence

D. Excessive lateral communication

65. Which channel would have been MOST effective for initial communication of the policy?

A. Written circular

B. Email

C. Face-to-face or video conference

D. Informal grapevine

66. Which communication channel is MOST appropriate for conveying ambiguous and emotionally sensitive information?

A. Formal written report

B. Email

C. Face-to-face communication

D. Notice board announcement

67. According to Media Richness Theory, which channel is considered the richest?

A. Video conferencing

B. Telephone

C. Email

D. Face-to-face interaction

68. Which factor MOST influences the selection of a communication channel in organizations?

A. Cost of the channel

B. Organizational size

C. Nature and complexity of the message

D. Sender's personal preference

69. Grapevine communication is BEST described as:

A. An unreliable and harmful channel

B. A formal communication network

C. An informal channel that supplements formal communication

D. A downward communication tool

70. Which of the following is a limitation of written communication channels?

A. Lack of legal validity

B. Absence of immediate feedback and emotional cues

C. High cost

D. Time inefficiency

71. In virtual teams, which communication channel MOST reduces misunderstandings?

A. Text messages

B. Emails

C. Video conferencing

D. Online notice boards

72. When speed is critical and record-keeping is not required, the BEST communication channel is:

A. Formal memo

B. Email

C. Telephone call

D. Circular

73. Which channel is MOST suitable for standardized and routine communication?

A. Face-to-face discussion

B. Informal conversation

C. Written manuals and reports

D. Video meetings

74. Which communication channel BEST supports two-way feedback in real time?

A. Written report

B. Email

C. Video conference

D. Circular

75. Formal communication channels are primarily designed to:

A. Encourage social interaction

B. Support organizational authority and accountability

C. Replace informal networks

D. Increase speed of communication

76. Which of the following channels is MOST prone to message distortion?

A. Written communication
B. Face-to-face communication
C. Informal grapevine
D. Official circulars

77. In cross-cultural communication, which channel minimizes cultural misunderstanding?

A. Email
B. Written notice
C. Face-to-face communication
D. Text messaging

78. The use of multiple communication channels for the same message is known as:

A. Channel redundancy
B. Channel filtering
C. Media displacement
D. Communication overload

79. Which situation BEST justifies the use of a written communication channel?

A. Resolving interpersonal conflict
B. Conveying policy changes requiring legal documentation
C. Motivating employees
D. Brainstorming ideas

80. Which channel MOST supports knowledge sharing in learning organizations?

A. Formal circulars
B. Informal communities of practice
C. Notice boards
D. Policy manuals

81. Communication channels that follow the chain of command are known as:

A. Informal channels
B. External channels
C. Formal channels
D. Horizontal channels

82. Which of the following is a key disadvantage of email as a communication channel?

A. Lack of speed
B. Absence of permanent record
C. Misinterpretation due to lack of non-verbal cues
D. High cost

83. Which channel is MOST effective for crisis communication?

A. Email
B. Written notice
C. Face-to-face or live video briefing
D. Informal grapevine

84. The choice of communication channel reflects management's:

A. Technical competence
B. Leadership and communication strategy
C. Personal communication style only
D. Organizational size

85. Which channel enhances coordination across departments at the same hierarchical level?

A. Downward communication
B. Upward communication
C. Lateral communication
D. External communication

86. Which channel is MOST suitable for communicating confidential information?

A. Email
B. Informal conversation
C. Face-to-face communication
D. Notice board

87. Noise in communication channels refers to:

A. Physical sound only
B. Any factor that distorts the message
C. Excessive use of informal channels
D. Technical language

88. Which channel is MOST appropriate for long-term reference?

A. Oral communication
B. Telephone conversation
C. Written documentation
D. Informal discussion

89. Effective managers select communication channels based on:

A. Habit
B. Organizational tradition
C. Message purpose and audience needs
D. Technology availability alone

90. Which communication channel encourages employee participation and engagement the MOST?

A. Circulars
B. Emails
C. Interactive meetings
D. Policy manuals

91. The strategic use of communication channels contributes MOST to:

A. Cost reduction
B. Organizational control
C. Alignment between strategy and execution
D. Reduction in informal communication

92. Which of the following is TRUE about formal communication channels in large organizations?

A. They are always faster than informal channels
B. They reduce flexibility but enhance accountability
C. They are mostly used for social interaction
D. They replace the need for informal networks

93. Which factor MOST affects the efficiency of upward communication?

A. Frequency of meetings
B. Power distance and organizational culture
C. Availability of email
D. Employee technical skills

94. According to the media richness theory, a lean channel is suitable for:

A. Complex negotiations
B. Routine messages
C. Conflict resolution
D. Crisis communication

95. Which channel is MOST suitable for gathering employee feedback in real time?

A. Circular
B. Online polls or interactive meetings
C. Emails
D. Policy manuals

96. Excessive reliance on informal channels may result in:

A. Accurate and timely information
B. Message distortion and rumors
C. Clear record-keeping
D. Strong alignment with organizational strategy

97. Which communication channel is MOST suitable for global teams across multiple time zones?

A. Face-to-face meetings only
B. Asynchronous channels like emails or collaborative tools
C. Physical memos
D. Notice boards

98. The greatest challenge of lateral communication in large organizations is:

A. Lack of coordination among hierarchical levels
B. Excessive record-keeping
C. Conflicts and interdepartmental competition
D. Low speed of message transmission

99. Which of the following BEST explains why video conferencing is preferred over emails for complex discussions?

A. It is cheaper
B. It allows multiple feedback cues and immediate clarification
C. It creates a permanent record
D. It requires less planning

100. Cross-cultural communication failures are MOST often caused by:

A. Lack of email access
B. Differences in perception, language, and non-verbal cues
C. Excessive use of video conferencing
D. Over-reliance on formal channels

Answers

1	2	3	4	5	6	7	8	9	10
D	B	C	D	C	A	D	B	C	D
11	**12**	**13**	**14**	**15**	**16**	**17**	**18**	**19**	**20**
C	A	C	B	D	C	C	A	C	C
21	**22**	**23**	**24**	**25**	**26**	**27**	**28**	**29**	**30**
A	A	D	B	D	B	C	B	C	B
31	**32**	**33**	**34**	**35**	**36**	**37**	**38**	**39**	**40**
B	C	C	C	C	B	C	C	D	C
41	**42**	**43**	**44**	**45**	**46**	**47**	**48**	**49**	**50**
B	C	C	C	C	C	B	C	C	C
51	**52**	**53**	**54**	**55**	**56**	**57**	**58**	**59**	**60**
A	B	B	C	A	A	D	A	C	A
61	**62**	**63**	**64**	**65**	**66**	**67**	**68**	**69**	**70**
D	A	D	B	C	C	D	C	C	B
71	**72**	**73**	**74**	**75**	**76**	**77**	**78**	**79**	**80**
C	C	C	C	B	C	C	A	B	B
81	**82**	**83**	**84**	**85**	**86**	**87**	**88**	**89**	**90**
C	C	C	B	C	C	B	C	C	C
91	**92**	**93**	**94**	**95**	**96**	**97**	**98**	**99**	**100**
C	B	B	B	B	B	B	C	C	B

◆◆◆◆◆

2601-RK

Administration & Finance

Multiple Choice Questions

1. Upgradation of a post means:
A. Abolition of the post in lower grade and creation in higher grade
B. Prescribing higher qualification for a post
C. Allotting heavier duties on a post
D. Expanding span of control over more employees

2. Which of the following sectors is not covered for non-entitled officers to travel by Air in Economy class in LTC?
A. Between Kolkata/Guwahati and any place in NER
B. Between Delhi/Mumbai and Dadra & Nagar Haveli
C. Between Delhi/Amritsar and any place in J&K
D. Between Kolkata/Chennai/Bhubneshwar and Port Blair

3. Which one of the following actions cannot be taken against a Govt. servant for misuse of LTC?
A. Disallowing the claim
B. A penalty under discipline rules
C. Pecuniary fine within prescribed ceiling
D. Forfeiture of next two sets of LTC

4. Please identify the item from amongst the following which cannot be deducted from subsistence allowance payable to a Govt. servant placed under suspension.
A. GPP subscription
B. House Rent (Licence Fees)
C. Income Tax
D. CGHS contribution

5. Which one of the following documents is not required to be supplied to the charged officer along with the charge sheet?
A. Copy of preliminary inquiry
B. Articles of charges
C. Statement of imputation of misconduct & misbehaviour
D. List of witnesses and documents by which the charges are proposed to be proved

6. Out-of-turn allotment of quarter on medical grounds is not permissible to patients of:
A. Heart ailments
B. Liver & Kidney Transplant
C. Tuberculosis
D. Cancer

7. The scheme relating to Compassionate Appointment of Dependents does not cover:
A. A Govt. servant who dies in service
B. A Govt. servant retired on medical grounds before attaining age of 55 years
C. An ex-employee serving jail term
D. A member of armed forces boarded out but unfit for civil service

8. Which one of the following transaction require permission under CCS (Conduct) Rules 1964?
A. To approach court of law for redressal of service grievance
B. To purchase property abroad
C. To open a bank account jointly with a non-Government servants
D. To appear before a parliamentary committee for evidence in official capacity

9. Which one of the following situations will not call for a review DPC?
A. Where eligible persons were omitted to be considered
B. Where ineligible persons were considered by mistake

C. When adverse remark in the APAR of an officer was toned down or expunged after the DPC had considered his case
D. When one of the members of DPC was absent and did not participate in its proceedings

10. Under which one of the following conditions the lien acquired by a Govt. shall be terminated?
A. While on deputation
B. While on leave
C. On joining another organisation on instant absorption
D. While under suspension

11. Navodaya Vidyalaya Samiti deputes a teacher for a day's training at NCERT New Delhi. The teachers travels from his residence in Delhi to the venue of training. The NCERT deputes him further to visit two schools in Delhi. What will be the T.A. entitlement of the teacher?
A. One day daily allowance & Travel Cost
B. Conveyance reimbursement to cover cost of travel to visit schools
C. Travel cost from home to venue of training and visited places
D. No re-imbursement on any count

12. In an inquiry under Rule 14 of CCS (CCA) Rules, 1965 the following persons participate, as mentioned in a private publication.
1. Inquiry officer
2. Presenting officer
3. Investigating officer who conducted preliminary inquiry
4. Witnesses listed in charge sheet

Which one of the following options is correct?
A. All the four
B. 1, 2 and 4
C. 1, 2, 4 and the charged officer and witnesses on his behalf
D. 1, 2 and 3

13. Additional quantum of 50% of basic pension shall be payable when the pensioner attains the age of:
A. 80 years
B. 85 years
C. 90 years
D. 95 years

14. Children Education Allowance will not be admissible to an employee:
A. under suspension
B. on extra-ordinary leave
C. for the period treated as *'dies-non'*
D. on study leave

15. The concept of 'confirmation' in service/post has undergone a major change since 1.1.1988. Which one of the following is not a feature of new process?
A. Confirmation is delinked from availability of permanent posts
B. One time confirmation in service, at entry level
C. Seniority is linked to confirmation
D. Lien is a right to hold post on regular basis

16. In which one of the following situation an APAR will be required to be written?
A. An officer is under suspension, having worked for more than 3 months before suspension
B. Honorary workers
C. Part-time workers
D. Workers who have worked for less than 3 months in the relevant year

17. In which one of the following cases the suspension period will not be treated as duty?
A. Official's death while under suspension
B. On re-instatement due to full exoneration
C. In cases where suspension is not considered wholly unjustified
D. When a minor penalty is imposed

18. Travelling Allowance in connection with an inquiry under CCS (CCA) Rules 1965 will not allowed to:
A. The Presenting Officer
B. Witness official non-official
C. Defence Assistant if the inquiry is held at his headquarters
D. The charged officer if inquiry is held at a station requested by him

19. In which one of the following eventuality the extraordinary leave will not count for increment?
A. on medical ground

B. for undergoing higher technical and scientific studies

C. for pursuing higher studies for appearing in competitive examination

D. inability to join duty due to civil commotion

20. Withdrawal of amount from GPF Account is not permissible:

A. for extensive repair of ancestral house

B. education outside India

C. payment of membership of elite club

D. meeting expenses in connection with illness of family member

21. While deciding an appeal under CCS (CCA) Rules, 1965 an appellate authority cannot:

A. confirm the penalty

B. enhance the penalty

C. reduce the penalty

D. refuse to entertain the appeal

22. An original application filed by a Govt. servant before Central Administrative Tribunal shall be time-barred unless:

A. filed within one year of rejection of request

B. within one year after waiting six month where the representation is unresponded

C. where the court has allowed condonation of delay

D. where the Govt. servant has good prima facie case in his favour

23. Which one of the following is not a benefit extended to officers posted to North-East Region?

A. Retention of Quarter

B. Benefit of two HRAs

C. Additional LTC facilities

D. Additional chances in appearing competitive exam

24. Which one of the following payment can be permitted by cash or cheque at the option of the Govt. servant?

A. Salary

B. Gratuity

C. Commuted value of pension

D. House building advance

25. Which one of the following is a major penalty under CCS (CCA) Rules 1965?

A. Recovery of heavy pecuniary loss caused to the Govt. by negligence or breach of rules

B. Withholding of promotion

C. Compulsory Retirement

D. Withholding of future increments of pay

26. The inquiry authority appointed under Rule 14 of CCS (CCA) Rules 1965 cannot summon:

A. the charged officer

B. the prosecution witness

C. the defence witness

D. the investigating officer who conducted the preliminary inquiry

27. A Govt. servant has to take permission for appearing before a committee for evidence if:

A. evidence to be given at an inquiry before the authority appointed by the Govt., Parliament or State Legislature

B. evidence to be given in any judicial enquiry

C. evidence to be given before an Arbitrator appointed in terms of a private contract

D. evidence to be given in Departmental inquiry

28. A sanction of GPF Advance/Withdrawal shall remain current:

A. even after expiry of three months in case of advance

B. when withdrawal is effected in installments till expiry of date mentioned in the sanction

C. after expiry of 3 months if withdrawal is to be effected in one installment

D. when withdrawal is effected in installments

29. Which one of the following is not a characteristic of child care leave?

A. LTC cannot be availed during child care leave

B. Child care leave is to be sanctioned like earned leave

C. There is no limit on no. of days or occasions in a year for sanctioning such leave

D. Child care leave shall be admissible for 2 eldest surviving children

30. When a Govt. servant covered under New Pension Scheme is transferred the DDO should clearly indicate in LPC details on the following items except:

A. Permanent Pension Account No.
B. The month upto which Govt. servant's contribution has been transferred to the Pension Fund
C. Details of amount standing at his credit in GPF A/c
D. The month upto which Govt. matching contribution has been sent to Pension Fund

31. A demi-official letter is:

A. similar to an ordinary official letter, written in urgent cases
B. is written in the nature of directions from a superior
C. written in a personal and informal tone to invite personal attention of the addressee
D. always written to dignitaries of high public repute

32. What is a 'starred' Parliament Question?

A. A question meant for written reply
B. A question of general public importance
C. A question for oral reply with provision for supplementary question
D. A question for oral reply without supplementaries

33. When an officer is deputed on training in India, which one of the following is not a correct statement about entitlement of DA?

A. Full DA for 180 day if Boarding/Lodging not provided
B. Full DA for 30 days if Boarding/Lodging provided
C. Half DA for next 150 days if Boarding/ Lodging provided
D. 1/4th DA beyond 180 days if Boarding/ Lodging not provided

34. Govt. policy on Reservation does not cover Appointment:

A. through Direct Recruitment
B. on Deputation
C. by Promotion
D. through Departmental Competitive Examination

35. Premature increments can be granted to a person appointed to a post, by an authority who is competent to sanction such post. Three such increments granted to an appointee are found to erroneously granted. Who is competent to refix the pay withdrawing such increments?

A. The appointing authority
B. The authority competent to create the post in question
C. The drawing and disbursing officer with approval of H.O.D.
D. Impermissible to withdraw such increments

36. While conducting sample verification of 'stores' in a library is found that from amongst 50,000 books over 20,000 volumes were consulted/issued and 100 volumes including one rare title were missing. Which one of the following option is open to the competent authority to take action in terms of GFR-194?

A. Ignore the loss being upto 5 per thousand volumes used and take appropriate action after investigation for loss of rare volume
B. Ignore the entire loss being within the prescribed ceiling of 5 per thousand of volume consulted
C. Report the matter to police for tracing the rare volume
D. Insist on accounting for each volume

37. A Govt. servant selected for discharge on account of abolition of his post is entitled to compensation pension.
Which one of the following is incorrect?

A. A Govt. servant retired as a measure of penalty is entitled to pension not less than 2/3rd of compensation pension
B. A Govt. servant who is dismissed from service is not entitled to any pension whatsoever
C. A dismissed person can be sanctioned compassionate allowance not more than 2/3rd of compassionate allowance
D. A person removed from service can be sanctioned compassionate allowance not exceeding 2/3rd of compassionate allowance

38. A Govt. servant who takes advance from Public funds has to give surety if:
A. he is a permanent Govt. servant
B. he is a permanent Central Govt. servant on deputation to State Govt.
C. he is a permanent State Govt. servant on deputation to Central Govt.
D. he is a temporary Central Govt. employee

39. Which one of the following is not a facility extended to the working spouses?
A. Posting at the same station to the extent possible
B. Double H.R.A., if Govt. accommodation not allotted
C. Counting of combined pay of both for the purpose of H.B.A.
D. Additional L.T.C., if the employer fails to post both of them to same station

40. An offence under POCSO Act 2012, regarding sexual abuse of a male child has been brought to the notice of school principal with an informal request from parent to keep the matter to himself to avoid bad name. What is the responsibility of the principal under law?
A. Warn the accused without naming the child
B. Report the matter to police
C. Get a reconciliation agreement signed by both the parties
D. Send the child for counselling, without action against the offender

41. The incentive scheme for promotion of working in Hindi covers the following categories except:
A. Officers who give dictation in Hindi
B. Officials working in 'A' & 'B' region who write more than 20,000 words in Hindi in a year in their official work
C. Officials who use Hindi in official meetings
D. Officials posted in C region who write not less than 10,000 words in Hindi in a year

42. In which of the following situation a Govt. servant will not get full pay and allowances on revocation of suspension?
A. When a minor penalty is awarded
B. In case when suspension is not held to be wholly unjustified
C. When the officer is fully exonerated in Departmental proceedings and no delay in proceeding was attributable to him
D. In case of erroneous detention and release without prosecution

43. A penalty of dismissal or removal from service is generally not imposed even in the proven case of:
A. Submission of False SC/ST Certificate
B. Possession of assets disproportionate to known sources of income
C. Violating conduct rules regarding prior permission for property transaction
D. Illegal gratification

44. Which one of the following concession is not admissible to persons with disability?
A. Age relaxation for appearing in competitive examination
B. Enhance no. of chances, over and prescribed no. of attempts
C. Exemption from payment of fees for examination
D. Exemption from passing type test for clerical posts

45. In terms of political neutrality under CCS (Conduct/Rules) 1964 and G.I.D. thereunder, neutrality does not imply:
A. Neutrality as Returning Officer
B. Neutrality while performing duty regarding scrutiny of nominations
C. Neutrality while casting his vote
D. Neutrality while working as Polling Officer

46. Which one of the following would not constitute an allegation of misconduct against a Government servant?
A. Disobedience of written orders of official superior
B. Habitual late coming and overstayal of leave
C. Performing at a level below outstanding
D. Negligence of family

47. Which one of the following is not an essential requirement for availing LTC for Escort?

A. The nature of disability warrants need of an escort

B. The employee is ready to travel by lower class and also to pay the cost difference, had he travelled alone

C. No entitled official availing LTC is accompanying

D. Prior permission of H.O.D. on each occasion

48. If husband and wife are Govt. servants and one of them dies. The other one will get:

A. own pay and family pension not pension

B. own pay or family pension

C. family pension and own pay while in service and family pension and own pension after retirement

D. family pension and pension not pay

49. In the matter relating to combination of appointments under FR49, which one of the following is not correct?

A. Additional pay for dual charge only upto 3 months in normal course

B. Additional charge pay beyond 3 month need to opt concurrence

C. Additional charge pay is admissible for holding charge for not less than a month

D. No additional pay for current duty charge

50. Which one of the following event does not amount to Breach of Allotment Rules of Govt. accommodation?

A. Furnishing incorrect information to procure allotment

B. Sharing accommodation with close relatives

C. Unauthorised structure erected

D. Tampering with electric connection

51. If a Junior Govt. servant is getting pay higher than his senior and the senior Govt. servant fulfills all the conditions for equating his pay with the junior, the pay of the senior can be effected by:

A. Stepping up of the pay

B. Grant of additional increment

C. Grant of advance increment

D. Grant of personal pay

52. Which form of Governance is created for Navodaya Vidyalaya?

A. Autonomous Body

B. Statutory Body

C. Society Registered under Society Registration Act

D. Non-Statutory Autonomous Body

53. Union Parliament Exercises control over NVS activities through a source other the following except:

A. while discussing budget of MHRD & Annual Report of NVS

B. through asking Parliament Questions

C. through Members of Parliament corresponding into HRD Minister

D. through Media

54. Teachers have been allowed 10 days Earned Leave in lieu of 20 days half pay leave. This is not applicable to:

A. KVS Teachers

B. NVS Teachers

C. Teachers of U.T. Govt. Schools

D. Teachers of State Govt. Schools

55. Which one of the following cases is not related to Reservation?

A. Indira Sawhney Case

B. R.K. Sabharwal Case

C. Ajit Singh II Case

D. TMA Pai Foundation Case

56. A meeting of Departmental promotion committee is being convened to fill up 12 vacancies. Which one of the following categories is not essential for being represented in the composition of D.P.C.?

A. Member belonging to SC/ST Community

B. A Woman Member

C. A Member belonging to Other Backward Community

D. A Member belonging to Minority Community

57. Reservation for persons with disability is not admissible to persons with:

A. blindness or low vision

B. hearing impairment

C. locomotor disability or cerebral palsy

D. persons suffering from cancer, tuberculosis, or AIDS

58. Invalid pension is granted to a Govt. servant:

A. who is retired on invalid grounds

B. whose initial appointment was invalid

C. who is declared by the competent medical authority to be permanently incapacitated

D. who is retired prematurely for valid reasons

59. Which one of the following statements is not true with reference to POCSO Act 2012?

A. POCSO Act covers a girl child only

B. Covers all children below 18 years of age

C. The Act is gender neutral

D. Withholding the information of offence from police is punishable

60. If both husband and wife are Govt. servants, in which situation both will get separate monetary benefit?

A. House Building Advance

B. Children's Education Allowance

C. House Rent Allowance, if Govt. accommodation is not allotted to either of two

D. House Rent Allowance, if allotted Govt. accommodation

61. Which of the following with reference to Home Town for LTC is **not** correct?

A. Every government servant should furnish a declaration within six months of his appointment

B. Ordinarily a declaration once made is final

C. A change may be authorized in exceptional circumstances by the Head of office

D. The above change is permitted only once during the entire service

62. Which of the following is **not** true when both the husband and wife are Central Government servants?

A. They can, at their option, declare separate home towns

B. Both may claim the concession separately in respect of their respective family members

C. Children shall be eligible for the benefit in one particular block as members of the family of both the parents

D. If husband or wife avails LTC as a member of the family of the other, he or she cannot claim the concession for self independently

63. Which of the following conditions for grant of advance is **not** correct?

A. The amount will be restricted to 90% of the estimated amount

B. Even where the Government servant and family members avail LTC separately, only one advance is to be drawn

C. The claim for reimbursement should be submitted within one month of the completion of the return journey

D. The advance can be sanctioned by Head of the office

64. With reference to the Medical Attendance Rules, which of the following is **not** a member of family?

A. A judicially separated husband

B. Wife of adoptive father

C. A 26 year old legally adopted son

D. Minor brother

It is given that those at (B) to (D) are wholly dependent on the government servant.

65. What is **not** correct with reference to admissibility of Medical Advance under M.A. Rules?

A. to all Government servants drawing a basic pay of ₹ 1,00,000 or less

B. for in-patient treatment in a recognized hospital

C. for purchase, replacement, repair and adjustment of admissible artificial appliances

D. for temporary officials, surety from permanent government servant is required

66. Which of the following is **not** true?

A. A pension once sanctioned can be withheld or withdrawn subsequently

B. A family pension can be withheld or withdrawn subsequently

C. If part of pension is withheld or withdrawn the balance should not be less than the minimum prescribed

D. A pension can be withheld or withdrawn only by the Appointing Authority

67. Which of the following is **not** correct?

A. Emoluments for retirement gratuity are Basic Pay + DA + NPA where applicable

B. Emoluments for death gratuity are Basic Pay + NPA where applicable

C. Emoluments for pension are Basic Pay + NPA where applicable

D. Emoluments for Family pension are Basic Pay + NPA where applicable

68. What is not correct with reference to the effect of dismissal and removal from service on pension and gratuity?

A. It entails forfeiture of past service and he is not entitled to any pension/gratuity

B. The competent authority may however grant a compassionate allowance

C. The amount of compassionate allowance will not exceed two-thirds of compensation pension

D. The amount of compassionate allowance will not be less than two-thirds of compensation pension

69. The maximum limit of retirement gratuity as per the 7th CPC has been raised to:

A. ₹ 15 lakh

B. ₹ 20 lakh

C. ₹ 25 lakh

D. No raise has been made

70. Normally family pension is admissible to one person at a time except in some cases. Which of the following cases is not an exception?

A. More than one widow

B. One widow and children from another

C. Twin children

D. Mother and Father of the government servant alive and dependent on the government servant

71. Which of the following is **not** true?

A. Single Tender Enquiry (STE) is permissible if it is in the knowledge of the user department that only a particular firm is the manufacturer of the required goods

B. STE is permissible if in emergency, the required goods are necessarily to be purchased from a particular source for reasons recorded and by obtaining the approval of the competent authority

C. STE is also permissible if for standardization of machinery to be compatible to the existing sets of equipment the required item is to be purchased from a selected firm

D. In the case of limited lender enquiry late bids can be considered with the approval of the competent authority

72. Purchase of goods costing upto what value on each occasion may be made on the basis of recommendation of a duly constituted Local Purchase Committee consisting of three members of an appropriate level as decided by the Head of the Department?

A. ₹ 1,00,000 B. ₹ 1,50,000

C. ₹ 2,00,000 D. ₹ 2,50,000

73. Barring exceptions invitation to tender by advertisement should be used for procurement of goods of estimated value of:

A. ₹ 10 lakh and above

B. ₹ 15 lakh and above

C. ₹ 20 lakh and above

D. ₹ 25 lakh and above

74. Which of the following is **not** true?

A. For purchasing high value plant, machinery etc. of a complex and technical nature, bids may be obtained in two parts

B. Technical bid will consist of all technical details along with commercial terms and conditions

C. Financial bid will indicate itemwise price for the item mentioned in the technical bid

D. The financial bid should be scaled while the technical bid may not be sealed but both should be in separate covers to be put in a bigger cover

75. Which of the following is **not** a member of family of a government servant for the purposes of CCS (Conduct) Rules?

A. Spouse who is no longer dependent on the government servant

B. Son or daughter wholly dependent on the government servant

C. Son or daughter who is no longer dependent on the government servant

D. Any other person related to the government servant or spouse, whether by blood or marriage and wholly dependent on the government servant

76. Which of the following is **not** true?

A. Permission is necessary for joining an educational institution after office hours

B. Permission is necessary for participation in "Shramdan" organized by a government department or Bharat Sevak Samaj

C. Permission is necessary for joining Civil Defence Service

D. Permission is necessary for seeking redress in courts of law for grievances arising out of employment or conditions of service

77. Which of the following is **incorrect**?

A. Every government servant shall at all times maintain absolute integrity and shall take all possible steps to ensure the integrity of those under his control and authority

B. Joint representation from government servants is treated as subversive of discipline

C. Conviction by a criminal court is a misconduct under CCS (Conduct) Rules

D. It is not necessary to obtain prior permission by the government servants for leaving station/headquarters

78. Which of the following is **not** true?

A. No government servant shall be a member of any political party

B. No government servant shall take part in any political movement/activity

C. The government servant shall endeavour to prevent his family members from taking part in any political activity

D. No government servant shall canvass or otherwise interfere with or use his influence in connection with an election to any legislature or local authority

79. By whom can the order of suspension against a government servant be revoked?

(*a*) By the authority which made the order of suspension

(*b*) By any authority to which the authority who made the order of suspension in subordinate

A. (*a*) only B. (*b*) only

C. By neither D. By both (*a*) and (*b*)

80. A Government servant is deemed to be placed under suspension when he is detained in custody for a period exceeding:

A. 24 hours B. 30 hours

C. 48 hours D. 60 hours

81. Within how much period an appeal may be preferred against the order passed by disciplinary authority?

A. 30 days B. 45 days

C. 60 days D. 90 days

82. Which of the following is a major penalty?

A. withholding of promotion

B. reduction to a lower stage in the time scale of pay by one stage for a period not exceeding three years, without cumulative effect and not adversely affecting his pension

C. withholding of increments of pay

D. reduction to a lower stage in the time scale of pay for a specified period with cumulative effect

83. Who shall be ex-officio Secretary of Kendriya Vidyalaya Sangathan?

A. Commissioner, KVS
B. Additional Commissioner (Administration)
C. Secretary, School Education & Literacy, MHRD
D. Joint Secretary, School Education & Literacy, MHRD

84. Who shall be the Member Secretary of Academic Advisory Committee of Kendriya Vidyalaya Sangathan?
A. Joint Commissioner (Administration)
B. Deputy Commissioner (Academic)
C. Additional Commissioner (Administration)
D. Additional Commissioner (Academic)

85. Who shall be the Internal Financial Advisor and Chief Accounts Officer of the Sangathan?
A. Deputy Commissioner (Finance)
B. Joint Commissioner (Finance)
C. Financial Advisor, MHRD
D. Commissioner, KVS

86. Who is the Reviewing Officer for Principals of Kendriya Vidyalayas, in respect of APAR?
A. Joint Commissioner (Academic)
B. Additional Commissioner (Academic)
C. Assistant Commissioner of the Region
D. Deputy Commissioner of the Region

87. The horizontal reservation in admission is applicable in Kendriya Vidyalayas for:
A. wards of soldiers died in harness
B. wards of Kashmiri migrants
C. divyang jan (Differently abled)
D. SC, ST and OBC category

88. A parent approached Kendriya Vidyalaya NTPC with KVTC (Transfer of the parent is not involved) for admission to class III. The present average enrollment in class III is 47. The principal:
A. refuses admission
B. refers to the Chairman, VMC
C. refers to the Deputy Commissioner of the Region
D. grants admission

89. An employee of Atomic Energy Central School seeks admission at a place of his final settlement with Transfer Certificate issued by Atomic Energy Central school in a KV. (No Atomic Energy Central school is available in the city). The principal:
A. refuses admission
B. grants admission immediately
C. refers to Chairman, VMC
D. grants admission after endorsement of J.C. by the Deputy Commissioner concerned

90. What is the maximum amount of concession granted to secure admission to class XI for students belonging to SC, ST and Divyang jan?
A. 0.4 points in CGPA
B. 0.6 points in CGPA
C. 0.8 points in CGPA
D. 1.0 points in CGPA

91. What is the timeline for forwarding first probationary report in respect of a PGT to the concerned Deputy Commissioner by the principal?
A. On completion of 9 months
B. On completion of 11 months
C. On completion of 12 months
D. On completion of 22 months

92. What is the condition to get summer/winter vacation pay for a newly joined TGT (Librarian)?
A. should have worked for a minimum period of 5 months in the preceding academic year
B. should have worked for a minimum period of 6 months in the preceding academic year
C. should have worked for a minimum period of 5 months before summer/winter vacation
D. should have worked for a minimum period of 6 months before summer/winter vacation

93. A lady teacher applies for Child Care Leave (CCL) for a period of one year. The principal:
A. forwards to the Chairman, VMC
B. forwards to Deputy Commissioner of the region
C. forwards to Commissioner through proper channel
D. disposes of at his/her own level

94. Who is Drawing and Disbursing Officer of a Kendriya Vidyalaya?
A. The Chairman, VMC
B. Principal
C. Vice-Principal
D. Office Superintendent

95. Who is responsible for preparing annual academic plan of a Vidyalaya?
A. Principal in consultation with teachers
B. Academic Committee of the Vidyalaya
C. Vice-Principal/senior most teacher in consultation with teachers
D. Assistant Commissioner concerned

96. Who shall provide special help and guidance to teachers newly entering the profession at Vidyalaya level?
A. Vice-Principal or senior most teacher
B. H.M. (Head Master)
C. Convenor, Subject Committee
D. Principal

97. Who shall be the competent authority to grant permission to non-teaching staff of Vidyalaya to appear in higher examinations?
A. Principal
B. Deputy Commissioner of the Region
C. Chairman, VMC
D. Additional Commissioner (Administration)

98. Who is the custodian of Service Books and Personal Files in respect of Principals?
A. Principal
B. Assistant Commissioner (Esst.-I), KVS (HQ)
C. Deputy Commissioner of the Region
D. Joint Commissioner (Administration), KVS (HQ)

99. An interruption or break in service caused in the circumstances laid down in FR 17-A will:
A. affect pay and allowance
B. affect increment
C. affect leave
D. not affect pension due to reduction of qualifying service for full pension

100. Which of the following is not true?
A. The term 'pay' is more comprehensive than 'substantive pay'
B. Presumptive pay means the pay to which a government servant would be entitled, if he had been holding the post substantively and was performing its duties
C. Personal pay is granted to an individual whereas special pay is attached to a post
D. Personal pay is an addition of the nature of pay to the emoluments of a Government servant in consideration of a specific addition to the work or responsibility

101. A Government servant shall not be treated on duty during:
A. service as a probationer if it is followed by confirmation
B. joining time
C. a course of training in India
D. service as an apprentice not followed by confirmation

102. A Government servant retains a lien on a post:
A. while on leave
B. while on foreign service
C. while under suspension
D. after his promotion to a higher post, the recruitment rules of which do not prescribe any probation

103. Which of the following is not true with reference to regulation of TA of a government servant who is required on any day to perform temporary duty at a place other than normal place of duty?
A. Local journeys should be performed in the same way as the government servant performs the journey to his duty point
B. DA admissible in addition to mileage allowance for the period of absence will be at half the rates prescribed
C. Prior permission of a superior authority should be obtained for journey by special conveyance
D. No Daily Allowance is admissible beyond 90 days

104. Which of the following is not true with reference to limitations on the payment of Daily Allowance?

A. It is not admissible for any period of Casual Leave or RH availed while on tour
B. It is not admissible for Sundays or holidays unless the government servant is actually and not merely constructively in office
C. It may not be drawn for any day on which the government servant does not reach a point outside a radius of 5 kilometres from the duty point
D. It may not be drawn for a continuous halt of more than 180 days at one and the same station

105. Which of the following is **not** true with reference to the absence from HQ for regulating Daily Allowance?
A. In case of journey by rail, with reference to the scheduled departure time
B. In case of journey by bus, with reference to the actual departure time
C. In case of journey by air, with reference to the scheduled reporting time at the airport
D. Where the train or plane is late by an hour or more actual arrival time will be taken

106. Which of the following is **not** true?
A. TA is admissible to and from examination centre in respect of departmental examination
B. TA is admissible to give evidence in a criminal case in official capacity
C. TA is admissible if the Government servant is compelled to travel to another station to obtain a medical certificate, payment of DA at the out station for the halt will not be admissible
D. TA is admissible for the journey when recalled to duty before the expiry of the leave if it is curtailed by not less than a month

107. With reference to LTC Rules, which of the following is **not** part of family of a Government servant if they are wholly dependent but not residing with the Government servant?
A. Step-children B. Step-parent
C. Divorced daughter D. Spouse

108. Maximum time allowed for extension of suspension at a time by the Review Committee is:
A. 90 Days B. 365 Days
C. 180 Days D. 730 Days

109. As per the provisions contained in the CCS (conduct) Rules, 1964, which of the following can be covered under the definition of dowry?
(*a*) A property
(*b*) A valuable security
(*c*) Streedhanam, among the Christians
(*d*) Dowar or Mahar to persons to whom Muslim Personal Law applies

Use the following codes to give the correct answer:
A. (*a*), (*b*), and (*c*) only
B. (*d*), (*b*), and (*c*) only
C. (*a*), (*c*), and (*d*) only
D. (*a*), (*b*), and (*d*) only

110. Suspension may be desirable in the circumstances indicated below:
(*a*) Any offence or conduct involving moral turpitude
(*b*) Desertion of duty

Which of the above is/are correct?
A. Only (*a*) B. Neither (*a*) nor (*b*)
C. Only (*b*) D. Both (*a*) and (*b*)

111. What is the time limit for preferring claims for reimbursement of medical expenses in respect of a particular spell of illness under the Central Services (Medical Attendance) Rules?
A. One Month B. Three Months
C. Two Months D. Six Months

112. Prior permission/sanction of the prescribed authority is necessary.
(*a*) To join an educational institution or a course of studies for a university degree.
(*b*) To seek redressal in courts of law or central Administrative Tribunals of grievance arising out of employment or conditions of service.

Which of the above is/are correct?

A. Only (*a*) B. Neither (*a*) nor (*b*)

C. Only (*b*) D. Both (*a*) and (*b*)

113. Which one of the following is correct in the context of admissibility of transport allowance?

A. No transport allowance where a tour covers full calendar month

B. Half of the transport allowance where tour covers half of the full calendar month

C. One third of the transport allowance where tour covers two thirds of a full calendar month

D. Two thirds of the transport allowance where tour covers one third of the full calendar month

114. In the context of Supplementary Rules, which of the following charges are not reimbursable?

A. Tatkal Seva Charges

B. Conveyance charges for collection of tickets

C. Service tax and education cess charges

D. Service charges for booking of tickets on LTC

115. Which of the following activity is permitted to a Government servant under CCS (conduct) Rules?

A. Acting as election agent of a Lok Sabha candidate

B. Proposing the nomination of an assembly candidate

C. Taking part in political movement

D. To exercise his right to vote in an election

116. Which was the year when the Service Tax was imposed for the first time through Finance Act?

A. 1990 B. 1994

C. 1992 D. 1996

117. What is the rail/air fare entitlement of a government servant who travels in his own car sent under its own propulsion?

A. Full fare B. 50% of the fare

C. No fare D. 25% of the fare

118. What is the extent of absence required from the headquarters to be entitled to full daily allowance?

A. Less than 12 hours

B. More than 18 hours

C. More than 12 hours

D. More than 24 hours

119. What is the rate at which daily allowance is admissible involving local journey of more than 12 hours duration?

A. Full rate B. Half the rate

C. Three-fourth rate D. One-fourth rate

120. Within how many days of completion of tour of an officer or on rejoining duty if he had gone on leave immediately on completion of tour, should the advance of TA on tour be adjusted?

A. 30 days B. 60 days

C. 45 days D. 15 days

121. Which of the following are the acts, conduct and commissions which amount to misconduct under CCS (conduct) Rules?

A. To participate in flag day collections

B. Habitual late attendance

C. To participate in sports activities as an amateur

D. To publish a book in discharge of duties

122. Which of the following activities does not require permission of the Government?

A. To join Civil Defence Service

B. To participate in the fund raising efforts of the National Foundation for Communal Harmony

C. To participate in 'Shramdan' organised by the 'Bharat Sewak Samaj'

D. To join Home Guards Organisation

123. Indicate the period during which the service book of an employee is required to be completed and certified in respect of previous service by the officers who maintain it.

A. In the 25th year of service or 5 years before the retirement, whichever is less

B. In the 20th year of service or 5 years before the retirement, whichever is less

C. In the 30th year of service or 5 years before the retirement, whichever is less
D. None of these

124. Indicate the rate of licence fee charged for out of turn allotment of a government quarter allotted to a Govt. servant.
A. 3 times of normal licence fee
B. 6 times of normal licence fee
C. 4 times of normal licence fee
D. 10 times of normal licence fee

125. LTC cannot be availed during:
A. Earned Leave
B. Child Care Leave
C. Casual Leave
D. Restricted Holiday

126. What is the rate at which a Government servant is required to make a contribution under the New Pension Scheme?
A. 10% of his basic pay plus DA
B. 12% of his basic pay plus DA
C. Only 10% of his basic pay
D. Only 12% of his basic pay

127. To whom is LTC admissible if an official is under suspension?
A. Family members only
B. Suspended official only
C. None of the family members including the official
D. Entire family, including the suspended official

128. Which of the following is not treated as part of the salary as per Income Tax Act/Rules?
A. Overtime Allowance
B. Leave salary
C. Travelling Allowance granted on transfer/tour
D. House Rent

129. Which of the following statements is correct in the context of a Central Govt. Servant?
(*a*) Duty includes service as a probationer or apprentice provided that such service is followed by confirmation.
(*b*) Duty does not include joining time.
A. Only (*a*)
B. Both (*a*) and (*b*)
C. Only (*b*)
D. Neither (*a*) nor (*b*)

130. What is the maximum limit prescribed under Fundamental Rules for grant of leave of any kind for a continuous period?
A. 3 years B. 7 years
C. 5 years D. 10 years

131. Which of the following is not part of Terms of Reference (TOR) to be prepared for hiring of consultants?
A. Precise statement of objectives
B. Schedule of Rates
C. Outline of the tasks to be carried out
D. Schedule for completion of tasks

132. What is the rate of additional Pension payable to a 96 years old pensioner?
A. 50% of basic pension
B. 100% of basic pension
C. 80% of basic pension
D. 75% of basic pension

133. What is the minimum period after retirement during which a retired Central Service Group A officer can take up commercial employment only after obtaining previous sanction of the Government?
A. Five years B. Two years
C. Three years D. One year

134. Who among the following is not included in family in accordance with Central Services (M.A.) Rules?
A. Unemployed son below 25 years of age
B. Parents
C. Unemployed Daughter
D. Major brother

135. At what stage before his retirement, are the pension papers of a Central Government Servant required to be sent by the Head of Office to the Concerned Accounts Officer?
A. 2 years before his retirement
B. 6 months before his retirement
C. 18 months before his retirement
D. One year before his retirement

136. To what extent is the HRA received by an employee living in his own house exempt from Income Tax?

A. Actual amount of HRA received
B. No exemption
C. 50% of HRA received
D. 20% of HRA received

137. How much DA is admissible for the first 180 days of continuous halt at a station on tour/ temporary transfer/training?

A. Full rate B. Half the rate
C. Three-fourth rare D. One-fourth rate

138. After reduction of pension on account of commutation becomes operative, what is the time frame prescribed after which commuted pension is restored?

A. 8 years B. 15 years
C. 12 years D. 20 years

139. What is the prescribed period beyond which a vacancy caused by the deputation of an officer to a Central Government approved training programme may be filled in the normal manner?

A. 90 days B. 60 days
C. 75 days D. 45 days

140. Which of the following does not normally form part of the Bidding document under a two bid system?

A. Conditions of contract
B. Specifications and technical details
C. Contractor's Ledger
D. Price Schedule

141. Which of the following is not a minor penalty?

A. Censure
B. Compulsory retirement
C. Recovery from pay of the whole or part of any pecuniary loss to Government caused by the official's negligence or breach of orders
D. Reduction to a lower stage in the time scale of pay by one stage without cumulative effect

142. Which of the following is not categorised as 'goods' in terms of the provisions contained in Rule 136 of General Financial Rules, 2005?

A. Material B. Furniture
C. Books for a library D. Machinery

143. What is the age above which the Group A Officers of the Central Civil Services are Covered for Annual Medical Examination?

A. 35 years and above
B. 45 years and above
C. 40 years and above
D. 50 years and above

144. For purchase of high value plant, machinery etc. of a complex and technical nature, which of the following bids are obtained under two bid system?

(*a*) Technical Bid
(*b*) Financial Bid
(*c*) Commercial Bid

A. (*a*) and (*b*)
B. (*b*) and (*c*)
C. (*a*) and (*c*)
D. None of these

145. Within how much period of the receipt of the order appealed against, an appeal has to be preferred to the Appellate Authority?

A. 30 Days B. 60 Days
C. 45 Days D. 90 Days

146. Which of the following received by a Government Servant is not fully exempt from Income Tax?

A. Transport Allowance
B. Leave Travel Concession
C. Gratuity
D. Commuted Value of Pension

147. In which of the following cases period of suspension is treated as non-duty?

A. On reinstatement due to full exoneration in departmental proceedings
B. When official's death occurs while under suspension
C. When minor penalty is awarded
D. In cases where suspension is not considered wholly unjustified

148. Fixed tenure prescribed for officers with more than 10 years of service for serving in the North-Eastern states is:

A. 5 years B. 2 years
C. 3 years D. 1 year

149. In which of the following cases does a Government servant not retain lien?

A. While on foreign service
B. While on leave
C. While proceeding on immediate absorption basis to a post outside his service/cadre
D. While under suspension

150. The service book in respect of a Central Government Servant is to be maintained in .... copy/copies.

A. one B. two
C. three D. four

151. A Government servant may seek voluntary retirement after completion of how much qualifying service?

A. 10 years B. 20 years
C. 15 years D. 12 years

152. .... composite transfer grant is admissible to a Govt. servant with compulsory change of residence at the same station involving distance of more than 20 kms.

A. Equal to full band pay plus grade pay
B. Equal to two-thirds of band pay plus grade pay
C. Equal to one-third of band pay plus grade pay
D. No grant is payable

153. (*a*) A divorcee need not seek permission to contract a second marriage with a divorcee or a person having no living spouse.

(*b*) When a Government servant gets married to a foreign national, the fact is not required to be intimated to the Government.

Which of the above is incorrect as per CCS (conduct) Rules, 1964?

A. Only (*a*)
B. Both (*a*) and (*b*)
C. Only (*b*)
D. Neither (*a*) nor (*b*)

154. What is the maximum period prescribed for foreign service to an International Organisation and Autonomous body, trust, society etc. not controlled by Government or a private body?

A. 3 years in one stretch and 5 years in entire career
B. 7 years in one stretch and 9 years in entire career
C. 5 years in one stretch and 7 years in entire career
D. 9 years in one stretch and 12 years in entire career

155. Which of the following is not a punishment under CCS (CCA) Rules?

A. Warning
B. Withholding of future increments
C. Censure
D. Reduction to a lower time scale

156. How is the date of death of a Government Servant treated as?

A. Non-duty B. Working day
C. Medical Leave D. None of these

157. What is the entitlement of TA to an employee who resigns from the Central Govt.?

A. No TA B. Half TA
C. Full TA D. One-third TA

158. Which of the following recoveries is not permissible from the subsistence allowance?

A. Income Tax
B. CGHS contribution
C. GPF subscription
D. Licence Fee of Government Residential Building

159. Booking of Air Tickets on LTC is **not** permitted:

A. under LTC-80 Scheme
B. from web portal of Air India
C. from private travel agents
D. from web portal of Ashoka Travels

160. When both husband and wife are transferred from one and the same station to another same station within 6 months and after 60 days of the transfer of the spouse, what is the extent of composite transfer grant that the spouse transferred later will get?

A. 100% B. 50%
C. 75% D. 25%

161. What is the value limit prescribed under CCS (conduct) Rules, 1964 beyond which a Group 'A' officer is required to report to the Government for accepting customary gifts from near relatives and personal friends having no official dealings with him?

A. ₹ 7,500 B. ₹ 20,000
C. ₹ 15,000 D. ₹ 25,000

162. What is the maximum period for which encashment of earned leave for availing the LTC facility can be done during the entire career of a Government servant?

A. 30 days B. 45 days
C. 60 days D. 90 days

163. Which of the following periods does not count for increment in a time-scale?

A. Extraordinary leave taken other than on medical grounds
B. Foreign service
C. Joining time
D. Entire period of duty in the posting

164. The age of superannuation in respect of nursing teaching faculty with M.Sc. in Nursing in the Central Government Institutions is .... years.

A. 58
B. 60
C. 62
D. 65

165. At what rate will the death gratuity be payable to the family of a Government servant, who dies while in service, with 4 (four) years of service?

A. 6 times of emoluments
B. 2 times of emoluments
C. 3 times of emoluments
D. 12 times of emoluments

166. What is the date from which New Pension Scheme has come into operation?

A. From 1.1.2006 B. From 1.1.2004
C. From 1.1.2005 D. From 1.1.2003

167. What is the maximum permissible period for which the Leave Travel Concession not availed during a block of four years can be carried forward during the next four year block?

A. first 6 months B. first 3 months
C. first year D. first 2 years

168. Who among the following is treated as a family member as per CS(MA) Rules, 1944?

A. Judicially separated wife
B. Married brother
C. Married daughter
D. Divorcee wife

169. Which of the following does not count towards Qualifying Service?

A. On probation
B. Temporary service followed by regular service
C. As an apprentice except in the case of SAS Apprentice in Indian Audit and Accounts Deptt. and Defence Accounts Department
D. Service rendered in State Government

170. What are the maximum number of increments that can be awarded to a sportsperson in his/her entire career for achieving excellence in national and international events?

A. 2 B. 4
C. 3 D. 5

171. Within how much period Disciplinary Authority should take final decision on the Inquiry Report?

A. 6 months B. 9 months
C. 3 months D. 18 months

172. An allowance granted to meet personal expenditure necessitated by the special circumstances in which duty is performed, is called:

A. subsistence allowance
B. risk allowance
C. compensatory allowance
D. None of these

173. Which of the following is the condition for treating training as duty regarding central government servants?

A. The training or instructions should be in India

B. The training or instructions should be connected with the post which the Government servant is holding at the time of placing him on training or instructions.

C. The period of training should not exceed one year

D. All these

174. Vacancies exceeding .... days caused by the deputation of Central Government officers to the approved training programmes may be filled in by the ministries in normal manner.

A. 15 B. 20

C. 30 D. 45

175. Subsistence grant means a .... grant made to a Government servant who is not in receipt of pay or leave salary.

A. daily B. monthly

C. half-yearly D. yearly

176. A Government servant who has completed the .... service including training period as on 1st July, will be eligible for increment.

A. three month's B. six month's

C. nine month's D. one year

177. For the grant of special increment for undergoing sterilization operation, a male Government servant should not be over .... years and his wife should be between 20 to 45 years of age.

A. 48 B. 50

C. 52 D. 55

178. A Central Government officer is eligible for foreign service only after he has completed .... years of service.

A. 5 B. 9

C. 10 D. 12

179. In the case of foreign service to various International organizations and autonomous bodies, trusts and societies, the maximum limit of service for a Government servant is .... years in one stretch and .... years in entire service respectively.

A. 3, 5 B. 4, 6

C. 5, 7 D. 5, 8

180. A request for change in the date of birth of a Government servant may be made within .... of his entry into Government service.

A. six months B. one year

C. two years D. five years

181. Cases in which the sanction for prosecution is required to be accorded in the name of the President, ... will advise the Ministry/ Department concerned and it would be for that ministry/department to consider the advice and to take a decision as to whether or not the prosecution should be sanctioned.

A. the Ministry of Home Affairs

B. the Ministry of Law and Justice

C. the Central Vigilance Commission

D. the Department of Personnel and Training

182. All Ministries/Department shall ensure submission of disagreement cases, where the competent authority proposes to disagree with the advice of the CVC regarding prosecution of a government servant, to the DoPT giving at least .... time for DoPT to finalize its views and communicate the same to the competent authority.

A. 15 days B. three weeks

C. one month D. three months

183. Retired Government Officers to be appointed as inquiry officers should not be more than .... years of age as on 1st of July of the year of his/her empanelment.

A. 65 B. 70

C. 68 D. 75

184. The number of disciplinary cases may be restricted to .... in a year with not more than 4 cases at a time for retired Government servants as inquiry officer.

A. 10 B. 15

C. 20 D. 24

185. As per existing instructions, a government servant who is the charged officer in a disciplinary proceedings, is allowed .... days time to submit his written statement in reply to the charge sheet.

A. 7
B. 10
C. 15
D. 30

186. If vigilance angle is not involved in a complaint against a government servant, the case should be put up to the disciplinary authority for taking decision to initiate disciplinary action for major or minor penalty against delinquent officer under CCS (CCA) Rules within .... from the date of receipt of investigation report.

A. 15 days
B. 1 month
C. 45 days
D. 2 months

187. After receipt of first stage advice of central vigilance commission, the case should be put up to the disciplinary authority for taking decision to initiate disciplinary action for major or minor penalty against delinquent government servant under CCS (CCA) Rules within .... from the date of receipt of 1st stage advice of CVC.

A. 1 month
B. 2 months
C. 3 months
D. 6 months

188. Which one of the following groups of Central Government employees is exempted from furnishing information in respect of their close relations on first employment?

A. Group A
B. Group B
C. Group C
D. None of these

189. A government servant shall be deemed to have been placed under suspension by an order of the appointing authority with effect from the date of his detention if he is detained in custody, whether on a criminal charge or otherwise, for a period exceeding .... hours.

A. 24
B. 48
C. 72
D. 96

190. A case of 'dowry death' as defined in section 304-B of the Indian Penal Code is registered where the death of a woman is caused by any burns or bodily injury or occurs otherwise than under normal circumstances within .... years of her marriage.

A. five
B. seven
C. nine
D. eleven

191. Members of family in relation to a Government servant include:

A. spouse of the Government servant
B. son or daughter or step son or step daughter of the Government servant, who is wholly dependent on him/her
C. any other person related, whether by blood or marriage to the Government servant or to his/her spouse, who is wholly dependent on him/her
D. All these

192. The period of training and duty of Central government servants as Home Guards, etc. is treated as:

A. leave
B. casual leave
C. special casual leave
D. compensatory leave

193. Which of the following statements is wrong regarding government offices?

A. Oral instructions should not, as far as possible, be issued by senior officers to their subordinates
B. If oral instructions are issued by any senior officer, they should be confirmed by him in writing immediately thereafter
C. A junior officer who has received oral orders from his superior officer should seek confirmation in writing as early as practicable
D. None of these

194. Ministries/Departments should immediately identify a senior officer at the level of .... or equivalent who should be charged with the responsibility of ensuring that the references from committees of parliament are attended to promptly.

A. Under Secretary
B. Deputy Secretary
C. Joint Secretary
D. Secretary

195. Each communication received by a government office from the Member of Parliament, a member of the public, a recognized association or a public body will be acknowledged within .... days, followed by a reply within the next .... days of acknowledgement sent.

A. 10, 20 B. 15, 30
C. 15, 15 D. 10, 30

196. In case, a reference from an ex-member of Parliament is addressed to a Minister or Secretary, reply may be sent by the concerned Divisional Head after obtaining approval of the .... of Ministry/Department.

A. Secretary B. Joint Secretary
C. Deputy Secretary D. Under Secretary

197. In the case of Government servants, time-limit for grant of permission regarding connection with press or radio, gifts and transaction in movable and immovable property is ...., beyond which permission may be assumed to have been granted by the competent authority in the absence of communication to the Government servant.

A. 15 days B. 30 days
C. 45 days D. 60 days

198. On occasions when the making of gift is in conformity with the prevailing religious and social practice, a Government servant may accept gifts from his near relatives or from his personal friends having no official dealings with him, but shall make a report to the Government if the value of such gift exceeds ₹ .... in the case of a Government servant holding any group 'A' post.

A. 5000 B. 7000
C. 10000 D. None of these

199. Which of the following conditions is incorrect regarding special sanction for massage treatment of a Government servant?

A. It may be undertaken on the advice of the authorized medical attendant
B. It should be carried out by a trained masseur
C. The progress of such treatment should be reported at stated intervals to the authorized medical attendant
D. None of these

200. A Government servant, being a member of the Indian delegation or otherwise, may receive and retain gifts from foreign dignitaries, if the market value of gifts received on one occasion does not exceed ₹ ....

A. 1000 B. 2000
C. 5000 D. None of these

201. No conveyance allowance is admissible unless the average monthly running on duty is more than .... kilometres.

A. 500 B. 250
C. 200 D. 100

202. In all cases where Government servants drawing conveyance allowance are away from their headquarters on tour, temporary duty, etc., for a period of .... days or more, the allowance will not be admissible for such periods of absence.

A. 10 B. 15
C. 20 D. 30

203. Leave travel concession to visit any place in India is admissible once in a block of four calendar years. The first block was ....

A. 1951-54 B. 1961-64
C. 1971-74 D. 1974-77

204. If both husband and wife are Central Government servants:

A. they cannot declare separate home towns independently
B. they can claim LTC for their respective families
C. the children can claim the concession as members of family of both the parents in a particular block
D. All these

205. Central Services (Medical Attendance) Rules, 1944 does not apply to:

A. persons in railway service
B. defence services personnel

C. Government servants who are on leave or deputation abroad
D. All these

206. No fees should be charged by the medical officers in receipt of .... allowance for the professional services rendered to the central government servants and members of their families either before, or during or after hospital hours.

A. non-practising B. training
C. split duty D. special duty

207. A Central Government Servant after completing 20 years of qualifying service and seeking retirement has to give a notice of not less than .... months to the appointing authority.

A. two B. three
C. four D. six

208. When the place at which a Government Servant falls ill is more than .... miles by the shortest route from the consulting room of the authorized medical attendant he/she shall be entitled to travelling allowance for the journey to and from such consulting room.

A. two B. three
C. four D. five

209. The subsistence allowance entitled to a Central Government Servant under suspension is to be reviewed at the end of .... months of suspension.

A. two B. three
C. four D. six

210. Allotment of ground floor residence on medical ground can be made to a Central Government Servant suffering from which of the following diseases?

A. Serious pulmonary tuberculosis
B. Cancer cases
C. Heart ailments
D. All these

211. As per new Contributory Pension Scheme a Central Government Servant has to contribute .... per cent of the basic pay + DA for Tier-I.

A. five B. ten
C. fifteen D. twenty

212. Which of the following are not covered by CCS (Pension) Rules 1972?

A. Central Government Servants
B. Union Territories Employees
C. Civilians in Defence Services
D. Railway Servants

213. When a Central Government Servant has worked in different departments of Government during his service, the pensionary liability will be borne by the department where he was:

A. first posted on appointment
B. last posted at the time of retirement
C. proportionately shared by departments where he worked
D. employee can choose the option

214. Re-employed military pensioners should exercise option within .... years(s) whether he wants previous military service to be counted for pension in the civil Central Government post.

A. two B. three
C. one D. four

215. A Central Government Servant completing .... years of service is to be intimated the period of qualifying service so determined by the Head of the Department.

A. 15 B. 18
C. 20 D. 12

216. President of India is the appointing authority in respect of all Central Government Servants belonging to which of the following Group(s) of posts?

A. A and B B. A, B and C
C. A, B, C and D D. Group A only

217. Which among the following is not a minor penalty in respect of a Central Government Servant?

A. Censure
B. Withholding of promotion
C. Recovery from pay
D. Reduction to lower stage in time scale

218. Which of the following is the minimum penalty to be imposed on a Central Government Servant where Departmental proceedings have been held under the relevant CCS (CCA) Rules?
A. Warning
B. Censure
C. Withholding of promotion
D. Withholding increments to pay

219. Disciplinary proceedings can be initiated against a Central Government Servant as per CCS (CCA) Rules on which one of the following occasions?
A. Misconduct
B. Refusal to work
C. Refusal to accept promotion
D. All these

220. Which of the following is not treated as marking a day as *dies non* in respect of a Central Government Servant as per CCS (CCA) Rules?
A. Absent without prior information
B. On duty leaves office without proper permission
C. In office but refuses to perform duty
D. Coming late to office

221. Which of the following Officers can conduct Inquiry for the purpose of imposing penalties against a Central Government Servant?
A. Disciplinary Authority
B. Any Appointed Authority
C. A retired Government Servant
D. All these

222. If the Central Government Servant fails to appear before the Inquiring Authority within the specified time or refuses to plead, the case can be adjourned to a later date not exceeding:
A. 15 days B. 30 days
C. 45 days D. 60 days

223. What is the maximum number of disciplinary cases which can be entrusted to a Serving Officer as Inquiry Officer against Central Government Servants in a year?
A. Four B. Six
C. Eight D. Ten

224. The statement of a witness in an Inquiry being held against a Central Government Servant under CCS (CCA) Rules is to be countersigned by:
A. witness concerned
B. accused official
C. inquiry officer
D. All these

225. The Disciplinary Authority is required to take a final decision on the Inquiry Report held against a Central Government Servant within .... months.
A. two B. three
C. four D. six

226. Against which one of the following categories of Order against a Central Government Servant no appeal is admissible?
A. Order of suspension
B. Withholding of pension
C. Order of dismissal
D. Order passed by Inquiry Officer under Rule 14

227. Review Petitions to the President by a convicted Central Government Servant are to be forwarded to the proper authorities within .... days of their receipt.
A. 30 B. 45
C. 60 D. 90

228. A Central Government Servant is deemed to be under suspension if he has been detained in custody for a period exceeding .... hours.
A. 24 B. 48
C. 72 D. 96

229. In cases involving criminal proceedings against a Central Government Servant charge-sheet is to be filed in a Court of Law within .... months of the date of suspension.
A. one B. two
C. three D. four

230. Which one of the following compulsory deductions can be enforced from the subsistence allowance being paid to a suspended Central Government Servant?

A. Income Tax B. House Rent

C. CGHS Contribution D. All these

231. Which one of the following categories of Central Government Servants is not governed by the CCS (Conduct) Rules 1964?

A. Employees of public undertaking financed entirely by Government

B. Members of committees appointed by Government

C. Personal staff of the Ministers

D. Railway Servants

232. Members of family in respect of a Central Government Servant as per CCS (Conduct) Rules include:

A. son and daughter B. step son

C. step daughter D. All these

233. As per CCS (Conduct) Rules every Central Government Servant shall at all times act in accordance with Government policies regarding:

A. age of marriage

B. preservation of environment

C. protection of wildlife

D. All these

234. Which of the following is not permitted for a Central Government Servant as per CCS (Conduct) Rules?

A. Joining Civil Defence Service

B. Joining Home Guards Organisation

C. Joining St John Ambulance Brigade

D. Participation in demonstrations

235. Each communication received from a Member of Parliament is to be properly acknowledged by the concerned Central Government Department within .... days.

A. 7 B. 10

C. 15 D. 30

236. As per normal recreation purposes, Central Government Servants can play indoor games in office up to .... p.m. only as per CCS (Conduct) Rules.

A. 5 B. 6

C. 7 D. 8

237. As per CCS (Conduct) Rules, representation from a Central Government Servant on service matters is not to be addressed to:

A. immediate superior officer

B. head of Department

C. lowest authority competent to deal

D. Secretary DoPT

238. As per CCS (Conduct) Rules, a Central Government Servant is not permitted to:

A. canvass for a political party

B. display electoral symbol on his vehicle

C. display electoral symbol at residence

D. All of these

239. Which of the following activities amounts to a strike by a Central Government Servant?

A. Mass abstention from work

B. Go-slow

C. Sit-down

D. All these

240. Government as per CCS Conduct Rules means:

A. State Government

B. Central Government

C. Both (A) and (B)

D. None of these

241. As per CCS Conduct Rules, the time limit for grant of permission to a Central Government Servant for communication with press or radio is .... days.

A. 15 B. 30

C. 45 D. 60

242. Observance of Government policies is defined in which of the following Sections of CCS Conduct Rules?

A. Section 3-A B. Section 3-B

C. Section 3-C D. Section 3-D

243. Which one of the following omissions of a Government servant amounts to misconduct?

A. Willful insubordination or disobedience

B. Habitual late attendance

C. Habitual absence without permission

D. All these

244. Criticism of Government as per CCS Conduct Rules means and includes actions which:
A. effect current and recent Government policies
B. may embarrass relations between Central and State Government
C. embarrass relations with a Foreign Government
D. All these

245. For violation of CCS (Conduct) Rule 20 for the second time, a Government employee is liable to be:
A. advised in writing to desist from such act
B. warned in writing
C. subjected to disciplinary proceeding
D. None of these

246. The maximum earned leave that may normally be granted at a time in the case of any Central Government servant employed in India is ...... days.
A. 100 B. 120
C. 180 D. 200

247. Maximum amount of study leave during entire service carrier which may be granted to Central government servant other than Central Health Service Officer is:
A. twelve months
B. twenty four months
C. thirty six months
D. six months only

248. A Central Government servant cannot have any claim to leave to his credit in the following cases except for:
A. Dismissed
B. Removed
C. Resigned
D. Reinstated on Appeal or Revision

249. A male Central Government Servant with less than two surviving children may be granted paternity leave for a period of .... days.
A. 10 B. 15
C. 20 D. 30

250. A female Central Government Servant with less than two surviving children may be granted maternity leave for a period of .... days.
A. 30 B. 45
C. 60 D. 180

251. Leave shall not be granted to a Government servant whom a competent punishing authority has decided to .... from Government service.
A. dismiss
B. remove
C. compulsorily retire
D. All these

252. The half pay leave account of every Central Government servant shall be credited with half pay leave in advance, in two installments of ten days each on the first day of:
A. March and September
B. April and October
C. January and July
D. June and December

253. Commuted leave not exceeding .... the amount of half pay leave due may be granted on medical certificate to a Central Government servant.
A. one third B. half
C. three fourth D. full

254. Extraordinary leave may be granted to a Central Government servant for the purpose of prosecuting studies certified to be in the public interest subject to maximum of .... months.
A. twelve B. twenty four
C. six D. three

255. A female Central Government Servant may be granted child care leave subject to a maximum of .... days during entire service career.
A. 300 B. 450
C. 730 D. 800

256. There are a total of .... Fundamental Rules applicable to the employees of Central Government in India.

A. 120 B. 130
C. 140 D. 150

257. There are a total of .... Supplementary Rules applicable to the employees of Central Government in India.
A. 135 B. 235
C. 335 D. 435

258. Which of the following are permitted for transportation of conveyance on transfer in respect of a Central Government Servant?
A. Motor car B. Scooter
C. Horse D. All these

259. Which of the following are not included as part of the family of a Central Government Servant?
A. Unmarried sisters B. Widowed sisters
C. Divorced sisters D. Married sisters

260. Public conveyance for the purpose of travel allowances in respect of a Central Government Servant include(s):
A. Rail B. Roadways Buses
C. Steamer D. All these

261. Special Pay is admissible to a Central Government Servant while performing:
A. arduous nature of duties
B. addition to the work
C. addition to the responsibilities
D. All these

262. Which of the following constitute 'strike' on part of a Central Government Servant as per CCS Conduct Rules?
A. Mass abstention from work
B. Refusal to work overtime
C. 'Go-slow'
D. All these

263. A member of Reservist of the Army or Air Force in Civil employ when called up for military training will receive:
A. military pay and allowances
B. civil pay and allowances
C. receive excess of civil pay over military pay
D. receive both civil and military pay in full

264. An order of penalty which purports withholding the 'next increment' for a specified period in respect of a Central Government Servant implies withholding:
A. only one increment
B. two consecutive increments
C. three increments
D. all increments during specified period

265. Lower Division Clerks in the Attached and Subordinate offices of the Central Government are exempted from passing the Typing Test provided they are above .... years of age.
A. 25 B. 35
C. 40 D. 45

266. Nursing Staff working in the Central Government Hospitals/Institutions who possess B.Sc. Nursing/Certificate will be granted .... non-absorbable increment(s).
A. one B. two
C. three D. four

267. Which of the following services is to be charged in addition to the standard licence fee payable by a Central Government Servant for residence provided to him?
A. Water supply
B. Sanitary fittings
C. Electrical installations
D. Furniture

268. The maximum honorarium payable to a Central Government Servant should not exceed ₹ .... per annum.
A. 3,000 B. 4,000
C. 5,000 D. 7,000

269. Concurrence of the Department of Personnel and Training is required to permit a Central Government Servant additional pay beyond .... months while holding additional post.
A. two B. three
C. four D. six

270. The mandatory 'Cooling Off' after every period of Deputation/Foreign Service in respect of a Central Government Servant of the rank of Joint Secretary and below is .... years.

A. one B. two
C. three D. five

271. A is transferred to North-Eastern region from outside the region. His family does not accompany him. What would be his entitlement to carry personal effects if he does not carry his personal effects?
A. Cash equivalent of carrying 1/4th of his entitlement.
B. Cash equivalent of carrying 3/4th of his entitlement.
C. Cash equivalent of carrying 1/2nd of his entitlement.
D. Cash equivalent of carrying 1/3rd of his entitlement.

272. In case of absence from Headquarters for more than 12 hours, the D.A. entitlement is at the rate of:
A. 100% B. 50%
C. 60% D. 70%

273. What is the maximum time limit upto which the charged officer can seek extension of the initial time limit for submitting his statement of defence?
A. 45 days B. 2 weeks
C. 20 days D. 30 days

274. State which is true.
CCS (CCA) Rules applying to:
A. Member of Indian Information Service
B. Railway servants
C. Member of All India Service
D. Person in casual employment

275. Which of the following is not true? CCS (Conduct) Rules are applicable to:
A. every person appointed to a civil post.
B. every person appointed to a civil service.
C. a member of All India service.
D. a person appointed as personal staff of the minister.

276. For entering into a transaction relating to immovable property with a person having official dealing with him/her a Government servant will have to:
A. give intimation within two months
B. give prior intimation
C. give within a month intimation
D. seek prior permission

277. Within how much time an appeal under Rule 25 may be preferred:
A. 60 days B. 15 days
C. 30 days D. 45 days

278. Within how much time can the Appellate Authority revise any order made under CCS (CCA) Rules?
A. One year B. One month
C. Two months D. Six months

279. Booking of Air tickets from whom is not permissible under TA Rules?
A. Any Travel Agent
B. Air India Booking Counter
C. Ashoka Travels and Tours
D. IRCTC

280. A Government servant was appointed on a contract for one year which was extended to three years. Is he eligible for L.T.C.?
A. Eligible only in cases the initial appointment on contract was for at least 2 years.
B. Eligible after one year of continuous service.
C. Contract Govt. Servants are not eligible for LTC.
D. Eligible only if he is a retired Govt. Servant.

281. As per LTC Rules, how many times can the Home Town be changed during entire service?
A. Three times B. Two times
C. Once D. Never

282. A Govt. servant does not retain lien on a post:
A. On his appointment in any autonomous body on direct recruitment.
B. While performing duties of another post
C. While holding a temporary post
D. While under suspension

283. Which one of the following is not correct regarding premature increment?
A. Reasons for grant not to be indicated.

B. Further increment has to be regulated in the ordinary course.
C. It can be granted by the President only.
D. It can be granted by the authority which has the power to create the post.

284. If an order of suspension has been reviewed by the Competent Authority and it is decided to extend the suspension, how much maximum period can the suspension be extended at a time?
A. 120 days B. 60 days
C. 90 days D. 180 days

285. All Government Drawing and Disbursing officers are required to file certificates of TDS by:
A. 31 July
B. 31 May
C. 5th of the following month
D. Not required

286. The privilege of flying National flag on motor car is not allowed to which one of the following?
A. Foreign dignitary travelling in his car
B. Speaker of Lok Sabha
C. Chief Justice of High Court
D. Executive councillors, Delhi

287. In which of the following cases TA to the families of the temporary employees is not admissible?
A. who have not rendered three years of continuous service
B. who retire on attaining age of super-annuation after service of not less than 10 years.
C. who are invalidated
D. who are retrenched from service without being offered alternate employment

288. Revised rates of CGHS subscriptions based upon the Implementation of recommendation of seventh central pay commission are applicable to the employees superannuating on or after.
A. 31.12.2016 B. 1.1.2016
C. 1.2.2017 D. 31.12.2015

289. The block to which the LTC is to be debited is decided from which of the following?
A. Date of submission of claim for reimbursement.
B. Date of application for leave
C. Date of outward journey
D. Date of completion of return journey

290. Which of the following shall not be considered to be part of cost of production for the purpose of Valuation under GST?
A. Interest and finance charges
B. Prime cost
C. Production overheads
D. Administrative overheads

291. What is the entitlement of composite Transfer Grant of a Government servant transferred to another office at the same station involving compulsory change of residence?
A. Half of 80% of last month's Basic Pay
B. 80% of that last month's Basic Pay
C. One-third of 80% of last month's Basic Pay
D. One-third of last month's Basic Pay

292. The Competent Authority for various purposes is:
A. The supervisory officer of an employee
B. The appointing Authority
C. The Secretary of a Department
D. The authority who has been conferred powers under FR-6

293. Which of the following is a major penalty?
A. Reduction by one stage for a period of three years without cumulative effect not affecting pension.
B. Reduction by one stage for a period of one year without cumulative effect not affecting pension.
C. Reduction by one stage for a period of one year with cumulative effect affecting pension.
D. Reduction by one stage for a period of two years without cumulative effect not affecting pension.

294. What is the level of the officer to be appointed as member of Authority for Advance Ruling?

A. Not below the rank of Superintendent
B. Not below the rank of Joint Commissioner
C. Not below the rank of Assistant Commissioner
D. Not below the rank of Deputy Commissioner

295. Additional secretary and DG, CGHS has power to settle the Hospital Bills at approved rates of CGHS pensioner beneficiaries to the extent of:

A. ₹ 25,00,000 B. ₹ 10,00,000
C. ₹ 15,00,000 D. ₹ 20,00,000

296. In which of the following cases filing of Income Tax Return is not obligatory for a Government servant?

A. Tax liability has been discharged through self assessment.
B. Income Tax has been duly deducted by the DDO and certificate issued.
C. Total income during the previous year is less than the maximum amount not chargeable to Income Tax.
D. No tax is due to be paid.

297. Which of the following rules determine forfeiture of LTC claim?

A. Rule 15 B. Rule 7
C. Rule 9 D. Rule 14

298. A Govt. Servant can contribute his contribution towards National Pension System:

A. upto 70 years of age, if one is so willing
B. upto 60 years of age
C. upto his date of superannuation
D. upto 65 years of age

299. Who is vested with the review powers?

A. President of India
B. Disciplinary Authority
C. Appellate Authority
D. Revisioning Authority

300. Donations for charitable purpose made to which of the following is not fully exempt for Income Tax?

A. National Defence Fund
B. Prime Minister's Draught Relief Fund
C. Prime Minister's National Relief Fund
D. National Sports Fund

301. To what extent reimbursement of local journeys at the station of visit and incidental expenses are admissible under LTC rules?

A. Only porter charges admissible
B. Incidental expenses admissible but local journeys not admissible
C. Not admissible
D. Only transport from house to Railway station/Airport/Bus station admissible

302. Verification of Income Tax Return filed is required to be submitted through Form ITR-V if the return has been filed:

A. Through transmitting data electronically
B. In paper form
C. Electronically under digital signature
D. Electronically under electronic verification code

303. Which of the following is correct? Every Government servant shall at all times:

(*a*) maintain high ethical standard and honesty
(*b*) take decisions solely in public interest
(*c*) not do anything contrary to law

Choice:

A. (*a*), (*b*) and (*c*) B. (*a*)
C. (*b*) D. (*c*)

304. For the purpose of Central GST Act the expression 'Supply' includes:

A. Importation of services for a consideration.
B. Activities or transactions undertaken by Central Government.
C. Activities or transactions undertaken by State Government.
D. Activities or transactions undertaken by any local authority notified by Central Government.

305. A Government servant wants to buy immovable property outside India. She/He applies for permission but does not receive a reply. After how many days from the date of receipt of his/her request can she/he presume permission:

A. 90 days B. 15 days
C. 30 days D. 60 days

306. Which of the following is not correct?
A. The charge may relate to matters which have already been the subject of previous inquiry and decision if it is one of inefficiency or incompetence.
B. The charges should be clear, specific and precise.
C. The wording of the charges should be a clear expression of opinion as to the guilt of the accused.
D. Multiplication of the charges on the basis of the same allegation is to be avoided.

307. A sum not exceeding which of the following is allowed as deduction for preventive health check-up of the assessee as per I-Tax Act:
A. ₹ 10,000 B. ₹ 5000
C. ₹ 25,000 D. ₹ 40,000

308. Which of the following is not Fee?
A. Income from occasional participation in sports
B. Scholarship received during study leave
C. Remuneration for writing of study reports for UNO
D. Dividend

309. Maternity leave is not admissible in case of:
A. Threatened abortion
B. Unmarried Govt. Servant
C. Widow Govt. Servant
D. Induced abortion

310. Which of the following activity is not subject to GST?
A. Sale of pledged goods by Bank.
B. Sale of unserviceable parts by transport undertaking.
C. School providing food in hostel to the students.
D. Sale of old machinery and scrap by manufacturer.

311. Which of the following does not constitute a permanent disability?
A. Mental Retardation
B. Blindness
C. Renal Failure
D. Hearing Impairment

312. Which of the following is not admissible for reimbursement under CS(MA) Rules?
A. Expenses incurred on medical termination of pregnancy.
B. Expenses incurred on treatment for venereal diseases.
C. Expenses incurred in connection with operation for sterilisation.
D. Treatment by a private dentist

313. In which case the CCS (Leave) Rules shall apply?
A. Persons locally recruited for service in Indian establishments in foreign countries.
B. Persons paid from contingency.
C. Persons employed in industrial establishments.
D. Deptt. Canteen employees.

314. GST council is the Apex Constitutional Authority to decide policies of GST. It is presently headed by:
A. Union Commerce and Industry Minister
B. Union Finance Minister
C. Union Home Minister
D. Prime Minister of India

315. Which of the following is not admissible under CGHS package rates?
A. Monitoring charges
B. Registration charges
C. Admission charges
D. Cost of toiletries

316. For how many days of continuous halt at a station on tour/temporary transfer/training full DA is admissible?
A. First 360 days B. First 30 days
C. First 100 days D. First 180 days

317. Which is not correct about foreign service of a Pensionable Government Servant?
A. The contribution must normally be paid by the borrowing organisation and not by the employee.

B. The pension contribution is required to be paid.
C. The leave salary contribution is required to be paid.
D. The leave salary contribution for the leave taken while in foreign service is required to be paid.

318. What is the limit upto which a Group B Government servant can receive gift on occasions other than those when making of gift is not in conformity with the prevailing social practice without the sanction of the Government?
A. ₹ 5000 B. ₹ 1000
C. ₹ 1500 D. ₹ 2500

319. Which is not the criterion for recommending retirement under FR 56(*j*)?
A. Ineffectiveness shall be counted even if the Govt. servant is retiring within one year.
B. Govt. servant's integrity should be doubtful.
C. Govt. servant must be found ineffective.
D. Consideration is ordinarily to be confined to preceding 5 years.

320. What is the time limit within which the charged officer has to respond to the charge sheet?
A. One month B. One week
C. 10 days D. 15 days

321. CCS Conduct Rules come into force on:
A. 1965 B. 1964
C. 1956 D. None of these

322. CCS Conduct Rules apply to:
A. Every person appointed to a civil service
B. Every civilian in defense service
C. Both A & B
D. None of these

323. CCS conduct Rules not apply to:
A. A member of All India Service
B. A holder of any post in respect of which the president has, by a general or special order
C. A Railway servant as defined in Section 3 of the Indian Railways act 1890
D. All the above

324. Short title, commencement and application are defined in _____ of CCS conduct rules.
A. Sec 2 B. Sec 3
C. Sec 1 D. Sec 4

325. Definitions are defined in _____ of CCS Conduct rules.
A. Sec 2 B. Sec 3
C. Sec 1 D. Sec 4

326. Government means in CCS Conduct Rules:
A. State government
B. Central government
C. Both A & B
D. None of these

327. Every government servant shall at all times:
A. Maintain absolute integrity
B. Maintain devotion to duty
C. Do nothing which is unbecoming of a government servant
D. All the above

328. In sec 3-A of CCS Conduct rules explained:
A. Observance of Government's policies
B. Prohibition of sexual harassment of working women
C. Promptness and Courtesy
D. All the above

329. No Government servant shall:
A. In the performance of his official duties, act in a discourteous manner
B. In his official dealings with the public or otherwise adopt dilatory tactics or willfully cause delays in disposal of the work assigned to him
C. Both the A & B
D. None of these

330. Observance of Government's policies is defined in ____ of CCS Conduct rules.
A. Sec 3-A B. Sec 3-B
C. Sec 3-C D. Sec 3-D

331. Prohibition of sexual harassment of working women is defined in _____ of CCS Conduct rules.

A. Sec 3-A B. Sec 3-B
C. Sec 3-C D. Sec 3-D

332. For the purpose of Sec 3-C of these rule "sexual harassment" includes such unwelcome sexually determined behaviour whether directly or otherwise as:
A. Physical contact as advances
B. Demand or request for sexual favours
C. Sexually coloured remarks
D. All the above

333. Mark the correct option:
A. Govt servant who may be convicted in a criminal court to inform his official superiors of the fact of his conviction and the circumstances
B. Failure to the part of any Govt servant so to inform his official superiors will render him liable to disciplinary action on this ground alone
C. Govt servant who may arrested for any reason to intimate the fact of his arrest and the circumstances connected therewith to his official superior promptly even though he might have subsequently been released on bail.
D. All the above

334. Mark the incorrect option:
A. To joining educational institution by Govt servants outside normal office hours should be take prior permission before joining educational institutions or courses of studies for universities degree
B. Participation in Shramadan organized by Govt department or the Bharat Sevak Samaj can be permitted
C. Participation in Shramadan or Bharat Sevak Samaj such activity does not interfere with the performance of this official duties
D. None of these

335. The following activities are requiring permission/sanction:
A. To enroll as member of St. John Ambulance brigade
B. To join territorial Army
C. To join foreign language classes conducted by Indo-foreign cultural organization
D. All the above

336. The following act, conduct and commissions of a Government servant amount to misconduct:
A. If the act or conduct is prejudicial or likely to be prejudicial to the interests of the master or to the reputation of the master
B. If the act or conduct is inconsistent or incompatible with the due or peaceful discharge of his duty to his master
C. If the act or conduct of a servant makes it unsafe for the employer to retain him in service
D. All the above

337. The following omissions of a Government servant amount to misconduct:
A. Willful insubordination or disobedience, whether alone or in combination with others, to any lawful and reasonable order of a superior
B. Habitual late attendance
C. Habitual absence without permission and overstaying leave
D. All the above

338. Employment of near relatives of Government servants in companies or firms is defined in _______ of CCS Conduct rules.
A. Sec 3 B. Sec 4
C. Sec 5 D. Sec 6

339. Mark the correct option:
A. No Govt. servant shall use his position or influence directly or indirectly to secure employment for any member of his family in any company.
B. A Govt. servant shall, as soon as he becomes aware of the acceptance by a member of his family of an employment in any company or firm, intimate such acceptance to the prescribed authority.
C. Both A & B
D. None of these

340. Elections are defined in _____ of CCS Conduct rules.
A. Sec 3 B. Sec 4
C. Sec 5 D. Sec 6

341. Mark the incorrect option:
A. A Govt. servant qualified to vote at such election may exercise his right to vote.
B. A Govt servant shall canvass or otherwise interfere with or use his influence in connection with or take part in an election in legislature election only
C. Govt servant endeavour to prevent any member of his family form taking part in elections.
D. None of these

342. The following action by a Govt servant does not amount of contravention of rule:
A. Making normal arrangement during election tours of ministers to enable them to carry out their responsibilities as ministers.
B. Arrangements by district officer for affording normal courtesies and security to Ministers on their visits connected with election campaign.
C. A only
D. All the above

343. Mark the correct option:
A. Prior permission is required to join Bharat Sevak Samaj
B. Participation of Govt servants in the Indo-Foreign cultural organizations to be avoided
C. Mere intimation sufficient to join Samyukta Sadachar Samiti
D. All the above

344. Joining of Associations by Government servants is defined in _____ of CCS Conducts rules.
A. Sec 3 B. Sec 4
C. Sec 5 D. Sec 6

345. Demonstration and Strikes are defined in _____ of CCS Conducts rules.
A. Sec 7 B. Sec 4
C. Sec 5 D. Sec 6

346. Strikes includes:
A. Mass abstention from work without permission
B. Refusal to work overtime where such overtime work is necessary in the public interest
C. Resort to practices or conduct which is likely to result in or results in the cessation or substantial retardation of work in any organization. What are called go-slow, sit-down, pen-down, stay-in etc
D. All the above

347. Connection with press or other media is defined in _____ of CCS Conducts rules.
A. Sec 8 B. Sec 7
C. Sec 9 D. Sec 10

348. Criticism of Government is defined in _____ of CCS Conducts rules.
A. Sec 8 B. Sec 7
C. Sec 9 D. Sec 10

349. Criticism of Govt means and includes:
A. Which has the effect of an adverse criticism of any current or recent policy or action of the Central Government or a State Government
B. Which is capable of embarrassing the relations between the Central Govt. and the Government of any State
C. Which is capable of embarrassing the relations between the Central Government and the Government of any foreign state
D. All the above

350. Evidence before committee is defined in _____ of CCS Conducts rules.
A. Sec 8 B. Sec 7
C. Sec 9 D. Sec 10

351. Rule 10 of CCS Conduct rules does not apply to:
A. Evidence given at an enquiry before an authority appointed by the Govt, Parliament or a State Legislature
B. Evidence given in any judicial enquiry
C. Evidence given at any departmental enquiry ordered by authorities subordinate to the government
D. All the above

352. Rule 11 of CCS Conduct rules explains:

A. Evidence before committee

B. Unauthorized communication of information

C. Election

D. Gift

353. Unauthorized communication of information means and include:

A. To which he is not authorized to have access

B. Which he is not authorized to keep in his personal custody

C. Both A & B

D. None of these

354. Subscription includes:

A. Contributions B. Funds

C. Collection in cash D. All the above

355. Gift is defined in _______ of CCS Conducts rules.

A. Sec 11 B. Sec 12

C. Sec 10 D. Sec 13

356. The date on which CCS (CCA) Rules, 1965 came into effect is:

A. 1st January B. 1st April

C. 1st September D. 1st December

357. According to the definitions of CCS (CCA) Rules, who is defined as a Government servant?

A. A member of a service who holds a civil post under the Union, who is temporarily placed at the disposal of the State Government

B. A member of a service who holds a civil post under a State Government, who is temporarily placed at the disposal of the Central Government

C. A person in service of a local or other authority, temporarily placed at the disposal of the Central Government

D. All the above

358. From the following, CCS (CCA) Rules, 1965 is applicable to:

A. Members of All India Services

B. Railway servant of Indian Railways Establishment

C. Civilian Government servant working in the Defence Services

D. Extra Departmental Agents of Postal Department

359. Central Government Civil posts are classified into ______ after implementation of Seventh CPC.

A. Three B. Four

C. Five D. Two

360. Name the Level to which a Government servant belongs to if he was appointed to a Central Civil post carrying the grade pay of ₹ 4,600 in the scale of pay of ₹ 9,300-34,800 in PB-2:

A. Level 6 B. Level 7

C. Level 8 D. Level 9

361. Name the Authority for appointment to Group ‘A’ services and posts of the Union without delegating any other authority:

A. Governor

B. President

C. Vice President

D. Head of the Department

362. Name the Authority for appointment to Groups ‘B’, ‘C’ and ‘D’ posts of the Union:

A. Vice President

B. Governor

C. Appointing Authority

D. Inquiry Authority

363. Suspension of Government servant means:

A. A kind of penalty

B. Temporary withdrawal of duties

C. Attending office without salary

D. None of the above

364. An Appointing Authority may not place a Government servant under suspension where:

A. A disciplinary proceeding against him is contemplated or pending

B. He has engaged himself in an activity prejudicial to the interest of the security of the State

C. A case against the Government servant in respect of any criminal offence is under trial

D. A Government servant has disobeyed his superior authority

365. From the following circumstances, under which can a Government servant be placed under suspension?

A. For attending office late

B. For a case against him in respect of any criminal offence

C. For disobedience

D. For petty quarrels amongst the Government servants

366. A Government servant is deemed to have been placed under suspension, if he is detained in custody for a period exceeding:

A. 24 hours B. 12 hours

C. 48 hours D. 6 hours

367. Name the authority competent to place a Government servant under suspension:

A. Appointing / Disciplinary Authority

B. Inquiry Authority

C. Leave Sanctioning Authority

D. Subordinate Authority of a Government servant

368. A Government servant shall be deemed to have been placed under suspension:

(*i*) With effect from the date of his detention, if he is detained in custody

(*ii*) With effect from the date of his conviction, if he is sentenced to a term of imprisonment exceeding 48 hours

A. Both (*i*) and (*ii*) B. (*i*)

C. (*ii*) D. Neither (*i*) nor (*ii*)

369. Where a penalty of compulsory retirement from service imposed upon a Government servant under suspension is set aside in appeal, whether the order of suspension is to be continued? If so from which date?

A. From the date of original order of compulsory retirement

B. From the date of original date of suspension

C. From the date of appeal

D. Order of suspension need not be continued

370. Can an order of suspension made or deemed to have been made, be modified or revoked? If so by whom?

A. Inquiry Authority

B. Leave Sanctioning Authority

C. An Authority competent to issue suspension order

D. Order of suspension cannot be modified / revoked

371. Mention the period up to which an order of suspension can be reviewed.

A. Before expiry of 30 days from the effective date of suspension

B. Before expiry of 45 days from the effective date of suspension

C. Before expiry of 60 days from the effective date of suspension

D. Before expiry of 90 days from the effective date of suspension

372. When will an order of suspension made or deemed to have been made, not be valid unless extended?

A. After a period of 30 days

B. After a period of 60 days

C. After a period of 90 days

D. After a period of 120 days

373. If an order of suspension made or deemed to have been made is not reviewed before expiry of ninety days, can it be valid?

A. Yes

B. No

C. Yes, subject to conditions

D. Yes, but with the approval of next higher Authority

374. What is the maximum period of suspension that can be extended at a time after review of the Competent Authority?

A. 120 days B. 150 days

C. 180 days D. 210 days

375. Within the meaning of Rule 11, which of the following does not amount to a penalty?

A. Stoppage of a Government servant at the efficiency bar

B. Compulsory retirement

C. Withholding of increments

D. Withholding of promotion

376. Of the following, identify those who are excluded from the purview of CS (Medical Attendance) Rules, 1944:
A. Railway employees
B. State Government servants on deputation with the Central Government
C. A Probationer
D. Central Government servants on leave preparatory to retirement

377. CS (Medical Attendance) Rules is not applicable to:
A. Defence Services Personnel
B. Government servants governed by CGHS
C. All India Service Officers
D. All the above

378. A Government servant is admitted to a hospital for treatment before retirement but is discharged from the hospital after retirement. Which of the following sentences is correct?
A. He has to bear his expenses from the retirement benefits that he will get
B. He will be reimbursed the expenses incurred by him by his office
C. The Controlling Officer can decide, whether the bills can be reimbursed or not
D. Special sanction from the Ministry of Health is required for reimbursement

379. Extension of medical facilities under CS (Medical Attendance) Rules, 1944 to Industrial Staff working in establishments run by various Ministries is given effect from:
A. 1-8-2010 B. 12-9-2016
C. 1-1-2006 D. 1-1-2016

380. When can a Medical Officer send a Government servant and his family to a private clinic / lab for bacteriological or pathological examination?
A. When it is essential owing to non-availability of such facility at a Government hospital with the consent of the Director of Health Services
B. At the request of Government servant
C. When the Medical Officer feels so
D. For better result

381. What is the amount refunded for massage treatment per visit of the masseur?
A. ₹ 50 per visit B. ₹ 25 per visit
C. ₹ 100 per visit D. ₹ 10 per visit

382. To a Government servant who is entitled to free accommodation in a Government Hospital in Delhi, what are the items that are not refundable?
A. Cottage booking fee
B. Admission fee
C. Dhobi charges
D. All the above

383. To determine the status of a re-employed pensioner for the purpose of medical attendance and treatment, which of the following will be taken into consideration?
A. Pension
B. Pay
C. A and B
D. Re-employed pensioners are not entitled to medical attendance

384. Who appoints a private medical practitioner as an AMA?
A. Ministry of Health and Family Welfare
B. Head of the Department
C. Medical Council
D. Health Minister of the State

385. From which date is Fixed Medical Allowance paid to Government employees working in interior / remote areas governed under CS (MA) Rules stopped?
A. 1-1-2015 B. 3-6-2015
C. 1-1-2016 D. 1-7-2015

386. What is the rate of first consultation fees paid to Medical Postgratuate / Specialists appointed as AMA?
A. ₹ 100 B. ₹ 200
C. ₹ 300 D. ₹ 500

387. What is the rate of first consultation fees paid to Medical Licentiates and Medical Graduates (MBBS or equivalent) appointed as AMA?
A. ₹ 100 B. ₹ 150
C. ₹ 75 D. ₹ 70

388. Who of the following has the power to recognize any private hospitals for treatment of beneficiaries and their family members under CS (MA) Rules, 1944?

A. District Health Officer
B. Ministry of Health and Family Welfare
C. CGEWCC
D. Respective State Health Minister

389. The rate of Intravenous Injection Fees prescribed for AMAs in their consulting room is ______

A. ₹ 40 B. ₹ 50
C. ₹ 60 D. ₹ 80

390. What is the period of stay in a hospital termed as average stay for "In patient" treatment under CS (MA) Rules, 1944?

A. Two weeks B. Three weeks
C. Four weeks D. Six weeks

391. Any hospital stay beyond _____ weeks should be considered as prolonged stay under CS (MA) Rules, 1944.

A. Three weeks B. Six weeks
C. Eight weeks D. Ten weeks

392. What is the pay limit as per Fourth CPC pay scale for reimbursement of diet charges in case of patients suffering from diseases other than TB and mental illness?

A. ₹ 1,350 B. ₹ 1,400
C. ₹ 1,500 D. ₹ 1,650

393. Define the circumstances under which special nursing charges are reimbursed:

A. When special nursing become essential for the recovery of the disease
B. For prevention of serious deterioration in the condition of the paitent
C. Both A and B
D. Neither A nor B

394. What is the ceiling limit for reimbursement of Attendant / Ayah charges per shift of 12 hours?

A. ₹ 75 B. ₹ 100
C. ₹ 150 D. ₹ 200

395. What is the age criteria for women undergoing IVF treatment to be eligible for reimbursement under CS (MA) Rules?

A. Between the age of 21 and 29 years
B. Between the age of 21 and 39 years
C. Between the age of 30 and 40 years
D. Between the age of 25 and 45 years

396. Reimbursement of expenditure incurred on IVF treatment will be allowed for how many cycles?

A. 2 (two) B. 3 (three)
C. 4 (four) D. 5 (five)

397. From which date is reimbursement cases of IVF (In-Vitro-Fertilization) treatment allowed under CS (MA) Rules?

A. 1-1-2006 B. 1-10-2010
C. 22-7-2011 D. 22-11-2011

398. When a claim for reimbursement is rejected by a Controlling Officer, what is the period within which an appeal is to be made?

A. Thirty days B. Forty days
C. Forty-five days D. Sixty days

399. What are the maximum number of consultations that are allowed in the AMA's consulting room for the outpatient treatment of a Government servant?

A. 2 (two) B. 3 (three)
C. 5 (five) D. 4 (four)

400. There should be ______ between the closing of the first spell of illness from one disease and recurrence of the same disease for a second time to justify a fresh claim in respect of Medical Attendance.

A. A reasonable gap B. 15 days gap
C. 20 days gap D. 30 days gap

401. What is the maximum number of days allowed for the treatment at the consulting room of the AMA in case the treatment is in Indian System of Medicines and in Homoeopathy?

A. 15 days B. 20 days
C. 25 days D. 40 days

402. What is the maximum number of injections administered in cases of treatment of non-prolonged nature of treatment at the consulting room of the AMA?

A. 10 injections B. 15 injections
C. 8 injections D. 6 injections

403. To become eligible for TA, what is the distance prescribed between a place where a patient falls ill and the consulting room?
A. More than five miles by the shortest route
B. More than eight miles by the shortest route
C. More than 5 kms by the shortest route
D. More than 12 kms by the shortest route

404. When can an AMA claim TA for treating a patient?
A. When it is mutually agreed between the patient and the AMA
B. When the patient is too ill to travel and treatment is given by the AMA at the patient's place
C. When the AMA is appointed is such terms to treat patients at their place of stay
D. An AMA cannot claim TA

405. Who is competent to refer a patient to consult a specialist / medical officer?
A. Any private doctor
B. Controlling Officer of the patient
C. AMA of the patient
D. The patient himself can consult a specialist

406. What is the frequency at which a Government servant may have his eye-sight tested?
A. Once in every two years
B. Once in every three years
C. Once in every four years
D. Once in every five years

407. A claimant can appeal to the Central Government within 45 days from ______ if his claim for medical attendance is rejected by a Controlling Officer:
A. Date of claim
B. Date of rejection
C. Date of receipt of the rejection order
D. Date of treatment

408. When can cases of prolonged treatment, not requiring hospitalization be referred to the OPD (Out Patient Department) of a Government hospital?
A. When more than four consultations are required within 10 days
B. When more than four visits are required within 10 days
C. When more than a course of 15 injections are required to be administered
D. All the above

409. In-patient treatment is permissible without consulting AMA in a ______.
A. Private nursing home
B. Private hospital
C. Private clinic
D. Government hospital / recognized hospital

410. What are the charges that are reimbursed in case of admission in nursing home / clinics (as in-patient) run by AMAs?
A. No reimbursement allowed
B. Medicines only
C. Consultation fees only
D. Injection charges / medicines

411. Charges of treatment for Immunizing and Prophylactic purposes are refundable for which of the following communicable diseases?
A. Tetanus B. Plague
C. Whooping Cough D. All the above

412. From which date is payment / reimbursement of medical expenses to Central Government pensioners allowed from two sources viz., from Insurance Company and CGHS?
A. 1-1-2006 B. 19-2-2009
C. 1-9-2008 D. 21-4-2006

413. Which of the following types of dental treatment obtained at Government hospitals recognized under CS (MA) Rules, 1944 is reimbursable?
A. Extraction
B. Scaling and gum treatment
C. Root canal treatment
D. All the above

414. What is the maximum ceiling limit for reimbursement of complete denture of one jaw?
A. ₹ 1,000 B. ₹ 2,000
C. ₹ 3,000 D. ₹ 5,000

415. Charges for which of the following treatment is not reimbursable under CS (MA) Rules?
A. Delirium Tremens

B. Treatment of sterility
C. Treatment from a private dentist
D. Operation for sterilization

416. Payment for purchase of artificial appliances is made by the Administrative Authority to:
A. The Government servant
B. The specialist, who prescribes the instrument / equipment
C. To the supplying agency
D. Any one of the above

417. What is the frequency and limit prescribed for reimbursement of cost of boot for patients of polio?
A. Once in 3 years for 3 times
B. Once in 3 years for 5 times
C. Once in 5 years for 3 times
D. No limits

418. Who will bear the maintenance cost of artificial appliances of beneficiaries?
A. Supplying agency
B. Central Government
C. Beneficiary
D. Any one of the above

419. What is the periodicity for re-issue of motorized wheel-chair and tricycle for beneficiaries?
A. Every year B. After 2 years
C. After 3 years D. After 5 years

420. Which certification is essential for reimbursement of prosthetic components and orthotic joints used in appliances?
A. BIS (India)
B. BIS / CE (Europian)
C. BIS (USA)
D. None of the above

421. What is the upper age-limit for reimbursement of sophisticated prosthetic appliances to Government servants and their dependent family members participating in State level sports activities?
A. 35 years B. 40 years
C. 42 years D. 45 years

422. Which item of expenditure is not admissible for reimbursement under CS (MA) Rules?
A. CT scan charges
B. Post-operative care of donor of kidney
C. Charges for surgery for transplantation
D. Cost of contraceptives

423. State the Rule that defines the term "treatment" under CS (MA) Rules:
A. Rule 2 (*a*) B. Rule 2 (*e*)
C. Rule 2 (*h*) D. Rule 2 (*f*)

424. Which item is not included in the package rate for Coronary Bypass surgery treatment taken in a private recognized hospital?
A. Room rent B. Service charges
C. Diet and toiletry D. Anaesthetist's fee

425. Which private hospital is recognized for Coronary Bypass surgery at Chennai for CS (MA) Rules beneficiaries?
A. Trinity Acute Care Hospital
B. Apollo Hospital
C. Madras Medical Mission
D. All the above

426. Who is the prescribing authority for a Deep Brain Stimulation Implant for CS (MA), beneficiaries?
A. secretary, Ministry of Health and Family Welfare
B. Additional-Director of CGHS
C. Any two Government Doctors
D. Neurologist of a Government hospital

427. What is the selection criteria for Cochlear Implant surgery under CS (MA) Rules for a pre-lingually deaf child?
A. Age group between 1 to 16 years
B. No retro cochlear lesion or central deafness
C. No mental retardation
D. All the above

428. The ceiling rate for reimbursement for cochlear implant shall be ....
A. ₹ 5,40,000 B. ₹ 5,35,000
C. ₹ 4,25,000 D. ₹ 3,75,000

429. Which type of bariatric surgery procedure is allowed under CS (MA) Rules?

A. Laparoscopic Gastric Banding surgery
B. Laparoscopic Sleeve Gastrectomy
C. Laparoscopic Gastric Bypass (GBP)
D. All the above

430. Which of the following documents is/are required for seeking permission / reimbursement for bariatric surgery under CS (MA) Rules?
A. Recommendation by specialist / surgeon / Government surgeon
B. BMI report
C. Report of tests for endocrine disorders and relevant reversible conditions that can cause obesity
D. All the above

431. What is the age prescribed for annual medical examination for the Group 'A' Officers of Central Civil Services?
A. 35 years and above
B. 40 years and above
C. 45 years and above
D. 50 years and above

432. What is the package rate prescribed for the purpose of annual medical examination in respect of men and women officers respectively?
A. ₹ 2,000 and ₹ 2,200
B. ₹ 2,200 and ₹ 2,000
C. ₹ 2,400 and ₹ 2,500
D. ₹ 3,000 and ₹ 3,500

433. State whether a Central Government servant is eligible to obtain medical treatment outside India under CS (MA) Rules?
A. Eligible under certification by the Standing Committee
B. Not eligible to obtain treatment outside India
C. Treatment can be taken outside India, if the facilities are good
D. Eligible if the Government servant wishes

434. Identify the medical treatment taken abroad which is not eligible for reimbursement under CS (MA) Rules—
A. Bone Marrow transplant
B. Complex / high risk Cardiovascular surgery
C. Complex medical and oncological disorders such as Leukaemia
D. Complicated delivery

435. Who can be a member of the Standing Committee constituted for purpose of consideration of application of a Central Government servant for taking treatment outside India?
A. Director-General of Health Services in the Ministry of Health in Central Government
B. Joint-Secretary in the Ministry of Health and Family Welfare
C. Director-General of Armed Forces Medical Services
D. All the above

436. When should a bill for reimbursement of medical claim be taken up for condonation?
A. Bills submitted after 45 days from the date of completion of treatment
B. Bills submitted after six months from the date of completion of treatment
C. Bills submitted after two months from the date of completion of treatment
D. Bills submitted after four months from the date of completion of treatment

437. Who is competent to condone a delay in submission of medical claims under CS (MA) Rules?
A. Ministry of Health
B. Head of the Department
C. Joint-Secretaries
D. All the above

438. What is the financial limit up to which powers are delegated to Heads of Department / Ministry to settle cases of reimbursement of medical claims for treatments obtained in emergency at a private hospital / nursing home / clinic?
A. ₹ 2,00,000 B. ₹ 3,00,000
C. ₹ 2,50,000 D. ₹ 4,00,000

439. Who will maintain a register of reimbursement of medical claims of Central Government Servants?

A. Head of Office
B. Controlling Officer
C. DDO
D. None of the above

440. What is the pay limit for grant of medical advance under CS (MA) Rules?
A. Government servants of Level 5 and below
B. Government servants of Level 8 and below
C. Government servants of Level 10 and below
D. No pay limit

441. What is the limit for grant of medical advance in respect of outpatient treatment?
A. Pay last drawn by the Government servant
B. Up to ₹ 10,000
C. 75% of estimated cost of treatment
D. 90% of estimated expenditure if the cost of treatment is more than ₹ 10,000

442. What is the maximum limit for grant of Medical Advance for inpatient treatment of Major / Minor illness?
A. 4 months' pay
B. 90% of the approved CGHS package rates
C. Amount recommended by the treating physician
D. 80% of the estimated cost

443. The advance will be paid to .... on receipt of an estimate from the treating Physician / Medical Superintendent of the hospital.
A. The Government servant
B. The treating doctor
C. The hospital concerned
D. Any one of the above

444. What is the maximum amount of advance that can be granted for the treatment of TB?
A. ₹ 50,000
B. ₹ 36,000
C. 80% of the estimated cost
D. Two months' Basic Pay

445. What is the time-limit prescribed for submission of medical bills for settlement of advance?
A. Forty-five days from the date of discharge from the hospital
B. One month from the date of discharge from the hospital
C. Two months from the date of discharge from the hospital
D. Three months from the date of discharge from the hospital

446. How are recoveries of medical advance granted for OP treatment made from the Government servant when no prolonged treatment is necessary?
A. In four equal monthly instalments from the pay bill
B. In one lumpsum from the pay bill
C. In future reimbursements of medical bills
D. Any one of the above convenient to the Government servant

447. How many hospitals, recognized by the Ministry of Health and Family Welfare under the National Cancer Control Programme, are approved for the treatment of "Cancer" under CS (MA) Rules?
A. 20 Hospitals
B. 27 Hospitals
C. 25 Hospitals
D. 18 Hospitals

448. Which fee is not eligible for reimbursement in cases of Central Government servants suffering from mental diseases?
A. Reimbursement of diet charges
B. Reimbursement of attendant charges
C. Reimbursement of special nursing charges
D. Reimbursement of capitation fees

449. What are the documents required to be submitted by a 'certified patient' for seeking admission in the hospital for Mental Diseases, Ranchi?
A. Two Medical Certificates, one of which should be from the AMA
B. A reception order from the Magistrate of the area
C. A certificate of physical fitness of the patient to undertake travel to mental hospital
D. All the above

450. What is the maximum period of TB treatment that is allowed from the date of detection of the disease for the purpose of reimbursement?

A. 30 months B. 24 months
C. 16 months D. 36 months

451. What is the rate of first and subsequent consultation fees for a specialist not below the rank of civil surgeon for suspected leprosy treatment?

A. ₹ 16 and ₹ 8 B. ₹ 4 and ₹ 2
C. ₹ 8 and ₹ 4 D. ₹ 8 and ₹ 2

452. From which date is the treatment of chronic active hepatitis, sub-set of Hepatitis 'C' and 'D' categorized as specialized treatment in the list of major diseases under CS (MA) Rules?

A. 1-1-2007 B. 1-1-2008
C. 9-4-2007 D. 1-4-2008

453. Which family member is not included in the definition of family for reimbursement of medical claims under CS (MA) Rules?

A. Wife/Husband
B. Parents
C. Brother aged 23 years
D. Stepmother

454. What is the age-limit of a son, suffering from permanent disability of any kind (Physical or Mental), for reimbursement of medical expenses under CS (MA) Rules?

A. 18 years B. 21 years
C. 24 years D. No age-limit

455. What is the age-limit applicable to the son of a Government servant to claim reimbursement of medical expenses under CS (MA) Rules?

A. 20 years
B. 18 years
C. Attaining the age of 25 years or starting to earn or getting married, whichever is earlier
D. No age-limit

456. What is the age-limit of a dependent daughter to be eligible for reimbursement of medical claims?

A. Age up to 18 years
B. Till she starts earning or gets married, irrespective of the age-limit, whichever is earlier
C. Age up to 21 years
D. Age up to 20 years

457. From the following, identify the dependent member who is eligible for reimbursement of medical expenses?

A. Divorced daughters
B. Widowed daughters
C. Widowed sisters
D. All the above

458. Which disability does not constitute a permanent disability for the purpose of medical reimbursement?

A. Renal failure
B. Leprosy-cured
C. Blindness
D. Hearing impairment

459. What is the income limit for dependency of the family members for reimbursement of medical expenses after implementation of Seventh CPC?

A. ₹ 7,000 *plus* the amount of DR admissible on the date of consideration of the claim
B. ₹ 9,000 *plus* the amount of DR admissible on the date of consideration of the claim
C. ₹ 3,500 p.m.
D. ₹ 12,000 p.m.

460. State which of the following sentences is correct for parents of a Government servant to claim medical expenses?

A. They must reside with the Government servant in the headquarters
B. They can reside separately other than in the Government servant's headquarters
C. They can reside either with the Government servant or with the family members at another station
D. They can reside anywhere in India

461. When is the declaration regarding the income and the residence of parents to be furnished by the Government servant to the Controlling Officer?

A. Beginning of every calendar year
B. Once in six months
C. Every financial year
D. At the submission of each claim

462. When can a female Government servant give a declaration regarding inclusion of her parents-in-law for reimbursement of medical expenses?
A. At the time of joining service
B. Immediately after her marriage
C. One year after the marriage
D. Any time after the marriage

463. How many times can a female Government servant change the declaration regarding inclusion of parents-in-law for reimbursement of medical expenses?
A. Only once during her entire service
B. Any number of times during her service
C. Two times in her entire service
D. Once every calendar year

464. Extension of medical facilities to permanently disabled dependent brother of a Government servant was allowed with effect from—
A. 1-9-2008 B. 1-1-2006
C. 19-6-2014 D. 1-7-2010

465. What is the percentage fixed for permanent disability for a disabled dependent brother of a Government servant to be eligible for reimbursement of medical claims?
A. 25% or more of one or more disabilities
B. 40% or more of one or more disabilities
C. 30% or more of one or more disabilities
D. 50% or more of one or more disabilities

466. Which of the following criteria is necessary for a permanently disabled dependent brother to avail medical facilities under CS (MA) Rules?
A. He should ordinarily reside with the Government servant
B. He should be unmarried and wholly dependent on the Government servant
C. The income limit for deciding dependency shall be as prescribed by the Ministry of Health and Family Welfare from time to time
D. All the above

467. What is the age-limit for a male child of a Government servant to take treatment in a recognized Women's Hospital under CS (MA) Rules?
A. 10 years B. 15 years
C. 6 years D. 18 years

468. What is the validity period for recognition of a private hospital?
A. 4 years at a time
B. 5 years at a time
C. 6 years at a time
D. No validity period

469. Which city is covered under special rules for the purpose of medical attendance and treatment of Central Government servants and their families?
A. Delhi B. Allahabad
C. Mumbai D. Kolkata

470. Which area of Central Government servant is excluded from the purview of "Special Arrangements" in Kolkata?
A. South Dum Dum Municipality
B. Airport Area
C. Howrah Municipality
D. Garden Reach Municipality

471. Under Indian Systems of Medicine and Homoeopathy, reimbursement of essential expenditure is done for a maximum of .... consultations at an interval of 10 days.
A. Six B. Four
C. Two D. Three

472. The Central Council for Research in Indian Medicine and Homoeopathy has been divided into .... Councils.
A. Six B. Five
C. Four D. Three

473. Can a Government servant and members of his family claim TA/DA for obtaining appropriate Medical Attendance or treatment?

A. TA only
B. Both TA and DA
C. Not eligible
D. DA only

474. What is the minimum distance specified for claiming Travelling Allowance when a Government servant undertakes a journey to obtain appropriate medical treatment?

A. 15 kms
B. 10 kms
C. 8 kms
D. 16 kms

475. Under what conditions will Government servants be entitled for reimbursement of charges paid for an ambulance used for the conveyance of self / family members for medical treatment?

A. If it is certified in writing by the Medical Authorities that conveyance of the patient by any other means of conveyance would definitely endanger the life of the patient
B. If the ambulance used belongs to Government or local fund or a social service organization such as the Red Cross Society, etc.
C. If the ambulance is used within the same city
D. All the above

476. State whether TA is reimbursed for journey undertaken by the donor of a kidney?

A. No reimbursement of TA is made
B. Expenses of the donor should be undertaken by the Government servant
C. Donor has to meet his expenses
D. TA will be admissible at the rates applicable to the recipient Government servant

477. What is the special railway concession available for a TB /Cancer patient who is travelling alone for taking treatment?

A. Single journey ticket on payment of 1/4th the normal fare due
B. Single journey ticket on payment of 1/2 the normal fare due
C. Single journey ticket on payment of 3/4th the normal fare due
D. No special concession is available

478. What are the circumstances to justify treatment in private Medical Institution in an emergency under CS (MA) Rules?

A. Accidents
B. Serious nature of disease
C. Patient was admitted by others when the beneficiary was unconscious
D. All the above

479. The AMA should prescribe such quantities of medicines as are necessary and sufficient for treatment of the disease within a period of .... days from the commencement of treatment.

A. 25
B. 20
C. 15
D. 10

480. Arrange the following sentences in the correct order to enable hazzle-free reimbursement for a Government servant—

(*i*) Whenever you are sick, consult your AMA
(*ii*) When you go to a hospital for admission, inform the AMA about the fact that you are a Central Government servant
(*iii*) Get all bills, receipts, Essentiality Certificate, etc. duly signed by the AMA
(*iv*) Prefer your claims within the time-limit

A. (*i*), (*ii*), (*iii*), (*iv*)
B. (*ii*), (*i*), (*iii*), (*iv*)
C. (*iv*), (*iii*), (*ii*), (*i*)
D. (*iii*), (*iv*), (*ii*), (*i*)

481. Consultation of AMA is not necessary, if the treatment is for a female family member as in-patient in a ....

A. Government recognized Hospital
B. Government Hospital
C. Recognized Women's Hospital
D. Private Hospitals

482. In case of treatment of female members receiving treatment at a recognized Women's Hospital, they should get the hospital bills, etc., countersigned by the .... of the hospital.

A. Treating Doctor
B. Medical Superintendent
C. Ward Doctor
D. AMA of the Government servant

483. For what purpose should the pay eligibility be taken into consideration for reimbursement of medical expenses under CS (MA) Rules?

A. For special nursing
B. Special attendant
C. Ayah charges
D. All the above

484. Medical claims of — are not referred to the Directorate General, H.S. / Ministry of Health and Family Welfare under CS (MA) Rules—
A. Employees of UT Administration
B. Employees of ABs
C. Employees of PSUs
D. All the above

485. Pathological, Bacteriological, Radiogical or other methods of examination for the purpose of diagnosis should be carried out at a ....
A. Private hospital
B. Private laboratory
C. Government hospital or laboratory
D. Any one of the above

486. If the treatment is expected to be prolonged requiring many consultations and several injections spread over a period of more than 10 days, the patient should be referred to an .... of a Government Hospital.
A. In-patient Department
B. Out-patient Department
C. ICU Department
D. Emergency Care Department

487. Identify the type of medicines admissible for reimbursement under CS (MA) Rules—
A. Siddha Medicines
B. Homoeopathic Medicine
C. Ayurvedic and Unani Medicines
D. All the above

488. Which authority is competent to investigate cases of medical reimbursement involving bribery and corruption?
A. Special Police Establishment
B. Area Sub-inspector of Police
C. Assistant Commissioner of Police
D. Department Vigilance Officer

489. Form of application for claiming refund of medical expenses incurred for taking treatment from an AMA and a hospital has to be made in ....
A. Med. 97
B. Med. 97-A
C. A-4 paper
D. Bills with a consolidated sheet

490. Can a Government servant who obtained a treatment in a private hospital be shifted to a Government/recognized hospital after the emergency is over?
A. He should get discharged only when the hospital authorities discharge him from the private hospital
B. He can choose any hospital for his treatment
C. Prior approval of the AMA is necessary
D. He should complete the treatment in the private hospital only

491. To whom does CCS (LTC) Rules apply?
A. Persons paid from contingencies
B. Persons appointed on contract basis
C. Members of the Armed Forces
D. Persons in casual and daily-rated employment

492. CCS (LTC) Rules shall not apply to:
A. Persons re-employed after their retirement
B. State Government employees on deputation with the Central Government
C. Employees of National Airlines
D. Persons appointed to Central Civil Services

493. What is the minimum service required to avail the LTC facilities?
A. Completion of one year's continuous service
B. Completion of two year's continuous service
C. Completion of three year's continuous service
D. Completion of five year's continuous service

494. Who of the following are not included in the term 'Family'?
A. Married daughters who have been divorced and wholly dependent
B. Stepmother residing with and wholly dependent
C. Father-in-law/mother-in-law of Government servant

D. Unmarried minor brothers residing with and wholly dependent on Government servant and whose parents are not alive

495. What is the income limit prescribed for dependency?

A. Income not exceeding pension of ₹ 9,200 p.m. and Dearness Relief thereon

B. Income not exceeding pension of ₹ 9,000 p.m. and Dearness Relief thereon

C. Income not exceeding pension of ₹ 9,500 p.m. and Dearness Relief thereon

D. Income not exceeding pension of ₹ 3,500 p.m. and Dearness Relief thereon

496. Dependency is not applicable to—

A. Son B. Daughter

C. Parents D. Spouse

497. Who is the Sanctioning Authority for LTC advance?

A. Head of Department

B. Controlling Officer

C. Drawing and Disbursing Officer

D. Head of Office

498. For the following members of family, condition of "residing with" is waived for?

A. Father and mother

B. Spouse and children

C. Brother and sister

D. Widowed daughter

499. Who can authorize a change of Home Town already declared?

A. Immediate Superior

B. Controlling Officer

C. Head of Department

D. Head of Office

500. How many times can Home Town be changed during the entire service?

A. Thrice B. Once

C. Twice D. Four times

501. Which of the following is correct?

A. The declared place of visit may be changed before commencement of journey

B. The declared place of visit can be changed during the journey

C. The declared place of visit can be changed after completion of the journey

D. The declared place of visit can be changed at the time of submission of LTC bill

502. Which of the following statements are not correct in the case of admissibility of LTC?

A. Admissible during Casual Leave

B. Admissible during Special Casual Leave

C. Admissible during Maternity Leave

D. Admissible during closed holiday without any leave

503. Will a Government servant, who proceeds on regular leave and then resigns his post without returning to duty, be entitled to LTC?

A. Yes

B. No

C. Yes, subject to condition

D. Yes, in respect of onward journey

504. Whether reimbursement of special supplementary charges for travel by superfast express trains be allowed?

A. Not allowed

B. Allowed only for home town LTC

C. Allowed

D. Allowed only for All India LTC

505. Whether LTC is admissible for journeys during weekend holidays without any leave?

A. Admissible

B. Admissible in exceptional cases

C. Admissible subject to conditions

D. Not admissible

506. Whether LTC is allowed to Government employees while on 'Study Leave'?

A. Not allowed

B. Allowed for self only

C. Allowed for family only

D. Allowed

507. Can a husband and wife, both being Government servants and residing together claim LTC?

A. Yes, subject to conditions

B. No

C. Only husband can claim

D. Only one of them can claim

508. Whether LTC facility is allowed to an escort accompanying single handicapped Government servant?
A. No
B. Allowed with conditions
C. Allowed
D. None

509. What is the entitlement of LTC to officials under suspension?
A. Entitled for self and family
B. Not entitled
C. Entitled for family only
D. Entitled for self only

510. Whether LTC is allowed during LPR?
A. Allowed, subject to conditions
B. Not allowed
C. Allowed only to Home Town LTC
D. Allowed only to All India LTC

511. Is there any distance limit from headquarter to Home Town / Place of visit on LTC?
A. Within 1000 kms B. Within 5000 kms
C. Within 3000 kms D. No limit

512. What is the entitlement of LTC to Home Town to unmarried Government servants?
A. Once in two years
B. Every year
C. Alternate years
D. Once in three years

513. What is the entitlement of LTC to fresh recruits in the first eight years of service?
A. Two occasions to Home Town, third and fourth occasion to anywhere in India in a block of four years
B. Three occasions to anywhere in India and Fourth occasion to Home Town in a block of four years
C. Three occasions to Home Town and Fourth occasion to anywhere in India in a block of four years
D. First four occasions to Home Town and the next four occasions to anywhere in India in a block of eight years

514. Can a Government servant and members of his family avail LTC in different groups at different times during a block of two or four years?
A. No
B. Yes
C. Allowed only for four year block
D. Allowed only for two year block

515. Whether some members of the family can avail concession to "home town" while some others for visiting "anywhere in India" in the same two-year block?
A. No
B. Yes, subject to conditions
C. Yes
D. Family members must avail the same LTC as Government servant

516. How is the carry over of Leave Travel Concession allowed?
A. Within the second year of next block of two years or four years
B. Carry over of LTC is not allowed
C. Within the first year of next block of two years or four years
D. Carry over of LTC is always allowed

517. Whether a Government servant and each member of his family is permitted to visit different places of their choice during a block of four years?
A. Permitted
B. Not permitted
C. Family should visit same place as Government servant
D. Government servant and family must travel together to same place

518. Whether travel by air is permitted between places not connected by rail and an alternative means of travel is either not available or is more expensive?
A. Permitted
B. Not permitted
C. Restricted to road mileage
D. None of the above

519. What will be the restriction of train fare in the case of air journey by non-entitled officers having concessional train fare for his family members?

A. 75% of train fare
B. Actual concessional train fare
C. 50% of train fare
D. If full air fare has been charged and paid, then full train fare will be reimbursed

520. Which of the following claim is admissible for travel on LTC by air?
A. Daily Allowance and Air fare ticket
B. Incidental expenses and Air fare ticket
C. LTC-80 fare of Air India
D. Expenditure on local journeys and Air fare ticket

521. By which mode can air tickets be purchased for travel on LTC?
A. By private agencies
B. Through Internet / Indian airlines directly / Authorized travel agents
C. By Spice Jet, Jet Airways
D. In make-my trip

522. Which of the following air travel is admissible in respect of entitled officers to travel on LTC by Air for stations connected by Air India?
A. By any private airlines
B. By Helicopter
C. By both private airlines and Air India
D. By Air India only

523. What is the amount admissible for reimbursement of LTC claim in respect of entitled officers and their families, travelling by any private airlines?
A. Actual cost of air fare
B. LTC-80 fare of India
C. Prevailing fare on the date of booking of LTC
D. None of the above

524. Which of the following is admissible for reimbursement in respect of Non-entitled Officers travelling by air on LTC?
A. Actual air fare
B. LTC-80 fare of India
C. Entitled class of rail fare
D. None of the above

525. Can "Facilitation Fee" levied by authorized travel agents on air tickets booked, be included in the bills raised for air tickets?
A. Yes
B. No
C. Subject to maximum of ₹ 300
D. ₹ 100 only

526. A Government employee travelled by Helicopter on LTC. State which of the following is correct?
A. A Government employee can travel by Helicopter
B. A Government employee can travel by Helicopter with the permission of the Competent Authority
C. A Government employee can travel by passenger plane only.
D. None of the above

527. Whether Entitled Officers can travel by private airlines to J&K from their Headquarters?
A. Yes
B. No
C. At the discretionary powers of the Competent Authority
D. None of the above

528. Can All India LTC be availed in combination with transfer / tour?
A. No
B. At the discretionary powers of the Competent Authority
C. Yes
D. None of the above

529. Whether reimbursement of fares is permissible in cases where an employee travels by a longer route or breaks the journey?
A. Actual expenses incurred is reimbursable
B. No reimbursement will be permissible
C. Reimbursement will be restricted to the shortest or the cheapest route
D. With the special sanction from the Competent Authority

530. Are the incidental expenses incurred during LTC admissible for reimbursement?
A. Admissible for reimbursement
B. Not admissible for reimbursement
C. With the sanction from the Administrative Department
D. None of the above

531. Which of the following is a type of school budget?

A. Cash budget B. Personal budget
C. Corporate budget D. Household budget

532. Assertion (A): The principle of economy ensures effective utilization of funds.

Reason (R): Economy means spending maximum resources without monitoring.

A. Both A and R are true
B. Both A and R are true, but R does not explain A
C. A is true, R is false
D. A is false, R is true

533. Assertion (A): A school budget promotes account-ability.

Reason (R): Budget allocation helps track and control expenditures.

A. Both A and R are true, and R explains A
B. Both A and R are true, but R does not explain A
C. A is true, R is false
D. A is false, R is true

534. Which of the following statements are true about school budgeting?

1. Budgeting helps in planning resources efficiently
2. It ensures accountability
3. It is only for record-keeping purposes
4. It prioritizes student learning and school goals

A. 1, 2, and 4 B. 1 and 3
C. 2 and 3 D. All of the above

535. A predictive or tentative budget is prepared:

A. After the academic year ends
B. Before the academic year begins
C. Only for building repairs
D. Only for salary payments

536. Which of the following statements are true about principles of school budgeting?

1. The budget should be flexible
2. It should promote accountability
3. It should prioritize school needs

It should focus solely on infrastructure

A. 1, 2, and 3 B. 1 and 4
C. 2 and 4 D. All of the above

537. Which statements about school budget preparation are correct?

1. Budget should be based on accurate estimates
2. Teachers' salaries are the only priority
3. It should align with school goals

It should include provision for contingencies

A. 2 and 3 B. 1 and 2
C. 1, 3, and 4 D. All of the above

538. Which statements are true about school budget control?

1. Regular monitoring ensures financial discipline
2. Budget control helps in decision-making
3. Overspending is acceptable if funds are available

Budget reports are unnecessary

A. 1 and 2 B. 2 and 3
C. 3 and 4 D. All of the above

539. Assertion (A): A school budget should be flexible.

Reason (R): Flexibility allows adjustments to unforeseen changes in resources or needs.

A. Both A and R are true, and R explains A
B. Both A and R are true, but R does not explain A
C. A is true, R is false
D. A is false, R is true

540. The main purpose of a school budget is to:

A. Control teachers' salaries
B. Plan, allocate, and regulate financial resources
C. Purchase only textbooks
D. Hire administrative staff

541. A well-prepared school budget should be:

A. Rigid and unchangeable
B. Limited to annual salaries
C. Flexible to accommodate unforeseen expenses
D. Focused only on building maintenance

542. The principle of economy in school budgeting emphasizes:
A. Spending maximum resources
B. Using resources efficiently and avoiding waste
C. Allocating funds only to teachers
D. Ignoring student needs

543. Which statements correctly describe the preparation of a school budget?
1. Budget estimates should be realistic
2. Budget should ignore teacher requirements
3. Contingencies must be included
4. It should reflect educational priorities

A. 2 and 3 B. 1 and 2
C. 1, 3, and 4 D. All of the above

544. Which of the following statements are true about budget monitoring?
1. Regular review helps prevent overspending
2. Monitoring is unnecessary if funds are sufficient
3. Helps in reallocating resources efficiently
4. Budget control reduces accountability

A. 1 and 3 B. 1 and 2
C. 2 and 4 D. All of the above

545. The principle of progressiveness in school budgeting emphasizes:
A. Allocating funds only for recurring expenses
B. Including innovative and future-oriented programs
C. Spending funds on old programs only
D. Ignoring new educational methods

546. Which of the following is NOT a key principle of school budgeting?
A. Flexibility
B. Economy
C. Accountability
D. Ignoring contingencies

547. The principle of accuracy in budgeting requires:
A. Estimates based on guesswork
B. Using realistic and verifiable data
C. Ignoring historical expenditures
D. Random allocation of funds

548. Which statement is true about cash budget in schools?
A. It focuses on income and expenditure over a period
B. It ignores cash flow
C. It includes only salaries
D. It is not part of school planning

549. Which of the following is true about contingency provision in school budgets?
A. It is optional
B. It is prepared for unforeseen expenses
C. It replaces all other allocations
D. It is unrelated to actual needs

550. Budget evaluation in schools helps in:
A. Ignoring past financial errors
B. Improving future budgeting decisions
C. Reducing transparency
D. Limiting educational goals

551. The Right to Information Act, 2005, aims to:
A. Promote transparency and accountability in government
B. Provide legal aid to citizens
C. Regulate elections
D. Control media

552. The RTI Act applies to:
A. Only central government ministries
B. All public authorities, including state and central governments
C. Private companies
D. Political parties

553. The maximum time limit for a public authority to provide information under RTI is:
A. 10 days
B. 30 days
C. 60 days
D. 90 days

554. Which body is responsible for overseeing the implementation of RTI in India?
A. Election Commission
B. Supreme Court
C. Central Information Commission
D. Finance Ministry

555. Under RTI, information can be denied if it affects:
A. National security
B. Personal convenience
C. Political debate
D. Public interest

556. Which statements about RTI are true?
1. Citizens can request information from any public authority
2. RTI applies to private companies with government funding
3. The Act guarantees access to classified military secrets
4. Applicants must pay a nominal fee

A. 1, 2, and 4 B. 1 and 3
C. 2 and 3 D. All of the above

557. Which statements correctly describe the duties of a Public Information Officer (PIO)?
1. Receiving and processing RTI applications
2. Providing information within the specified time
3. Delaying information for administrative convenience
4. Maintaining records and assisting applicants

A. 2 and 3 B. 1 and 3
C. 1, 2, and 4 D. All of the above

558. Which of the following statements about exemptions under RTI are true?
1. Information related to national security can be denied
2. Trade secrets or intellectual property can be protected
3. Personal information that harms privacy may be withheld
4. Information on government expenditure cannot be denied

A. 1, 2, and 3 B. 1 and 4
C. 2 and 4 D. All of the above

559. Assertion (A): RTI promotes transparency in government.

Reason (R): Citizens have the right to access information about government functioning.

A. Both A and R are true, and R explains A
B. Both A and R are true, but R does not explain A
C. A is true, R is false
D. A is false, R is true

560. Assertion (A): Public authorities can refuse to provide information if it threatens national security.

Reason (R): The RTI Act has specific exemptions to protect sensitive data.

A. Both A and R are true, and R explains A
B. Both A and R are true, but R does not explain A
C. A is true, R is false
D. A is false, R is true

561. Assertion (A): RTI applications can be submitted orally in some cases.

Reason (R): The Act allows verbal requests to reduce barriers for illiterate applicants.

A. Both A and R are true, and R explains A
B. Both A and R are true, but R does not explain A
C. A is true, R is false
D. A is false, R is true

562. Which statements about filing an RTI application are correct?
1. Applications can be submitted online
2. Applicants must pay a nominal fee
3. Applications must be handwritten
4. Requests should be addressed to the Public Information Officer

A. 1 and 3 B. 1,2 and 4
C. 2 and 3 D. All of the above

563. Which statements correctly describe the role of the Central Information Commission (CIC)?
1. Hearing complaints from applicants
2. Ensuring compliance with the RTI Act
3. Setting government salaries
4. Issuing directions to public authorities

A. 1, 2, and 4 B. 1 and 3
C. 2 and 3 D. All of the above

564. Which statements about exemptions under RTI are true?

1. Information affecting sovereignty, security, or strategic interests may be withheld
2. Trade secrets can be denied
3. Personal details affecting privacy may be withheld
4. Information on government expenditure cannot be exempted

A. 2 and 4
B. 1 and 4
C. 1, 2, and 3
D. All of the above

565. The maximum appeal under RTI can be made to:

A. Public Information Officer
B. First Appellate Authority
C. Central Information Commission or State Information Commission
D. Supreme Court

566. Which of the following are grounds for rejecting an RTI application?

1. Threat to national security
2. Trade secrets
3. Political opinions
4. Personal privacy

A. 1, 2, and 4 B. 1 and 3
C. 2 and 3 D. All of the above

567. Which section of the RTI Act mandates the appointment of Public Information Officers?

A. Section 2
B. Section 5
C. Section 12
D. Section 19

568. Which of the following statements is true about fees under RTI?

A. No fees are required under any circumstance
B. Nominal fees are required for filing applications
C. Fees vary according to political preference
D. Fees are mandatory only for corporate applicants

569. Which of the following statements are true about information disclosure under RTI?

1. Information should be provided promptly
2. Information can be denied if it threatens sovereignty
3. Citizens can request any information, including classified military secrets
4. Time limit for providing information is generally 30 days

A. 1, 2, and 4 B. 1 and 3
C. 2 and 3 D. All of the above

570. Which of the following are responsibilities of public authorities under RTI?

1. Maintain records properly
2. Assist citizens in obtaining information
3. Deny all information without reason
4. Ensure timely response to RTI requests

A. 1 and 2 B. 1 and 3
C. 1, 2 and 4 D. All of the above

571. The main objective of the Income Tax Act, 1961 is to:

A. Promote exports
B. Levy tax on income of individuals and companies
C. Control inflation
D. Regulate banks

572. GST (Goods and Services Tax) in India is:

A. A direct tax
B. An indirect tax
C. A personal tax
D. A luxury tax only

573. Income from salary is taxable under:

A. Income from house property
B. Income from other sources
C. Income from business or profession
D. Income under the head "Salaries"

574. GST replaced which of the following taxes in India?

A. Excise duty, service tax, VAT
B. Income tax
C. Wealth tax
D. Customs duty

575. Individuals with an annual income below the basic exemption limit:
A. Must pay full tax
B. Are exempt from paying income tax
C. Must pay GST
D. Must pay corporate tax

576. Which statements about GST are correct?
1. GST is levied at multiple stages of the supply chain
2. Input tax credit avoids double taxation
3. GST is a direct tax
4. GST is levied only on services
A. 1 and 2 B. 1 and 3
C. 2 and 3 D. All of the above

577. Which of the following are taxable under income tax?
1. Salary income
2. Agricultural income (in most cases exempt)
3. Income from business or profession
4. Capital gains
A. 2 and 3 B. 1 and 2
C. 1, 3, and 4 D. All of the above

578. Which statements correctly describe GST registration?
1. Businesses with turnover above a threshold must register
2. GST registration is optional for all businesses
3. Every registered person must file GST returns
4. Registration is applicable only to service providers
A. 1 and 2 B. 1 and 3
C. 2 and 4 D. All of the above

579. Assertion (A): GST reduces the cascading effect of taxes.
Reason (R): Input tax credit allows offsetting taxes paid at previous stages.
A. Both A and R are true, and R explains A
B. Both A and R are true, but R does not explain A
C. A is true, R is false
D. A is false, R is true

580. Assertion (A): Income tax is a direct tax.
Reason (R): Direct tax is levied on the income of an individual or entity.
A. Both A and R are true, and R explains A
B. Both A and R are true, but R does not explain A
C. A is true, R is false
D. A is false, R is true

581. Assertion (A): GST is levied on both goods and services.
Reason (R): GST is a comprehensive indirect tax replacing multiple taxes.
A. Both A and R are true, and R explains A
B. Both A and R are true, but R does not explain A
C. A is true, R is false
D. A is false, R is true

582. Which of the following statements about GST are true?
1. GST is collected at each stage of supply
2. GST is a single tax applicable throughout India
3. GST registration is mandatory for all businesses
4. Input tax credit helps reduce tax burden
A. 1 and 3
B. 2 and 3
C. 1, 2, and 4
D. All of the above

583. Which statements about income tax filing are correct?
1. Individuals must file income tax returns if income exceeds exemption limit
2. TDS (Tax Deducted at Source) is a method of tax collection
3. Only companies are required to file income tax returns
4. Advance tax is applicable to salaried individuals
A. 1 and 2
B. 1 and 3
C. 2 and 3
D. All of the above

584. Which of the following statements about GST rates are true?

1. GST rates are uniform for all goods and services
2. Different goods and services attract different GST rates
3. GST rates are decided by the GST Council
4. GST rates never change

A. 2 and 3 B. 1 and 4
C. 2 and 4 D. All of the above

585. Which of the following are types of GST in India?

1. CGST
2. SGST
3. IGST
4. VAT

A. 2 and 4 B. 1 and 4
C. 1, 2, and 3 D. All of the above

586. Income tax is calculated based on:

A. Gross income
B. Net taxable income
C. Expenditure
D. GST collected

587. Which of the following are benefits of GST?

1. Simplifies indirect tax structure
2. Reduces tax cascading
3. Promotes ease of doing business
4. Eliminates income tax

A. 1, 2, and 3 B. 1 and 4
C. 2 and 4 D. All of the above

588. The threshold turnover for mandatory GST registration for services is:

A. 10 lakh B. 20 lakh
C. 50 lakh D. 1 crore

589. Which of the following statements are true about TDS?

1. TDS is deducted at source from payments like salary, rent, interest
2. TDS ensures timely collection of tax
3. TDS is applicable only for GST
4. TDS is refundable if excess deducted

A. 1, 2, and 4 B. 1 and 3
C. 2 and 3 D. All of the above

590. GST Council in India is responsible for:

1. Determining GST rates
2. Making recommendations on exemptions
3. Levying income tax
4. Coordinating between center and states

A. 1 and 3 B. 2 and 3
C. 1, 2, and 3 D. All of the above

591. The Prevention of Sexual Harassment (POSH) Act, 2013, was enacted with the aim of ensuring a safe working environment for women in workplaces by preventing sexual harassment. Which of the following statements correctly reflects the primary purpose of the POSH Act?

A. It applies only to private organizations and their employees
B. It aims to prevent sexual harassment of women at workplaces and ensure safe working conditions
C. It penalizes all male employees in an organization
D. It promotes women-only workplaces

592. Employers have certain responsibilities under the POSH Act to ensure a safe and harassment-free workplace. Which of the following is a key responsibility of employers under this Act?

A. Ignoring complaints to protect the company's image
B. Organizing awareness programs and training employees about sexual harassment and redressal mechanisms
C. Discouraging the formation of an Internal Complaints Committee
D. Terminating all male employees to avoid harassment cases

593. According to the POSH Act, sexual harassment includes a variety of unwelcome behaviors in the workplace. Which of the following activities are explicitly considered sexual harassment under the Act?

A. Physical contact or advances, request for sexual favors, or using derogatory remarks or emails

B. Monitoring attendance and performance
C. Discussing appraisal or promotions
D. Supervising work hours

594. The Internal Complaints Committee (ICC) is a critical component of the POSH Act. Which of the following statements about ICC is correct?
A. It can dismiss complaints without inquiry
B. The committee must complete its inquiry within 90 days and submit a report
C. It can function with only male members
D. It can indefinitely delay the inquiry process

595. Employers who fail to comply with the provisions of the POSH Act can face penalties. Which of the following correctly describes the penalties or consequences for non-compliance?
A. Employers may be fined, and ICC can recommend disciplinary action against the perpetrator
B. Employers face no penalties under the Act
C. Complainants are imprisoned for filing false complaints
D. Employers are exempt from action if harassment occurred outside office hours

596. Awareness programs on sexual harassment are essential for workplaces. Why are these programs considered important under the POSH Act?
A. They are designed only to entertain employees
B. They help employees identify, prevent, and report incidents of harassment, promoting a safe workplace
C. They delay the formation of ICC
D. They are completely optional and not recommended

597. The POSH Act applies to:
A. Adult women employees in all workplaces covered by the Act
B. Men only
C. Children under 18
D. Senior management only

598. Filing a complaint under the POSH Act requires certain procedures. Which of the following is correct regarding the manner in which complaints can be submitted?
A. Complaints can be oral only
B. Complaints must be submitted in writing, either physically or electronically
C. Complaints can be submitted only after six months from the incident
D. Complaints must be submitted to an external NGO only

599. The role of external members in the ICC is crucial to ensure fairness in the inquiry process. Which of the following statements is correct about external members?
A. External members must be from NGOs or persons familiar with issues of sexual harassment to provide an unbiased perspective
B. External members can overrule the ICC decisions
C. External members are optional and not recommended
D. External members must always be government officials

600. Preventive measures under the POSH Act aim to promote a safe workplace. Which of the following are considered preventive measures?
A. Creating a hostile work culture to discourage complaints
B. Framing policies, conducting awareness sessions, and providing counseling to victims and perpetrators
C. Ignoring complaints to maintain company reputation
D. Punishing all employees regardless of involvement

601. The Protection of Children from Sexual Offences (POCSO) Act, 2012, was enacted to protect children from sexual abuse and exploitation. Which of the following statements correctly identifies the age group covered and key provisions of the Act?

A. Only boys under 18 are protected
B. Children below 18 years are protected, and the Act mandates reporting of abuse and establishment of special courts
C. Only adult women are covered
D. Only employees in schools are protected

602. The POCSO Act defines several sexual offences against children. Which of the following are explicitly punishable under the Act?
A. Using children for pornography, penetrative sexual assault, and sexual harassment
B. Corporal punishment
C. Filing income tax
D. Filing complaints in civil court

603. Reporting of child sexual abuse is mandatory under the POCSO Act. Which of the following statements about reporting is correct?
A. Reporting is optional for everyone
B. Any person who knows of child sexual abuse must report it, and failure to report is punishable
C. Only police officers can report such cases
D. Parents are exempt from reporting

604. Special courts have been established under POCSO to ensure speedy and sensitive justice. Why is this necessary?
A. Child sexual abuse cases require quick and sensitive handling to protect the child
B. To reduce the workload of the police
C. Only adults are tried in these courts
D. To deliberately delay trials

605. Punishments under the POCSO Act vary depending on the severity of the offence. Which of the following is correct regarding penalties under the Act?
A. Only fines are imposed
B. Rigorous imprisonment and fines can be imposed depending on the offence
C. Community service is the only penalty
D. Warning letters are sufficient

606. Child protection officers have special duties under POCSO. Which of the following are correct?
A. Recording statements of children in a child-friendly manner, ensuring safety and confidentiality, and facilitating rehabilitation and counseling
B. Conducting court trials independently
C. Avoiding rehabilitation of children
D. Ignoring counseling for victims

607. Certain individuals are legally required to report child sexual abuse. Who is included in this mandatory reporting?
A. Parents and teachers
B. Only police officers
C. NGO members only
D. No one is legally required

608. The POCSO Act applies to children below 18 years. Which of the following is correct?
A. Adults above 18 are included
B. Children below 18 are included, and they are protected from sexual offences
C. Senior citizens are included
D. Only school-going children are included

609. Child-friendly procedures are a key part of the POCSO Act. Which of the following describes these procedures?
A. Using legal jargon to intimidate the child
B. Avoiding confrontation with accused in the presence of the child, and allowing support persons during investigation
C. Ignoring the child's presence during trials
D. Conducting cross-examination harshly

610. FIRs under POCSO must follow certain rules. Which of the following is correct?
A. FIRs must be registered immediately upon receiving information of abuse
B. FIRs are optional
C. FIRs can be delayed until convenient
D. FIRs are not required if the child is scared

611. The Rights of Persons with Disabilities Act, 2016 was enacted to ensure that persons with disabilities (PwD) are able to participate in society on an equal basis with others. Which of the following is a key provision of the Act?

A. It mandates that only government offices accommodate PwD.

B. It ensures the right of PwD to access government services and public transportation

C. It provides exclusive jobs only for PwD.

D. It allows discrimination against PwD in private organizations.

612. The Economically Weaker Sections (EWS) category was introduced to provide reservation to individuals who are not covered under the reservation for SC, ST, or OBC but face economic challenges. Which of the following is true regarding the criteria for EWS reservation?

A. EWS reservation applies to individuals with a family income above ₹ 8 lakh per annum.

B. EWS category is applicable to families with an annual income of ₹ 8 lakh or below

C. EWS applies only to students and not to job seekers.

D. EWS applies only to urban families.

613. Which of the following is a significant constitutional safeguard for the Scheduled Castes (SC) and Scheduled Tribes (ST) in India?

A. They are provided with affirmative action in the form of reservations in education and employment.

B. They are given the right to own land in any part of the country.

C. They are excluded from government benefits and schemes.

D. They are not eligible for any government services.

614. The National Commission for Scheduled Castes (NCSC) is an important body established under the Constitution to safeguard the interests of SCs. Which of the following are the primary functions of the NCSC?

A. To supervise elections in tribal areas

B. To investigate and monitor matters related to the rights and welfare of SCs

C. To implement laws for OBCs

D. To conduct business-related training for SCs

615. According to the Constitution of India, which Article specifically deals with reservation for Scheduled Castes (SCs) and Scheduled Tribes (STs) in legislatures and public employment?

A. Article 46

B. Article 15

C. Article 335

D. Article 29

616. Which of the following is a policy initiative aimed at improving the socio-economic conditions of Scheduled Tribes (STs) in India?

A. The Tribal Sub-Plan (TSP) aims to allocate resources for the development of tribal areas.

B. The government focuses solely on urban areas, leaving rural tribes behind.

C. The TSP does not provide any financial assistance.

D. The TSP applies only to Scheduled Castes (SCs).

617. The Reservation for PwD in educational institutions and government jobs was implemented to provide equal opportunities. Which of the following statements correctly reflects this reservation?

A. PwD are not entitled to any reservation in government jobs or educational institutions.

B. A certain percentage of seats in higher education and jobs are reserved for PwD under the Rights of Persons with Disabilities Act, 2016.

C. Only private sector jobs can reserve seats for PwD.

D. PwD only have reservation in educational institutions but not in jobs.

618. Scheduled Castes (SCs), Scheduled Tribes (STs), and Other Backward Classes (OBCs) are provided with special provisions under the Indian Constitution. Which of the following is NOT a provision under Article 46 of the Constitution?

A. Promotion of education and economic interests of SCs and STs

B. Protection from social injustice and exploitation

C. Prohibition of reservation for SCs and STs in private institutions

D. Measures for the welfare of weaker sections of society

619. The Protection of Civil Rights Act, 1955 was enacted to abolish untouchability. Which of the following actions does the Act prohibit?

A. Prohibits discrimination in educational institutions based on caste.

B. Prohibits discrimination in access to public places such as temples, restaurants, and shops.

C. Allows the practice of untouchability in rural areas.

D. Allows discrimination in government jobs for SC/ST.

620. The Constitution of India provides for special provisions for the Scheduled Tribes (STs) in areas related to land rights, social security, and development. Which of the following provisions ensures protection of ST land rights?

A. The Forest Rights Act, 2006 ensures that forest-dwelling STs have legal access to land and resources

B. The Indian Forest Act, 1927 denies tribal rights over land

C. The Land Acquisition Act mandates that all ST land be sold to non-tribals

D. The Mineral Laws Amendment Act permits unrestricted mining on ST land

621. The Constitution of India under Article 17 abolished untouchability and provided for legal protection. What penalty is prescribed for practicing untouchability?

A. Fine and imprisonment of up to one year

B. Fine and imprisonment of up to five years

C. Only fines, no imprisonment

D. Social exclusion without legal penalties

622. Under the Rights of Persons with Disabilities Act, 2016, which of the following measures is mandated to promote accessibility for PwDs in public spaces?

A. Providing special seating arrangements only for PwDs

B. Making transportation and public buildings accessible, including ramps and elevators

C. Exempting PwDs from any government procedures

D. Limiting PwD accessibility to government buildings only

623. Article 338 of the Indian Constitution establishes the National Commission for Scheduled Castes (NCSC). Which of the following is a function of the NCSC?

A. To safeguard the rights of SCs, review laws affecting SCs, and recommend measures for their welfare

B. To oversee the welfare of economically backward groups

C. To administer the welfare of scheduled tribes only

D. To manage only financial resources for SCs

624. The Economically Weaker Sections (EWS) category for reservation was introduced in the General Category. Which of the following is a key criterion for a family to be classified under EWS for reservation benefits?

A. The family must have a total annual income of ₹ 8 lakh or below

B. The family must have an annual income of ₹ 10 lakh or above

C. EWS benefits are only applicable to urban families
D. EWS benefits are applicable only to rural families

625. Which of the following provisions ensures the right to education for children from disadvantaged groups including SC, ST, OBC, and PwD?
A. The RTE Act, 2009 mandates free education only for children from scheduled tribes
B. The Right to Education (RTE) Act mandates free and compulsory education for all children, including those from disadvantaged backgrounds
C. The RTE Act excludes children from backward classes
D. The RTE Act applies only to private schools

626. The National Policy for the Empowerment of Women focuses on improving the condition of women from disadvantaged backgrounds. Which of the following does the policy emphasize?
A. Providing special educational opportunities only for women in urban areas
B. Enhancing economic, social, and educational opportunities for women, including SC, ST, OBC, and PwD women
C. Limiting government employment for women from disadvantaged groups
D. Reducing the number of women in education programs

627. The Scheduled Tribes and Other Traditional Forest Dwellers (Recognition of Forest Rights) Act, 2006 is also known as the Forest Rights Act (FRA). What is its primary objective?
A. To reduce the forest area available for tribal communities
B. To provide legal rights over forest resources to forest-dwelling STs and other traditional forest dwellers
C. To limit the rights of tribals to forest resources
D. To convert forest lands into commercial areas

628. Article 330 of the Constitution of India mandates reservation of seats for Scheduled Castes (SCs) and Scheduled Tribes (STs) in the Lok Sabha. How does this provision help ensure political representation for these groups?
A. It provides direct representation for SC/STs, ensuring they are heard in the legislative process
B. It gives full autonomy to SC/STs in government functions
C. It provides a 10% seat allocation in local elections only
D. It allows SC/STs to vote for others only

629. The Central Civil Services (Pension) Rules, 2021 are applicable to which of the following categories of employees?
A. All employees of the state government
B. All central government employees
C. Employees of public sector undertakings only
D. Only employees in the Ministry of Finance

630. Under the CCS (Pension) Rules, 2021, what is the minimum qualifying service required for an employee to be eligible for pension?
A. 5 years
B. 10 years
C. 15 years
D. 20 years

631. Which of the following is a pensionary benefit under the CCS (Pension) Rules, 2021?
A. Gratuity
B. Leave encashment
C. Family pension
D. All of the above

632. According to the CCS (Pension) Rules, 2021, the amount of pension is based on:
A. The employee's last drawn basic pay
B. The employee's average emoluments for the last 10 months
C. The employee's highest pay drawn in the last 12 months
D. The employee's average pay in the last 5 years

633. Under the CCS (Pension) Rules, 2021, the pension of a government employee is reduced if the employee has:

A. Completed less than 10 years of service
B. Completed more than 20 years of service
C. Less than 15 years of service and resigned voluntarily
D. Retired on medical grounds

634. The family pension under the CCS (Pension) Rules, 2021 is payable to:

A. Only the employee's spouse
B. Spouse, children, and dependent parents
C. Only dependent children
D. Only dependent parents

635. What is the maximum family pension allowed under the CCS (Pension) Rules, 2021 for a government employee?

A. 50% of the last pay drawn by the employee
B. 100% of the last pay drawn by the employee
C. 30% of the basic pension
D. 50% of the basic pension

636. Under the CCS (Pension) Rules, 2021, the rate of pension for an employee who has completed 10 years of qualifying service is:

A. 40% of last pay drawn
B. 50% of last pay drawn
C. 30% of last pay drawn
D. 60% of last pay drawn

637. The gratuity payable to a government employee under the CCS (Pension) Rules, 2021 is calculated based on:

A. The last pay drawn by the employee
B. The number of years of service completed
C. The employee's monthly basic pay
D. The employee's total annual income

638. In case of death in service, the family pension under the CCS (Pension) Rules, 2021 is payable:

A. Only to the surviving spouse
B. Only to dependent children
C. To the spouse and children (if any) of the deceased employee
D. To the deceased employee's dependent siblings

639. According to the CCS (Pension) Rules, 2021, a pensioner is eligible for a revised pension when:

A. The pensioner completes 5 years post-retirement
B. The government decides to implement a pay commission revision
C. A revision of pay structure is approved by the government
D. A pensioner submits an application for pension revision

640. The minimum pension under the CCS (Pension) Rules, 2021 is:

A. ₹ 5,000 per month
B. ₹ 7,500 per month
C. ₹ 10,000 per month
D. ₹ 15,000 per month

641. Under the CCS (Pension) Rules, 2021, a pensioner can receive a pension only after the completion of:

A. 1 year after retirement
B. 6 months after retirement
C. 3 months after retirement
D. 2 months after retirement

642. A government employee who voluntarily retires after completing at least 20 years of service is eligible for:

A. Full pension
B. Reduced pension based on qualifying service
C. No pension
D. Gratuity only

643. Under the CCS (Pension) Rules, 2021, the pension of an employee can be withheld or reduced if:

A. The employee is found guilty of misconduct
B. The employee resigns voluntarily
C. The employee opts for early retirement
D. The employee is absent without leave

644. A government employee who has been dismissed or removed from service under the CCS (Pension) Rules, 2021 is:

A. Entitled to full pension if the dismissal is not upheld

B. Denied any pension benefits
C. Eligible for a reduced pension
D. Eligible for pension after completion of 5 years of service

645. Under the CCS (Pension) Rules, 2021, a pensioner can nominate the following for receiving the pension in case of the pensioner's death:
A. Only legal heirs
B. Only the spouse
C. Spouse or children or dependent parents
D. Any person designated by the pensioner

646. According to the CCS (Pension) Rules, 2021, the family pension for an employee who dies while in service is payable to:
A. Spouse only
B. Spouse and children, in case of eligibility
C. Only dependent children
D. Dependent parents

647. Under the CCS (Pension) Rules, 2021, an employee retiring on medical grounds is eligible for:
A. Full pension
B. Pension at reduced rates based on qualifying service
C. Family pension only
D. Gratuity only

648. Which of the following pension-related benefits is not provided under the CCS (Pension) Rules, 2021?
A. Gratuity
B. Leave encashment
C. Provident fund
D. Medical allowance after retirement

649. The National Pension Scheme (NPS) is managed by:
A. Reserve Bank of India (RBI)
B. Employees' Provident Fund Organization (EPFO)
C. Pension Fund Regulatory and Development Authority (PFRDA)
D. Ministry of Finance

650. The National Pension Scheme (NPS) was launched in India in which year?
A. 1999 B. 2000
C. 2004 D. 2009

651. The NPS is applicable to which of the following?
A. Only government employees
B. Only private sector employees
C. Both government and private sector employees
D. Only employees working in public sector undertakings

652. In the NPS, what is the minimum annual contribution required from an individual?
A. ₹ 1,000
B. ₹ 2,000
C. ₹ 5,000
D. ₹ 10,000

653. Under the NPS, which of the following is NOT a type of account?
A. Tier 1 account
B. Tier 2 account
C. Pension Preservation Account
D. Tier 3 account

654. What is the maximum age limit for joining the National Pension Scheme (NPS)?
A. 45 years
B. 55 years
C. 60 years
D. 65 years

655. Under the NPS, which of the following is eligible for tax benefits?
A. Contribution to the Tier 1 account
B. Contribution to the Tier 2 account
C. Both Tier 1 and Tier 2 accounts
D. Only the government's contribution

656. The Tier 1 NPS Account is meant for:
A. Long-term retirement savings and cannot be withdrawn before retirement
B. Short-term savings and can be withdrawn anytime
C. Day-to-day savings
D. Investment in real estate

657. In the NPS, the individual can invest their contributions in which of the following asset classes?
A. Equities
B. Corporate bonds
C. Government securities
D. All of the above

658. The contribution to NPS is divided into two parts, one of which is the Pension Fund. What is the other part?
A. Insurance Fund
B. Annuity Fund
C. Tax Fund
D. Social Security Fund

659. The NPS allows you to invest in a maximum of how many asset classes?
A. 1 B. 2
C. 3 D. 4

660. The NPS has been designed to provide retirement benefits primarily for which of the following?
A. Individuals employed in the public sector only
B. Any Indian citizen between the ages of 18 and 65 years
C. Only senior citizens
D. Only corporate sector employees

661. Under the NPS, the amount invested in the scheme is:
A. Fully taxable at the time of withdrawal
B. Partly taxable, depending on the amount invested
C. Exempt from taxes during the accumulation phase and partially taxable at withdrawal
D. Exempt from taxes at all stages

662. Under the NPS, what percentage of the total corpus can an individual withdraw as a lump sum at retirement?
A. 40% B. 60%
C. 70% D. 80%

663. The remaining corpus (after the 40% lump sum withdrawal) in the NPS is used to:
A. Pay off outstanding debts
B. Purchase an annuity plan to provide regular income after retirement
C. Invest in mutual funds
D. Reinvest in stocks

664. Under the NPS, the government employees' contribution is:
A. 10% of their basic pay
B. 12% of their basic pay
C. 14% of their basic pay and dearness allowance
D. 5% of their basic pay

665. An NPS account holder is allowed to exit the scheme before the age of 60 years. Which of the following is the condition for early exit?
A. Completion of 3 years of service
B. Compulsory purchase of an annuity at the time of early exit
C. Exit can only be allowed after 5 years of contribution
D. Withdrawal of the full amount at exit is allowed, but 80% must be used for annuity purchase

666. Which of the following is true about the Tier 2 NPS Account?
A. It is mandatory for all NPS subscribers
B. It allows for withdrawal at any time and is a voluntary savings account
C. It provides tax benefits similar to the Tier 1 account
D. It is intended only for government employees

667. The NPS is designed to:
A. Provide fixed returns for contributors
B. Offer market-linked returns, which can vary based on investment performance
C. Be completely tax-free for withdrawals
D. Provide pension only after a contributor reaches 80 years of age

668. Under the NPS, the default option for fund management is:

A. Actively managed by government agencies
B. A mix of government securities and corporate bonds
C. The Auto Choice (which allocates funds automatically between equity, government bonds, and corporate bonds based on the subscriber's age)
D. Equally distributed between all asset classes

669. The Universal Declaration of Human Rights (UDHR), adopted by the United Nations (UN) in 1948, is a landmark document outlining fundamental human rights. Which of the following is a key provision of the UDHR?

A. It guarantees the right to free speech, education, and participation in government
B. It mandates a global system of governance for all member states
C. It states that all citizens are entitled to free healthcare
D. It restricts the freedom of movement to certain countries

670. The International Covenant on Civil and Political Rights (ICCPR), adopted by the UN, ensures various civil and political rights. Which of the following rights is explicitly protected under this covenant?

A. Right to free healthcare
B. Right to work in any government office
C. Right to life, liberty, and security of the person
D. Right to free education

671. The Right to Equality is a fundamental right guaranteed by the Indian Constitution. Which of the following is a provision under Article 14 of the Constitution?

A. Prohibition of discrimination based on religion, race, caste, sex, or place of birth
B. The right to equal pay for equal work
C. Prohibition of untouchability
D. Right to form associations

672. The Convention on the Elimination of All Forms of Racial Discrimination (CERD) is an international human rights instrument. Which of the following is a key provision of CERD?

A. Prohibition of racial discrimination in any form, including employment, education, and public services
B. Ensuring equal pay for all ethnic groups
C. Encouraging migration from under-developed countries
D. Restricting the entry of people from specific racial backgrounds into a country

673. The Right to Freedom of Speech and Expression is guaranteed under Article 19 of the Indian Constitution. Which of the following is a permissible restriction on this right?

A. Freedom of speech cannot be curtailed under any circumstances
B. Speech that incites violence or threatens national security can be restricted
C. Restrictions based on religion or race
D. Restrictions based on political opinions

674. The Convention on the Elimination of All Forms of Discrimination Against Women (CEDAW) is a key international treaty. Which of the following is a key provision of CEDAW?

A. It guarantees gender equality in all aspects of life, including education, work, and political participation
B. It mandates the protection of women's rights in only rural areas
C. It provides preferential treatment for men in education and employment
D. It prohibits women from holding political office

675. According to the Universal Declaration of Human Rights (UDHR), which of the following is a universal human right?

A. The right to own property
B. The right to a fair trial and due process of law

C. The right to marry only within one's caste
D. The right to reside in any country for indefinite periods

676. The Right to Education Act (RTE) in India ensures free and compulsory education for children. Which of the following is a key provision of the RTE Act?
A. Only children from economically weaker sections are entitled to free education
B. Children aged 6-14 years must be provided free and compulsory education
C. The Act does not apply to private schools
D. The Act guarantees free education only up to 5th grade

677. The International Labour Organization (ILO) Convention No. 111 deals with the elimination of:
A. Child labor
B. Gender inequality in labor markets
C. Discrimination in employment and occupation
D. Forced labor in armed forces

678. Article 21 of the Indian Constitution guarantees the Right to Life and Personal Liberty. Which of the following is the judicial interpretation of this right?
A. Right to live with dignity includes the right to a clean and healthy environment
B. Right to personal freedom includes the right to access free healthcare
C. Right to personal liberty excludes the right to privacy
D. Right to life is limited to physical survival only

679. The Right to Information Act (RTI), 2005, empowers citizens in India. Which of the following is a provision under the RTI Act?
A. Citizens can request information only from government departments
B. The government is obligated to provide information within 30 days of the request
C. Only government employees can access information under RTI
D. Information about national security is always exempt from disclosure

680. The Convention Against Torture and Other Cruel, Inhuman or Degrading Treatment or Punishment aims to:
A. Provide a global framework for prosecuting war criminals
B. Prevent any form of cruel, inhuman, or degrading treatment or punishment, including torture
C. Protect the right to life for prisoners only
D. Allow exceptions in the case of national emergencies

681. The International Covenant on Economic, Social and Cultural Rights (ICESCR) guarantees which of the following rights?
A. Right to free legal assistance
B. Right to participate in government
C. Right to adequate standard of living, including access to housing, food, and healthcare
D. Right to access to free and compulsory education

682. The Protection of Children from Sexual Offences (POCSO) Act, 2012 is an Indian law aimed at:
A. Preventing child labor
B. Protecting children from sexual abuse and exploitation
C. Ensuring equal opportunities for disabled children
D. Providing free education for all children

683. The UN Declaration on the Rights of Indigenous Peoples (UNDRIP) protects the rights of indigenous people. Which of the following is a key provision of the UNDRIP?
A. Indigenous peoples have the right to maintain their distinct cultural practices and traditions
B. Indigenous peoples have no rights to natural resources

C. Indigenous peoples are prohibited from using modern technology
D. Indigenous peoples must abandon their languages and adopt the national language

684. Which of the following is a provision under the Indian Constitution related to Human Rights?
A. Article 15: Prohibition of discrimination on grounds of religion, race, caste, sex, or place of birth
B. Article 45: Right to free and compulsory education for all children
C. Article 21: Right to life and personal liberty
D. All of the above

685. The Human Rights Council (HRC) of the United Nations is responsible for:
A. Ensuring peacekeeping missions in conflict areas
B. Reviewing the human rights records of UN member states
C. Providing economic aid to impoverished nations
D. Overseeing arms control treaties

686. The National Commission for Protection of Child Rights (NCPCR) was established to:
A. Provide scholarships for children
B. Protect the rights of children and ensure their well-being
C. Provide healthcare to children
D. Regulate children's educational curriculum

687. The NCPCR guidelines for school safety and security focus on:
A. Academic curriculum improvements
B. Protection from physical and emotional harm, and ensuring a secure learning environment
C. Providing uniforms and textbooks
D. Enhancing the digital infrastructure of schools

688. According to NCPCR guidelines, which of the following is a primary responsibility of schools to ensure child safety?
A. Providing free meals
B. Ensuring the safety and security of children from physical, mental, and sexual abuse
C. Organizing extracurricular activities
D. Managing school buses

689. Under the NCPCR's child protection framework, schools are required to:
A. Report all incidents of child abuse immediately
B. Conduct regular health check-ups for students
C. Provide financial assistance to needy students
D. Teach students about financial management

690. Which of the following is true about the NDMA guidelines for school safety during disasters?
A. Schools are not required to have any disaster management plans
B. Schools should have a Disaster Management Plan that includes evacuation procedures and first aid training
C. Disaster management only applies to schools located in earthquake-prone zones
D. Schools can ignore disaster management plans if they are located in urban areas

691. According to NDMA guidelines, what is a key component of school disaster management?
A. Organizing cultural programs
B. Creating safe zones and evacuation routes for students and staff
C. Providing free textbooks to students
D. Offering rewards for good academic performance

692. According to NCPCR and NDMA guidelines, schools must ensure:
A. Complete isolation of children from all external contacts
B. Only basic infrastructure for disaster preparedness
C. The presence of adequate first aid and medical support during emergencies and disasters
D. Student participation in politics

693. The NCPCR guidelines recommend that schools should establish which of the following to ensure child safety?
A. Regular sessions on child rights and responsibilities
B. A dedicated Child Safety Committee for addressing concerns
C. Restricting children from interacting with other schools
D. Hiring only male teachers

694. In case of a disaster, the NDMA guidelines suggest that schools should:
A. Allow students to leave the school on their own
B. Wait for the government to take action
C. Activate the school's disaster response team immediately
D. Ignore minor emergencies

695. According to NDMA guidelines, schools are advised to conduct:
A. Annual fire drills and evacuation exercises
B. School cleanliness drives only
C. Only theoretical disaster management training
D. Outdoor sports activities

696. Which of the following is part of the NCPCR's framework for creating a safe environment for children in schools?
A. Preventing students from attending outdoor activities
B. Limiting student-teacher interactions
C. Ensuring that students have access to safe spaces in the school premises
D. Only hiring teachers with educational qualifications

697. The NCPCR encourages schools to promote which of the following to prevent child abuse?
A. Restricting interaction between students and teachers
B. Allowing corporal punishment to discipline children
C. Ignoring complaints of bullying
D. Educating children about their rights and safe boundaries

698. Which of the following does NDMA emphasize for post-disaster school recovery?
A. Schools should be completely rebuilt after every disaster
B. Mental health support and counseling for children and staff
C. Immediate closure of the school for long periods
D. Restricting student activities in the aftermath

699. According to NCPCR guidelines, the school safety committee should include:
A. Only the principal and teachers
B. Only government officials
C. Only parents
D. A mix of teachers, parents, and student representatives

700. Under NCPCR guidelines, schools must address which of the following?
A. Ensuring only physical safety measures
B. The emotional well-being of children
C. Limiting the number of extracurricular activities
D. Restricting student interactions with teachers

701. The NDMA guidelines suggest that schools should be made disaster-resilient by:
A. Ensuring that school buildings meet safety standards for different types of natural disasters
B. Allowing students to make their own evacuation plans
C. Closing the school during every disaster alert
D. Focusing only on structural safety, ignoring other safety measures

702. Under the NCPCR guidelines, it is recommended that schools provide which of the following to ensure the safety of children?
A. Limited interaction with parents
B. No extra-curricular activities for children

C. Complete control over students' personal relationships
D. Establishment of an effective grievance redressal mechanism

703. The NCPCR's focus on school safety includes:
A. Building sports infrastructure only
B. Aiming to prevent any physical, mental, or sexual abuse of children in the school environment
C. Expanding the curriculum to international standards
D. Preventing students from attending school during the rainy season

704. According to the NDMA, schools should ensure that all staff are trained in:
A. Basic first aid and emergency response skills
B. Financial management
C. Public speaking
D. Advanced computing skills

705. The National Pension System (NPS) was introduced by the Government of India to provide which of the following benefits to citizens?
A. To provide tax-free income for all pension contributions made during the individual's working years
B. To allow individuals to invest in government bonds and receive returns after retirement
C. To provide a fixed monthly pension after retirement through a market-linked savings scheme
D. To offer a lump sum amount as a pension based on the amount invested during working life

ANSWERS

1	2	3	4	5	6	7	8	9	10
A	B	C	A	A	B	C	B	D	C
11	**12**	**13**	**14**	**15**	**16**	**17**	**18**	**19**	**20**
B	C	D	C	C	A	C	D	C	C
21	**22**	**23**	**24**	**25**	**26**	**27**	**28**	**29**	**30**
D	D	D	A	C	D	C	D	C	C
31	**32**	**33**	**34**	**35**	**36**	**37**	**38**	**39**	**40**
C	C	D	B	D	A	B	D	D	B
41	**42**	**43**	**44**	**45**	**46**	**47**	**48**	**49**	**50**
C	B	C	B	C	C	B	C	D	B
51	**52**	**53**	**54**	**55**	**56**	**57**	**58**	**59**	**60**
A	C	D	D	D	C	D	C	A	C
61	**62**	**63**	**64**	**65**	**66**	**67**	**68**	**69**	**70**
C	C	B	C	A	B	B	D	B	D
71	**72**	**73**	**74**	**75**	**76**	**77**	**78**	**79**	**80**
D	A	D	D	C	D	D	C	D	C
81	**82**	**83**	**84**	**85**	**86**	**87**	**88**	**89**	**90**
B	D	B	D	B	D	C	C	D	A

91	92	93	94	95	96	97	98	99	100
B	A	D	B	A	D	B	C	D	D
101	**102**	**103**	**104**	**105**	**106**	**107**	**108**	**109**	**110**
D	D	D	C	D	C	C	C	A	D
111	**112**	**113**	**114**	**115**	**116**	**117**	**118**	**119**	**120**
D	A	A	D	D	B	C	C	B	D
121	**122**	**123**	**124**	**125**	**126**	**127**	**128**	**129**	**130**
B	C	D	A	B	A	A	C	A	C
131	**132**	**133**	**134**	**135**	**136**	**137**	**138**	**139**	**140**
B	A	D	D	B	B	A	B	D	C
141	**142**	**143**	**144**	**145**	**146**	**147**	**148**	**149**	**150**
B	C	C	A	C	A	D	B	C	B
151	**152**	**153**	**154**	**155**	**156**	**157**	**158**	**159**	**160**
B	A	C	C	A	B	A	C	C	B
161	**162**	**163**	**164**	**165**	**166**	**167**	**168**	**169**	**170**
D	C	A	D	A	B	C	A	C	D
171	**172**	**173**	**174**	**175**	**176**	**177**	**178**	**179**	**180**
C	C	D	D	B	B	B	B	C	D
181	**182**	**183**	**184**	**185**	**186**	**187**	**188**	**189**	**190**
C	B	B	C	B	B	A	D	B	B
191	**192**	**193**	**194**	**195**	**196**	**197**	**198**	**199**	**200**
D	C	D	C	C	A	B	D	A	D
201	**202**	**203**	**204**	**205**	**206**	**207**	**208**	**209**	**210**
C	B	D	B	D	A	B	D	B	D
211	**212**	**213**	**214**	**215**	**216**	**217**	**218**	**219**	**220**
B	D	B	C	B	D	D	B	D	D
221	**222**	**223**	**224**	**225**	**226**	**227**	**228**	**229**	**230**
D	B	D	D	B	D	C	B	C	D
231	**232**	**233**	**234**	**235**	**236**	**237**	**238**	**239**	**240**
D	D	D	D	C	C	D	D	D	B
241	**242**	**243**	**244**	**245**	**246**	**247**	**248**	**249**	**250**
B	B	D	D	B	C	B	D	B	D
251	**252**	**253**	**254**	**255**	**256**	**257**	**258**	**259**	**260**
D	C	B	B	C	B	C	D	D	D
261	**262**	**263**	**264**	**265**	**266**	**267**	**268**	**269**	**270**
D	D	C	D	D	B	D	C	B	C

271	272	273	274	275	276	277	278	279	280
D	A	A	A	C	D	D	D	A	B
281	282	283	284	285	286	287	288	289	290
C	A	C	D	D	A	A	C	C	A
291	292	293	294	295	296	297	298	299	300
C	D	C	B	A	C	D	A	A	B
301	302	303	304	305	306	307	308	309	310
C	A	A	A	D	C	B	D	A	C
311	312	313	314	315	316	317	318	319	320
C	D	D	B	D	D	D	C	A	D
321	322	323	324	325	326	327	328	329	330
D	C	D	C	A	B	D	C	C	B
331	332	333	334	335	336	337	338	339	340
C	D	D	D	D	D	D	B	C	C
341	342	343	344	345	346	347	348	349	350
B	D	D	D	A	D	A	C	D	D
351	352	353	354	355	356	357	358	359	360
D	B	C	D	D	D	D	C	A	B
361	362	363	364	365	366	367	368	369	370
B	C	B	D	B	C	A	A	A	C
371	372	373	374	375	376	377	378	379	380
D	C	B	C	A	A	D	B	B	A
381	382	383	384	385	386	387	388	389	390
D	D	C	B	B	A	D	B	A	A
391	392	393	394	395	396	397	398	399	400
A	A	C	A	B	B	D	C	D	A
401	402	403	404	405	406	407	408	409	410
B	B	A	B	C	B	C	D	D	A
411	412	413	414	415	416	417	418	419	420
D	B	D	A	C	C	A	C	D	B
421	422	423	424	425	426	427	428	429	430
D	D	C	C	D	D	D	B	D	D
431	432	433	434	435	436	437	438	439	440
B	A	A	D	D	B	D	A	A	D
441	442	443	444	445	446	447	448	449	450
D	B	C	B	B	A	B	D	D	B

451	452	453	454	455	456	457	458	459	460
A	C	C	D	C	B	D	A	B	C
461	**462**	**463**	**464**	**465**	**466**	**467**	**468**	**469**	**470**
A	B	A	C	B	D	C	A	D	B
471	**472**	**473**	**474**	**475**	**476**	**477**	**478**	**479**	**480**
B	C	B	C	D	D	A	D	D	A
481	**482**	**483**	**484**	**485**	**486**	**487**	**488**	**489**	**490**
C	B	D	D	C	B	D	A	A	A
491	**492**	**493**	**494**	**495**	**496**	**497**	**498**	**499**	**500**
B	C	A	C	B	D	D	B	C	B
501	**502**	**503**	**504**	**505**	**506**	**507**	**508**	**509**	**510**
A	D	B	C	D	D	A	B	C	A
511	**512**	**513**	**514**	**515**	**516**	**517**	**518**	**519**	**520**
D	B	C	B	C	C	A	A	D	C
521	**522**	**523**	**524**	**525**	**526**	**527**	**528**	**529**	**530**
B	D	D	C	B	C	A	C	C	B
531	**532**	**533**	**534**	**535**	**536**	**537**	**538**	**539**	**540**
A	C	A	A	B	A	C	A	A	B
541	**542**	**543**	**544**	**545**	**546**	**547**	**548**	**549**	**550**
C	B	C	A	B	D	B	A	B	B
551	**552**	**553**	**554**	**555**	**556**	**557**	**558**	**559**	**560**
A	B	B	C	A	A	C	A	A	A
561	**562**	**563**	**564**	**565**	**566**	**567**	**568**	**569**	**570**
A	B	A	C	C	A	B	B	A	C
571	**572**	**573**	**574**	**575**	**576**	**577**	**578**	**579**	**580**
B	B	D	A	B	A	C	B	A	A
581	**582**	**583**	**584**	**585**	**586**	**587**	**588**	**589**	**590**
A	C	A	A	C	B	A	B	A	C
591	**592**	**593**	**594**	**595**	**596**	**597**	**598**	**599**	**600**
B	B	A	B	A	B	A	B	A	B
601	**602**	**603**	**604**	**605**	**606**	**607**	**608**	**609**	**610**
B	A	B	A	B	A	A	B	B	A
611	**612**	**613**	**614**	**615**	**616**	**617**	**618**	**619**	**620**
B	B	A	B	C	A	B	C	B	A
621	**622**	**623**	**624**	**625**	**626**	**627**	**628**	**629**	**630**
B	B	A	A	B	B	B	A	B	B

631	632	633	634	635	636	637	638	639	640
D	B	A	B	A	B	B	C	C	B
641	**642**	**643**	**644**	**645**	**646**	**647**	**648**	**649**	**650**
C	B	A	B	C	B	A	C	C	D
651	**652**	**653**	**654**	**655**	**656**	**657**	**658**	**659**	**660**
C	C	C	D	A	A	D	B	C	B
661	**662**	**663**	**664**	**665**	**666**	**667**	**668**	**669**	**670**
C	B	B	C	D	B	B	C	A	C
671	**672**	**673**	**674**	**675**	**676**	**677**	**678**	**679**	**680**
A	A	B	A	B	B	C	A	B	B
681	**682**	**683**	**684**	**685**	**686**	**687**	**688**	**689**	**690**
C	B	A	D	B	B	B	B	A	B
691	**692**	**693**	**694**	**695**	**696**	**697**	**698**	**699**	**700**
B	C	B	C	A	C	D	B	D	B
701	**702**	**703**	**704**	**705**					
A	D	B	A	C					

●●●